Sport in Latin America and the Caribbean

Jaguar Books on Latin America

Series Editors

WILLIAM H. BEEZLEY, Professor of History, University of Arizona
COLIN M. MACLACHLAN, John Christy Barr Distinguished Professor of History, Tulane University

---

Volumes Published

John E. Kicza, ed., *The Indian in Latin American History: Resistance, Resilience, and Acculturation* (1993; rev. ed., 2000). Cloth ISBN 0-8420-2822-6 Paper ISBN 0-8420-2823-4

Susan E. Place, ed., *Tropical Rainforests: Latin American Nature and Society in Transition* (1993; rev. and updated ed., 2001). Cloth ISBN 0-8420-2907-9 Paper ISBN 0-8420-2908-7

Paul W. Drake, ed., *Money Doctors, Foreign Debts, and Economic Reforms in Latin America from the 1890s to the Present* (1994). Cloth ISBN 0-8420-2434-4 Paper ISBN 0-8420-2435-2

John A. Britton, ed., *Molding the Hearts and Minds: Education, Communications, and Social Change in Latin America* (1994). Cloth ISBN 0-8420-2489-1 Paper ISBN 0-8420-2490-5

David J. Weber and Jane M. Rausch, eds., *Where Cultures Meet: Frontiers in Latin American History* (1994). Cloth ISBN 0-8420-2477-8 Paper ISBN 0-8420-2478-6

Gertrude M. Yeager, ed., *Confronting Change, Challenging Tradition: Women in Latin American History* (1994). Cloth ISBN 0-8420-2479-4 Paper ISBN 0-8420-2480-8

Linda Alexander Rodríguez, ed., *Rank and Privilege: The Military and Society in Latin America* (1994). Cloth ISBN 0-8420-2432-8 Paper ISBN 0-8420-2433-6

Darién J. Davis, ed., *Slavery and Beyond: The African Impact on Latin America and the Caribbean* (1995). Cloth ISBN 0-8420-2484-0 Paper ISBN 0-8420-2485-9

Gilbert M. Joseph and Mark D. Szuchman, eds., *I Saw a City Invincible: Urban Portraits of Latin America* (1996). Cloth ISBN 0-8420-2495-6 Paper ISBN 0-8420-2496-4

Roderic Ai Camp, ed., *Democracy in Latin America: Patterns and Cycles* (1996). Cloth ISBN 0-8420-2512-X Paper ISBN 0-8420-2513-8

Oscar J. Martínez, ed., *U.S.-Mexico Borderlands: Historical and Contemporary Perspectives* (1996). Cloth ISBN 0-8420-2446-8 Paper ISBN 0-8420-2447-6

William O. Walker III, ed., *Drugs in the Western Hemisphere: An Odyssey of Cultures in Conflict* (1996). Cloth ISBN 0-8420-2422-0 Paper ISBN 0-8420-2426-3

Richard R. Cole, ed., *Communication in Latin America: Journalism, Mass Media, and Society* (1996). Cloth ISBN 0-8420-2558-8 Paper ISBN 0-8420-2559-6

David G. Gutiérrez, ed., *Between Two Worlds: Mexican Immigrants in the United States* (1996). Cloth ISBN 0-8420-2473-5 Paper ISBN 0-8420-2474-3

Lynne Phillips, ed., *The Third Wave of Modernization in Latin America: Cultural Perspectives on Neoliberalism* (1998). Cloth ISBN 0-8420-2606-1 Paper ISBN 0-8420-2608-8

Daniel Castro, ed., *Revolution and Revolutionaries: Guerrilla Movements in Latin America* (1999). Cloth ISBN 0-8420-2625-8 Paper ISBN 0-8420-2626-6

Virginia Garrard-Burnett, ed., *On Earth as It Is in Heaven: Religion in Modern Latin America* (2000). Cloth ISBN 0-8420-2584-7 Paper ISBN 0-8420-2585-5

Carlos A. Aguirre and Robert Buffington, eds., *Reconstructing Criminality in Latin America* (2000). Cloth ISBN 0-8420-2620-7 Paper ISBN 0-8420-2621-5

Christon I. Archer, ed., *The Wars of Independence in Spanish America* (2000). Cloth ISBN 0-8420-2468-9 Paper ISBN 0-8420-2469-7

John F. Schwaller, ed., *The Church in Colonial Latin America* (2000). Cloth ISBN 0-8420-2703-3 Paper ISBN 0-8420-2704-1

Ingrid E. Fey and Karen Racine, eds., *Strange Pilgrimages: Exile, Travel, and National Identity in Latin America, 1800–1990s* (2000). Cloth ISBN 0-8420-2693-2 Paper ISBN 0-8420-2694-0

Joseph L. Arbena and David G. LaFrance, eds., *Sport in Latin America and the Caribbean* (2002). Cloth ISBN 0-8420-2820-X Paper ISBN 0-8420-2821-8

Sport in Latin America and the Caribbean

Joseph L. Arbena and David G. LaFrance
Editors

Jaguar Books on Latin America
Number 23

A Scholarly Resources Inc. Imprint
Wilmington, Delaware

First published 2002
Printed and bound in the United States of America

Scholarly Resources Inc.
104 Greenhill Avenue
Wilmington, DE 19805-1897
www.scholarly.com

Maps prepared by Robert E. Schultz.

Library of Congress Cataloging-in-Publication Data

Sport in Latin America and the Caribbean / Joseph L. Arbena and David G. LaFrance, editors.
p. cm. — (Jaguar books on Latin America ; no. 23)
Includes bibliographical references.
ISBN 0-8420-2820-X (alk. paper) — ISBN 0-8420-2821-8 (pbk. : alk. paper)
1. Sports—Latin America. 2. Sports—Caribbean Area. I. Arbena, Joseph. II. LaFrance, David G. (David Gerald), 1948– III. Series.

GV586 .S64 2002
796'.098—dc21 2001054270

♾ The paper used in this publication meets the minimum requirements of the American National Standard for permanence of paper for printed library materials, Z39.48, 1984.

To Chelito, who has rejuvenated

a fading veteran, and to Richard and Jeffrey,

brothers and sports enthusiasts, too

Acknowledgments

This collection in its present form would not exist were it not for the sacrificial labors of Dean Charles "Chuck" Tatum (University of Arizona) and Harold Hinds (University of Minnesota, Morris). As cofounders and longtime editors of *Studies in Latin American Popular Culture (SLAPC)*, they brought academic attention to the previously ignored area of popular culture, including sports, in Latin America, through both their journal and their periodic gatherings of intellectual and social benefit. It was they who invited us to organize volume 13 (1994) of *SLAPC*, devoted to sports in Latin America, and they who encouraged us to edit an anthology on that topic built around that issue. The process proved more complicated and arduous than they, or we, anticipated.

In addition, we owe much to William "Bill" Beezley (University of Arizona), who in one of his various apparitions wrote on sports and who, as guest editor, arranged volume 13, number 2, of the *Journal of Sport History* (Summer 1986), moving along the early analysis of our field of interest. He was later joined by Colin MacLachlan (Tulane University), and they, as coeditors of the Scholarly Resources Jaguar Series, skillfully dragged us along to finish this project. Our thanks also go to Richard "Rick" Hopper of Scholarly Resources for his patience and encouragement.

Contents

Introduction

Joseph L. Arbena and David G. LaFrance

History

Contemporary sports in Latin America and the Caribbean evolved from three sources: indigenous games and recreation; activities introduced by the middle of the nineteenth century, primarily under colonial rule; and those distinctly modern sports that have arrived as part of the diffusion outward from the North Atlantic community, mainly England and the United States.[1] When the Spaniards arrived in the Americas they found such recreational activities as swimming, running, wrestling, and games of chance. Only in *chueca*, similar to field hockey and played in southern South America, and in the Mesoamerican ball games did they see anything resembling modern team games. But these games, like much of indigenous culture, were sacred and ritualistic in content, provoking the Spaniards to try to suppress them by force. Few Europeans participated in the remnants of these games or athletic activities, some of which have survived in marginal communities.

In their place, the Iberians introduced diversions brought from home, though gradually modified by local environmental and African and Amerindian influences to form a regionally diverse American sporting culture, often involving animals and gambling. Thus, whites and mixed ethnic groups derived pleasure from many activities. Among the most prominent of these games and sports were bullfighting (especially in Mexico, Peru, Colombia, and Venezuela, which persists in those countries today), cockfighting (in Mexico and Central America), jai-alai and other Basque ball games (in the Southern Cone and selected circum-Caribbean areas), various card and board games (such as *patolli*, a Mexican version of Parcheesi), horse racing, and other equestrian activities related to ranching. The most common of the latter is *charrería*, the source of North American rodeo, played in Mexico. Various Argentine gaucho competitions such as *pato*, which is rather like playing basketball on horseback, and *sortija*, in which riders try to place a thin needle through a hanging ring, also exist. Some of these sports and games are little played today (*patolli*) or relegated to discrete segments of society; *pato*, for example, has moved from the rural pampa to be adopted by upper-class urban whites, while *tejo* (stones tossed underhand to explode blasting caps set on a target at a measured distance) is practiced by hard-drinking, lower-class, Colombian mestizos.

By the mid-1800s, three interrelated trends in the area of physical games and sports had become obvious. First, the few persisting indigenous forms virtually disappeared. Second, folk culture was attacked as an impediment to progress. The suppression of folk sports was particularly noticeable. Bullfighting was temporarily banned in Mexico, and it and cockfighting were prohibited elsewhere on grounds of cruelty and links to Spain. *Pato* and other gaucho diversions were suppressed in Argentina as part of an effort to impose capitalist control over the pampa and its labor force, although in the twentieth century gaucho games would be revived as elite, folkloristic activities.

Third, sport became increasingly tied to the spread of so-called modern, European culture and its evolving recreational practices. These activities came to Latin America mainly with British or French and, later and mostly around the Caribbean, North American businessmen, missionaries, teachers, sailors, and workers as well as Hispanics who studied on either side of the North Atlantic. They were practiced in the schools and social or athletic clubs opened by foreigners or by progressive locals who gradually displaced the foreigners as leaders of the sporting community. These newer, imported sports spread from the capitals and major ports into secondary cities and eventually rural areas. Thus, most popular sports in Latin America today have little connection with traditional society, not much with colonial society, and even less with pre-Columbian civilizations.

Following North Atlantic models, Latin Americans around 1900 began to organize athletic clubs, restructure school curricula, establish national associations, and later form physical education faculties, which they argued would improve health and morals, teach discipline, cultivate national identity and integration, and earn them respect in the civilized world. They likewise affiliated with the emerging international sports network: the Olympics after 1896; the International Federation of Association Football (FIFA), soccer's governing body, after 1904; and other sports federations, which appeared in later decades. Resources, however, rarely matched ambitions.

The British amateur ideal did not prevail for long. Institutionalization, commercialization, and professionalism soon became part of the game. The desire to improve performance led to longer practice sessions, the paying of salaries, and the acceptance of lower-class and darker-skinned players. The increase in free time allowed workers to become recreational athletes and spectators. The chance to make money led to charges for admissions, souvenirs, and broadcasting rights. Those countries with the closest ties to the North Atlantic economy (Mexico, Cuba, Brazil, and the Southern Cone) and those sports with the broadest appeal among the masses (boxing, horse racing, baseball, and soccer) combined to create the earliest forms of professionalism.

Professionalization also encouraged unionization, codification of contract law, and welfare legislation for players. In truth, despite higher selective player incomes, at least in soccer, baseball, and boxing, such efforts protected few athletes from exploitation. Furthermore, efforts to redress the situation, such as the Argentine soccer strike of 1948 and the Mexican baseball players' (ANABE) movement of the early 1980s, have generally ended in failure for the athletes.

Dominating the sports map in the region is soccer (football to the British, *fútbol* in Spanish, *futebol* in Portuguese), the principal participant and spectator sport in virtually all of South America and most of Central America and Mexico. It spread as a result of British influence and of its simplicity and adaptability. Initially played by white elites, by 1930 it had socially and racially democratized, developed a popular base, moved toward professionalization, and become a foundation of emerging national identities. In other words, some Latin Americans did with soccer what Cubans and Dominicans have done with baseball and West Indians with cricket: they made the sport of the white foreigner and colonizer their own and used it as an anticolonial force to establish their own dominion, if only symbolic, over those who previously dominated them.

In the 1920s, Uruguay became the premier soccer power, winning Olympic gold medals in 1924 and 1928, four South American championships, and the first World Cup, which it hosted in 1930. Since then four other Latin American countries have hosted the Mundial (Brazil, 1950; Chile, 1962; Mexico, 1970 and 1986; and Argentina, 1978), while Colombia was awarded the competition in 1986 but had to withdraw due to a lack of infrastructure and resources. Since Uruguay's victory in 1930, Latin Americans have won the Cup seven additional times: Uruguay (1950), Brazil (1958, 1962, 1970, 1994), and Argentina (1978, 1986). Brazil is the only country to qualify for all sixteen so-called finals and to win a title outside its own hemisphere (1958), and the first to win three championships. Also, within Latin America every year the region's top clubs compete for the Copa Libertadores, and every two years the national teams pursue the Copa América. Subject to substantial debate is the frequent assertion that Brazil's Pelé (Edson Arantes do Nascimento) and Argentina's Diego Armando Maradona are the two best players the world has ever seen; both men, like most Latin American players, are from humble socioeconomic origins. In December 2000, FIFA named the two to share the designation as Best Player of the Last Seventy Years, with plans to announce the Best Player of the Century in 2004. At the same time, FIFA also honored Spain's Real Madrid as the best soccer club of the twentieth century and France's Zinedine Zidane as the world's best player in the year 2000.

American football, by contrast, has found adherents mostly only in Mexico (not counting American schoolboys in the old Panama Canal Zone), where it has been played since the 1920s. There currently is a collegiate-level league made up of teams from the central and northern regions of the country. Local as well as satellite television carries National Football League (NFL) contests, and its teams occasionally schedule exhibition games south of the border. A few Mexicans, mainly place kickers, have played in the NFL, as have an even greater number of Mexican Americans. Other versions of American football are played by small numbers of devotees, partly as a result of the impact of televised Super Bowl extravaganzas.

Soccer's popularity, however, is not unchallenged or evenly distributed, either by place or by social group. On the island nations of Cuba, Puerto Rico, and the Dominican Republic; in northern Mexico and along its Gulf Coast, including Yucatán; and in Nicaragua, Panama, and the Caribbean zones of Colombia and Venezuela, baseball is king. The game, made attractive by its leisurely pace, low cost, and association with more politically and economically progressive societies, began arriving in the region in the 1870s, carried by U.S. sailors, engineers, educators, and military personnel as well by enthusiasts from Cuba, where it was first embraced. All these countries, as in soccer, have their own professional or organized leagues. Since 1970, the winners of the winter league in the Dominican Republic, Mexico, Puerto Rico, and Venezuela have played a reborn, yearly Caribbean championship series; Cuba, which frequently won the older series, no longer participates since it ended professional sports. Host Mexico, winner only three times in thirty-one years, finished second in February 2001 to the Dominicans, who have won seven of the last twelve competitions.

Cuba, the Dominican Republic, Nicaragua, and Venezuela have each won the world series of amateur baseball at least once. In recent years, Cuba's powerful "amateur" team has particularly dominated the nonprofessional circuit, winning gold medals in the 1992 and 1996 Olympic Games; they finished, for them, a disappointing second to the United States in 2000. Although these countries produced outstanding players before 1947, few of them made it to the North American major leagues because of racial barriers. At first, Cuba sent the most to the majors, but once Fidel Castro came to power in 1959, such movement proved more difficult, and major league baseball shifted its attention to Puerto Rico, Venezuela, and the Dominican Republic, although the number of Cuban baseball defectors was rising by the mid-1990s. San Pedro de Macorís, on the southeastern coast of the Dominican Republic, may have more players per capita in the major leagues than any other city in the world. Due to special legal problems, several leagues of its own, and its shared interest in soccer, Mexico's per capita output of baseball stars is not high, despite the achievements and popularity in the 1980s of Sonoran pitcher Fernando Valenzuela.

By the late 1990s, some 20 percent of players on major league rosters were from Latin American countries, driven by a love of the game, a strong desire to gain recognition, and the hope for economic achievement. Perhaps the greatest player ever, the one most cited as a model and hero, was Pittsburgh Pirate Hall-of-Famer Roberto Clemente (Puerto Rico), who died in a plane crash trying to deliver supplies to Nicaraguan earthquake victims in 1972. In the 1990s Dominican slugger Sammy Sosa gained popularity in the United States and at home as he engaged Mark McGwire in record-breaking home run races.

Baseball's counterpart, cricket, dominates the English-speaking Caribbean. What has made West Indian cricket distinctive is its lively style and carnival-like context as well as its ties to national identity, black ethnicity, and the pursuit of political independence. Although cricket, along with religion and education, was part of the white colonial regime, these three ultimately shaped the evolving culture of the transplanted African and creole (mixed-blood) population. With its emphasis on civility and recognition of achievement, cricket allowed West Indians a chance to emulate mainstream society while also challenging both British colonial rule and white domination.

Cricket matches between English and West Indian clubs began in the 1890s, although the first Test Match was not held until 1928. While several blacks represented early West Indies teams, the first black captain was Frank Worrell, named in 1959 following increasing criticism of white control of the sport in the islands. Later international Tests have earned the West Indians a reputation as the world's best for much of the last generation. If emotions surrounding such matches have engendered occasional riots among Caribbean fans, success has also stimulated great pride in such black stars as Worrell, Learie Constantine, George Headley, the great all-rounder Garfield (Gary) Sobers, and, more recently, Brian Lara.

Boxing is often the means of escape from poverty for whites and nonwhites all across Latin America. Given the number of international sanctioning bodies, it is impossible to cite all the past and present world champions, especially in the lighter weight divisions. Boxers who brought their countrymen thrills include Carlos Monzón and Pascual Pérez (Argentina), Alexis Argüello (Nicaragua), Al Brown, Luis Ibarra and Roberto Durán (Panama), Juan Guzmán (Dominican Republic), Vicente Rondón (Venezuela), and Julio César Chávez (Mexico). In 1994, Chávez was

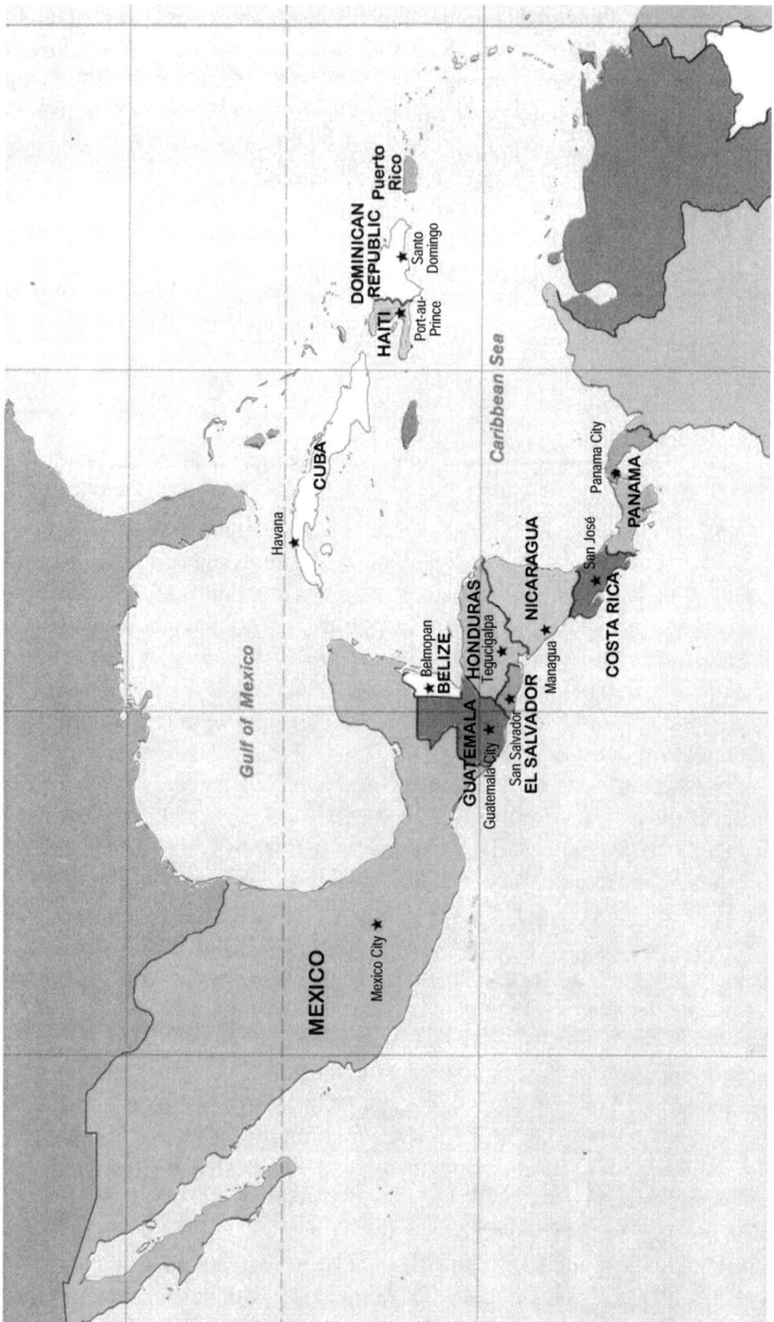

Middle America (Mexico, Central America, and the Caribbean)

South America

knocked down and defeated, both for the first time, after ninety fights and three world titles. Today, Cuba rules the amateur sphere as seen in the Pan American games, the Olympics, world boxing tournaments, and binational competitions with the United States. Best known among the Cubans has been heavyweight Teófilo Stevenson, who dominated the Olympics in the 1970s and later successfully coached his national team. Unlike boxing's near universal appeal, professional wrestling (*lucha libre*) has achieved extensive popularity among Mexico's working classes, yet less acceptance elsewhere.

Basketball has been played throughout Latin America since early in the twentieth century, and several countries, such as Brazil and Cuba, have succeeded on the international level. Argentina hosted and won basketball's first world championship in 1950. Uruguay has a limited professional league, and Mexico has a collegiate-level circuit. Recently, due in part to satellite transmission and possibly to racial identification, basketball, as exemplified by the National Basketball Association (NBA) and goodwill tours by its stars such as "Magic" Johnson, has become popular across the Caribbean. Within most countries, basketball remains an important part of physical education and recreation programs; Mexico, for example, introduced the sport into its public schools as early as the 1930s. Several players from the Caribbean as well as Mexico are now playing in the NBA.

Less extensively but also spreading is volleyball, carried worldwide by YMCA workers. Brazil, Cuba, and Peruvian women have excelled in international competition. Brazilians of both genders also rated very high at the 1996 Olympics in the newer beach volleyball sport and won both the men's and women's finals in the first world championships in 1997, a reflection perhaps of Brazilians' love of the beach.

As for other ball games, Latin American tennis stars, including several women, have increasingly populated world rankings since the glory days of Anita Linzana (Chile), Pancho Segura (Ecuador), Pancho González (Mexico), and Maria Bueno (Brazil). Out of the 1970s and 1980s emerged such stars as Guillermo Vilas (Argentina), Alex Olmedo (Peru), Andrés Gómez (Ecuador), and Gabriela Sabatini (Argentina). The temperamental Marcelo Ríos (Chile), upon winning the French Open in 1998, became the first Latin American man ever to be ranked number one in the tennis world; in 2000, Gustavo "Guga" Kuerten (Brazil) matched Ríos's achievement. Their success has promoted the game as a recreational activity for a limited middle class in their home countries. On the golf links, Roberto De Vicenzo (Argentina) competed among the best in the 1950s and 1960s; Juan "Chi Chi" Rodríguez (Puerto Rico) continued through the 1990s to play on the Professional Golf Association (PGA) Senior Tour, as did Lee Trevino (Treviño) a Mexican American. Finally, Mexico, selected Andean countries, and Cuba have long been promoters of jai-alai. Like jai-alai, handball and several other related court ball games derive from old Basque sports labeled *pelota vasca*.

Racing, too, attracts much attention in selected parts of Latin America. Perhaps because of their early industrialization, Argentina and Brazil embraced auto racing, both track and open road, and produced international champions such as Argentina's Juan Manuel Fangio (five-time world Formula I winner) and Oscar Gálvez and Brazil's Emerson Fittipaldi, Nelson Piquet, and Ayrton Senna, whose tragic death during a race in Italy in 1994 was mourned both in his native country and across Latin America. Cycling, an early import from Europe because of its ties to technology, exercise, and French leisure, has been more prominent in mountainous countries such as Colombia, Costa Rica, and Mexico. Finally, horse racing also plays a part on the sport scene. In areas under British influence the horses run clockwise on grass.

At different times, Latin American athletes, including women, also have shown their skills in a wide range of other sports. Claudia Poll (Costa Rica) became a national hero upon winning a gold medal in swimming at the 1996 Summer Olympics; her sister, Silvia, had starred in the 1987 Pan American Games. Skater Nora Alicia Vega (Argentina) won five world titles in a sport usually dominated by Europeans. Track and field events bring to mind the Brazilian runner Joaquim Cruz (1984 Olympic gold medalist) as well as the Cuban greats, sprinter Alberto Juantorena, high jumper Javier Sotomayor, and javelin thrower María Caridad Colón, who took the gold in the 1980 Olympics. Raúl González Rodríguez (Mexico) walked, mainly at a distance of fifty kilometers, to three world championships, two Olympic medals, and numerous records, overcoming a lack of support for a nonprofessional and not very glamorous sport. Weight lifter Soraya Jiménez (Mexico) also caught her country's attention by winning a gold medal in the 2000 Olympics. Chess, which, too, is considered a sport in the region, was led for years by the Cuban grand master, José Raúl Capablanca. More recently, Latin Americans have also shown increasing interest in noncompetitive participatory sports and recreational activities such as hiking and climbing, camping, survivalism, boating, and sport fishing.

In addition to soccer (Latin Americans joined FIFA, the sport's governing body, in 1913), the last century has also witnessed the region's participation in other international sports competitions, particularly in the Olympics and related games. They began to take part in Olympics as early as 1900. In 1968, Mexico was the first Third World and only Latin American country to sponsor the Summer Olympics. In 1922, on the centenary of its independence, Brazil organized the now-defunct South American Games; in 1926, encouraged by the Olympic leadership in Paris in 1924, Mexico hosted the first Central American and Caribbean games. (Overwhelmed by Mexico and Cuba in particular, the isthmian countries started a more limited Central American Games in Guatemala in 1973.) In 1938, on the 400th anniversary of its capital, Colombia initiated the Bolivarian Games. In 1951, Juan Perón's Argentina inaugurated the Pan American Games, a competition likewise encouraged by the Olympic leadership as early as the Los Angeles Olympics (1932) and originally scheduled for Buenos Aires in 1942. A smaller winter version of the Pan American Games debuted in 1990, but it has had only minimal success given the lack of suitable training sites, except for in the United States, Canada, and the Southern Cone.

In recent decades, no single country of the region has had the degree of success in international competition as Cuba, thus underlining that nation's unique system and the relative weakness of the rest of Latin America in sport. After 1959 and at a controversial cost, Cuba, in part through a Communist model administered by the National Institute for Sports, Physical Recreation, and Recreation (INDER), eliminated open professionalism and expanded domestic athletic activities to raise health standards at all age levels and for both sexes. Aided at first in this project by the socialist countries of Eastern Europe, in recent decades Cuba has become self-sufficient and even an exporter of coaches and technology.

The nation's high point came in the 1990s. First, in 1991, it successfully hosted the XI Pan American Games. Under severe economic and political difficulties, the Cubans not only prepared the facilities for thirty-nine countries and over 4,500 athletes but also won ten more gold medals than did the United States (140–130), although the total medal count favored the latter (352–265). Then, in 1992 at the Barcelona Olympics, Cuba's medal count totaled thirty-one, placing the island nation fifth overall in gold medals and sixth in total medals. In Atlanta in 1996 Cuba placed seventh and ninth, respectively. Within Latin America that year, Cuba won more medals than Brazil, Argentina, and Mexico combined—more also than Canada—which illustrates that without the Cubans the overall Latin American performance in 1996 was lower than for any region on the globe. At Sydney in 2000 they were eighth in total medals and tied for ninth in gold, surpassing Great Britain and all Western Hemisphere countries except the United States. Still, these successes have not kept Cuban athletes from fleeing the island's economic failures and political restrictions. Some forty Cuban athletes, for example, defected during the 1993 Central American and Caribbean Games in Puerto Rico, suggesting that dissatisfaction runs high even among the privileged—a conviction reaffirmed by the similar flight of an increasing number of players from Cuba's Pan American, world amateur, and Olympic championship baseball teams, several of whom signed professional contracts in North America. Among these a few, such as New York Yankee pitcher Orlando "El Duque" Hernández, have become World Series heroes.

Issues

Given the long history of sport, it still is necessary to define exactly what one means by the term. Broadly, sport is a form of diversion or recreation. Nevertheless, so are many other activities such as movie going, or beer drinking, or even sex. Therefore, sport consists of something else, a physical and mental endeavor that involves competition against others or with oneself. Competition here is used in the sense of pushing oneself toward a goal—even something as mundane as a daily walk around the block—in an effort to enhance one's well-being. It could also cover other informal activities not always construed as sport, such as chess, cyclists on tour, or even hopscotch. Clearly, however, the more common idea of sport includes not only competition but also some degree of organization and systematization with rules and procedures and generally score keeping. In Allen Guttmann's models, sport is defined as organized, physical, competitive play. Thus, there are differences between, say, tossing a ball and playing in a baseball game. The latter is more commonly thought of as sport, although the former may be shaped by and in turn contribute to the more refined practice of true sport.

Another issue to be considered is modern sport, the topic of this volume, as opposed to its so-called earlier counterpart. Here, a time factor clearly divides the two; according to most periodizations, sporting activities that took place before approximately 1850 are considered premodern. Nevertheless, certain endeavors, such as foot or horse racing and even hitting or throwing a ball can be traced back for centuries; consider the Mesoamerican indigenous peoples, for example, who, divided by teams, competed by using their bodies to place a sphere through vertical stone hoops.

What then, besides chronology, divides modern from ancient? Again, one must return to the idea of organization and systematization. In the late nineteenth and early twentieth centuries, societies, or at least segments of those societies, in certain parts of the world gained enough leisure time and material resources to dedicate themselves and their money to regularized sport. Again citing Guttmann, modern sports are characterized by secularism, equality, bureaucratization, specialization, rationalization, quantification, and an obsession with records. Clearly there seems to be a connection between the rise of modern sport and industrial capitalism both in an economic and a bureaucratic sense; note the increasing emphasis during that later period on record keeping, rules, training, and professionalism in all walks of life (such as, for example, the rise of discrete social science and humanities disciplines in universities and the requirement that doctors and lawyers be licensed). Few societies before this time had the means or motivation to apply such regimentation and importance to nonwork endeavors.

Furthermore, it was not only a question of resources and motivation that promoted the development of modern sport in the late nineteenth and early twentieth centuries. As William Beezley demonstrates for Mexico in *Judas at the Jockey Club*, sport was much more than merely tangential to the modernizing process; indeed, it was an integral part of that very process and helped to allow people to adjust to and perform better in that rapidly changing era.[2] Cycling, for example, not only offered something to do during one's spare time but also maintained or even improved one's health, an important consideration in an age in which hard physical labor was no longer a part of daily life for middle-class urbanites.

Organized boxing epitomized the individualistic competition of the period's stage of economic development. Team sports provided another type of competition, attuned to the expanding factory system, in which team/firm competed against team/firm, while within the organization players/workers learned to cooperate as a cohesive unit following certain rules and procedures and operating under the guidance of a coach/foreman. In addition, baseball, soccer, basketball, and the like were well suited to and even made more compelling by elaborate record keeping, again another parallel between sport and the bureaucratic modernization of the time. Furthermore, modern sport stimulated, through equipment manufacturing and repair, commercial sales, facility construction and maintenance, and, of course, ticket purchases, the very development of capitalism that it reflected. After all, who would deny that sport and Coca-Cola or Nike sportswear, to take two recent examples, go hand in hand?

In this same vein, some observers would also argue that sport enslaves the individual to his or her society. In other words, participation in modern sport, either as player or fan, reinforces societal norms and one's acceptance of them, even though these practices may be exploitative. Here, one might point out as an example the average factory worker or teacher who spends a lot of money on tickets to watch millionaire ball players, accepting the fact that he is, one could say, being exploited for the benefit of overpaid, self-indulgent professionals who produce, unlike the worker or teacher, little of concrete value. Another example might be the casual runner who, convinced by advertisements, thinks he needs the latest model of Nike athletic shoes; again, this purchase enriches a huge corporation and the professional athletes who endorse its products. Nevertheless, other students of sport and its relationship to society have argued that this idea of enslavement is simplistic. They posit, instead, that sport is mostly neutral. People participate in it or watch it for benign, but not unimportant, reasons of health, relaxation, and entertainment. Once having taken part, however, the experience does not necessarily carry with it any ulterior baggage such as an acceptance or reinforcement of society's social structures or one's own personal exploitation.

Other observers claim that while sport does reflect and strengthen the dominant norms of society, it also provides individuals with a means to challenge those very structures, whether social, economic or political. In other words, according to this argument, one gets out of sport what one sees as appropriate to one's own desires or needs. One player or fan, for example, may participate in or view a game with little other motivation than to have fun; afterward he walks away feeling satisfied about his team's performance and, by extension, views his life and his place in it (at least for the moment) positively. Another person may enter or view the same contest with the intention of taking out his frustrations about life, or boss, or spouse, and therefore challenging the status quo through the security of the ritual of sport. What we have here is a safety-valve phenomenon, in which sport allows the angry and frustrated person to let off steam in a relatively harmless way, thus preventing more serious "blowups" in the society at large. As Richard D. E. Burton observes regarding Caribbean cricket, the significant fact for West Indians is "not that they regularly beat Massa at his own game and regularly make him *look foolish*, but that they are playing his game in the first place." The consequence is that "the System itself survives—strengthened, not weakened by its merely symbolic defeat."[3]

A fourth issue that one must consider when analyzing the nature of sport is the debate between amateurism and professionalism. Basically, the controversy swirls around whether one is superior to the other, or, more accurately, whether professionalism has ruined the ideals of amateurism. Traditionally, those advocating amateurism have taken the high road, claiming that sport's principal objective should be the betterment of our health and moral condition; we should all play for the fun of it. According to this line of thinking, paying someone to take part in what amounts to a game not only corrupts players and turns them into elitists but also transforms likely participants into fans. Those people who defend professionalism argue, however, that if the public wants to pay for sedentary diversion, then the entertainers should be duly compensated for their work. (Note here the transition from player as entertainer to worker and the implications this differentiation has in how one views and treats athletes.) After all, are athletes as entertainers/workers/artists any different from opera and rock singers, actors, novelists, or fashion models?

Attitudes about the superiority of amateurism have a fairly long history, going back to the origins of the modernization of sport in the mid-to-late nineteenth century. In that period, only people of some economic means had the resources and leisure time to participate in sport; they also had no need to be paid for their activity and shunned so-called public spectacles. Furthermore, the requirements of money and time generally kept out the lower classes, who had neither in sufficient amounts to join in, at least in any organized form of sport of the day. Over time, however, as the popularity of organized sport spread to the lower rungs of society, the working classes began to form their own teams (sometimes with the help of bosses and owners), and more and more people were attracted to the contests as fans. Entrepreneurs, less concerned about elitism and amateurism, saw the opportunity to attract the best players of any social class because this superior product attracted paying fans. Thus, a semi-professional system arose in which ad hoc payments to athletes and volunteer donations by observers became the norm. Eventually, these sometimes illegal or at least condemned practices became tolerated and accepted, thus resulting in full-blown professionalism. Nevertheless, the tension between amateur and professional sports still exists today. Witness the debate among countries over whether the Olympics should permit professional players to take part in the games or the insistence on the part of Cuba that its athletes, though provided with special benefits, privileges, and training, are amateurs and not professionals.

In recent years, as students of sport (economists, historians, political scientists, sociologists, and others) have increasingly examined its relationship to human life, other avenues of inquiry and speculation have evolved, most of them not as philosophical as the issues addressed above but nevertheless relevant to an understanding of this complex and constantly changing phenomenon, which touches in one way or another the life of nearly every human being. Most attention in this regard has been paid to sport in the developed countries of Europe, North America, and Austral-Asia. However, a growing body of work exists on other areas of the world, including Latin America.[4]

One theme is the internationalization or the diffusion and globalization of sport. No so-called modern sport originated in Latin America either during its pre-Columbian or colonial eras (to the 1820s). All, including football/soccer, baseball, basketball, volleyball, boxing, cycling, tennis, swimming, wrestling, *charrería*, automobile racing, and even bullfighting, originated in Europe or North America and were adopted in Latin America. As a result, each sport now practiced there has a history of transferal to the middle and southern zones of the Western Hemisphere. Nevertheless, it should not be assumed that the transferal process was one in which the sport arrived intact. Latin America as a whole and even areas within the region adapted these sports to their specific needs and cultures. Over time many of these sports have continued to evolve, making them in some instances increasingly different from those in their countries of origin.

This process has been studied comprehensively by Tony Mason, who, in *Passion of the People?*, traces football (soccer) from England to South America, particularly in Argentina, Brazil, and Uruguay.[5] Mason argues that within three to four decades of football being introduced to South America, the working classes had adopted the heretofore elite sport as their own and began to modify it, giving it more flair, passion, and emotion than that of Europe where almost formulaic structure and technique dominated. Indeed, commentators today still talk about the "difference" between the sport on the two continents. Nevertheless, Mason goes on to say that as football has become more internationalized in the mid- to late-twentieth century via the World Cup and other intercountry and intercontinental competitions, including the establishment of FIFA and its universal body of rules, the sport has begun to revert to a more homogeneous form that undermines the differences between regions of the globe. Obviously depressed by a perceived tendency of world soccer and culture to become standardized and conservative, Uruguayan historian and avid soccer fan Eduardo Galeano predicts that "in this end-of-century world, whoever doesn't die of hunger dies of boredom."[6]

The fact that sport has been imported into Latin America raises the question of whether this process has produced or at least contributed to a relationship of dependency or hegemony between the originating and recipient country or region. Likewise, the growth of Latin America's athletic pool, the region's uneven and relatively dependent economic development, and the growing international sports dimension have resulted in the migration of players and coaches within and from Latin America and the sale within the region of foreign sporting equipment and televised sporting events. The best performers move from small town to city and small country to large one. They start with small clubs, then are transferred to better known ones, although these also lack funds and sell their rights to the players abroad. Soccer players, especially from the Southern Cone, commonly play their peak years in Europe. Building on a tradition that dates back to the 1930s, for example, over 400 Argentine soccer players were estimated to be playing in other countries in the 1990s. Cricket and baseball players from the circum-Caribbean earn fame and fortune in Britain and North America, respectively. Before 1959, Cuba was the major source mined for baseball talent, but since 1970 the mother lode has been the Dominican Republic. Other countries provide jockeys, boxers, and American football place kickers. On the amateur level they also help fill rosters of American university swimming, tennis, soccer, and track teams. Although the foreign exploits of their former hometown heroes may warm the hearts of locals, their home clubs suffer a loss of fans, and national teams lack time together to prepare for international competitions. In other sports, such as track and field, the best athletes often reside and train abroad; in sports such as tennis and auto racing, most competition is out of the country. In short, except via television, most people have little contact with their athletic heroes. Moreover, whatever their sport and wherever they choose to live, Latin America's best athletes traditionally have had to travel abroad to earn major recognition and rewards.

Most observers would agree that in some important ways, particularly economic and cultural, the region is subject to the undue and, many would argue, unhealthy influence of Europe and the United States. While other people would accept the dependency idea in general, many of them would add that sport is also used to resist outside influences; this can take on symbolic importance, such as in the modification of an imported sport as mentioned above, or in a more direct form in international competition, in which both players and fans evaluate successes or losses in nationalistic terms.

Two works by Alan Klein have explored the intricacies of this dependency-nationalism idea. In *Sugarball*[7] he shows that Dominicans admire U.S. culture and ways, aping much of what the larger country does and sending many of its talented athletes northward to play. Nevertheless, the author argues that baseball is used in this Caribbean nation to create a sense of nationalism; its people take tremendous pride in the success of its exports to the center of world-class ball. The irony, of course, is not only that the Dominicans employ a foreign cultural import to assert their patriotism but also that the more they imitate U.S. baseball, the more they undermine the distinctiveness of their own game and thus its ability to challenge the hegemony of their northern neighbor.

In a second book, *Baseball on the Border*,[8] Klein examines different forms of nationalism and how they are manifested by Mexican players who were members of the unique binational (Mexico and the United States) baseball team, the Tecolotes de los Dos Laredos (Owls of the Two Laredos), which shared two cities, Laredo, Texas, and Nuevo Laredo, Tamaulipas. According to Klein, players and the larger communities demonstrated three types of nationalism depending on given situations: autonationalism, the most traditional, which pits one's own country against another; binationalism, or the pragmatic sharing of interests, especially along a border; and transnationalism, or the fusion of the other two forms into what amounts to the creation of a border region that sees itself as unique and apart from the power centers (in this case, Washington and Mexico City) of each country.

No major sport, and few minor sports that are played internationally, escape the fact that governments have a close connection to them. Thus, sport and politics are often closely intertwined. All countries have, however poorly funded and ineffective, some version of an integrated national sports federation, such as Chile's DIGEDER, Colombia's COLDEPORTES, Cuba's INDER, and Mexico's CONADE. In addition, there are national associations for most sports, Olympic organizing committees, a physical education institute, and periodic "national games" at different age levels.

Some people bemoan this aspect of government involvement, while others applaud it; whatever the case, it is an important component of sport studies. Sports people, commonly without adequate resources, have looked to the government for support. In turn, officials readily have understood the value of backing sport to one degree or another. First, it has not been lost on politicians that sport is widely popular. Take note, for example, of the candidates for office who show up at contests or Argentine president Carlos Menem who, in the 1990s, was often seen playing soccer wearing the shirt of the national team.[9] Second, teams and events, many argue, bring economic as well as psychic well-being to a community. In this vein, one hardly needs mention the rhetoric surrounding the building of professional-level stadiums and other facilities to attract and support teams or events.

Third, authorities in many areas promote sport as a means to improve the physical (and mental) health of the society at large; many countries and states and provinces have physical education requirements in the public school system and even in universities. Finally, returning to the nationalism idea, leaders back sport as a means to enhance a country's image both at home and abroad, thus helping to legitimize incumbent regimes and attract foreign aid, investment, and tourism. This phenomenon goes back to the 1930s when President Getúlio Vargas of Brazil gave his government a formal role in the promotion of sports. A decade later, Juan Perón of Argentina (1946–1955) moved even further in funding training and travel for national athletes, organizing youth sports and competitions, diverting money to professional soccer clubs, arranging public appearances with famous athletes, attending high-profile events, and hosting the Pan American Games. Since coming to power in 1959, Fidel Castro in Cuba has done much the same, only on an even larger and more successful scale. Mexico hosted the Olympic Games in 1968, in part to project an image of development and modernity, but the event was marred by the shooting of hundreds of protesters in central Mexico City. Perhaps the most notorious example of this political use of sport occurred during the Latin American military dictatorships of the 1960s to the 1980s, especially those in the Southern Cone. Officer-run regimes promoted international competition in a blatant attempt to curry favor and burnish their tarnished images; in contrast was Chilean strongman Augusto Pinochet who, after taking power in 1973, suppressed all sports clubs and events that might give voice to critics and protesters.

In another perspective on this issue, Janet Lever, in her pioneering study *Soccer Madness*,[10] connects official support for sport to the goal of national integration. Brazil, despite its many cleavages (region, ethnicity, religion, class), she argues, demonstrates a unique ability to remain a whole, thanks at least in part to football/soccer. Participation in and observance of the sport from the local through the state and national levels to the international level help to overcome these divisions and thus create unity through competition. Brazilian leaders from bottom to top thus expend public monies on sport on soccer's behalf.

A consideration of sport and politics moves on to a closely related inquiry: the difference between a judgment about sport in socialistic and capitalistic nations. From the socialist perspective, capitalist nations treat sport as a commercialized, individualized endeavor that may benefit the athlete personally yet does little or nothing for the populace or nation as a whole. Furthermore, this view would posit that socialist countries have proven to be international sport powerhouses despite, in most instances, their relatively smaller population and resource bases. The capitalist would counter by saying that socialist systems smother personal initiative, overly regiment society, and deny successful athletes their economic due. Another less visible position maintains that all organized sport is inherently exploitative and repressive and should be abolished in favor of true play and games.

Paula Pettavino and Geralyn Pye have taken the closest look at arguably the only truly socialistic sport system in the Americas, that of Cuba.[11] They trace the history of sport in Cuba, comparing the pre- and post-revolutionary periods, and point out the difficulty in developing a socialistic sport system in a primarily capitalistic world. Castro's efforts, the authors assert, have come close to meeting several socialistic ideals such as mass participation, a healthier populace, and national integration. Nevertheless, with the increasing difficulty of supporting economically such an extensive sport system and the temptation to focus on the training of world-class elite performers, both to bring in hard currency and to boost Cuba politically on the international scene, there is the danger of losing sight of or even undermining many of the heretofore impressive achievements regarding mass, egalitarian sport. Recently the results of this process have been manifested in the defection of Cuban athletes, especially baseball players, to the United States, in which their officially expressed desire for freedom is difficult to separate from the motivation of earning undreamed-of salaries.

No matter whether capitalistic or socialistic, however, every government views, at least to some extent, sport in terms of the good it can do for the physical and mental well-being of society as a whole. In other words, sport, through direct participation as well as the diversion it creates, is seen as the key factor in the development of a healthy, contented, and vice-free people. Political entities at all levels (not to mention private efforts—note the proliferation of exercise facilities as standard perquisites at many businesses) expend large amounts of resources on playgrounds, parks, summer leagues, coaches, equipment, and related items that are used both by adults and children. Consider, for example, the nature of the arguments employed by advocates of sport in the public schools when faced with cuts in programs due to tax shortfalls.

Furthermore, for those officials, a healthy, satisfied, and vice-free populace is more productive in an economic sense. This concept is illustrated by a term commonly used in Latin America, San Lunes, which translates as Saint Monday, and refers to the one day of the week that many workers take off after weekend binges. In the United States, too, it is not unusual to be cautioned not to buy a car or some other product manufactured on either Monday or Friday for the same reason. In both cases officials would rather see workers playing than partying, even during days off.

Another aspect of sport, touched only briefly upon above, is its relationship to culture, ethnicity, race, class, and gender. Using any one or a combination of these concepts of social analysis, one can examine the greater society through sport. Given sports are played differently by different cultures; baseball in Latin America, for example, is not exactly like that of the United States. People of one ethnicity or race may prefer to play one sport as opposed to another, or people who play the same sport may be segregated to certain teams or leagues, either voluntarily or involuntarily. Some sports are clearly elite dominated (take polo, for example) as opposed to having mass or explicitly lower-class appeal. And no one can deny that certain sports tend to be played largely by men as opposed to women, and vice versa, as well as the fact that few sports are mixed. Indeed, except for those of Cuba, few Latin American women have achieved the widespread recognition enjoyed by their male counterparts. Financial and social constraints in part reflect the lower value placed by their societies on female competitors. With the exception of a handful of tennis players as well as the Peruvian volleyball team, mentioned above, most women, such as swimmer Jeanette Campbell (Argentina), silver medalist at the Berlin Olympics in 1936, have won and been forgotten. Finally, other ills of society at large, such as drug consumption (note the situation of former Argentine soccer star Diego Maradona) and spousal abuse, can be viewed through sport. These issues must not be overlooked when studying sport's relationship to society as a whole.

The student of sport also must not forget the effects of its links to the media, particularly the fact that modern communications gives it access to a mass audience and subsequently to the impact of commercialization. After all, without the publicity provided first by newspapers, later by radio and television, and now by the computer, sport would have remained largely a local and fairly isolated phenomenon, preventing its evolution into a national and even international spectacle with huge audiences and with considerable sums of money at stake. Indeed, in recent years it can be argued that many sports are driven by the money that the media offers. Television contracts, especially, provide the economic wherewithal for teams and leagues and transnational organizers to pay athletes huge salaries and stage extravagant events.

Consider, moreover, the common use of sport jargon in the ordinary language and of sport themes in artistic expression. While the language of sport was built on the Hispanicized pronunciation of imported, usually English, terms (golf, round, football), more recently, under pressures of mass involvement and nationalism, either Spanish or Portuguese linguistic inventions have replaced many foreign words (*boxeo* for boxing, *gol* for goal, *arquero* for goalie) or reasonable translations have been identified (*fuera de lugar* for offside, *lanzador* for pitcher, *árbitro* for referee). Politicians often "move pieces on the board" in the hope of "getting to the head of the pack" in order to "score more goals." Popular songs praise the skills of Pelé and Fernando Valenzuela; poems glorify the talents of Brazilian soccer star Garrincha, Puerto Rican baseballer Roberto Clemente, and Argentine jockey Irineo Leguisamo; works of art illustrate the physical beauty of athletics. Great writers such as Julio Cortázar (boxing, Argentina) and Antonio Skármeta (cycling and soccer, Chile) have long used play or game settings to convey their ideas. Increasingly, authors depict sport as physical activity rather than spectacle and as a means to represent social and psychological conflicts among literary characters, as in the boxing plays of Eduardo Pavlosky (Argentina) and Vicente Leñero (Mexico) and the novels of Isaac Goldemberg (soccer, Peru) and José Agustín (baseball, Mexico). Humorists Roberto Fontanarrosa (Argentina) and Oscar Conti (Chile) have contributed numerous collections of sports-related cartoons. A final expression is seen in widely read sports periodicals such as *El Gráfico* (Argentina), *Placar* (Brazil), and *Esto* (Mexico). Clearly, sport fills an important place in and reflects Latin American society.

Notes

1. This section is based on Joseph L. Arbena, "Sport," in Daniel Balderston et al., eds., *The Encyclopedia of Contemporary Latin American and Caribbean Cultures* (London: Routledge, 2000); Joseph L. Arbena, "Sport in Latin America and the Caribbean," in Simon Collier et al., eds., *The Cambridge Encyclopedia of Latin America and the Caribbean* (2d ed.; Cambridge and New York: Cambridge University Press, 1992); and Joseph L. Arbena, "Sports," in Barbara A. Tennenbaum, ed., *Encyclopedia of Latin American History and Culture* (New York: Charles Scribner's Sons, 1996).

2. William Beezley, *Judas at the Jockey Club and Other Episodes of Porfirian Mexico* (Lincoln: University of Nebraska Press, 1987).

3. Richard D. E. Burton, *Afro-Creole: Power, Opposition, and Play in the Caribbean* (Ithaca, NY: Cornell University Press, 1997), 185–86.

4. For more complete listings of works on sport in Latin America, see Joseph L. Arbena, ed., *An Annotated Bibliography of Latin American Sport: Pre-Conquest to the Present* (Westport, CT: Greenwood Press, 1989); and *Latin American Sport: An Annotated Bibliography, 1988–1998* (Westport, CT: Greenwood Press, 1999).

5. Tony Mason, *Passion of the People? Football in South America* (New York: Verso, 1995).

6. Eduardo Galeano, *Soccer in Sun and Shadow* (London: Verso, 1998), 209.

7. Alan M. Klein, *Sugarball: The American Game, the Dominican Dream* (New Haven, CT: Yale University Press, 1991).

8. Alan M. Klein, *Baseball on the Border: A Tale of Two Laredos* (Princeton, NJ: Princeton University Press, 1997).

9. On the historical connection between sports and Argentine presidents and politicians, see Ariel Scher, *La patria deportista* (Buenos Aires: Editorial Planeta, 1996); and Pablo A. Ramírez, "Política y fútbol," *Todo Es Historia*, 21:248 (February 1988): 34–43.

10. Janet Lever, *Soccer Madness* (Chicago: University of Chicago Press, 1983).

11. Paula J. Pettavino and Geralyn Pye, *Sport in Cuba: The Diamond in the Rough* (Pittsburgh: University of Pittsburgh Press, 1994).

1

The Catholic Church and the Origins of Soccer in Costa Rica in the Early 1900s

Chester Urbina Gaitán

During more than three hundred years of colonial rule, the Roman Catholic Church played a crucial role in Latin America, one so important that at times it was difficult to distinguish it from the nonecclesiastical structures of the state. Independence in the early nineteenth century, however, initiated a long process in which the Church's powerful and privileged position came under challenge as governments, backed by so-called liberals, sought to free themselves from the clerics' influence. In some countries, such as Colombia and Mexico, this conflict over who would be in charge of the state became so heated that civil wars broke out. By the turn of the twentieth century, urban workers, their numbers growing because of increased trade, commerce, and industrialization, became the target of recruitment by both religious and secular authorities. In Costa Rica, as Chester Urbina shows, football (soccer in the United States) became the vehicle through which both clerics and civil officials attempted to attract workers to their cause.

Urbina's study brings out some interesting ideas. First, by supporting the playing of football/soccer, the Church linked the game to God, thus enhancing its legitimacy. Second, over time the game became so popular that it itself became a "god," challenging the institutionalized Church for attendance and even allegiance as more people attended matches rather than Masses. Third, the Church's backing for soccer backfired as it played into the hands of the state, whose "goal" all along had been to wean the general populace from priestly influence. Consequently, in Costa Rica, as most elsewhere in Latin America, today's Catholic Church, although not inconsequential, ranks much below its formerly powerful status; the civilian state now universally rules. Football/soccer played an important role in this fundamental transformation in Latin American life.

The objective of this article is to examine the position of the Costa Rican Catholic Church as an institution toward the play and popularization of soccer (known locally as *fútbol*, or football) in the first two decades of the twentieth century. Or, to put it another way, to explore whether the Church understood and took a position regarding the new cultural changes that were beginning to have an increasing impact on the Costa Rican mentality.

Early in the last century the perceived dangers of liberal ideas in America that closed in upon the Church forced it to rethink its work of pastoral action. In Costa Rica the vacancy left by the death of Bishop Thiel in 1901 was assumed by the new bishop of Costa Rica, Dr. Juan Gaspar Stork, a German Paulist priest, former director of the seminary, and close friend of Thiel. With the new century there also came to power a new generation of liberals made up of men with solid intellectual training, especially in law. Moreover, they had significant political experience acquired over the years by occupying important public positions; the most notable among them were Presidents Cleto González Víquez (1906–1910) and Ricardo Jiménez Oreamuno (1910–1914).

Since the beginning of the century, the creation and development of a working class in Costa Rica had been taking place, and it began to assume the characteristics of a structured and organized movement. In addition, the new group that began to administer the state found itself opposed on two fronts. On the one hand was the traditional bourgeoisie that controlled the agro-export sector. On the other was a younger, popular movement organized around the artisans' guilds and trade unions. This second group began to create an extensive social welfare network of night schools and reading and lecture rooms, which had as one of their central objectives the enhancement of laborers' knowledge not only in relation to labor issues but also in general.

Within this context of increasing adversity and defiance, the new sector of the dominant class, which moved to take control of the state at the beginning of the century, found itself obliged to look to the Church as an ally despite the fact that the two had become distanced from each other because of the former's promulgation of anticlerical laws. A conciliatory attitude on the part of the Vatican made the alliance possible.

During the period under study, possibly the most dangerous enemy of the urban workers' movement was the Church. It attacked not only labor organizations as well as their political clubs, press, and popular libraries but also the ideas professed by their members, whether liberal or socialist. Through the organization of Catholic artisans' circles, the Church aimed to divide the nascent workers' movement.

According to Mario Oliva, on the one hand there existed a secular movement, aligned with the nationalist objective of the state and which created its own press. On the other hand, there was a movement that incorporated workers into a conservative Catholic project, which offered them the consolation of eternal life and made them forsake any possibility of improvement in their temporal situation. With the coming to power of a new generation of liberals and the naming of a new bishop, Monsignor Juan Gaspar Stork, who served during the period from 1904 to 1921, there arose conditions for the beginning of a slow but steady rapprochement between the Church and state.

A Beneficial Relationship

The figure of the priest in the nation's communities has been, perhaps, one of the most notable and visible; his conduct, opinion, support, and guidance in a number of ways—for example, moral, spiritual, political, and that of drawing together and creating bonds among the faithful—have played a key role for Costa Ricans, giving the priest a deserved and indisputable position of leadership in the society. The loss of power and political leadership experienced by the Church toward the end of the nineteenth century, above all with the suppression of the Catholic Union Party (Partido Unión Católico), was not, however, accompanied by a total loss of prestige, power, and leadership by the national clergy at the community level.

On the contrary, some priests were able to consolidate their role as local leaders in a new way—by organizing and directing soccer/football associations in numerous towns. One of the first was organized in August 1904 in San Pedro de Poás where the local priest, Father Porras, also founded and served as the football club's president. This new phenomenon in which religious personnel directed social and sports organizations began in a "coincidental" way in 1904, the same year in which Bishop Stork came to power, and in the same geographical area.

It is worth mentioning the founding in November 1904 of the club Blue Sport Josefino, whose chaplain was Andrés Vilá y Alba, a priest of Spanish origin. Also, at the initiative of the players there arose the idea of staging benefits with the objective of aiding social causes. In June 1905 various members of the Club Sport from Santo Domingo de Heredia undertook a comedy production to raise funds for the construction of a new church building in the town. Slowly but surely other communities began to form their own sport clubs with the help of their local priests. On Sunday, October 21, 1906, the Club Paraiseño Foot Ball was installed, with a Nicaraguan, Father Alfredo Jarquín, named its honorary president. With considerable enthusiasm he transformed the town's central square into an area suitable for the practice of athletics. Also, the fathers of the seminary and its students in 1906 created the Club Foot Ball del Seminario, thanks mostly to the presence of German Paulist clerics who taught at the institution and imbued their pupils with their passion for sport.

An examination of San Isidro de Coronado (1906), San Pedro de Poás (1907), and San Antonio de Belén (1907) along with their respective priests, Gregorio de Jesús Benavides, Mardoqueo Arce, and Antonio

Monestel, makes it clear that these men combined their deep religious commitment with an effort to develop healthy and restorative recreational activities for young people. In other words, they used their positions to create sports organizations in their communities. As such, in their effort to strengthen relations with other towns for the purpose of gaining religious followers, the priests organized football matches. Most often, fiestas celebrating patron saints became the means for this end: an interesting program of activities alternated religious festivities with athletic competitions.

Everyday identity in Costa Rica revolved around the parish church, given that here was found the highest concentration of people, especially at the time of religious services. But with the arrival of football, the playing field, located in front of the church, slowly complemented religion's role regarding the development of a shared Costa Rican outlook.

This development of a common identity that football helped to create can be attributed in large part to the support provided by priests, both national and foreign. They understood the fraternal significance of this sport to parishioners. Given the great sympathy and appreciation enjoyed by priests in their communities, it was not uncommon for some football matches to be dedicated to them. In some towns, following the games, players and spectators gathered at the local cleric's residence. It played an important role in the search for companionship among winners and losers.

Although many ecclesiastics certainly supported and even actively promoted football, not all looked favorably upon it when competitions interrupted the holding of religious services. This fact is apparent in a report about a game that took place in Barva de Heredia on Monday, January 27, 1908:

> In yesterday's match in Barva between "Renacimiento" and "El Coronel Aguilar," the former won by two goals. During the action, a priest tried to stop the game on the pretext of holding rosary. The official and players became angry. Consequently, the competition continued without further problem despite the fact that the priest appealed to the *jefe político*, who took the attitude that it was better to wait. The public preferred diversion to devotion.

In this quotation, one clearly can see the cultural subordination of the Church to the state. Football, a cultural element promoted by liberalism, already had managed to distance Costa Ricans from religiosity and its manifestations, for example, the rosary and Mass. Attendance fell at church-related activities, especially on Sundays when football matches attracted large numbers of believers. Indeed, in some cases, such as in San Rafael Heredia, the ball even interrupted religious services because some people played soccer in the plaza located directly in front of the church. The origin of these sport plazas can be traced to the urban design created by the Spaniards during the colonial period. They established in the center of the community a space one block square for public use. This area also served as the site for the two principal buildings of the town: the parish church, which was nearly always built on the east side of the plaza, and the municipal government building on the west side.

As with all innovations that alter the prevailing values of society, there were various reactions to that of soccer. Some Costa Ricans, based on their values and form of explaining reality, believed that football disturbed the traditional routines of daily life. As such, these people resorted to popular religion to help understand this new phenomenon. For example, take the case of a woman from the city of Heredia in November 1908: "A concerned woman has decided for penance to peruse all the newspaper articles reporting about bothersome football, an act to be completed on San Silvestre Day or, in other words, on December 31. She reads them while kneeling on a 'shield' that looks like a 'Catholic' one, with pleasant thoughts. May she be contented!"

It is possible that some Costa Ricans, men as well as women, chose on Sundays to watch soccer matches rather than fulfill their duty to hear Mass, therefore opting for recreation over religion because the former activity was more attractive. Football allowed them the freedom to express themselves, to shout and say whatever they wanted, while a church service, by comparison, demanded a certain discipline and respectable behavior.

In the 1910s sport associations contributed enormously to the stamping of a secular character on Easter Week through the organization of excursions and outings to the port of Puntarenas. Especially important in this process was the Club Sport Alfonso XIII. Little by little, fueled by such trips organized by clubs combined with the public's expectations that soccer provoked, the game continued to grow in popularity and eventually drew more attention than official religious activities. This trend finally obliged Bishop Stork to issue Pastoral Letter Number 11 in 1912, "The Sanctification of Sunday and Holidays," which advocated not only attendance at Mass but also an end to the excuse of not going to church in order to travel to games. The bishop did not oppose as such the playing and viewing of football and sports in general; he only objected to the amount of time spent on these activities on Sundays, thus ignoring the original significance of the day—that of dedicating oneself to the Lord. Moreover, Monsignor Stork claimed that it was precisely on Sundays that the lack of moral constraint most manifested itself in the typical Costa Rican. According to him, on that day of the week, matches and other activities of an excessive nature encouraged the passionate behavior that had been at least partially contained during the workweek.

One thus can infer that soccer played the role of an escape valve through which Costa Ricans relieved the tensions, frustrations, and routine of daily life. In ending an exhortation, Bishop Stork offered the following advice:

> Venerable Brothers and Beloved Sons, we tell you again: Celebrate the day of the Lord as a duty of conscience, and do not allow yourselves to profane it because of various vain pretexts provided by diversions, nor by bad example, nor because of demands from men without religion or conscience. If such men mock our faith, if they threaten you or want to persuade you to go along with them, vigorously answer them with the Maccabean Saints: Save us, God, from him; we do not want to abandon the Law of God.

This message directly questioned the Church's advocacy of football, a liberal cultural project that had as its ends the secularization of customs and outlook. This stance was made clear by the official position of the Church as presented in the words of Monsignor Stork, although he only urged people to comply with religious duties, not to impede the already-mentioned state project. Nevertheless, Stork himself became an "indirect" collaborator of this project when he provided athletic equipment to the Club Sport "Juventud Mariana," which was made up of low-level workers.

The effort to reach out to Costa Ricans through football meant that the Church sought to use the same weapon to combat a phenomenon that the state itself was promoting, the secularization of customs and mentality, yet the latter was doing so in a more aggressive manner. Aside from immersing itself in a process of adjustment to an atmosphere of action against the state, the Church tried to find new mechanisms that would permit it to survive, thus neither losing its domination of nor its presence in society.

It also needs to be pointed out that the role played by the Church, by promoting football, amounted to a desperate attempt to dismantle workers' ideas and organizations that were considered hostile to it as well as to the state. In this way the Church aimed to divide the increasingly strong labor movement.

It would be an error to suppose that the thoughts of Dr. Stork, even though he certainly represented the official position of the Church, were shared and put into practice by all worshippers who made up the broad base of the institution. Despite his warnings and advice, Costa Ricans more and more identified with the liberal cultural project that employed football as its means to penetrate society. As such, during those years, Costa Ricans got into the habit of attending football matches on Sundays, a tradition fundamentally encouraged by the example that fathers passed on to their sons.

Conclusion

Undoubtedly, the social practice of football in Costa Rica can be accounted for because of its great popularity. This condition can be attributed, in part, to the role played by different clerics who, in their efforts to promote the sport, also aimed to proselytize and build a closer relationship between religious leaders and the faithful as well as among the public in general. Moreover, it is clear that these priests understood football in its global dimension. Basically they saw the sport as able to be manipulated for beneficial and restorative ends, thus hoping through it to gain the adherence of significant numbers of citizens.

This process came about as a result of the introduction of football as a new form of festivity, added to those that had a traditionally religious character such as Mass and patron saint commemorations. As a result, spiritual and moral benefits accrued—among them brotherhood, support, and solidarity—that over time became consolidated into a strong sense of common identity that still exists among Costa Ricans who were influenced by the religious element. In the end this condition made possible the achievement of goals heretofore unreachable, for example, the construction of new church buildings or the restoration of existing ones, not to mention allowing a rapid organization of the community.

What Costa Ricans did not always understand, despite the advice of Monsignor Stork, was that playing and watching football on Sundays might lead one to the failure to fulfill one's duties and obligations as a Christian. This is not to say that football need be considered a "sin," yet one should not fall into error and extremism by failing regularly to attend religious services.

The effort to tear down those ideas and forms of workers' organizations that the Church as well as the state considered hostile and prejudicial to their interests should also be noted. Indeed, an increasingly active labor movement established the need for new and significant changes that sought the construction of a more just and egalitarian society on Earth.

Finally, it is necessary to comment on the process of "adaptation," "collaboration," and "response" that the Church, as seen through Bishop Stork, experienced in relation to civil authority before about 1920. This process allowed the liberal cultural project to penetrate without great difficulty all aspects of Costa Rican life and, as a result, establish a strong identification among many of the country's citizens with soccer/football.

Bibliography

Betrano Valverde, Sonia, et al., "El Estado costarricense y la Iglesia Católica, 1900–1939: La participación de los sacerdotes en el Poder

Legislativo." Licenciatura thesis in history, Universidad de Costa Rica, 1994.

Oliva Medina, Mario. "Movimientos sociales en Costa Rica, 1825–1930," *Nuestra Historia*, 13 (San José: EUNED, 1992).

Urbina Gaitán, Chester, *Costa Rica y el deporte (1871–1921): Un estudio acerca del origen de fútbol y la construcción de un deporte nacional* (Heredia, CR: Editorial Universidad Nacional, 2001).

Urbina Gaitán, Chester. "El fútbol en San José: Un estudio histórico social acerca de su origen, 1898–1921." Licenciatura thesis in history, Universidad de Costa Rica, 1994.

2

The Case of Soccer in Early Twentieth-Century Lima

Steve J. Stein

Soccer (called football in many countries outside the United States) is Latin America's premier sport, equivalent to, one might argue, U.S. baseball, football, and basketball rolled into one in terms of popularity and its impact on society. This degree of success, however, has not always been the case. Soccer first arrived in South America via the British during the last half of the nineteenth century, and in the beginning it was played mainly by foreigners and a handful of local elites with close connections to these outsiders. How and why, then, did soccer become such a widely played and watched sport?

The University of Miami's Steve Stein, an expert on labor in Latin America, provides some answers to these questions in his study of soccer in early twentieth-century Lima. He also points out the intersection of such issues as urbanization, class, race, and institutionalization, all of which played key roles in the development of the sport in Peru's capital and largest city. According to Stein, lower-class workers, many of them black, found in soccer a chance to improve their generally oppressive lives. At the same time, elites, mainly whites, saw in soccer an opportunity to channel and control potentially threatening lower-class energy. Therefore, they moved to create a systematized and commercialized version of soccer—one that persuaded the masses to take part (the material rewards were substantial while the psychological release of yesteryear remained) and at the same time one that functioned as a mechanism to help ensure social tranquillity. Hence, soccer served as both a liberating and restrictive force that served the interests of people of all walks of life, thus helping in part to explain its great attraction.

From *Sport and Society in Latin America: Diffusion, Dependency, and the Rise of Mass Culture*, ed. Joseph L. Arbena (Westport, CT: Greenwood Press, 1988), 63–84. Reprinted by permission of Greenwood Press.

It might seem redundant and not particularly profound to state that the principal characteristic of the life of Latin America's poor has always been misery. Nevertheless, this simplistic redundancy carries with it a series of questions that students of Latin American society have long been trying to answer with varying success. If misery has acted in different situations and at different times as a kind of sieve through which the life of the poor has passed, how has it shaped popular values and institutions? On another level, how have the essentially oppressive societies of Latin America—oppressive at least from the standpoint of the poor—survived during years, decades, centuries? What have been the major forces of cohesion, both external and internal to the Latin American popular sectors, that have helped hold these societies together?

An essay on soccer in early twentieth-century Peru could hardly purport to answer such complex questions.[1] Yet this case study of the development of the sport among the growing popular sectors in Lima from 1900 to 1930 reveals a variety of significant forms of social control, from the production and dissemination among the urban poor of conservative ideological norms to the preemption of potential popular self-consciousness and unrest through the institutionalization of one of this group's primary forms of diversion and autonomous expression. At the same time, we may see through the emergence of soccer how the popular sectors in an expanding metropolis created new forms of space—living space—in a world highly stratified in social and economic terms, which offered them precious little of such space. In short, the growth and progressive institutionalization of popular soccer exercised a dual impact on the urban poor. First, the consolidation of greater "living space" through participation in and attendance at soccer games made the life of some members of the popular sectors more bearable, at least in psychological terms. Second, the increasing institutionalization of popular sport made for greater identification between lower-class players and fans on the one hand, and the dominant elite and the state on the other.

Popular soccer began as the most informal of diversions at the turn of the century in Lima; thirty years later, when Peru fielded its first national team in World Cup competition, the sport seemed to have come full circle, from being a major form of autonomous lower-class expression to being a major form of elite supportive social control. This study traces the drama of soccer as popular expression versus soccer as social control and attempts to explain its resolution.

Throughout Latin America the emergence of popular soccer was directly related to the birth of mass cities. The close intertwining of these two processes was evident in Lima during the first three decades of this century. In these years the Peruvian capital began to undergo an almost revolutionary transformation. For the first time the urban area began to extend geographically beyond its colonial limits. New paved streets and avenues, new houses for the rich and to a lesser extent for the poor, new public plazas, and new multistoried edifices all combined to give the city the image of a rapidly expanding modern metropolis. But even more than the physical evidence of change, the most dramatic feature of a growing Lima was expressed in the human dimension. Between 1900 and 1931 the total number of inhabitants rose over 125 percent, from approximately 165,000 to 376,000. The popular masses grew even more spectacularly, by more than 200 percent in the same period. The largest scale rural-urban migration in Peruvian history to that date was the major cause of this overall growth.

Simultaneously, the urban masses became plainly visible on the urban landscape: they labored on the numerous construction projects that exemplified the city's growth; they sold everything from vegetables in the city's expanding markets to lottery tickets in the new public squares; they worked in the textile, shoe, and beer factories; they inhabited the growing number of *callejones*, *casas de vecindad*, and *casas subdivididas* that had sprung up to meet the need for lower-class housing. The emergence of the popular masses as a political force was also undeniable. This was clear in the initial organization of bakers and textile workers, in the general strikes of 1913 and 1919, and in growing support for political candidates, first in street demonstrations and later as members of Peru's earliest organized populist parties.

In terms of popular culture, soccer quickly became the most significant expression of the massification process. The fact that by the 1920s more than 25,000 people would have gathered in a stadium in Lima to watch a soccer match, as they often did, is testimony to both the emergence of Lima as a mass city and the importance of soccer as a mass sport.

Lima's first recorded soccer match took place in 1892, and in its initial form popular participation and appeal were totally absent. As in the case of all the sports practiced in Peru around the turn of the century—riflery, bullfights, bicycle and boat racing—soccer was restricted to Lima's elite groups and was a foreign import. Peru's elite, increasingly integrated into the international economic system, was quick to imitate the cultural patterns of the core's elites. As with other European imports, soccer arrived in Peru in the 1880s aboard an English ship. The sport's English origins were immediately apparent, for example, when the first press account of the sport (1892) referred to it as "Football," a term which is retained today:

> On Sunday, August 7, a *Football* challenge will occur, between Limeños and Chalacos [residents of the port city of Callao] in Santa Sofia, Lima, organized by señores Larranaga and Fonkes, beginning at three in the afternoon.[2]

Still today in Peruvian soccer one speaks of the "offside," "corner," "forward," and "wing." These terms were also used in the early twentieth century and represented a clear expression of elite cultural dependency on Europe, specifically Great Britain.

In 1893 two exclusive soccer clubs were formed: Lima Cricket and Football Club, composed almost exclusively of foreigners resident in Peru; and Unión Cricket, composed both of foreigners and of Lima's young "gentlemen," or sons of the elite. These clubs combined soccer with other sorts of games such as cricket, polo, boat racing, and fencing. This was also true of the Club Cyclist Lima at the turn of the century, where members participated in both bicycle races and soccer matches. The kind of young men who were active in these clubs conformed to a specific social type: the "eminent *sport-man*" ("*conocido sport-man*"). The typical "sport-man" was energetic, athletic, carefree, and the member of a wealthy and prominent family.[3]

In the final years of the nineteenth century, soccer matches were often organized among groups—not always through such formal institutions as Lima Cricket or Unión Cricket—from areas that included central Lima, Callao, and the wealthy suburbs or summer retreats of Barranco and Chorrillos. There was a gradual increase in the number of spectators at these games, played on open fields, although no seating was available and no admission charged. Spectators, who were still almost exclusively members of the elite, began to have "favorite" teams with which they identified and whose progress they followed. In 1897 admission was charged for the first time at a soccer game; soccer began to have a more public character, although its participants were still drawn from the elite. By the turn of the century people began regularly to attend soccer games (*ir el fútbol*).

In sum, when soccer first became absorbed into the Peruvian cultural panoply, it conformed to the mold of various other elite, exclusivist sports and institutions of the era. Later, against the backdrop of a changing social context, soccer would come to play a very different role.

Among the effects of early urbanization and industrialization in Lima was that ever larger numbers of people were thrown into ever more densely concentrated social spaces: neighborhoods, factories, etc. Possibly this generalized process of collectivization favored the popularization of collective sports. It was in the port city of Callao where soccer as a working-class sport first took root. Sailors from English vessels demonstrated the sport to the inhabitants of this poor city. Later, spontaneous matches would occasionally be played between the young aristocrats of Lima Cricket and workers who had observed their play with curiosity.

Soon these informal matches between dock workers or fishermen and English sailors in Callao, or between players of Lima Cricket and workers in the capital, led to growing popular participation in soccer. In some instances, the patronage of the aristocratic clubs allowed working-class clubs to be established, which in turn would provide competition for the patron clubs. The aristocratic clubs encouraged workers' teams, paying them small "tips" or quotas for matches in which the two teams met. More frequently, workers began to form their own teams without upper-class patronage. In February 1901, the first such "spontaneous workers" club was formed, "Club Sport Alianza," later to become well known as Alianza Lima. A year later, Alianza's early rival, Club Atlético Chalaco, was established in Callao. By 1910 a whole series of working-class teams had appeared; these included: Sport José Gálvez, Sport Tarapacá, Miraflores Sporting Club, Club Atlético Grau, Sport Inca, Sport Jorge Chávez, Club Atlético de Lima, Sport Vitarte, Sport Progreso, and Sporting Tabaco (later Sporting Cristal).[4]

These clubs, composed of players from the lowest social strata, were formed in a variety of ways. Some began with the enthusiastic backing of the working-class neighborhoods or districts of the city where the players lived. Such was the case of Unión Buenos Aires Callao, located in the Buenos Aires district of the port city, and of Sport Alianza, which had its home and original allegiance with the new factory district, La Victoria. These types of clubs were usually formed spontaneously and autonomously by workers who played together regularly. Alianza, for example, was originally established by men who were employed to care for the racehorses of Augusto B. Leguía, future president of Peru. They would play soccer near the stables every afternoon after work. According to one account: "One fine day the idea came up to found a soccer club just like the *gringos* of Lima Cricket and the 'whites' of Unión Cricket."[5] One worker who recalls the early days of working-class soccer in Peru reflected on the growing importance of these neighborhood teams during this period:

> Each neighborhood had its club, but these clubs were informal, and their interest was in playing. You would see soccer from eight o'clock in the morning until eight in the evening. All those teams! All different kinds of teams with their uniforms. Boys who played for the sport of it, no? There were no other motives; they played for sport. When Alianza [Lima] won, La Victoria won.[6]

In the first decade of the twentieth century, when these initial neighborhood or district teams were formed, Lima was more a series of semi-autonomous neighborhoods than an integrated city. One's identification was first with one's *barrio* or district—El Rímac, La Victoria—and only second with Lima as a whole. And these soccer teams were often the most visible symbol or representative of the *barrio*. The victory of one club over another in a soccer match symbolized the victory of one area over another.

But in the early years of the century, most workers experienced soccer through less formalized channels than established clubs. On the way home from school, or just walking around the neighborhood, one would inevitably stumble upon spontaneous soccer games played in the streets or in vacant fields. The early experience of Antonio Maquilón, who was to become the first captain of a Peruvian team to participate in a World Cup match (Montevideo, 1930), was probably typical of most: "I began to play in school. I would even play hooky in order to play soccer. We used to play in pastures where we had to clear out rocks to make a playing field."[7] Miguel "Quemado" Rostaing, a working-class black who would become a renowned player in the 1910s and 1920s, tells of a similar initiation into the sport: "We used to play in the neighborhood, sometimes five against five. In the kind of field that you found all over then. In those days Lima was still all farms. Groups of us boys used to play"[8]

Neighborhood soccer, then, was played with few material objects. The playing fields were simply open spaces with goals delineated by stones. The teams played with "rag balls" (*pelotas de trapo*), which were made of women's stockings filled with rags, wool, and sometimes a stone for weight. The more established teams played with rubber balls and began wearing uniforms "thrown together any which-way," according to one player.[9] These uniforms, usually nothing more than T-shirts of a given color and style, were paid for with the players' own small monthly contributions or, in some cases, with a donation from a better-off neighbor who would then be named president of the club.[10]

For young men of the poorest social sectors, who lacked resources and support institutions, soccer came to have an importance in daily life beyond casual recreation. Through the sport, they began to expand their "living space" in a variety of ways. For example, the small soccer team grew into a close-knit network of friends who were involved in each others' lives, on and off the soccer field. According to Maquilón: "We on the team were very close. We used to go to the movies. We would fool around together, play with tops, make mischief. My best friends were the ones who played [soccer] with me."[11]

On a more basic level soccer came to represent a significant form of autonomous popular expression. From the dawn of the sport to the present day, the distinctive characteristic of Peruvian popular soccer has been what is called *picardía*. Miguel Rostaing explains clearly what *picardía* meant on the soccer field and how, in his experience at least, a dominant style of play was simply a reflection of a dominant style of living:

> The *pícaro* player is the guy who doesn't let himself get kicked all the time. They weren't going to be kicking us. So you had to find [a way], jumping here, jumping there. And sometimes you had to give back a little so that they would be afraid of you. You're born with it, you're born with *picardía*. A quick-witted person is called a *pícaro*. To be quick witted when you play is not to let yourself get kicked. To face life, be-

> cause life is like a soccer game, you have to be quick so that you don't get hit that way in life.[12]

Rostaing's concern with maneuvering more than with winning is not unusual in a world where, as Peruvian sociologist Abelardo Sánchez León has stated, political, social, and economic power was "so immense, vast, and unfathomable that you could not directly confront it. Rather you had to deal with it by dribbling around it, making feints, dodging so that with a strange psychological reasoning, the lower-class person opposed a power superior to him by trying to weaken it or wear it out."[13]

Soccer as self-expression and intangible personal reward was most clear in the experiences of the early players, even from the most prestigious clubs like Alianza Lima or Atlético Chalaco, who through the beginning of the 1920s played largely for love of the sport, since participation in soccer at that point represented a material sacrifice rather than material rewards. Nevertheless, certain special benefits did exist. Some players were attracted by the admiration and enthusiasm of the spectators: "The crowd began to buzz," according to Miguel Rostaing, "when one player faked out another, dribbling around him. And the crowd would join in and shout for you."[14] Another player of the era recounts that "when you made a good play and they cheered you, you felt like God. You really felt you could do anything."[15] Or on an even more basic level, Rostaing states: "You feel pride, pride that you're worth something."[16] For the Lima poor who suffered the humiliation and "defeats" of daily life, these feelings had enormous significance. In a society that continually denigrated their basic human worth, soccer was one of the few areas in which players who were poor could feel valuable, whole, accepted, and even revered.

More concrete than this relatively amorphous sense of personal fulfillment was that, for many working-class players, success in soccer led to the attraction of friends, male and female. "In those days that was the satisfaction of the soccer player, to attract women to dance. Then came respect, special consideration, the esteem of friends."[17] Often this esteem was expressed in the rounds of beer the fans bought the players and in the neighborhood parties that fans and family members sponsored after games. Israel Bravo Ríos, who played on Sporting Tabaco, remembered that

> . . . games never ended without dances following them. The most important thing for us, the players, was getting together after the game at the club's locale. Girls would come, and there would be music, a party. And you were like a hero, you got a lot of attention from the girls. Of course, you didn't have only low intentions, it wasn't all a question of excesses. Respect and esteem were foremost. Of course we knew what we wanted; that's part of human nature.[18]

In addition, as the 1910s became the 1920s, there were increasingly more tangible rewards for soccer players and clubs. The clubs organized tournaments in which certificates, medals, and sometimes trophies were given out. The players themselves, together with other members of the clubs and their presidents, contributed toward the purchase of these prizes. For many players, winning a certificate or a "gold medal" —usually made of copper—was an event of great importance. Even players of the stature of Miguel Rostaing, who went on to play in international competition, placed a high personal value on those early prizes. Asked in 1982 what had been the most important part of his career, Rostaing insisted that "For me, the gold medals, the certificates, those are the most gratifying memories. But it costs a lot to frame them. In hard times I've had to pawn the medals."[19]

This world of soccer, created by the working-class players themselves, had become a genuine manifestation of popular culture. Allowed to evolve autonomously, the solidarity that emerged between players and fans might have later translated into forms of class solidarity and perhaps class consciousness among the popular sectors as a whole. Nevertheless, just as the seeds of soccer as popular expression were visible in this early period, so were the seeds of soccer as social control. The first evidence of attempts on the part of other social sectors to utilize the sport to fortify their own positions vis-à-vis the urban poor was the establishment and financing of soccer clubs for lower-class players by members of the dominant elites. A clear example of this—and also a first step toward the professionalization of soccer—was the creation of clubs by the owners of the principal textile factories of Lima and in the nearby factory town of Vitarte. Apparently the idea for such clubs emerged when managers saw workers playing soccer after work in empty fields near the factories. First the managers established teams from different sections of the same factory and gave one *sol* to the winning team in intrafactory matches. Slightly later, teams were formed to represent entire textile factories: Sport Inca, of the Inca Cotton Mill; Sport Progreso, of the Fábrica del Progreso; Sport Vitarte, of the Fábrica de Tejidos Vitarte; and José Gálvez of the Fábrica de Tejidos de La Victoria. The founding of José Gálvez was described in the following manner:

> The José Gálvez Club was formed on May 2, 1907. It was made up of the workers of the factory. The man in charge of it all was Sr. Ricardo Tizón y Bueno [president of the factory]. The factory donated uniforms, shoes, everything. They gave the team a free locale. They didn't charge them rent. And everyone who played for the team was given work in the factory.[20]

In recruiting players with offers of relatively privileged and well-paying jobs (compared with nonindustrial occupations), the textile factories pushed soccer one step further toward professionalization. Frequently it was the player who approached the company's management, either directly or through a friend already there. According to a man who came to play for Sporting Tabaco in just such a manner,

> The manager would say, "we'll give him a chance. Let's see him play." Then they would watch him. If they liked what they saw, they gave him a job, even though it might just be cleaning up, or sweeping. The important thing is that you were working in the factory. You had a good salary.[21]

And there were some additional benefits as well. The soccer players left work early for practice, without losing any income. Some occasionally received from management loans that were not available to other workers.

These practices occurred mainly, but not solely, in the textile factories. In addition to the Club Sporting Tabaco, created by the cigarette factory, the owners of various haciendas around Lima created "company teams."

For their part, the hacienda and factory owners' motives probably went beyond pure sportsmanship. In the case of the factory teams, their creation clearly corresponded with the desire of owners and managers to forge bonds of loyalty between themselves and their workers. By sponsoring the teams, buying their equipment, providing the clubs with locales, and sometimes subsidizing the post-match celebrations, the presidents/owners/managers created strong clienteles among their workers. This description, provided by a player of Sporting Tabaco, illustrates the strong element of paternalism inherent in these initiatives:

> The president, who at that time was don Juan Carbone, would arrive [at the post-game party]. Carbone was very lively. Whether we had won, lost, or tied the game, he always came with a contribution and to see if we were getting along with each other. He would come, stay for a little while, then get in his car and say, "Have fun. Here's a donation for your beer." And then all of us, grateful, would continue the party. And we were in such good physical condition in those days that we'd get up at 6 A.M., and by seven we were in the factory. The president didn't participate in the party. He looked in to make sure there were no bad feelings among us, difficulties, problems. He was like a father. Really. And we all came through with our obligations, because we admired him, like he admired us.[22]

A player from another club interpreted the gestures of his "patron" differently: "The thing is that those people are smart. You take care of him, the Señor. If you have workers, you have to reward them. So that the workers will watch out for you, instead of robbing you."[23]

For the owners of factories and haciendas, the sponsoring of popular soccer produced another even more tangible benefit. Matches between factory or hacienda teams distracted some workers from political or union-related concerns, and created divisions among members of the working class. According to some union leaders of the era, these actions had a negative impact on their ability to forge worker solidarity:

> It was in the interest of the factory to use sports to break the labor movement. It pulled people away. They had tournaments between factories, and the union struggle suffered somewhat. Because everybody in the factory liked sports, pushed sports. It was a tactical move on the part of the owners to create disunity in the organization. That's where rivalries began; there were actual fights between the clubs. In Vitarte, when the soccer team played against La Victoria, there were fights.[24]

Workers who had fought among themselves on the soccer field found it more difficult afterward to unite in seeking social revindication.

Working-class soccer also created rivalries in contests between neighborhood or *barrio* teams. Independent of the influence of upper-class patrons, these matches sometimes ended in brawls between players and fans, who identified with different districts of the city. These forms of internal conflict surfaced in both the "spontaneous" and "institutionalized" forms of the sport.

This picture of the emergence of popular soccer in early twentieth-century Lima is one filled with contradictions. The same sport that seemed to have the potential for stimulating class unity also produced conflicts between members of the popular classes. The game that constituted a highly significant form of popular self-expression and self-affirmation seemed to be easily turned to the purposes of elite social domination and ideological hegemony. Yet even within these uses of the sport for social control, there appeared important popular responses. As we have seen, at least some workers were well aware of factory owners' manipulative motives. And popular sector players were equally willing to manipulate the game for their own purposes. As one player from a hacienda recalls:

> When I worked on the hacienda, I played soccer also, with the other peons. We made don Enrique Pardo, the hacienda owner's son, president of the team. He gave us a set of shirts, so we made him president. He gave us a trophy and paid for meals. We used to go on Sundays to other haciendas to play. We played because we loved the game. We made the hacienda owners captains, not so they would play, but so they would give us something. They were the owners. They gave us shirts, shoes, balls. We took advantage of it.[25]

This player astutely observed that the peons encouraged the owners' patronage, not only because it facilitated their play, but because in doing so they saw themselves as "taking advantage" of the hacienda owners. Hence, within these attempts of upper-class sponsors to use the sport to consolidate their own positions, workers played at a similar game. At the same time that soccer became an effective means of social control, a way of reproducing the existing class structure through new mechanisms and clientage, workers did not seek to escape these mechanisms, but rather to exploit them for their own benefit. The very efforts on the part of the upper classes to use the sport to promote their self-interest led to the creation of opportunities for increased living space, in material and psychological terms, for lower-class players at least. While some of these players might have been induced to sincere expressions of clientelistic loyalty to their patrons—"He was like a father . . . we admired him"—others found in the relationship that emerged elements of class opposition as well as elements of vertical social cohesion—"They were the owners . . . We took advantage of it."

With the coming of the 1920s, soccer would begin to take on a much greater importance in the life of the city's popular sectors. That decade marked soccer's transformation into a major spectator sport. It would be in the burgeoning soccer stadiums that seated the growing numbers of spectators where the battle between soccer as popular expression versus soccer as social control would be decided.

One immediately evident feature of the new decade was the virtual disappearance of elite soccer clubs composed entirely of the rich, the white, the *gente decente de buena familia* [decent people of high lineage]. Unión Cricket and Lima Cricket were the only representatives extant in the early 1920s of the old guard, and soon they too were inundated by the new popular clubs. Various factors led to the retreat of oligarchic teams from the top ranks. They found themselves continually defeated on the soccer field by lower-class teams that could recruit their players from a much larger pool. Furthermore, for the exclusive members of Lima Cricket, it would have been absolutely unacceptable to play on the same team with a black or a mestizo; this would mean not only close contact with their "inferiors" in training and in games, but also—what was much worse—contact in the locker rooms.

What was happening with soccer teams reflected a larger social trend: public life in general, and specifically the sphere of organized sports, was becoming dominated by the popular sectors. In the case of soccer another cause and an important effect of this domination was the growth of sports consumers, the spectators who in ever larger numbers attended soccer matches. The overwhelming majority of these spectators belonged to the urban lower classes. Soccer crowds were made up of working men and women: taxi drivers, textile workers, construction workers, fishermen, stevedores, maids, and peons from the haciendas surrounding the capital. They came together in their scarce moments of leisure, on Sundays and holidays, to watch this magical game played by their peers. Soccer matches were a form of amusement, a way of escaping, at least momentarily, from the heavy burdens of working-class life. Soccer was a spectacle, a social occasion, a kind of collective release, for fans as well as players, a new kind of "living space."

Before the 1910s, soccer "stadiums" had no walls or seats. They were simply open fields surrounded on a Saturday or Sunday by a hundred or so spectators, who, in the early years, were mostly relatives or friends of the players. Of course, admission was rarely charged for those early games. During the decade 1910–1920, however, these arrangements gave way to more formal settings, as benches began to be placed around the fields, and people now had to pay to see most games. Even in these makeshift stadiums a division between first- and second-class seats was established; in 1914, for example, typical ticket prices were 50 *centavos* for the "Preferential" section and 20 for the "Popular" seats.[26] With the sale of food and beer, matches turned into true fiestas. To give some idea of the size of these events, contemporary reports estimated that some 7000 people attended a game in 1918 between Atlético Chalaco and José Gálvez, a record for the period.[27]

By the end of the 1920s not only had the number and size of soccer stadiums increased, but also the price and variety of tickets. The following types of seats were available for a 1930 game between the two top teams, Alianza Lima and Universitario de Deportes: first class, child's seat in first class, first class unreserved, railing unreserved, and second class.[28]

Although it is very difficult to confirm exact numbers of spectators for these games, the report on the above match gives a good idea of the massive nature of these events:

> Days before the date fixed for the playing of the game . . . the demand for tickets was truly extraordinary. . . . The demand for tickets greatly exceeded the capacity of the National Stadium to seat the spectators in a normal fashion. As a consequence, violence broke out . . . thousands of people were unable to enter the stadium in spite of having in their hands their legitimate tickets.[29]

One important facet of the growing number of soccer spectators was the appearance of the *barras*, or rooting sections, for specific teams. The affection of the *barra* and of the individual fan for the club was a function of the growth of the city and of changing urban lifestyles. There existed a long tradition of identity with one's neighborhood, and many soccer teams had become informal institutional expressions of that identity. On a broader level, the teams responded to a need for identification on the part of a growing, heterogeneous urban mass population. Like the regional associations that integrated new migrants, religious brotherhoods that integrated the faithful, and labor unions and political parties that integrated those with common concerns for their own welfare and that of the larger body politic, soccer clubs provided a sense of belonging, a sense of place in the ever-changing, at times uncertain, metropolis.

The *barras* emerged with particular energy in the 1920s, above all on the occasions of the first *clásicos*, the games between the archrival teams

Alianza Lima and Atlético Chalaco, that informally represented Lima against the neighboring port city of Callao. As Callao did not yet have a soccer stadium, the games generally took place in Lima. The *barra* of Atlético Chalaco, made up largely of fishermen and stevedores, was greatly feared by the Lima populace, as well as by the Alianza Lima players. The *barra* from Callao would arrive by train and, according to the account of Antonio Maquilón, "They went on foot to the stadium. The mobs that came! And through all the streets [screaming] *chimpún* Callao, *chimpún* Callao![30] (The term *chimpún* comes from the small sticks of dynamite carried by the fishermen.) Pedro Frías further describes the behavior of the *barras* during the games:

> People started fighting each other. It was a terrible thing when the Callao team played the Lima team. It was like a war. It was like the Chileans and the Peruvians, natural enemies. There was tremendous passion. If a Callao team lost, if Alianza won, uf![31]

The enthusiasm of the *barras* affected the players as much as the spectators. Miguel Rostaing, who played for a period with Alianza Lima, relates his experiences with the inflamed fans from the perspective of those on the field:

> We had to play with a knife in our hand to stick any of those fans who got mean, to scare them. They were tough, those guys from Callao. Lots of bad people. The fishermen came with dynamite. They had their dynamite ready. So the Lima *barra* couldn't take it. How could they defend themselves? They had to leave on the run. Those fishermen almost blew up a back who we had when they threw a stick of dynamite next to where he was going to kick the ball. And another time they beat us when some fans, who were in back of the goal, stuck a knife through the net and cut Segalá [the Alianza goalie] in the behind. Segalá turned around, and the ball went in the net. They had to take Segalá out and give him five stitches. Their *barra* was terrible. You had to run off the field at the end of the game with your pants in your hands.[32]

Among other things, these experiences demonstrate that soccer had taken root in the consciousness of the Lima popular masses. It had, in fact, become almost the sole sport of the urban popular sectors and, for many, a central concern in their daily lives. In the words of one who felt the attraction of soccer:

> When I was young [in the 1920s], I liked soccer more than anything else. There was no other sport except soccer. And besides Independence Day and Carnival, there was nothing, nothing else. But soccer really stirred me up because it had everything, even better than girls.[33]

Related to the general popularization of soccer and the emergence of the *barras* was the appearance of the so-called idols, of players of clearly lower-class origins, who filled the sports pages and the conversations of all groups attracted to soccer. These were men with whom the young and even the old of working-class Lima could identify, one of the few positive role models that came from the same social and racial strata as themselves. The idols were men to imitate; they represented forms of behavior to which to aspire. And they were essentially spontaneous creations in an age prior to broadcast media, one in which even the print media was just beginning to devote substantial coverage to sports.[34]

The impressive growth in soccer's popularity did not escape the attention of Peru's dominant elites. The large crowds, unbridled enthusiasm, and frequent outbreaks of violence at the games provoked a degree of fear in the upper classes. To many, "savage soccer mobs" and "violent soccer emotions" must have seemed to be particularly dangerous manifestations of the growing mass presence in Lima. The excesses of soccer would need to be curbed just like the more obvious dangers of popular sector emergence, such as strikes and political demonstrations. The creation of a series of formal institutions to regulate sports activities constituted a major response to these concerns. The first signs of this enthusiasm for institutionalization were the tournaments organized by those factories that had teams: trophies and pennants were awarded to the winners, and the events were invariably followed by parties paid for by the firms. In 1912 the first step was taken to organize soccer on a wider plane with the foundation of the Peruvian Soccer League (Liga Peruana de Fútbol). It is interesting to note the social origins of the two presidents of the league: Eduardo Fry, a member of Lima's social elite, and H. G. Redsaaw, a prominent representative of the local British community. The English sportsman Sir Thomas Dewar donated a silver plaque to be awarded to the winning club each season. It was with the foundation of the league that admission was normally charged for soccer games.

Despite its yearly championships between 1912 and 1921, the league was plagued with difficulties from the outset. It did not have an office and suffered from a perpetual shortage of funds. Ultimately the league was unable to impose its authority over its member clubs, and in 1922 an internal schism developed that led to its demise. One faction of the league thereupon founded the Peruvian Soccer Federation (Federación Peruana de Fútbol) in August 1922, and in 1924 the latter affiliated itself with the international soccer organization, FIFA.[35] The emergence of the federation coincided with the opening of Lima's National Stadium, a gift of the British community in Lima on the occasion of Peru's centennial celebrations. Decisive steps had been taken in the institutionalization of soccer and its recognition as an "official sport." This marked the initiation of a process through which sport as an expression of popular culture would be distorted by the state acting as a mediator and a control. Peruvian soccer continued to be practiced on an amateur level, but the popular spontaneity connected with its early days, particularly in regard to the formation and functioning of clubs, began to decline at a rapid pace.

The full impact of institutionalization would not become evident until Peruvian national teams were formed in the late 1920s to compete in international tournaments. Throughout that decade, however, there were other forces that increasingly militated against spontaneous popular soccer. The most important of these was the progressive use of so-called "tips" to pay players informally. These payments were made possible with the charge for admission to the games. During the 1920s, particularly after the founding of the federation, tips became the norm for nearly all the major teams. The tip was not a fixed salary, but rather a percentage of the gate. The federation received its share, the club took another 20 percent, and the rest was divided equally among all the players. Although, in the eyes of the fans, specific soccer idols had clearly emerged, this fact was not reflected in higher payments to the best players.

Despite the extension of the payment of tips and the growing crowds at the games, until the 1930s there was not a single soccer player who made a living exclusively from his play. The case of the famous right wing of Alianza Lima and the national team, José María Lavalle, is illustrative in this context. A brickmaker by trade, Lavalle got up every morning at 4 A.M. to prepare his bricks, after which, according to his longtime friend and teammate Miguel Rostaing, "he worked all day, and he went to Santa Beatriz in the afternoons to train. And when the tickets were so cheap, how much did they pay him? A pittance. He had nothing."[36]

The tendency toward the integration or co-optation of popular soccer by the dominant elites, either through institutionalization or through tips, did not have the same effect on all clubs. The majority of the best clubs quickly succumbed to the new order. Others never played outside their neighborhoods, competing entirely on the local level. The contradiction between soccer as popular expression and soccer as social control was no more clearly seen than with the premier team of the period, Alianza Lima. At the same time that Alianza continued through the 1920s to be a faithful representative of spontaneous popular soccer, it was also subject to the same pressures toward informal professionalism as the rest of the teams. In fact, because of its superior performance on the field, Alianza was the focus of additional forces promoting its integration into institutionalized soccer. The story of Alianza in these years illustrates the tensions within popular soccer, and its response to institutional pressures at the end of the decade, in moments when Peru was fielding its first national teams in international competition, would mark the end of the formative era in Peruvian soccer.

From its formation in 1901, Alianza was like the other local teams; it had no ambitions outside the boundaries of its own neighborhood, the working-class *barrio* of La Victoria. But the very quality of its players, the increasing competitiveness of the sport, and the simple desire to become known soon lured Alianza beyond those local streets and makeshift fields. By the 1920s, it had become Lima's most popular soccer club for various reasons. First, Alianza was truly popular in its origins. Never linked to a factory or any particular firm, its players worked at a variety of jobs, including construction, printing, textiles, and truck driving. Furthermore, the Alianza of the post-World War I years distinguished itself through its unusual ethnic composition; unlike most teams, its players were largely black. Alianza represented a mixture of what was clearly identifiable as lower class, and this was nowhere more evident than in the color of its black "idols," especially Alejandro "Manguera" Villanueva, José María Lavalle, Miguel "Quemado" Rostaing, and Alberto "Culebra" Montellanos.

The fact that a black team was able to gain prominence as not only the best but also the most popular club had implications that went far beyond the sports sphere. In some ways Alianza's success put a positive value on blackness, on the particular qualities of society's traditionally lowest racial stratum.

"Soccer is the sport of the blacks" became an oft-heard refrain, which not only recognized obvious virtues, but could also be interpreted to imply the incapacity of this group to excel in other activities, such as business or politics. With the success of Alianza, we see the self-affirmation of the individual lower-class soccer player being acted out on a larger social canvas. Whatever the interpretation, the dominance of lower-class and black soccer players meant that, in at least one area of society, the recreational area, the popular sectors could reign supreme.

But this supremacy too was ambiguous. Alianza's appeal and its successes constituted one of the instances for the exploited to defeat their exploiters, for the poor to defeat the rich, for the blacks to defeat the whites. Soccer was a mirror that reflected larger social conflicts, but it was an imperfect mirror that inverted or distorted them. Democracy reigned on the soccer field, while it was missing from the general society. Hence, the victories of popular soccer remained largely symbolic. After the match ended, life resumed its normal course: the worker returned to the factory, the black or mestizo to his marginal existence.

Although popular dominance through soccer was mainly symbolic, it was not meaningless or illusory. Indeed, the virtual hegemony of Alianza in the 1920s was a primary motive for the creation of a new team in 1927 to mount an upper- and middle-class challenge to the lower-class supremacy of Alianza. The Universitario de Deportes, made up largely of university students and appealing to a "higher category" of spectators, quickly became and remains the major rival of Alianza. The matches between Alianza and Universitario, which on occasion took the form of virtual warfare, became cultural representations of class and ethnic conflict. A popular sports magazine of the period openly described that "class conflict" in the following terms:

> The University team, made up mainly of young men who have always aspired to take first place in Peruvian soccer, is the incarnation of the idea of a renewal of our values in this sport. . . . Alianza Lima, a popular team which has garnered the support and admiration of all good fans, represents the athletic abilities of the more modest class: the people. On one side are the youthful students and on the other the workers.[37]

This same magazine characterized Alianza-Universitario games in terms of racial conflict by referring to the teams as coffee and milk:

> A coffee with milk,
> with Quality milk [read Universitario]
> and coffee highly esteemed
> as is Alianza Lima. . . .
> The match of the little blacks [*negritos*]
> with the doctors will be a competition between
> milk and coffee in which the best qualities
> of these products will decide the winner.[38]

The players themselves recognized this element of racial antagonism in the Alianza-Universitario games, and it appears to have had an effect on their output. According to ex-Alianza player Miguel Rostaing, "These games turned into fights between blacks and whites. The newspapers built them up as such to attract spectators. . . . Of course, we played with greater intensity against Universitario because there was this rivalry: Alianza blacks, Universitario whites."[39]

These conflicts transcended the playing field to involve the fans who attended the games in support of their particular teams. Universitario attracted ethnically white, upper- and middle-class fans, while Alianza maintained enormous lower-class backing. Miguel Rostaing described the two groups of fans:

> The Alianza fans were from different neighborhoods, of course, the majority from La Victoria, but also from Abajo el Puente, from Malambo [a major black neighborhood]. Alianza was the people, the workers. The Universitario fans were connected to the University. Alianza represented the poor people and Universitario the rich people. That's why they called them black and white.[40]

These fans often engaged in the same racial warfare they saw being played out in front of them. Pedro Frías recalls the virulence of racial insults on the occasion of one Alianza-Universitario match:

> It was a game with Universitario that all of a sudden in less than five or ten minutes they kicked two goals against Valdivieso [the Alianza goalie], and Alianza lost. When the Alianza players were leaving the field, [the Universitario fans] called them "blacks, slaves, cooks from Alianza Lima."[41]

Despite all precautions, it appeared that by the late 1920s, with the creation of Universitario, the elites had unwittingly made soccer more than ever before the focus of the profound tensions within the society of the massifying city. Indeed, in those years two sets of related contradictions were brewing at the core of Peruvian soccer: poor/black versus rich/white; and spontaneous/social expression versus institutionalization/social control. Their resolution would take place in the context of the two international soccer competitions in 1929 and 1930, the South American Cup in Buenos Aires and the World Cup in Montevideo.

The 1929 South American Cup marked the first official Peruvian participation in a major international tournament. The Soccer Federation announced the selection of a national team made up of the best players from the Lima clubs. To ensure successful recruitment and to focus public attention on the national team, the federation canceled regular local play. Ironically, those decisions, which seemed to emerge from a growing recognition of Peru's national identity, indicated an overriding interest in "international culture" on the part of Soccer Federation members and constituted a form of contempt for local culture. Given their continued supremacy on the soccer field, a large proportion of the national team was to be composed of players from Alianza Lima. In the majority of cases, however, these players did not share the priorities of the federation leaders. Alianza's main concern was to maintain close relations with their working-class fans and to compete with their traditional rivals. Furthermore, the tips derived from these games represented a significant form of supplementary income. To spend a full year dedicated entirely to the national team, without being able to fulfill its role as the popular club in local competition, went against the grain and interests of Alianza Lima. Alleging that they "did not want to be held responsible for any 'failure' of the national team," after some indecision the majority of the Alianza players decided not to participate.[42]

Racial discrimination appears to have been another strong motive for the withdrawal of the Aliancistas. It became clear from the first practice sessions that Alianza's players were being segregated from the more "distinguished" players of Universitario, and that they would be relegated to the role of reserves in the actual competition. This determination on the part of the team's management may have emerged from the perception that, were Peru to be represented in Buenos Aires by a team composed largely of blacks, the country might be viewed internationally as a nation of "barbarians." A newspaper story in 1930 openly explained these fears: "How are we going to send a team of blacks to a championship. . . . They will say that we are a country of people from this race!"[43] In the end racial concerns appeared to outweigh all else when it came to Peru's international image, on and off the soccer field.

The withdrawal of the Alianza players from the national team, despite their subordination to the "doctors of soccer," provoked a bitter response from the Soccer Federation. This rebellion of "the blacks from La Victoria" could not be permitted. The federation's incensed directors expelled the club from their ranks, thereby prohibiting it from playing in any official league game or tournament—in other words, from any event in which admission was charged. This "unpatriotic, undisciplined" team found itself abolished, or at least banished, a club with no official status.[44]

The response of Alianza to this sanction was fascinating. The players fell back on the more spontaneous popular soccer of earlier years. Prohibited from using the stadiums, Alianza returned to the open dirt fields, seeking out teams from Lima's working-class neighborhoods and from the provinces. The reports of their games harken back to an era of sport for pure enjoyment that seemed to have passed away in the surging institutionalization of Lima soccer:

> Alianza Lima's players have become even more popular, if that is possible, as they have partied in Lima and vicinity. . . . We say that they are partying because they have a good time, inside and out. On the outside they make goals against their adversaries like there was no tomorrow, and inside they eat wonderfully with abundant *anticuchos* [barbecues] which they wash down with *chica de jore* [corn beer] or delicious Peruvian cane liquor or pure grape brandy from Ica, depending on what is served. . . . In Pachacamac [a village south of Lima] the thing was fantastic. A band, lots of applause, and a creole style lunch that made people's mouths water a mile away.[45]

So, despite the absence of the customary percentage of the gate, the Aliancistas certainly did receive concrete material, as well as moral, benefits. If the Soccer Federation would not permit them the "space" to play, they showed themselves capable of creating their own space on their own terms.

In light of the striking success of Alianza's new/old form of competition, the team did not appear to have been terribly disappointed by its expulsion from the Soccer Federation. Rather, the players seemed to be initiating a redirection of Peruvian soccer back toward the seeking of fulfillment *within* the world of Lima's popular masses. Alianza's actions are all the more noteworthy in that they were occurring at the same time that official Peruvian soccer was linking its identity, with a great deal of success, to that of the state in the international arena.

It is evident that the Aliancistas were at least partially conscious of the implications of their actions, as demonstrated by the following dialogue between the captain of the team, Jorge Kochoy Sarmiento, and a sports reporter:

"They say, Señor Kochoy, that the expulsion of Alianza will be lifted. . . ."
"Alianza doesn't need to have the expulsion lifted. Its players are happy with the attention everybody pays us when we play with the people. . . ."
"Yes, but you don't make enough money to even buy a pair of shoes or a shirt."
"With the federation it's the same thing. We don't make anything and they screw us."
"So Alianza is content with its situation?"
"You can say in the paper that Alianza is content."[46]

Despite Kochoy's statements, the disastrous performance of Peru's national team in the South American Cup, where they lost all their games, in most cases by wide margins, abruptly changed the panorama. Comparisons between the disgraceful defeats in Buenos Aires and Alianza's successes on the local scene filled Lima's sports pages. Public indignation with the national team was matched by public admiration for the Aliancistas, more than ever recognized as "the idols of the day."[47] But this admiration did not produce the consolidation of Alianza's "people's soccer." Rather it had something of an opposite effect.

In the face of the extensive criticism and painfully conscious that the World Cup was less than a year away, the Soccer Federation approached Alianza with an offer to reinstate the team if they would simply sign a letter of apology. The spokesmen of the federation understood, so they stated, that "after all, these people who lack culture are not fully conscious of what they are doing."[48] Alianza agreed to the federation's terms.

Alianza's readiness to return to the official fold was the product of a complex set of circumstances. The players may have truly missed the relatively steady income derived from their weekly percentage of the admissions; also, they probably were not happy at being the target of criticism from many segments of Lima's society. Perhaps the Aliancistas too were looking forward to proving their athletic quality at the Montevideo World Cup. What is clear is that when Alianza resumed its place as part of official soccer, it had lost none of its touch. In their first game, they beat 3–0 an Argentine team that had soundly drubbed every other local club. At the game and subsequently, the Lima fans reconfirmed en masse their support for the ever popular team:

> The public's reception of Alianza when they ran on the field was without precedent. They were given a thunderous ovation which must be interpreted at the least as the recognition of their controversial quality.[49]

At the same time that Alianza once again became a "legitimate team," a new club president, Juan Bromely, was named, a high-ranking official in Lima's municipal government. It is not clear to what extent the choice of Bromely was a condition of Alianza's rehabilitation, nor was it clear then that he would be successful in "establishing order" over the "undisciplined" Aliancistas. As one magazine of the period speculated:

> There are those who doubt the ability of don Juan Bromely to manage Alianza with success. His personal integrity, his class, together with his lack of knowledge about the world in which soccer is played are considered hindrances for a task in which you need, more than ability in sport, a "native sharpness" [*viveza criolla*]: he'll have to spend a lot of time burning incense around certain personalities and he'll have to keep up with the thousands of intrigues that occur on a daily basis.[50]

There is no evidence that Bromely actually burned incense, but he had more potent weapons with which to achieve the pacification of his players: hard cash and the offer of relatively well-paid jobs. Proceeding on the paternalistic model that had been introduced years earlier by the factory clubs, Bromely secured city hall jobs for all those players who wanted them, and he made customary personal loans to all who requested them.

Alianza, a team that had never had a president with sufficient material resources to offer such benefits and pressured by official soccerdom, ended up abandoning its own soccer. The last significant bastion and most effective representative of popular soccer finally joined the tide against the sport as autonomous popular culture. Its actions seemed to severely dim the prospect that popular soccer could generate worker solidarity and class consciousness.

While Alianza and similar teams continued to attract mass followings despite their institutionalization and later professionalization, a series of strong forces—from impoverished conditions to an increasingly interventionist state—forced players to set aside, if not abandon, soccer as popular expression. Soccer became more formally professionalized through the decade of the 1930s and in subsequent years. With the construction of stadiums, larger in size and number, and with the radio and (later) television broadcast of games, soccer gained even greater popularity, if not autonomy, than in its formative years. Disseminated throughout ever-larger segments of the Peruvian populace, the sport expanded its capacity to provide living space to the masses, at the same time that it became an increasingly effective mechanism for social control.

Notes

1. This paper, originally presented at the Annual Meeting of the American Historical Association, Chicago, December 1984, is the product of joint research with José Deustua Carvallo of the Instituto de Estudios Peruanos (Lima), and Susan C. Stokes of the Department of Political Science, Stanford University. Data was collected and earlier versions written by the three of us during 1981–1982. Results of that earlier collaboration appeared in *Studies in Latin American*

Popular Culture (1984 and 1986), and in my *Lima obrero* (Lima: Editorial de la Univer-sidad de Lima, 1985), vol. 1.

2. *El Callao* (3 August 1892); emphasis in the original.

3. For a perceptive caricature of the "sport-man" of this period, see the novel written in 1928–1929 by José Diez Canseco, *Duque*, 3rd ed. (Lima: Ediciones Peisa, 1973).

4. *El Comercio* (January–December 1900); *Variedades* (July–November 1911); and Jorge Basadre, *Historia de la República* (Lima, 1968–1969), vol. 16, pp. 216–221.

5. César Miró, *Los intimos de La Victoria* (Lima: Editorial El Deporte, 1958), pp. 22–23.

6. Interview with Pedro Frías (November 10, 1981).

7. Interview with Antonio Maquilón (June 19, 1982).

8. Interview with Miguel Rostaing (April 15, 1982).

9. Interview with Frías (November 13, 1981).

10. Rostaing comments (May 6, 1982), that when he played for his first lower division team, Huáscar, between 1914 and 1918, he paid fifty *centavos* per month to the team. Israel Bravo Ríos, who played for Sporting Tabaco after 1930, recalled (June 20, 1982) that in the 1920s he paid 20 *centavos* per week to play on "minor division" teams.

11. Interview with Maquilón (June 19, 1982).

12. Interview with Rostaing (April 29, 1982).

13. Comments made during round table, "Fútbol en el Perú, Historia y Pasión" (Universidad de Lima, August 1982).

14. Interview with Rostaing (June 17, 1982).

15. Interview with Francisco Real (April 28, 1982).

16. Interview with Rostaing (April 29, 1982).

17. Interview with Israel Bravo Ríos (June 3, 1982).

18. Ibid.

19. Interview with Rostaing (May 13, 1982).

20. Interview with Frías (November 13, 1981).

21. Ibid.

22. Interview with Bravo Ríos (June 3, 1982).

23. Interview with Pedro Méndez (May 24, 1982).

24. Interview with Bravo Ríos (May 3, 1982).

25. Interview with Méndez (May 24, 1982).

26. Interview with Frías (November 13, 1981). The cost of a seat in the "Popular" section was equivalent to approximately 10 percent of an average worker's daily wage.

27. Roco Borodi, *Historia de la selección: en campos de antaño* (Lima, 1982), p. 28.

28. *El Sport* (19 April 1930): 5.

29. Ibid. (26 April 1930): 4.

30. Interview with Maquilón (July 19, 1982).

31. Interview with Frías (November 13, 1981).

32. Interview with Rostaing (April 22, 1982).

33. Interview with Real (April 28, 1982).

34. Soccer was indeed a major factor in the appearance of sports journalism. As the sport grew in popularity, so did the number of sports publications in Lima, rising from two in 1918 to nineteen in 1930. See República del Perú, *Extracto estadístico del Perú* (Lima: Ministerio de Hacienda, 1943).

35. For information on the league and the federation, see Borodi, *Historia de la selección*, pp. 24, 32–33, and *El Intimo* 1:1 (1962) 23–24.
36. Interview with Rostaing (May 13, 1982).
37. *El Sport* (19 April 1930): 5.
38. Ibid.
39. Interviews with Rostaing (April 15 and 22, 1982).
40. Interview (April 24, 1982).
41. Interview with Frías (April 13, 1982).
42. *Toros y Deportes* (21 December 1929): 2. Also, Alianza had been offered a possible tour of the United States, and many players refused to give up such a potential opportunity—which never was realized—to follow the uncertain enterprise of the national team.
43. *Toros y Deportes* (22 February 1930): 2.
44. Ibid. (7 December 1929): 6.
45. Ibid.: 13.
46. Ibid. (14 December 1929): 15.
47. Ibid. (7 December 1929): 13.
48. Ibid. (15 February 1930): 2.
49. Ibid.: 15.
50. *El Sport* (5 April 1930): 15.

3

Soccer Madness: *Futebol* in Brazil

Joseph A. Page

*Sports have interacted repeatedly with a variety of processes in the history and culture of Latin America. Perhaps no country illustrates this interaction more than Brazil and its passionate relationship with "the people's game" of soccer/*futebol. *Like many so-called modern activities, soccer arrived from Europe and spread outward geographically from the major cities and socially from the whiter, Europeanized sectors to the darker-skinned, less internationalized classes. As the sport gained in popularity and came to display aspects of Brazil's mixed origins, at its highest club and national team levels it became racially integrated. And as an expression of the country's complex national identity, it was perhaps the only institution with which a majority of Brazilians could identify.*

*In turn, soccer/*futebol *produced players who were beloved, popular heroes, and these idols were courted by politicians who sought to enhance their own images through affiliation with such figures. At the same time, professionalization and globalization infused into the sport increasingly large amounts of money. For many Brazilians the fortunes of their clubs, national teams, and favorite players determined their own sense of worth. Since Joseph Page, professor of law at Georgetown University, wrote this essay, Brazil finished second to host France in the 1998 World Cup; shared with the world Ronaldo and Romario, among the best and most popular stars of the current generation; and qualified for the 2002 World Cup in Japan and Korea.*

On July 16, 1950, as the world's largest stadium embraced the largest crowd ever to witness a soccer game, a palpable sense of unease blanketed the more than two hundred thousand Brazilians who thought they had gathered to celebrate the consecration of their national team as the best on the planet. A mere tie would enable the host squad to drink champagne from the coveted World Cup, since this was the final contest in a round-robin championship series and Brazil had entered with a slight lead in the standings. But when the Uruguayans knotted the score at 1–1 early in the second half, the anxiety emanating from the huge throng began to weigh heavily on the Brazilian players, and the team's overconfidence quickly gave way to hesitation and excessive caution.

Then, with eleven minutes remaining in regulation time, there came a moment that remains emblazoned in the collective consciousness of a nation otherwise noted for its lack of historical memory. Alcides Ghiggia, a slender Uruguayan winger nicknamed Perrito (Puppy), worked a perfect give-and-go pass with a teammate and darted past his defender, Bigode. Deep on the right side, he pushed the ball into the penalty area. Juvenal, another Brazilian defender, retreated in a desperate but tardy effort to mark his opponent but left a Uruguayan attacker free in front of the net. The Brazilian goalkeeper, Barbosa, anticipated a centering pass, but Ghiggia opted to shoot from a very difficult angle, and he put the ball past the goalie on the short side and into the twine.

When the English referee blew his whistle to end the game, the assembled multitude as well as a radio audience composed of the rest of the country wept tears of blood. In the words of a local reporter, the Brazilian team left the field "like sleepwalkers." Dazed spectators exited in slow motion, "a battalion of living dead," as one author described them. It was a catastrophe the extent of which is difficult for outsiders to grasp. A number of Brazilians reportedly took their own lives. Many could never again bring themselves to set foot in Maracanã stadium.

Athletes expecting enshrinement in the national pantheon found themselves plunging into a lifelong nightmare. The secret police summoned Barbosa to headquarters to ask him whether he was a Communist. Bigode had been voted the most popular player in Rio, but after the game the company sponsoring the poll refused to pay him the prize money that was due him. Juvenal could not bring himself to set foot outside his home for weeks. The team's top goal scorer suffered a temporary loss of memory.

More than four decades after their bitter loss, the players still talk about it, point fingers of blame at one another and their coach, and provide grist for books and newspaper articles. Barbosa continues to claim that Ghiggia meant to pass the ball, but somehow the misdirected spheroid found its way into the goal. His assertion is an understandable yet vain attempt to erase the indelible stain of the phrase "Barbosa's chicken" ("chicken" being Brazilian soccer slang for an easy shot that somehow eludes the goalkeeper), which will follow him to the grave.

On that fateful afternoon, Brazil took second place in the World Cup competition, a result that would have produced some degree of satisfaction in most other countries. But Brazilians felt only frustration, betrayal, anguish, and despair. For them soccer was not just a game; it was the embodiment of their Brazilianness, a sport they had elevated to an art form, and a game they had taken to new heights. All they lacked was the stamp of official recognition a World Cup championship would bring. Their loss was all the more painful because it occurred at home where they were heavily favored, at a time when the traditional European soccer powers had still not fully recovered from the effects of World War II, and in a showdown match against a team from a tiny neighboring country.

This tragic loss also brought to the surface not only the self-doubt Brazilians have always harbored, but also the racism that lurked beneath their inferiority complex. Both Barbosa and Bigode, the principal scapegoats, were dark-skinned, and many Brazilians were willing to believe that their country would never win the World Cup with a racially mixed team.

~

The soccer madness that has never relaxed its hold on Brazil began at the turn of the century, caused the entire nation to plunge into depression in 1950, later lifted it to peaks of euphoria between 1958 and 1970, contributed to the malaise caused by the political, social, and economic difficulties afflicting the country in the 1980s, and in 1994 gave Brazil's collective self-esteem a badly needed boost.

The oft-used expression "Soccer Country" defines Brazil as accurately as the descriptive "Carnival Country." Indeed, the game has managed to captivate Brazilians in every corner of the land, from Amazônia to the deep south, with an equal measure of devotion; in fact, it has sustained a degree of popularity that even Carnival had never been able to match. The sport has played a major role in unifying both nation and community. Everyone follows the national team and takes great pride in its successes. Newcomers, whether from abroad or from another part of the country, are able to integrate themselves into the social life of a city or town by becoming fans of a local team or by participating in the game themselves.

Sailors from Great Britain, where the game of soccer originated, were the first to play soccer on Brazilian soil, but it was a teenager named Charles Miller who receives credit for introducing the sport to Brazilians. In 1894 this native-born son of British parents brought back with him from a trip to England two soccer balls and a rule book. He had played soccer during his trip abroad, and upon returning helped organize several teams in São Paulo.

At first soccer players were mostly British employees of British-owned firms. Then Mackenzie University organized a squad composed primarily of Brazilians, the first such soccer club. Enthusiasm for the game spread among young Brazilians from the upper class, many of whom had been exposed to soccer during visits to Europe, and they began to organize teams of their own. The formation of a league in São Paulo inspired sportsmen in Rio de Janeiro to follow suit.

Many of the early soccer teams in São Paulo and Rio were sponsored by societies that catered to the wealthy, and games were played on fields provided by exclusive clubs. This atmosphere made it respectable as well as fashionable for young women of good breeding to don their Parisian finery and attend matches.

In the second decade of the twentieth century, soccer received a further boost with the influx of European immigrants who began to form teams of their own. Many of the employers for whom the newcomers worked encouraged them to play the game, since it diverted them from involvement in trade-union militancy, which was beginning to disrupt labor relations in Brazil.

At the same time, the sport was spreading rapidly throughout the country. Leagues in Pernambuco, Bahia, Minas Gerais, Paraná, and Rio Grande do Sul were established, and soccer clubs were organized even in faraway Amazônia.

For a long time soccer in Brazil remained very British. Beginning with the name of the game, "football" (later evolving into the Portuguese word "*futebol*"), the terminology generally used was English. Players who committed fouls that injured an opponent customarily apologized by saying, "I'm sorry." Teams exchanged the "Hip, hip, hooray" salute after a match.

Lower-class Brazilians soon developed their own fascination with soccer. For the poor it was an ideal sport, requiring only a ball and some empty space. They would stand on walls surrounding playing areas or on the fringes of unfenced fields to watch games in progress. Before long they too were practicing the sport. However, with very few exceptions, nonwhites found themselves excluded from high-level competition. Those who were permitted to play were either fair-skinned or used rice powder to lighten their complexions.

The color line was not really breached until 1923, when Vasco de Gama, a club founded by Portuguese immigrants, fielded a squad composed primarily of black and mulatto workers, and the team won the Rio championship. Initially there was much resistance to integration on the soccer fields, but by the 1930s it receded.

By this time the face of soccer in Brazil had changed dramatically. It was no longer a pastime for aristocrats. The elegant young ladies who once graced the sidelines withdrew to more genteel surroundings. Ordinary people took the game to their hearts and shaped it accordingly.

Soccer swept Brazil in large part because there was no other sport to compete with it. In the United States, baseball was already the national pastime, so immigrants and their children found it prudent to embrace the sport as a means of asserting their Americanness. Brazil, on the other hand, had lacked a sport to call its own. Soccer filled that void. Indeed, it became as much a monoculture as the production of sugar or coffee.

These explanations alone, of course, do not adequately explain why soccer ignited the passions of Brazilians throughout the country. The game proved ideally suited to the Brazilian temperament and became a consummate mechanism for both individual and collective self-expression. It seemed as though soccer had been invented just for Brazilians. They adopted it as their own, identified with it, and went about transforming it.

What Brazilians imprinted on the game was their strong reliance on individuality and improvisation, a faith in magic (exemplified by the conviction that in the relationship between the human body and the soccer ball, anything was possible), the slyness of Pedro Malasartes (a legendary folk hero who survived by outwitting his social superiors), and, above all, the sense of overwhelming joy shared by players and spectators alike.

Betty Milan has aptly described the improvisational style of Brazilian soccer as deriving from the Brazilian way of overcoming poverty. "The Brazilian player invents in every possible way, for . . . he has been schooled in invention. If we have no money, then we'll make a tambourine out of an old tin can. We haven't got a hat for a fancy dress? An old cheese box will serve the purpose."

Soccer seemed to merge sport and samba. During games fans often beat drums from start to finish, and in so doing they reinforced the rhythms of the players, who converted dribbling into a form of dance. Their moves always exuded spontaneity, one of the characteristics of the samba.

Anthropologist Roberto de Matta and others have advanced another explanation for soccer's popularity. They regard the existence of fixed, universally respected rules as the key to the sport's hold over the Brazilian masses. In a society where laws that inconvenience the rich and powerful are either ignored or easily changed, soccer stands apart as an enterprise governed by norms with which everyone is familiar, and which guarantee that talent, rather than money or personal ties, will prevail. The sport thus demonstrates to the common people of Brazil that the social justice they do not see in their everyday lives is possible, and their love for the game represents their embrace of that possibility.

Sociologist Gilberto Freyre hit upon yet another aspect of soccer's appeal to Brazilians when he observed, in the course of a television documentary, that when ordinary people took soccer away from the elite and adopted it as their national pastime, "[i]t ceased to be a sport for Apollos, and became a sport of the Dionysia." Indeed, over the years soccer became "carnivalized."

Thus crowds attending major matches are not mere onlookers; they are participants in an ecstatic rite that begins when the teams take the field. Waving banners, setting off firecrackers, tossing talcum powder, and chanting cheers, the fans enter into a symbiotic relationship with the players, who feed off the energy that comes from the stands. The mass frenzy reaches the point of orgasm with the scoring of a goal.

It was only natural that Brazilian soccer, with its emphasis on individual genius, should develop idols. One of the earliest was Arthur Friedenreich, who could trace his green eyes and steely determination to a father of German descent, and his dark skin and irreverence to a mulatto mother. The first nonwhite to gain recognition as a topflight player in Brazil, the "Tiger" scored 1,329 goals during his career—a record not even Pelé would match.

Another hero was Leônidas da Silva, the legendary "Black Diamond," who has been credited with inventing the "bicycle kick" (an acrobatic maneuver he performed by doing a half somersault backward and at the same time kicking the ball in the direction opposite to that which he had been facing). He was the top goal scorer in the 1938 World Cup tournament in France.

The chance to play in international soccer matches permitted Brazilians to test their skills against the rest of the world. A necessary prerequisite was the organization of a national body that would supervise the scheduling of these contests and the formation of national teams. In 1914 the Brazilian Sports Federation came into being, and soon a Brazilian squad was competing sporadically against other South American teams. But Brazilian soccer was not up to the level of play in Argentina and Uruguay, where the sport had been introduced several decades before its arrival in Brazil and had been immediately taken up by working-class youths.

Brazil did not send a soccer team to participate in the 1924 Olympic Games in Paris, nor in the 1928 Amsterdam Games. Teams from Uruguay won gold medals in soccer at both events, and in so doing astonished the Europeans with their style of play—fast and tricky.

It was during this period that soccer became a professional sport in a number of European countries. This meant that many of the world's best players would be ineligible to compete in the Olympic Games. As a consequence, FIFA (the International Federation of Football Associations), an organization founded in 1904 to encourage and standardize international soccer competition, decided to sponsor a new tournament, called the World Cup, that would be open to professionals. As a result of their Olympic triumphs, the Uruguayans were selected by FIFA in 1930 to host the first of what would become a quadrennial event. They agreed and proceeded to win the Cup.

For the first several tournaments, participation was by invitation rather than through qualification in preliminary matches. FIFA asked Brazil to play in the 1930 World Cup. In 1934 and 1938 Brazil also took part in the event, to replace other South American countries that were not able to send teams to Italy and France, where the matches were held.

By this time soccer in Brazil had also become professionalized. There had been some opposition to the change, but when Argentine play-for-pay teams began to lure away Brazilians in the early 1930s, Brazil had no option but to permit the teams in its various leagues to compensate their players.

The Brazilian national teams showed great progress and promise during their performances in the three World Cup tournaments in the 1930s. Their lack of experience and organization cost them dearly, and they were ousted in the first round in Uruguay (although a 4–0 victory over Bolivia served notice to the world that the Brazilians could score goals). In 1934 the team did not survive a single-elimination preliminary round, but in 1938 it at last came into its own. Leônidas put on a spectacular offensive show, and Brazil made it to the semifinals, where the team self-destructed and lost, 2–0, to the eventual World Cup winner, Italy.

By now Brazilians were convinced that they were the best in the world at soccer, but because of World War II they had to wait twelve years for another chance to prove it. When FIFA decided to resume the competition in 1950, it accepted Brazil's offer to host the event, and a nation of soccer-crazed fans reached new peaks of frenzy.

To provide an appropriate backdrop for the games, the Brazilians embarked on a prototypically "pharaonic" project, the construction of a stadium the likes of which had never been seen anywhere on earth. On the site of a racetrack not far from Rio de Janeiro's downtown, work began in 1948 on what would become soccer's most grandiose temple, its most splendid cathedral, its most magnificent theater.

Nearly two years and five hundred thousand sacks of cement later, Brazilians could look with pride on what came to be known as Maracanã stadium, an area capable of seating 178,000, and of crowding (cheek by jowl) 42,000 standees in a sunken area surrounding the playing field. A moat ten feet wide and ten feet deep separates the field from the fans and makes it impossible for them to reach the players and the officials, who enter through tunnels. Maracanã represented Brazilian architecture at its most imaginative. It was a facility expressly designed for the future (although locating it in a densely populated area that provided no separate space for parking has turned out in the long run to be a serious shortcoming).

Because of its size, Maracanã does not offer the average spectator a close-up view of the action on the field. But the arena does serve as a perfect setting for soccer madness. Brazilians go to matches not just to watch but to participate, and the antics of the crowds are often as diverting as the plays on the field. Maracanã merely increased the scale of the spectacle.

Brazilians rejoiced in the construction of Maracanã because they believed that it would be on its grass that their beloved all-stars would win their first World Cup. Few doubted this. After all, the home advantage had been decisive in two of the first three World Cup tournaments. Germany, Hungary, and Argentina, perennial favorites to win the Cup, were not sending squads to Brazil, and the Italian team had been decimated by the loss of ten players in a 1948 airplane crash. The bottom line was that the Brazilians would field a team with talent far superior to that of the competition.

In its first appearance in the stadium, the Brazilian team trounced Mexico 4–0 to open Cup play, and the home team went on to compile a near perfect record (blemished only by a tie with Switzerland) in the preliminaries. Brazil, Sweden, Spain, and Uruguay qualified for the championship series, which would be round-robin rather than single-elimination. (Constant modification of its format has been a feature of the World Cup.) The Brazilians overwhelmed the Swedes, 7–1, and the Spaniards, 6–1. The latter contest was one big party, as a throng of two hundred thousand waved handkerchiefs, released yellow and blue balloons, and sang "Touradas de Madrid" ("Bullfights in Madrid"), a popular Brazilian song that seemed appropriate for the occasion.

Now only Uruguay remained. The Uruguayans had struggled to beat Sweden and had tied their game with Spain. Hence, a draw would give Brazil the coveted Cup. At this point the optimism of the locals was out of control. An unwise decision was made to move the team's training camp closer to Maracanã. In the several days before the final game, publicity-seeking politicians (1950 was an election year), endorsement-seeking merchants, and well-wishers in general were so relentless in imposing themselves on the team that the players had no respite from their attentions. The press assured readers that Brazil would not only win but would run up a lopsided score.

On that fateful, memorable afternoon the unreserved sections of the stadium were packed solid by noontime. When the Brazilians took the field, pandemonium erupted. The mayor of Rio, in a pre-game speech, hailed the team as "world champions."

The Uruguayans had nothing to lose. Before the match their captain led them in a ceremonial mass urination on a stack of copies of a Rio newspaper heralding Brazil's impending triumph. He then led them to the most stunning upset in World Cup history.

One interpretation of Brazil's loss likens it to a Greek tragedy—a classic case of punishment visited by the gods on a people whose fatal flaw was hubris. But perhaps immaturity is a more suitable explanation. The Brazilians were behaving like adolescents, flaunting an overconfidence that gave them a sense of invincibility. This overestimation of their skills put too much pressure on the players who turned out to be human after all. So the Brazilian people would have to wait a while, until the lessons of 1950 had been fully absorbed, and until a new crop of superheroes arrived on the scene.

Among the millions who sat by their radios and wept on that Sunday afternoon in 1950 was a skinny little nine-year-old black boy in the city of Bauru in the interior of the state of São Paulo. His given name was Edson Arantes do Nascimento, but his friends called him Pelé, the meaning and origin of which remain unknown even to the present day. His father played soccer professionally but never made it to the top leagues. Pelé would more than make up for this by becoming the greatest soccer star the planet has ever seen.

Pelé was shining shoes at the age of seven and had only four years of formal education. But his uncommon skill with a soccer ball brought him to the attention of talent hunters, and he soon left home to play for the Santos team, in the port of the same name not far from the city of São Paulo. Although it was expected that he would remain for a while with the Santos youth squad, within a short time he found himself promoted to the main team, which competed with the major clubs from São Paulo. On September 7, 1956, the five-foot-eight, 130-pound, fifteen-year-old phenomenon scored his first goal in an official game against topflight competition.

The youthful Pelé converted a strong Santos team into what one author has called "an astonishing goalscoring machine." His offensive abilities were prodigious. He had it all: speed, mobility, a sense of oneness with the ball, uncanny vision, a fearsome shot off either foot, and, the crowning touch, an audacious, instinctive creativity. On July 7, 1957, Pelé made his debut on the national team in Maracanã. Entering a South American championship game against Argentina in the second half, he scored Brazil's only goal in a 2–1 loss. A year later, despite his tender years, he was called to join the squad that would travel to Sweden for the World Cup tournament.

Brazil had still not recovered from its calamitous 1950 defeat at the hands of the Uruguayans. In 1954, under a new system of regional qualifying matches, Brazil beat Chile and Paraguay to earn a chance to compete for the Cup in Switzerland. But in a bloody, brawl-marred quarterfinal match against a Hungarian team that had not lost in four years, the Brazilians bowed out, 4–2.

But in 1958 things were different. The team benefited from better organization and coaching. The new crop of stars was truly exceptional, clearly the best group that the Brazilians had ever assembled. There were no weaknesses at any position. The attacking front line displayed awesome talent. The squad that would travel to Sweden for the 1958 World Cup featured not only Pelé, but Mané Garrincha, a twenty-four-year-old mulatto forward who brought to the game an exuberant artistry that endeared him to spectators on both sides of the Atlantic.

Garrincha did not look much like a soccer player. But his hunched body and crooked legs, the results of malnutrition, enabled him to perform "now-you-see-it-now-you-don't" feats of legerdemain once he gained control of the ball. When he embarked on one of his patented dribbling sorties, he would more often than not leave in his wake a trail of frustrated defenders.

Garrincha came from Pau Grande, thirty-one miles from Rio at the foot of the steep climb to Petrópolis. The descendants of slaves seeking work at a nearby textile factory were the first settlers of Pau Grande, and to this day it remains an impoverished backwater. Garrincha was born Manoel dos Santos, but as a boy he received the nickname Garrincha, after a small bird indigenous to the region. The additional sobriquet Mané would come later.

As a teenager, Garrincha liked to drink, chase girls, and play soccer, pursuits at which he excelled. Because of his threadbare clothes and unathletic physique, he had difficulty obtaining a tryout with the professional teams of Rio. One coach, upon seeing his twisted legs, remarked, "They're bringing everyone here now—even cripples." But Garrincha eventually secured a chance to show off his talents to the officials and fans of one of the elite Rio teams. He played in a preliminary game for the junior team of Botafogo and scored three goals. It was a quick trip from there to full-fledged stardom, and in 1958 he earned a berth on the national squad that would play in Sweden.

Brazil entered the World Cup tournament with a reputation for choking in critical games. In an attempt to turn this around, the coach installed a new formation better suited to the freewheeling talents of his players. He also followed the advice of the team psychologist (one of the additions to the Brazilian contingent), whose tests told him that Pelé was too immature and Garrincha too undisciplined to be effective in World Cup play. (Some say that the two players were also too dark, since Brazilian officials seemed to want to field as white a team as possible.) The two sat on the bench as Brazil beat Austria and tied England in its first two matches.

The next game, against a strong squad from the Soviet Union, would decide who got a berth in the quarterfinals. On the night before, some of the players urged the coach to turn loose Pelé and Garrincha, and he gave in to their entreaties.

From the opening whistle Garrincha drove the Soviets to distraction with his dribbling. Pelé, though nervous at first, flashed the brilliance that suggested his capacity to transcend mere stardom. Although neither player scored, they were instrumental in Brazil's 2–0 triumph.

Victories over Wales, France, and host team Sweden brought the Cup to Brazil at long last. Pelé, Garrincha, and the rest of the team put on a display of crowd-pleasing soccer that left spectators breathless. The Brazilian style of play had clearly established itself as transcendent. Moreover, several ghosts had finally been put to rest. The Brazilians had demonstrated that they could win when the chips were down, and that they could do so with a racially mixed team. All Brazil exploded in celebration.

In 1962 Brazil captured its second World Cup championship in Chile. Most of those who had played on the Brazilian squad in Sweden returned. The extent of the Brazilian players' talent became obvious when Pelé suffered a serious groin pull in the second game and was lost to the team for the rest of the tournament, yet the irrepressible Garrincha and his teammates did not miss a beat.

A third championship would have allowed Brazil to retire the Cup permanently, but the 1966 event in England turned out badly for them. This time the squad as a whole was less talented. Moreover, World Cup officials had apparently decided that European teams would have a better chance against Brazil and the other South American teams if the referees allowed a more "manly" (that is, rough) brand of play. Against Bulgaria, Pelé was fouled incessantly, and in a subsequent game a defender on the team from Portugal finally put him out of action with a brutal, blatant foul. An angry Pelé swore he would never play in World Cup competition again. Brazil did not survive the first round.

By 1970 Pelé had changed his mind, and the regenerative faculty of Brazilian soccer had given the national team another crop of gifted athletes to compete for the Cup, this time in Mexico. Though perhaps not quite at the overall level of the 1958 squad (the goalkeeper, for example, was a bit unsteady), the team featured a mature Pelé at his prime and other splendid offensive players whose talents more than compensated for defensive lapses. Jairzinho, for example, scored a spectacular goal off a pass from Pelé to beat England 1–0 in a critical first-round match. In the semifinals, the Brazilians downed Uruguay, 3–1, and satisfied themselves with a large measure of revenge for 1950. Then, with an impressive 4–1 victory over Italy in the championship match, Brazil became the first country ever to capture three world titles.

~

In the course of two decades Brazilian soccer had gone from pit to pinnacle. This trajectory mirrored certain trends in Brazilian society as a whole during this same period. Indeed, there was a complex interrelationship between the course of the national soccer team and larger events that were transforming the country. This was especially true in 1950, 1958, and 1970.

Midcentury found Brazil still searching for an identity, still uncertain of its destiny, still seeking to realize its aspirations. The nation's self-image continued to reflect serious reservations about its racially mixed heritage and doubts about whether an underdeveloped tropical nation could ever compete successfully with the countries of Europe and North America, countries where Brazilians felt they were regarded as "savages." What happened on the grass at Maracanã in 1950 intensified their worst fears.

By 1958 Brazilians had reason to believe that they were at last on the verge of finding themselves. The Kubitschek era had begun, and the country at last was moving forward toward a realization of its potential. The victory in Sweden was a tremendous confidence booster. Moreover, winning had not required slavish imitation of foreign models. The Brazilians could win in their own way, and the rest of the world admired not only their triumph but also the Brazilianness they stamped on it.

In the late 1960s the military regime in Brazil decreed a new economic policy designed to encourage rapid growth, and the "Brazilian miracle" dawned. In order to divert the millions of Brazilians left out of the "miracle" and to defuse any discontent they might harbor, the government took full advantage of the opiate qualities of soccer.

Thus, for the first time teams from all over the country (not just the powerhouses of Rio and São Paulo) were permitted to compete in a tournament for the national championship. As an important component of the regime's ambitious program of "pharaonic" public works, a number of large stadiums mushroomed in population centers throughout the country. A national lottery based on results of major soccer games was instituted. The TV networks improved their technical capacity to transmit games involving the national team from anywhere in the world.

Clearly, as far as the military was concerned, as an instrument for promoting national integration, soccer was on a par with building highways to the Amazon, and its promotion even became a matter of national security. To the surprise of no one, Brazil's rulers gave top priority to the winning of World Cups, and they spared no expense in the effort.

General Emílio Médici, who took over as president in 1969, was a passionate devotee of the game, and his public-relations people made the most of the leader's love for the game. Indeed, most of the popularity he achieved during his presidency came from his image as Brazil's number one soccer fan. He boldly predicted that Brazil would bring home the Cup from Mexico in 1970, and he even tried to influence the selection of the squad. Moreover, many suspect that the president engineered the ouster of the team's coach (who had once belonged to the Communist Party and had ties to opposition politicians) five days before its departure for the tournament in order to monopolize the political dividends he would reap from a Brazilian victory.

When Brazil won its third championship, Médici seemed to assume personal credit for it. He flew the team directly to Brasília, where he presented cash bonuses to the players and posed with them for photographers. The government organized a reception in Rio, where a carnival-like celebration reached such a pitch of uncontrolled frenzy that forty-four people lost their lives.

The success of the Brazilian style of play delighted soccer connoisseurs. One analyst described it as "soccer with a smile, fluid, entertaining, immensely skilled and acrobatic." The Europeans traditionally relied on technical factors such as hard-nosed tackling (as practiced by the English), brute strength and physical conditioning (German characteristics), tactical discipline (a Soviet specialty), and cautious defensive play (the contribution of the Italians). All this added up to dull soccer when compared to the way the Brazilians performed.

After the 1970 victory the glory soon faded. The pressures of international competition grew more intense, yet at the same time the Brazilian people came to expect nothing less than championships. Other countries improved their level of play. The Europeans further refined their defensive tactics and physical approach to the game. It became increasingly evident that although Brazilian soccer entertained spectators, it no longer guaranteed favorable numbers on the scoreboard.

Indeed, the very Brazilianness at the heart and soul of Brazilian soccer now seemed to be a drawback. Improvisation, creativity, and slyness might once have bewildered opponents, but the element of surprise had worn off, and the lack of discipline inherent in the Brazilian approach to the game made adjustments to opposing countertactics difficult.

Moreover, Brazilian soccer put great reliance on individual effort, which meant that success in international competition depended on the genius of superstars. Brazilians cherished the conviction that because they were inherently superior at the game, there was no need for them to train, and that their genes could consistently produce soccer prodigies who would maintain Brazil's position at the top of the soccer world. This was yet another version of the extractive mentality that has long plagued the country. This mind-set led the Brazilians to believe that they could dispense with thoughtful preparation and hard work, because all that was required was the harvesting of a crop of plentiful talent that grew naturally in the country's soccer-rich environment.

The government did everything it could to field a squad that would win again in 1974, and it spent an estimated $6 million in preparations for the event, which was to be hosted by the West Germans. But the military advisers with no special soccer expertise who received appointments to Brazil's burgeoning soccer bureaucracy interfered clumsily with the management of the team. Moreover, Pelé and a number of other stars from the 1970 squad decided not to play, and their replacements were less talented. The Brazilians had to struggle to reach the semifinals, where an excellent Dutch team trounced them.

At this point Brazilian soccer found itself at a crossroads. One option was to maintain the status quo and hold fast to the notion that the country would continue to produce uncommonly talented players who could win World Cups if they were allowed free rein on the field. The other choice was to "Europeanize."

In the wake of the 1974 defeat, the military men who controlled the Brazilian soccer program chose the second option, deciding to mimic the transatlantic strategies of defensive play and teamwork. An army officer who specialized in physical education became the coach of the national team and tried to convert his players into Europeans by exalting tactics and physical conditioning over raw talent. At the 1978 World Cup in Argentina, the Brazilians were neither themselves nor a passable imitation of European players. Although they did not lose a game, they nonetheless suffered the sting of elimination in the second round.

This disappointing outcome settled nothing about the direction Brazilian soccer should take. A debate continued to rage, with some urging a return to the freewheeling days, and others insisting that Brazil had to adapt its game to the European style. Yet at the same time it was obvious that certain aspects of the European style, such as long passes and constant running, were ill-suited to a tropical climate.

Those in the status quo camp could point to the difficulty some Brazilians with rare natural talent had when forced to play within a structured system. They argued that an overly disciplined approach to soccer could kill off the type of idiosyncratic genius that had been the foundation of Brazil's extraordinary successes in international competition.

On the other hand, those who endorsed the Europeanization of Brazilian soccer could point to the national team's failures in 1982 and 1986, when aggregations of extremely talented Brazilian players delighted World Cup spectators with their dazzling performances, only to suffer heartbreaking defeats in critical matches against European opponents.

It was not until 1994 that a Brazilian national team successfully melded the soccer styles of both Brazil and Europe. The squad that won the World Cup in Pasadena, California, featured a skilled, disciplined, well-conceived defense playing behind a pair of uncommonly gifted goal scorers. Although the championship team displayed less flair than prior Brazilian teams (much to the dismay of critics back home), it proved that greatness was still within Brazil's grasp.

The plight of Brazilians in international play between 1974 and 1994 mirrored the deterioration of the game within Brazil. This latter aspect of the "soccer crisis," in turn, reflected trends and developments within Brazilian society at large during this same period of time.

The game suffered from the economic problems that beset the country after the collapse of the "miracle." The overcrowding of cities by migrants from the countryside drove up property values and caused the utilization of empty spaces that had previously served as soccer fields. Urban children thus had fewer opportunities to play the game. Depressed wages made it difficult for fans to afford tickets to matches, and attendance slipped, imposing financial hardships on the various local teams.

European soccer clubs found it easy to purchase Brazilian players from their cash-starved teams. The players preferred to go abroad, where they could earn more. Before long, a number of Brazilian *craques* (crack, or star, players) were performing in Europe. In 1991 there were thirteen of them in the top Italian league alone. Their departures lowered the quality of the professional game in Brazil. It became difficult to put together a cohesive national squad every four years, since those invited to participate had a limited time to practice as a team.

For those Brazilians not playing overseas, the quadrennial World Cup became a showcase for them to market their individual talents and secure lucrative contracts with European teams. So the players did not have the kind of team spirit needed to bring the championship back to Brazil. The Brazilian public became resentful of what it perceived as the mercenary motives of its quondam heroes. In 1990, after an indifferent performance by the team in the World Cup tournament in Italy, disenchanted fans met returning players at the airport in Rio and pelted them with coins.

The structure of organized soccer in Brazil has also contributed to the slump the game has experienced. Although soccer has long been a professional sport, the people who run it are amateurs in the worst sense of the term and have coped clumsily with changing conditions in the country.

Unlike North American pro teams, many of which are the private property (and often playthings) of millionaires or the subsidiaries of corporate conglomerates, soccer teams in Brazil have always remained under the sponsorship and control of nonprofit clubs that serve a particular local community. These entities make available to members a wide range of social and recreational activities.

This organizational structure dates back to the turn of the century, when clubs catering to the upper classes or organized by immigrants to serve their leisure-time needs put together soccer squads composed of their own members. The subsequent professionalization of the sport did not change its club-based structure. The clubs simply sent out and hired players, who became employees. In time the clubs not only stocked Brazil's topflight soccer leagues but also created teams for younger players in various age groups as a means of discovering and developing new talent.

Clubs are organized in democratic fashion, so that members in good standing elect the directors and officers. The administrators serve two-year terms and manage social and recreational activities as well as the soccer team. They are not professionals and hence receive no direct payment for their efforts.

Many directors are self-made men devoted to their clubs and prone to acting emotionally rather than rationally. As one Rio soccer expert put it, "they do in the clubs all kinds of stupid things they would never think of doing in their businesses." Since their terms in office are limited, they have been known to make shortsighted decisions, such as taking out heavy loans to sign a star player, that in the long run have devastating financial consequences.

Service as an officer or director may have its rewards. A position in the leadership of a major urban club can function as a springboard for entering politics, or it can facilitate the cultivation of important business contacts. Directors and officers also gain a substantial amount of community prestige, which helps explain why bankers of Rio's illegal lottery have become involved with the administration of certain clubs.

The financial straits into which Brazilian soccer has fallen have, of course, had a negative impact on the players. Like the rest of the country's workers, they have been hit hard by the economic downturn and have been powerless to do anything about it. Exploitation has always defined the relationship between employers and employees in Brazil, and the boys and men who play professional soccer are no exception.

The physical demands on them are brutal, to say the least. The schedule may cover as many as forty-nine weeks of the year. Occasionally, the elite teams play exhibition games in other parts of the country or abroad in the middle of state or national competitions, and keeping to that kind of schedule requires exhausting travel. In addition, playing in tropical heat can subject players to the sort of wear and tear that can shorten careers.

The majority of Brazil's professional soccer players receive meager wages. Their contracts tie them to a team for long periods of time, and they are usually at the mercy of their employers during salary negotiations. They have no agents and no unions to represent their interests.

Until recently, professional soccer has been in large part the sphere of boys from impoverished backgrounds, who look on it as a vehicle for social advancement. Dreaming of fame and fortune, they devote their early years to the game, and more often than not acquire very little formal education along the way. This pattern has produced the stereotype of the ignorant soccer player, best illustrated by the anecdote about the member of the national team who, while participating in the 1966 World Cup in Munich, refused to buy a Telefunken radio because it "spoke only German." Ill-prepared for life after soccer, many of these men eventually slide back into the poverty from which they thought they had escaped.

There is some evidence that this pattern is beginning to change. A 1991 survey of soccer teams in the state of São Paulo found that players were predominantly white, middle class, and reasonably well educated. One-fourth had attended university classes. More than 50 percent identified as the main factor motivating them to become professional athletes the pleasure they derived from playing the game.

The Brazil of the 1990s differs significantly from the nation that produced World Cup champions in 1958, 1962, and 1970. Soccer has found itself competing with other sports, such as basketball and volleyball, with the latter gaining a tremendous boost when the men's team won an Olympic gold medal in 1992. Images of the youthful, yuppie-ish president Collor practicing karate and windsurfing set a tone that was difficult to ignore.

Attendance at soccer matches has suffered because of an increase in the savage behavior of fans and the security problems confronting spectators who leave large urban stadiums like Maracanã in Rio. The toll of such violence has not yet reached the level of casualties experienced at soccer stadiums elsewhere in the world, but it should come as no surprise that the violence afflicting Brazilian society at large has spread to soccer stadiums.

Despite its problems, soccer continues to reign supreme as the country's most popular sport. Brazil has more stadiums (five) with a capacity in excess of one hundred thousand than any other country. The terminology of the game remains embedded in everyday conversation. The favorite fantasy of boys and grown men alike is to imagine themselves playing on the grass at Maracanã in front of a huge crowd. That Brazil is the only country in the world to have participated in every single World Cup tournament since the Cup's inception and that it is the first country to win the Cup four times remain matters of enormous national pride.

4

Soccer Conspiracies: Maradona, the CIA, and Popular Critique

Jeffrey Tobin

Soccer is not only a highly popular participant as well as spectator sport in nearly all of Latin America; even more intriguing is the fact that it has also become associated with and complexly tied into national identification. The old saying—in order to know the United States one must understand baseball—can be applied even more closely to much of Latin America in terms of soccer. There, people live and (literally) die by the game, passionately equating the fortunes of their team not only to themselves but also to their nation.

Except perhaps for Brazil, no country in the region demonstrates the degree of allegiance to soccer than Argentina does. To say, "soccer is Argentina," is hardly an exaggeration. Indeed, when the national team loses, it is not uncommon for fans and the press to look for international conspiracies, even believing that the U.S. Central Intelligence Agency may be involved. Jeffrey Tobin, Occidental College, Los Angeles, examines this nationalistic aspect of the game in Argentina and how star player Diego Maradona fits into it. Tobin also analyzes the way in which average Argentines, as opposed to intellectuals, view the game, which in turn is linked to another question he explores: whether the game is hegemonic or counterhegemonic—in other words, does it help people to accept the political and socioeconomic systems in which they live, or does it help them to defy such strictures?

Critique is a capacity that we intellectuals tend to see in ourselves and to doubt in others. We presume to locate and expose connections that lie beneath the surface of everyday life, hidden from the view of less contemplative persons. Our superior attitude toward the people transcends even the political differences that otherwise separate one intellectual from another. This fact is clear in the case of soccer. There are intellectuals with politics spanning the spectrum from the Marxist left to the rationalist right who agree that soccer serves to distract the people from contemplating more important issues—whether those issues have to do with the exploitation of workers or the privatization of state services. Whatever the critic's own agenda happens to be, soccer is not on it. In this paper I review some intellectual critics' approaches to soccer, focusing on texts by and about Argentines. This review leads me to a discussion of intellectual-populists' theorization of embodied resistance. Without wanting to minimize the value of nonverbal political actions, I proceed from considering nonverbal actions to considering popular verbal critique.[1] In particular, I examine how soccer fans' discourse can serve to theorize the workings of global capitalism. In conclusion, I reflect on the politics of the distinction between serious intellectual work and playful populist diversions.

Soccer Theology

"In what way does soccer resemble God?" The riddle is posed by Eduardo Galeano. The answer, according to Galeano, is "in the devotion placed in it by many believers and in the distrust placed in it by many intellectuals" (Galeano 1995: 36). Similarly, Umberto Eco connects his disillusion with soccer to his disillusion with religion: "And one day, as I was observing with detachment the senseless movements down there on the [soccer] field, I felt how the high noonday sun seemed to enfold men and things in a chilling light, and how before my eyes a cosmic, meaningless performance was proceeding. Later, on reading Ottiero Ottieri, I would discover that this is the sense of the "everyday unreality," but at the time I was thirteen and I translated the experience in my own way; for the first time I doubted the existence of God and decided that the world was a pointless fiction" (Eco 1986: 167–68).

The 13-year-old Eco may have felt alone among thousands of cheering soccer fans, but, in observing the spectacle of soccer "with detachment," he was already well on his way to joining the community of intellectuals who sometimes have little in common other than their positions as professional thinkers and their conclusion that soccer, like religion, is an "opium of the people" (see Marx 1978: 54). As intellectual soccer coach Jorge Valdano concludes, "When all is said and done, few were the times intellectuals expressed amicable opinions with respect to soccer" (Valdano 1995: 13).

The intellectual critique of participating in popular activities may translate into a disinclination to study those activities. There were few intellectual studies of Argentine soccer published before 1994. Among those that were, Juan José Sebreli's 1981 book *Fútbol y masas* (Soccer and masses) stands out as by far the weightiest in both its scholarship and influence, but, significantly, Sebreli was apologetic about devoting an entire volume to soccer. He hoped, rather defensively, that:

> it is not wholly gratuitous to dedicate oneself to the task—like that which I have attempted with this book—of demystifying the ideological fallacies of contemporary society, and among these fallacies one of the most powerful, sports and soccer used as means of indoctrinating the youth and the masses, in order to depoliticize them and accustom them to alienated labor, to pure compliance, to competition, to social aggression, to sexual repression, to fanaticism, to irrational activism, to the disparagement of the individual in favor of the cult of idols, to the submission to authoritarianism, to the suspension of the critical spirit and of independent thought, to mystical fusion into totalitarian collectivisms (Sebreli 1981: 184).

Whether they would find his book "wholly gratuitous" or only partially so, most of the intellectuals who have written about soccer—in Argentina and elsewhere—agree with Sebreli that soccer either distracts the people from what ails them or trains them for submission to fascist or capitalist discipline. Sebreli and many other Latin American scholars were influenced by Gerhard Vinnai's argument that sports, including soccer, were used to promote patriotism in Nazi Germany (Vinnai 1974: 131). Similarly, Sebreli observed that Mussolini, Franco, Stalin, Perón, and Pétain were "great proponents of sport and their example has been followed by the majority of contemporary world leaders for whom totalitarianism triumphs without violence" (Sebreli 1981: 154). More recently, intellectual critics of soccer have adopted the 1978 World Cup, held in the midst of Argentina's so-called Dirty War, as the paradigm for understanding the relationship between soccer and politics. José Luis Ponsico and Roberto Gasparini have produced the definitive work on how the 1978 World Cup served the interests of the military junta, who used the competition to show the world "an image of an organized, well-behaved, and efficient country under military guidance" (Gasparini and Ponsico 1983: 78).

According to Eco, to the extent that we ponder sports instead of politics, we are all like the Argentines who welcomed the spectacle of the World Cup as an escape from thinking and talking about the military dictatorship:

> [S]ports debate is the easiest substitute for political debate. Instead of judging the job done by the minister of finance (for which you have to know about economics, among other things), you discuss the job done by the coach; instead of criticizing the record of Parliament you criticize the record of the athletes; instead of asking (difficult and obscure questions) if such-and-such a minister signed some shady agreements with such-and-such a foreign power, you ask if the final or decisive game will be decided by chance, athletic prowess, or by diplomatic alchemy. In short, it allows you to play at the direction of the government without all the sufferings, the duties, the imponderables of political debate. . . . And at a moment like this, concerning oneself with the

> running of the government (the real one) is traumatic. So faced with such a choice, we are all Argentines (Eco 1986: 171).

For Eco, sports debate is not political, but what, then, is political? Note that he argues that "sports chatter has all the characteristics of a political debate . . . [o]nly the object is not the city (or the corridors of the statehouse) but the stadium, with its locker rooms" (ibid.: 163), and that sports debate "deceitfully passes itself off as talk of the City" (ibid.: 165). Given Eco's heightened linguistic consciousness, it comes as no surprise to observe that his understanding of the word "political" is etymological. It seems that for Eco the political is that which pertains to the *polis* in the narrowest sense of "city" or "city-state." Eco's understanding of the political never strays from "the corridors of the statehouse," "the record of Parliament," or "the running of the government" (ibid.: 171). He even specifies that when he says "government" he means "the real one" (ibid.) as opposed to an ersatz government, such as the "governing body" of a soccer club.

Anthony Mason also identifies politics exclusively with affairs of state and nation. In a chapter on "Fútbol and Politics," he offers a chronological list of government involvement in soccer clubs and competitions. Later in his book, *Passion of the People?*, Mason does mention in passing that soccer "can occasionally be used to dramatize social conflict," but the only example he gives is of a soccer club that "became involved in the campaign to restore free elections in Brazil" (Mason 1995: 129). Again, the example defines the political as pertaining only to government per se and not to cultural politics, which is the domain in which soccer does most of its political work.

In Argentina, on those frequent occasions when soccer intrudes onto the front page of the national newspapers, certain intellectual, political commentators—most notably, television journalist Bernardo Neustadt—lament that "soccer is not the *patria*" (Alabarces and Rodríguez 1996: 43), that is to say, the "motherland" (Taylor 1997: 4). These commentators share Benedict Anderson's recognition that newspapers are central to the imagining of the nation, so they are upset when *La Nación*, the newspaper of record, devotes half its front page to yesterday's game between Boca Juniors and River Plate. Such contemporary complaints about soccer's role in defining the Argentine nation are reminiscent of an earlier generation's complaints about the tango, as documented by Marta Savigliano. Soccer, like the tango, is "a practice close to the identity of a different/inferior class of *argentinos*" (Savigliano 1995: 140). Argentine tango "conquered" Europe in the years immediately preceding the First World War and became one of the principal images that Europeans had of the country. Argentine soccer clubs began to gain fame touring Europe in the 1920s. By the time that the national soccer team won the World Cups of 1978 and 1986, soccer joined the tango among the principal images that masses of people around the world have of Argentina. In both cases, members of the intellectual, professional, and elite classes resented the way that they, as Argentines, were identified abroad. They believed that "legitimate representatives of a nation can be distinguished from illegitimate ones and that the morally superior sectors should represent the morally inferior ones, usually meaning that the civilized, wealthier ones should represent the uncivilized, poor ones" (ibid.: 141).

Consider the case of a contemporary engineer from Argentina who, like many men of his class, considers Diego Maradona an uneducated, misguided, and drug-addled soccer player. Traveling abroad, the engineer comes in contact with taxi drivers, waiters, and even fellow engineers who, upon hearing that he is from Argentina, inevitably and infuriatingly respond, "Argentina? Maradona!" (see Alabarces and Rodríguez 1995: 43). The contemporary engineer's resentment is analogous to the beef baron who eighty or ninety years earlier found his nationality reduced to "Argentina? The tango!" Now, as before, the superior Argentine believes that his country should be known for the industry, education, or refinement of its best citizens and not for the passionate physical antics of its lower sectors.

Popular Culture and Big "P" Politics

Sebreli is especially critical of his fellow leftist-intellectuals who romanticize soccer in an attempt to establish a link to "the people":

> The declarations of "national and popular culture" self-proclaimed by populist writers who "reach out to the people" do not, of course, have the least impact on the people themselves. The fan has a need alienated from something that, lacking any other name, we continue calling "culture," "knowledge," and that in reality is nothing more than something to talk about. But the fan's culture does not consist, to be sure, in reading poems, sociological essays, or narratives by populist writers. The fan whose life is stripped of all useful knowledge, just as of all thought, is impelled by mass media to memorize with obsessively minute pedantry the players' career statistics, the dates of the games won or lost for each squad over the years, and even the rosters of other countries and all types of superfluous data related to soccer, about which he speaks and debates all day long as if it had to do with something truly important and serious (Sebreli 1981: 150–51).

Sebreli's critique of "popular culture" can be traced back to century-old disputes, in English as well as in Spanish, concerning the definition of "culture." Is culture something that is attained by those individuals who are properly educated, refined, and, in a word, cultivated? Or is a culture something that everyone has regardless of the class of education he or she has received? For Sebreli, "popular culture" is not culture precisely because it is popular and the people—that is, *el pueblo*, as opposed to *la gente*—are not cultured. The people are oppressed, and one of the great tragedies of their oppression is that they are deprived of true culture and in its place are left with opiates such as soccer and the tango. Sebreli concludes that rather than valorize "supposed popular, national, or proletarian culture," intellectuals should "endeavor so that the people will learn to assimilate classic culture, accepting the rich inheritance of the past, that up until now has been the privilege only of the enlightened elites" (Sebreli 1981: 152).

I suspect that I am far from alone in being troubled by Sebreli's argument that popular culture is not culture, and in Eco's definition of "the political" as pertaining to the state. Many anthropologists would be troubled by limiting "culture," in effect, to that which literary critics or art historians have traditionally studied, or by the restriction of "the political" to mark, in effect, what has been studied by political scientists, economists, and historians. There are, to be sure, those among us who do focus on "culture" as defined by Sebreli or on "the political" in Eco's narrow sense of the term. Archaeological studies of palace art or of state formation spring easily to mind, as do ethnographic studies of elites or of resource management, but so do studies of popular cooking, dancing, healing, child rearing, and tending cattle. We anthropologists are also "Argentines" to the extent that what we study is indistinguishable from what Eco calls "sports chatter." A similar observation is at the heart of Orin Starn's critique of Billie Jean Isbell (Starn 1992; Isbell 1985) and, by extension, of all of us who in the midst of governmental turmoil, general strikes, and even revolutions, persist in asking such questions as: "How did you become a Boca fan?" "Who taught you that dance step?" or "Do you salt the meat before or after putting it on the grill?"

I hesitate to make too much of the fact that Starn is a man and Isbell is a woman, but I observe that the engendering of their dispute is consistent with standard academic engenderings of "the political." To a great extent, "the political"—as defined by Eco and Starn—coincides with the public as opposed to the private, with the weighty as opposed to the frivolous, and with the male as opposed to the female. The feminist claim that "the personal is political" is a move to disrupt these oppositions, but the disruption is only partially successful. A feminist theorist's study of a Hollywood film is likely these days to be recognized as "political" but not in the same way as is a political scientist's study of voting behavior. Gay and lesbian studies, queer theory, and cultural studies are also all fields devoted primarily to political analyses, but those analyses are construed as somehow lacking the weightiness of political science.

This distinction between the little "p" politics studied by feminist theorists and other cultural field types and the big "P" Politics studied by political scientists, political economists, and traditionally oriented historians is related to the distinction between the little "c" culture studied by anthropologists and the big "C" Culture studied by critics of serious music, art, and literature. Not coincidentally, in the little "p" political fields, female scholars are either dominant or at least well represented, whereas the big "P" Political fields tend to be dominated by men. As is usual in disciplinary categorizations, anthropologists are a marginal case. For a few decades now, women have comprised around half of anthropology's new Ph.D.s in the United States. Anthropology is also split between those who tend to focus on big "P" Politics, which usually correspond with men's activities, and those who tend to focus on little "p" politics, which are often women's activities. Soccer in Argentina is a thoroughly male sport, but Eco locates it in the little "p" political camp and Sebreli puts it in the little "c" culture camp. In part, these lower-case locations can be attributed to soccer's being a physical activity. Playing soccer, like dancing and cooking, is "manual" labor as opposed to mental labor,[2] so even if soccer is thoroughly masculine, it is still disparaged by intellectuals for being related to the wrong class of masculinity.

Opium or Stimulant?

There are a handful of intellectuals who defend soccer against the opium charge. Franklin Morales argues that soccer is frequently used by oppressive governments to control the working class but that it is "absurd to confuse the fever with the thermometer" (Morales 1969: 9). According to Morales, any activity can be and is exploited by oppressive governments, but it does not follow that the activity itself is soporific. Whereas Sebreli accuses working-class fans of scapegoating intellectuals (Sebreli 1981: 33), Morales accuses intellectuals of scapegoating working-class fans. "To unload collective responsibility comfortably onto soccer is a typical attitude of intellectuals who seek scapegoats to expiate their own impotence" (Morales 1969: 9). The implication is that intellectuals would do better to examine our own complicity or ineffectiveness in oppressive regimes than to blame soccer and its working-class fans for their complicity and ineffectiveness.

Mason also argues that it is "fundamentally mistaken" to argue that soccer is "an opiate of the people, a phenomenon commanding such intense interest over a long period of time that it deflects large portions of the population from confronting the endemic economic, social and political problems" (Mason 1995: 129). Instead, he argues, "Great victories are momentary distractions but the harsh realities of poverty and unemployment, class and race quickly return. Football may aid the rule of the rich but it does not by itself eliminate social conflict" (ibid.: 129). One problem with Mason's argument is his distinction between "momentary distractions" and "intense interest over a long period of time." No one who argues that soccer is an opiate of the people claims that the drug's effects are complete or everlasting so that soccer "by itself eliminate[s] social conflict." Rather, they argue precisely what Mason argues, that soccer games—and other popular passions, such as *telenovelas* [soap operas], rock music, and social dances—"aid the rule of the rich" by temporarily distracting the people from the harsh realities of poverty or political repression.

Another problem with Mason's argument is that it misses South American soccer's capacity to serve counterhegemonic as well as hegemonic interests. Mason calls attention to a chant at Argentine soccer games that begins, "Hay que saltar! / Hay que saltar! / El que no salta / es . . . " ("You must jump! / You must jump! / He who does not jump / is . . . "). Mason observes that in the final match of the 1978 World Cup between Argentina and Holland, he who did not jump was a Dutchman, and that in the midst of the Malvinas/Falklands War, he who did not jump was an Englishman (Mason 1995: 73). Mason concludes that the chant has served nationalist and pro-junta interests, but he fails to note that during the same period, he who did not jump was just as likely to be *un militar* (pro-military) as to be a foreigner.[3] As Eduardo Archetti and Amílcar Romero observe, "since 1979 stadia have been used by fans for protesting against the military junta and many matches were and are still transformed into political happenings when fans loudly comment upon political events and judge governments and politicians" (Archetti and Romero 1994: 68).

The question is, does going to a soccer game on Saturday or Sunday afternoon interfere with a fan's capacity to confront political problems from Monday through Friday? Does Eco's observation that there cannot be a revolution on World Cup Sunday mean there can be no revolution any day of the year so long as the World Cup remains the planet's most successful media event? Does soccer fandom inhibit labor organizing or other forms of political involvement? Does soccer serve fascist interests by promoting complacency or national identity? In addressing these questions in his response to Sebreli and others, Galeano acknowledges that "the diffusion of soccer around the world was the result of an imperialist maneuver to keep oppressed people in a state of infancy," but he observes that this imperialist maneuver is frequently subverted. "[T]he club Argentinos Juniors was born calling itself club Martyrs of Chicago, in homage to the anarchist workers, and May First was the day chosen to give birth to the club Chacarita, baptized in an anarchist library in Buenos Aires. In those first years of the century, there was no lack of leftist intellectuals who celebrated soccer in place of repudiating it as an anesthetic of consciousness. Among them, the Italian Marxist Antonio Gramsci, who praised 'this kingdom of human loyalty exercised in the open air' "(Galeano 1995: 37).

Galeano acknowledges that soccer has been used to promote patriotic fervor in favor of fascist regimes. He points out, however, that it has also been one of the principal sites in which opposition to such regimes has found expression. "In the years of Franco's dictatorship, the two stadia, Barcelona's Camp Nou and Bilbao's San Mamés, served as refuge for forbidden national sentiments. There the Catalonians and the Basques yelled and sang in their own languages and waved their clandestine banners. And the place where a Basque flag first appeared without police pummeling those who carried it was a soccer stadium: One year after [Francisco] Franco's death, the players of Athlétic and Real Sociedad appeared on the field clutching the flag" (ibid.: 127; see also MacClancy 1996).

Similarly, Sebreli acknowledges that with [Juan] "Perón fallen in 1955, soccer clubs became the refuge of outlawed Peronists, following in this the example of the Radicals of 1930" (Sebreli 1981: 167). Sebreli is antinationalist and, especially, anti-Peronist, so for him these are examples of soccer serving regressive interests, but for Galeano, these same incidents are examples of soccer fostering oppositional—working-class or separatist—causes, and they are not incidental.

Galeano finds soccer intrinsically oppositional because it is a playful physical activity and as such it resists capitalist rationalization. For Galeano, the history of soccer is a history of Third World dwarfs conquering First World giants, of skinny and crooked South Americans showing up Europeans, despite all attempts to fix it so that games will be won by the bigger, the stronger, the swifter, and the more disciplined. FIFA plays a major role in stacking the deck in favor of Western Europe, but there is another, subtler struggle in soccer. A club struggles not only against opposing clubs but also against its own coach. The players resist their coach, much as a dance company, according to Randy Martin, becomes a social body in "opposition to an initial domination of language-based authority in the figure of the choreographer" (Martin 1990: 96). Even though they share an interest in producing a successful performance, there is an oppositional relationship between the dancers who move and the choreographer who speaks.[4]

Martin suggests that "the dance company could be replaced by any collective body, articulated as labor, gender, or race, against a controlling authority" (ibid.: 96), and, indeed, I find Martin's analysis of dance relevant to the study of soccer. Coaching, too, is language-based, mental labor. Coaches demand obedience and respect from their players, and they are quick to take an important share of the credit for any victory. In fact, following a major victory, it is standard operating procedure in the Río de la Plata region for a coach to write (or ghostwrite) a book with the title "Así Ganamos" (This is how we won) (for example, Bilardo 1986; Núñez

1995). Almost all of the experts who comment on soccer strategy observe that good coaching is needed to produce a solid defense. The problem for coaches is that a well-coached defense is not threatened by a well-coached offense. To score goals, it is considered necessary to have a "creative" player who is capable of "thinking with his feet": one who has mastered "the art of the unforeseen" or who has "an artistic feel for the game" (Valdano 1996: 9). Fans go to the soccer stadium to see the player who is able to score goals despite the plans of the opposing coach, the discipline of the opposing defenders, the skills of the opposing goalkeeper, the limits of his own coach's offense, the offside rule, the rule that denies him the use of his hands, the boundaries of the playing field, the penalty area, and the goal itself.

"Even if it is a *golcito*," a little goal, as opposed to a big goal, *golazo*, Galeano observes that "it always comes out goooooooooooooooooooal in the throat of the radio commentators" (Galeano 1995: 9). This cry is comparable to what José Limón, observing *mexicanos* in South Texas, calls "the *gritos*, long cries of celebratory approval, coming from the men sitting or standing at the bar, as they watch a particularly artful execution on the [dance] floor" (Limón 1994: 163–64). An important difference is that the Mexican-American men whom Limón describes celebrate the virtuosity of women and men on the dance floor, while the virtuosity celebrated by Argentine soccer fans is exclusively male. Nevertheless, there are similar class politics in Argentine soccer and Mexican-American social dance, despite the very different politics of gender and sexuality. Drawing on Martin's work, Limón explains: "to hear the sharp, well-formed class-consciousness of the *grito*, is to realize that, for a moment, some measure of artful control over [the forces of hard, working-class labor, substance use, and sexual desire]—some measure of victory—has been achieved in the never-ending struggle against the choreography of race, class, and, one has to say, gender" (ibid.: 165). Similarly, a soccer goal is a blow not only against the rival team but also a physical blow against the mental strategies, rules, and regulations that conspire to make the goal every day less frequent. As such it is celebrated by the working-class male fans who take political pleasure in witnessing the creative capacity of a fellow male, working-class body.

Maradona and Argentine Cultural Studies

Galeano, Martin, and Limón argue that popular physical activities such as soccer or dance can be leftist political actions. In each case, subversion is silent or barely articulated. What makes a physical activity subversive, according to these authors, is its refusal to speak intelligibly and thus to enter the dominant ideological discourse. Sergio Levinsky makes a similar argument about Maradona. In addition to criticizing the U.S. boycott of Cuba and expressing great admiration for Fidel Castro, Maradona has spoken out against North/South discrimination within Italy and between Europe and South America (Levinsky 1996: 284 passim). Thanks to such declarations, many of the arguments in Argentine cultural studies about opposition and resistance, class and (neo)colonial relations can and are routinely applied to Maradona. Levinsky argues that intellectuals thereby "find in him an ideology that he does not have" (ibid.: 268). In Maradona's own words, "I am of the left, completely of the left, my foot, my faith, my head. But not in the sense that you give to the political term in Europe. I am of the left in the sense that I am for [former President Raúl] Alfonsín, for my country's progress, for improving poor people's quality of life, for everyone having peace and freedom" (Maradona quoted in Levinsky 1996: 274).

Levinsky cites such statements to demonstrate that Maradona is rebellious without having a consistent political position. In effect, Levinsky's argument is that political coherence is a peculiarly bourgeois expectation, which Maradona effectively resists. Argentine intellectuals made much of Maradona's inconsistency in praising both Cuba's Castro and then Argentine minister of the economy Domingo Cavallo. Their point was that it is impossible to reconcile Castro's socialist politics with Cavallo's commitment to free-market ideology. Levinsky makes it clear that neither Maradona nor his working-class fans are troubled by the charge of political inconsistency, and that they do not accept the intellectuals' political categories. Levinsky writes, "I do not believe Maradona has his ideology clear but he returns to Cuba and says intuitively positive things about that country" (Levinsky 1996: 267). Similarly, he argues that Maradona's support for Cavallo "was, as always, because of common sense and not because of ideologisms that he does not know" (ibid.: 352), and that Maradona struggles "against the established order, against nameless power, because his struggle is against Power as such" (ibid.: 21).

My main quibble with *Maradona, Rebelde con Causa* is the title, which Levinsky clearly likes very much, since he also used it for newspaper articles he published in 1991 (ibid.: 232) and 1996 (ibid.: 273) and for a public lecture in 1992 (ibid.: 372). *Rebelde con Causa* is, of course, a play on the title of the film *Rebel without a Cause*. What I do not understand is why Levinsky changed the title from "Rebel *without* a Cause" to "Rebel *with* a Cause" (my emphasis). His strongest point is precisely that Maradona, much like the film's Jim (played by James Dean), does not have a cause but rather is a rebel in search of one. For example, Levinsky's 1991 "rebel with a cause" article deals with Maradona's suspension by FIFA for testing positive for cocaine use, whereas the 1996 article deals with Maradona's determination to participate in a benefit game despite again being under suspension by FIFA. As Levinsky demonstrates throughout the book, Maradona is a rebel whose struggle is against "nameless power." As such, that struggle itself defies naming.

María Graciela Rodríguez also attempts to use Maradona as a key to understanding Argentine culture. Her approach involves comparing and contrasting Maradona and O. J. Simpson. Rodríguez claims that Maradona and Simpson are comparable because "both are examples of characters that are hard to classify" since they were raised in lower-class environments—one *cabecita negra* (dark and low class) and the other black—but both have made money through sports, and their money allows them to mingle with the upper class. Rodríguez proceeds to argue that because of these parallels, the differences in the media discourse surrounding each man are indicative of differences in their respective societies. In particular, she argues that the Simpson case raises issues of racism since racism is the unresolved conflict confronting the United States, while the Maradona case raises issues of national identity since nation-building projects in peripheral countries, such as Argentina, are not as developed as in core countries, such as the United States. She concludes that "if the two cases are compared (and the characteristics that their protagonists present seem to permit this), the difference is more in the topics and the debates that both generate than in the attributes that are attributed to them" (Rodríguez in Alabarces and Rodríguez 1996: 51).

It is true that both athletes had humble origins, but it is misleading to equate being black in the United States with being *cabecita negra* in Argentina. Moreover, Simpson abandoned his black first wife and used his celebrity to befriend white businessmen and lawyers. Maradona, by contrast, never separated from his lower-class background and used his celebrity primarily to befriend populist heroes such as Fidel Castro. If Simpson has a counterpart in the soccer world, it would be Pelé, also a black man who has chosen to court the favor of white businessmen, while Maradona's closest counterpart in U.S. society must be Muhammad Ali, with whom he shares a gift for speaking out in defense of leftist causes.

Conspiracy Theorizing

Maradona and political critique also come together in *Inocente* (Innocent), one of the best-selling novels in Argentina in 1995. The novel is coauthored by Fernando Niembro, a prominent Argentine sports journalist, and Julio Llinás, an Argentine novelist and essayist. *Inocente* offers a far-fetched explanation for Maradona's expulsion from the 1994 World Cup, held in the United States, and for Colombia's disappointing performance in that same competition. According to one of the many CIA agents in *Inocente*, Maradona was targeted by the CIA because "he was [Cuba's] principal apologist, the most effective, the most credible. . . . Nobody believed Castro. But [. . . Maradona] they believed in London, in Moscow, in Jakarta, in Teheran. He is the great white-washer, the great danger" (Niembro and Llinás 1995: 34–35). It stretches credulity to call Maradona Cuba's most effective or most credible apologist, but it is true that prior to the 1994 World Cup he promised to dedicate the Cup to "Fidel and the people of Cuba" if Argentina won. Colombia was favored by many soccer experts to win the 1994 World Cup, and, according to *Inocente*, that caused concern in the CIA since "we cannot allow the team of the greatest cocaine-exporting nation to win this championship" (ibid.: 73).

With the motives established, the novel's action begins when agent Anthony Llás is sent undercover to Colombia. On the plane he meets a beautiful and wealthy Argentine, Rubra Robirosa, the president of the largest public-relations firm in Latin America. Once landed, Llás meets up with Coco Cardo, a Colombian CIA operative. Under Llás's orders, Cardo arranges for the Colombian team to be provided with a skin cream doctored with an undetectable drug that will make them lethargic. After Llás leaves Colombia, Robirosa uses her great charm and some champagne to loosen Cardo's tongue, getting him to reveal that he and Llás work for the CIA and that thanks to their employers, Maradona "is finished" (ibid.: 170). Despite her executive position, Robirosa is naive about soccer and, as she explains, "Soy argentina, no argentino" (I am a female Argentine, not a male Argentine) (ibid.: 79). That is to say, the nationality that would qualify her as an expert on soccer is negated by the gender that excuses her from attending to her country's national game. Robirosa's female intuition tells her that something is up, but she lacks the masculine skills—pertaining to soccer and politics—needed to figure out what that something is. She figures that the CIA is going to assassinate Maradona as part of a plot to have the United States win the World Cup. As an *argentina* rather than an *argentino*, she does not understand that even in a novel as far-fetched as is *Inocente*, the United States could not be a candidate to win the World Cup. As Galeano observes, "Here [in the United States] soccer is the sport of the future, and always will be" (Galeano 1995: 223).

Robirosa rushes off to New York to tell the World Cup organizers of the plot. One of them, Alan Rothenberg, dismisses her warning that Maradona's life is in danger by explaining that "the Cuban groups [in Miami] are completely under control" (Niembro and Llinás 1995: 210). Meanwhile, Llás directs CIA agent Mel Kennedy to finish Maradona by framing him for doping. Kennedy happens to have a boyhood friend who is a native speaker of Spanish as well as a priest, so he arranges for the priest to administer a drugged communion wafer to Maradona before Argentina's match with Nigeria. In one of the book's many felicitous inventions, FIFA's medical director is not only a former CIA agent but also an accomplished magician, which lands him in the right place with the right skills to select Maradona's number in the lottery that determines which two players will be tested for drugs at the conclusion of the match. Maradona's urine sample tests positive for the drugs that the CIA agent had put in his communion wafer, so he is expelled from the tournament. The book concludes with Robirosa arranging a meeting with Maradona in order to tell him, "I do not really know how they did it, but they framed you" (ibid.: 275).

I take Robirosa's words to be a commentary on the novel itself. Niembro and Llinás note that actual observers of Colombia's loss to the United States in the 1994 World Cup knew something happened but not exactly what that something was. "The experts, frustrated, did not know what to say. Men such as Menotti, Sívori, Pelé, and Zico proposed multiple theories, all of them possible, all of them empty, trying to explain the unexplainable" (ibid.: 186). Niembro and Llinás present their own entertaining but implausible theory of how and why and who framed Maradona, but they are the first to acknowledge that they, too, have no idea of how or why "they" did it—or even who "they" are. Like Robirosa, all the authors pretend to know is that Maradona was framed.

As an ethnographer, I find *Inocente* of interest because it neatly corresponds with my fieldwork among soccer fans in Buenos Aires, during which I heard many theories about why Maradona was expelled from the 1994 World Cup. Most of the fans I interviewed speculated that his previous suspension for drugs was also a frame-up, ordered by the Italian mafia to retaliate against Maradona for leading Argentina to a victory over Italy in the 1990 World Cup. Such speculations are common in soccer circles. Experts and fans alike try out theories to account for game results and, more often than not, these theories evoke back-room deals and international intrigues. In Argentina, no event or result in the soccer world passes without conspiracy theorizing. All losses are explained by stories of bribes paid to players or referees, or of deals struck between players or referees, or of players unhappy with their coach or their paychecks. Argentina's loss to England and Uruguay's loss to West Germany in the 1966 World Cup are widely rumored to be the result of an arrangement involving the Englishman who refereed the West German game and the West German who refereed the English game. Argentina's 6–0 victory over Peru in the 1978 World Cup is also rumored—though usually not by Argentines—to be the result of a behind-the-scenes deal. And Rácing Club's repeated failure in recent years to measure up to its promise is often rumored to be the result of its disgruntled players' complaints about being paid late.

These explanations correspond with Frederic Jameson's observations regarding the relationship between conspiracy theories and cognitive mapping. Jameson argues that at an earlier stage of capitalism, it was a fairly straightforward process to link one's "lived experience" to "the true economic and social form that govern[ed] that experience" (Jameson 1988:

349). A serf, for example, worked in the fields from which most of his own food came, and he could see the lord who profited from his labor. If the serf's point of view did not provide a complete picture of the social relations in which he was enmeshed, it still provided a less partial picture than that given by any late twentieth-century point of view. Now, Jameson argues, "the truth of that limited daily experience no longer coincides with the place in which it takes place. The truth of that limited daily experience of London lies, rather, in India or Jamaica or Hong Kong; it is bound up with the whole colonial system of the British Empire that determines the very quality of the individual's subjective life. Yet those structural coordinates are no longer accessible to immediate lived experience and are often not even conceptualizable for most people" (ibid.: 349).

A cook in London, for example, may work in a Japanese-owned restaurant, using knives made in Germany, drive a South Korean car, and eat a steak from Argentina while watching a Brazilian score a goal for his local London soccer club. In Salman Rushdie's words, "The trouble with the English is that their history happened overseas, so they don't know what it means" (Salman Rushdie quoted in Bhabha 1990: 317). According to Jameson, all contemporary history happens overseas or at least out of any individual's sight and away from anyone's "immediate lived experience." Conspiracy theories, in his view, are often attempts to imagine "the unimaginable decentering of global capital" (Jameson 1988: 351): "Conspiracy, one is tempted to say, is the poor person's cognitive mapping in the postmodern age; it is a degraded figure of the total logic of late capital, a desperate attempt to represent the latter's system, whose failure is marked by its slippage into sheer theme and content" (ibid.: 356).

Jameson does not argue that conspiracy theorizing is peculiarly postmodern. He is surely aware that there have been conspiracies and conspiracy theories across cultures and epochs. Jameson's point is that in the age of late capitalism, conspiracy theorizing is a popular form of representing economic and political relations that are increasingly hidden from view.

In the case of Argentine soccer, conspiracy theories produce a map of the occult economic and political forces that structure the soccer fan's everyday life. The theories serve to construct an image of the world in which "fair play," like "free trade," is exposed as an illusion, trusted only by *giles* (suckers). Eco argues that in talk about soccer, "the strength that the citizen had at his disposal for political debate is vitiated and disciplined" (Eco 1986: 163) and Sebreli writes that thinking about soccer "is a sort of training in escaping from oneself, in not doubting, not criticizing, not discussing, not thinking" (Sebreli 1981: 151), but I would argue that conspiracy theorizing trains soccer fans precisely to doubt, to criticize, to discuss, and to think.

Critical thought is not a scarce resource that is depleted in talk about soccer. Thinking critically about any topic, including one as frivolous as soccer, leads to more, not less, critical thought about other topics. Moreover, in contemporary Argentina, big "P" Political debate is almost entirely a technocratic discussion of the Chicago school's macroeconomic theory, misleadingly divorced from discussions of social justice. Given the technocratic boundaries of what passes for political debate in contemporary Argentina, I would argue that reading the politics and economics sections of most Argentine newspapers vitiates more political energy than does reading the sports section. Soccer, more than monetary policy, provides many Argentine men with a topic of discussion that addresses the continuing politics of colonialism, class, and ethnicity in their nation's society. There are also many examples of talk about soccer being talk about politics per se. Working-class men who gather in a café to speculate on how soccer games are fixed often speculate on how the affairs of state and of multinational corporations are also fixed. Following Argentina's loss to Cameroon in the 1990 World Cup, there was a conspiracy theory that the players threw the game because President Carlos Menem was in attendance, and Menem immediately stopped attending games played by the national team, presumably for fear of being blamed for any subsequent losses. Many players endorse political candidates or otherwise comment on political issues while club officers routinely run for "real" political office, and many clubs have definite partisan political connotations (Aizpeolea 1994; Scher and Palomino 1988: 194–97).

The Stadium and the Street

Is the soccer stadium a transformative space, where oppositional consciousness is raised and honed, or is it a conservative space, where critical thought is vitiated and confined? The question calls attention to the wall that purportedly separates the stadium from the street as well as play from politics. In addressing the relationship between the soccer stadium and the street, Alabarces argues that the soccer stadium is a ritual space, separated from the world of commerce and history:

> *[I]n soccer one acts what one is, one simulates what one wants to be/to do*. In soccer, as in a ceremony, one experiences the victory that does not abound in commercial time; in soccer, dribbling, madness permit the weak to defeat the powerful, the oppressed to humble the oppressor. Two feats that [Juan] Sasturain recalls: the *caño* among Argentines, the *sombrero* among Brazilians, the feats that for Corbatta or Garrincha are the risk, the adventure, the *play* at the corner of the ledge of life where both finally slipped off: because soccer is the suspension of history, and there is no punishment for the transgressor. With the reestablishment of historical time, sanctions appear: misery, cirrhosis of the liver

(Alabarces in Alabarces and Rodríguez 1996: 31–32, emphasis in the original).[5]

Alabarces sees the soccer stadium as a liminoid setting in which the poor can triumph over the rich, and the Third World over the First. He uses Garrincha's and Corbatta's post-soccer destitution as an allegory for the ephemerality of what happens within the stadium. Alabarces turns to anthropological studies of ritual to argue that the stadium is "the classic ahistoric space of ritual . . . a zone that is imagined as free, as if it were removed from the time of history and economy" (Alabarces in Alabarces and Rodríguez 1996: 69). It seems that he would agree with critics of other rituals, such as Brazilian carnival, that the subversive inversions that occur within ritual space and time are safely contained and do not contaminate the space and time of everyday life. Accordingly, Alabarces argues that "in Argentina, politics will continue for many years to be constructed outside of the stadium" (ibid.: 160), not inside it. Maradona may be a soccer player who speaks out about politics, but he is not, according to Alabarces, a political player.[6]

Like Alabarces, Sebreli argues that transgressive behavior within a soccer stadium is insulated from transgressive behavior outside. His reasoning is that what happens inside the stadium happens there precisely in order to keep it from happening outside, on the street. "As happened with the Roman circus, and the Byzantine racetrack, the modern stadium is converted on some occasions into the last refuge of the confusingly political discontent of the masses" (Sebreli 1981: 167). Sebreli explains that the soccer stadium is so filled with passion that oppositional displays there leave fans mystified and spent, not enlightened and mobilized. To enlighten and mobilize the people, according to Sebreli, reason, not passion, is required. At other times, of course, soccer stadiums are sites of conformity, not of resistance, as was the case in the 1934 World Cup in Italy. On such occasions, Sebreli argues, soccer is no longer insulated from the outside world of big "P" Politics but is intimately connected with that world. Somehow the same passion that prevents oppositional displays from being effective becomes effective when it is put at the service of a fascist regime.

Roberto Da Matta questions the boundaries between seriousness and play, between the stadium and the street, and between "society" and "soccer":

> *Soccer* is an opium of Brazilian society, in the same way that the economic domain is its base, as if *soccer* and economics would be exogenous realities that could exist in isolation from society. From this point of view, *soccer* is seen as a way to divert the attention of the Brazilian people away from other more fundamental problems. If we were, however, faced with a political party or with an economic activity, the same equation could be established, but, in all probability, the social scientist

would be more cautious in saying that a certain party is "an opium of the people," simply because in his conception of society, the "political" or the "economic" are things that are more serious and relevant than "sports" or *soccer* (Da Matta 1982: 21–22, emphasis in the original).

Da Matta follows Marshall Sahlins (1976)—and therefore Jean Baudrillard (1981 and 1975)—in finding that utilitarian and functionalist paradigms reproduce the logic of capitalism that constitutes "work" and "war" as "real," while constituting "religion" and "sports" as "illusory." Da Matta's argument is that "sports are a part of society, as much as society is also a part of sports" (Da Matta 1982: 23). The two are not "exogenous realities" that could exist apart from one another, nor is theirs a hierarchical relation. Rather, according to Da Matta, sports and society are "two sides of the same coin." The sides cannot be separated, nor does the coin always land with the same side facing up.

The boundaries that would separate sports from society, soccer from politics, and play from work are everywhere blurred. These are "the paradoxes of abstraction" that Gregory Bateson finds in all but the very simplest communications (Bateson 1972: 193). For the professional soccer player, to play is to work. Similarly, Richard Schechner observes that gladiators' combat had life-or-death seriousness for the gladiators at the same time that it was an afternoon of entertainment for the audience (Schechner 1985: 298). The game of soccer is big business in Argentina and in most of the rest of the world. Billions of real dollars are circulated globally, buying and selling players, athletic equipment, and broadcast rights (Levinsky 1995). In Argentina, and throughout Latin America, "real" political careers are often launched in the "marginal" world of soccer, and soccer terms are regularly employed to discuss political events (Aizpeolea 1994). President Menem is only one of millions of Argentine men who usually seem more concerned with the national soccer team than with the national bank.

Real wars have also started because of soccer games, and soccer games have taken on special meanings because of real wars. In 1986, four years after the Malvinas/Falklands War, Argentina and England played a World Cup soccer match. Ten years later, Maradona reflected on what that match meant:

I felt—and I feel, I do not deny it—that with this [victory] we won something more than a soccer game. We defeated a country. It was our contribution, in our way. We all declared before the game that soccer had nothing to do with the Malvinas War . . . A lie! . . . *In our skin was the pain of all those kids who had died there, so close and yet so far.* Emotionally, I blamed every one of the English players—our rivals—for what had happened. And my goals—both of them—had special significance: the first was like sticking my hand in the pocket of an Englishman and removing the money that did not belong to them; the

> second . . . topped everything (Maradona quoted in *El Gráfico* no. 4003, 25 June 1996: 78, emphasis in the original).

Maradona recognizes that the absolute distinction between the game and the war was a lie. I am not suggesting—and neither is he—that there is no difference between dying on a battlefield and giving up a goal on a soccer field, or between maintaining political sovereignty over a territory and maintaining control of a soccer ball. There are differences, but there are also blurrings. The Malvinas/Falklands War was a board game before a single shot was fired, much as for many North Americans the Gulf War was a video game or a CNN miniseries. I have no doubt that for many soccer fans in both Argentina and England, the 1986 soccer game was more "real" than was the 1982 war, and there are indications that many North Americans do not believe that the Gulf War really happened (see Barry Levinson's film, *Wag the Dog*).

It could be argued that it is a mystification to believe that a victory in the World Cup was a victory for the Argentine people, but it could also be argued that it is a mystification to believe that a victory in the Malvinas/ Falklands War was a victory for the English people, and not just for the multinational corporations who control the islands' oil and fishing industries. Is the jersey that soccer players so frequently invoke any less real than "the flag which men will die to save"? (Bateson 1972: 183)

Notes

1. Perhaps it is necessary to specify when one uses the words "people" and "popular" in the strict sense referring to the lower classes. I find useful Néstor García-Canclini's distinction between the terms *la popularidad* (popularity) and *lo popular* (popular-ness) (García-Canclini 1992: 241). Applied to soccer, "popularity" would refer to its being "prevalent" or "widespread," whereas "popularness" would refer to its being "common" or "low class."

2. I recognize that "manual" has etymological roots associated with the hand, a part of the body infrequently used by soccer players. Perhaps, then, "pedal labor" would be more precise a term than "manual labor" to describe what soccer players do.

3. This was the case on Sunday, 24 March 1996, when I attended a soccer game in Buenos Aires between Boca Juniors and Platense. Because this was the Sunday closest to the twentieth anniversary of the military coup that launched the Proceso, the Asociación del Fútbol Argentino ordered a minute of silence before the start of each game played that weekend (*Clarín* 25 March 1996, política: 4). The players were all in position on the field, with Maradona and Caniggia standing in the middle of the central circle, ready for the kickoff when the silence began. A few seconds into the mandated minute, Maradona began to jump up and down, and immediately the vast majority of the more than 45,000 fans in attendance began to jump up and down in unison with him, and to chant that he who did not jump was promilitary. Meanwhile, in the San Lorenzo soccer club's Nuevo Gasómetro stadium, the fans chanted, "Paredón, paredón, a todos los milicos que vendieron la Nación" (The firing squad, the firing squad, for all the military men who sold out the Nation) (*Clarín* 25 March 1996: 4).

4. It is typical for theorists of the body to invoke a natural body whose desires are thwarted, contained, and harnessed by disciplinary practices such as choreography and soccer coaching, but Martin is careful to avoid appeals to a naturally meaningful body. He argues that "the body takes shape and social purpose [only] against the limits of a physical culture, that is, within a social construction of time, space, and motion" (ibid.: 51). The body, according to Martin, becomes meaningful and resistant within the context of a culture that disciplines it.

5. Note that the *caño* involves dribbling the ball between the legs of an opponent (Suburú 1968: 35), while the *sombrero* involves kicking the ball over an opponent's head and then running around him to receive the ball just kicked (Pablo Alabarces, electronic communication, 3 August 1997). Juan Sasturain attributes the former move to the Argentines and the latter to the Brazilians (Sasturain 1994: 49), and he identifies the Brazilian Garrincha and the Argentine Corbatta as the masters of the *caño* and the *sombrero*, respectively (ibid.: 63–67). Garrincha was the star wing for the Brazilian national teams that won the World Cup in 1958 and 1962, while Corbatta was the star wing for Rácing Club's championship teams of 1958 and 1961, but each player sank into alcoholism and poverty after his retirement from soccer.

6. María Graciela Rodríguez, Alabarces's coauthor, disagrees, suggesting that soccer can "supplement politics" (Rodríguez in Alabarces and Rodríguez 1996: 45). She writes that "in the face of the decline of public debates, other forms of political action have appeared that, without replacing them, would alter dramatic arguments and the spaces for entering the debate" (ibid.: 48). Rodríguez supports her speculation by providing examples of soccer serving to intervene in big "P" Political debates, on both the conservative and progressive sides.

References Cited

Aizpeolea, Horacio
1994 Política en el fútbol. *Viva: Revista de Clárin* 24 July: 28–34.

Alabarces, Pablo, and María Graciela Rodríguez
1996 *Cuestión de pelotas: Fútbol, deporte, sociedad, cultura*. Buenos Aires: Atuel.

Archetti, Eduardo P., and Amílcar G. Romero
1994 Death and violence in Argentinian football. In *Football, Violence and Social Identity*, edited by Richard Giulianotti, Norman Bonney, and Mike Hepworth, pp. 37–72. London: Routledge.

Bateson, Gregory
1972 A theory of play and fantasy. In *Steps to an Ecology of Mind*, pp. 177–93. New York: Ballantine Books.

Baudrillard, Jean
1975 *The Mirror of Production*, translated by Mark Poster. St. Louis: Telos Press.
1981 *For a Critique of the Political Economy of the Sign*, translated by Charles Levin. St. Louis: Telos Press.

Bhabha, Homi K.
1990 DisemiNation: Time, Narrative, and the Margins of the Modern Nation. In *Nation and Narration*, edited by Homi K. Bhabha, pp. 291–322. London: Routledge.

Bilardo, Carlos S.
1986 *Así ganamos: La verdadera lucha por la Copa*. Buenos Aires: Sudamérica-Planeta.

Da Matta, Roberto
1982 Esporte na sociedade: Um ensaio sobre o futebol brasileiro. In *Universo do futebol: Esporte e sociedade brasileira*, edited by Roberto Da Matta, pp. 19–42. Rio de Janeiro: Edicoes Pinckotheke.

Eco, Umberto
1986 *Travels in Hyperreality*, translated by William Weaver. San Diego: Harcourt Brace Jovanovich.

Galeano, Eduardo
1995 *El fútbol a sol y sombra*. Buenos Aires: Catálogos.

García-Canclini, Néstor
1992 *Culturas híbridas: Estrategias para entrar y salir de la modernidad*. Buenos Aires: Editorial Sudamericana.

Gasparini, Roberto, and José Luis Ponsico
1983 *El director técnico del proceso*. Buenos Aires: El Cid Editor.

Isbell, Billie Jean
1985 *To Defend Ourselves: Ecology and Ritual in an Andean Village*. Prospect Heights: Waveland Press.

Jameson, Frederic
1988 Cognitive mapping. In *Marxism and the Interpretation of Culture*, edited by Cary Nelson and Larry Grossberg, pp. 347–57. Urbana: University of Illinois Press.

Levinsky, Sergio
1995 *El negocio del fútbol*. Buenos Aires: Corregidor.
1996 *Rebelde con Causa*. Buenos Aires: Corregidor.

Limón, José E.
1994 *Dancing with the Devil: Society and Cultural Poetics in Mexican-American South Texas*. Madison: University of Wisconsin Press.

MacClancy, Jeremy
1996 Nationalism at Play: The Basques of Vizcaya and Athletic Club de Bilbao. In *Sport, Identity and Ethnicity*, edited by Jeremy MacClancy, pp. 181–99. Oxford: Berg.

Martin, Randy
1990 *Performance as Political Act: The Embodied Self*. New York: Bergin and Garvey.

Marx, Karl
1978 *The Marx-Engels Reader*, edited by Robert C. Tucker. Second edition. New York: W. W. Norton.

Mason, Anthony
1995 *Passion of the People? Football in South America*. London: Verso.

Morales, Franklin
1969 *Fútbol: Mito y realidad*. Nuestra Tierra 22. Montevideo: Editorial Nuestra Tierra.

Niembro, Fernando, and Julio Llinás
1995 *Inocente*. Buenos Aires: Grijalbo Mondadori.

Núñez, Héctor
1995 *Así ganamos la Copa América 1995*. Montevideo: Últimas Noticias.

Sahlins, Marshall
1976 *Culture and Practical Reason*. Chicago: University of Chicago Press.

Sasturain, Juan
1994 *El día del arquero*, illustrated by Fontanarrosa. Second edition. Buenos Aires: Ediciones de la Flor.

Savigliano, Marta E.
1995 *Tango and the Political Economy of Passion*. Boulder: Westview Press.

Schechner, Richard
1985 *Between Theater and Anthropology*. Philadelphia: University of Pennsylvania Press.

Scher, Ariel, and Héctor Palomino
1988 *Fútbol: Pasión de multitudes y de elites*. Buenos Aires: CISEA.

Sebreli, Juan José
1981 *Fútbol y masas*. Buenos Aires: Editorial Galerna.

Starn, Orin
1992 Missing the Revolution: Anthropologists and the War in Peru. *Rereading Cultural Anthropology*, edited by George E. Marcus, pp. 152–80. Durham: Duke University Press.

Suburú, Nilo J.
1968 *Primer diccionario del fútebol*. Montevideo: Ediciones Tauro.

Taylor, Diana
1997 *Disappearing Acts: Performing Gender in Argentina's "Dirty War."* Durham, NC: Duke University Press.

Valdano, Jorge
1995 *Cuentos de fútbol*. Buenos Aires: Extra Alfaguara.
1996 Un mal de ausencias. *Clarín* 8 June, deportivo: 9.

Vinnai, Gerhard
1974 *El fútbol como ideología*, translated by León Mames. Mexico City: Siglo Veintiuno Editores

5

Three Kings Day in Consuelo: Cricket, Baseball, and the Cocolos in San Pedro de Macorís

Rob Ruck

Perhaps no event has had a greater impact on U.S. major league baseball over the last half century than the breaking of the color bar by Jackie Robinson in 1947. This step permitted not only black players to enter the majors but also athletes from the Caribbean Basin, a phenomenon that has accelerated as scouts increasingly have sought talent abroad. Latin American players now make up a significant percentage of every team's roster, over 20 percent for the major leagues as a whole by the turn of the century. Of all the foreign nations that have contributed individuals to the majors, none in 2001 has a higher profile than that of the Dominican Republic. Furthermore, within the Dominican Republic, one town, San Pedro de Macorís, has accounted for more players than its size might warrant. And finally, many of these players are of black, West Indian stock. Why?

This is the question that the University of Pittsburgh's Rob Ruck tackles in his study of San Pedro. He comes up with an instructive thesis that involves the issues of class and race and the role of sport to help people resist oppressive societal forces. Ruck traces the history of the poor black, English-speaking, West Indian immigrants of San Pedro back to the turn of the century when they first arrived in the Dominican Republic to cut sugarcane. These people, Ruck argues, used cricket, originally learned in the British-colonized islands from which they came, to develop a sense of self and community in their new and often difficult surroundings. Over time, as a second and third generation came to the fore, these feelings of self-confidence and discipline were transferred to the playing of baseball, already the country's principal pastime among the mestizo majority, and one at which the West Indians not only excelled but also through which they finally became accepted as full-fledged Dominicans.

From *Studies in Latin American Popular Culture* 13 (1994): 129–42. Reprinted by permission of *Studies in Latin American Popular Culture*.

William Joseph and Roberto Caines sit under a grapefruit tree in Guachupita, a barrio in the shadow of *Ingenio* Consuelo's smokestacks. While the sugar mill's plume of smoke signals the beginning of another grinding season in the Dominican Republic, these men reflect upon the making of their community. It is a story that says much about why San Pedro de Macorís became baseball's Mecca in the 1980s. Yet their tale begins at the turn of the century in the British West Indies and is as much about cricket as about baseball.[1]

Only a few hours before and ten miles away, Alfredo Griffin stood in the driveway of his home in San Pedro as several hundred young boys swarmed the compound's walls, chanting "*Reyes*! [Kings!] Griffin! Griffin!" It is the morning of January 6—Three Kings Day—the traditional Dominican day of holiday gift giving and a time when politicos and other notables dispense toys. The children had been outside Griffin's house since dawn, spilling over from neighbor Joaquín Andújar's annual distribution of sporting goods. And the sight of the Toronto Bluejay shortstop heading down the driveway in a tan BMW 635CSi sets off a stampede that blocks his exit.

No one had stood chanting outside William Joseph's or Roberto Caines's concrete block homes in Consuelo that morning. But seventy-eight-year-old Joseph, a blacksmith pensioned after fifty-one years in the *ingenio*, and sixty-two-year-old Caines, who tends to the sugar mill's recalcitrant water pumps, had years before given their gifts to the youth of Consuelo and the surrounding sugar estates—boys like Rico Carty, Alfredo Griffin, Pedro Guerrero, George Bell, Tony Fernández, and Julio César Franco. And Griffin, hands on hips, wants badly to get back to Consuelo so that he can give his.

"How can you come over and ask for a gift when Joaquín has already given you a bat, a shirt, or a glove and other children haven't yet got anything?" Griffin implores in Spanish. Relenting, he hands gloves to a score of boys who seemed so far to have missed out and seizes the moment to ease his vehicle onto the streets of the town that currently sends more of its native sons to the major leagues on a per capita basis than any other town ever has.

For the West Indian migrants who ventured to San Pedro de Macorís early this century, and later their children and grandchildren, sport fostered a spirit of self-celebration in which a sense of community and ethnic identity were forged. It provided these *Cocolos*, as they came to be called, a vehicle to assert that collective identity within a larger, frequently hostile society. And that cultural role, perhaps even more than sport's lure as a means of mobility, explains its extraordinary importance and staying power in this community.

Sport has often been seen as a vehicle for asserting ethnic and cultural identity. The *Cocolo* experience suggests that ethnic and cultural identity can also become a vehicle for advancing sport.[2]

San Pedro offered little in the way of social amenities or economic security, although the hope for material gain was then sufficient to attract unprecedented numbers of migrants from the British, Dutch, and French West Indies. Clustered in a half-dozen mill town enclaves in and around San Pedro, these *Cocolos* were politically powerless and socially scorned. Their fragmentation along the lines of island of birth and Dominican residence only contributed to their disorganization. These conditions lent sport an extra significance as a force for cohesion and consciousness. And that helps to explain why baseball has become virtually an art form in the region.[3]

Driving past Rico Carty's house, Griffin stops near the home of his friend, George Bell, to pull out gloves for a trio of shoeshine boys. As Alfredo drives away, the boys run after his car, holding their prizes aloft. Weaving his car through a helter-skelter swirl of motor scooters, pedicabs, and the occasional Mercedes Benz, Griffin passes Tetelo Vargas Stadium, home of the Estrellas Orientales, his winter ball club, and heads north to Consuelo, the largest of the six sugar mills that have made San Pedro the center of the Dominican sugar industry since late last century.

During the late 1970s, when Macorísanos started to appear on major league baseball diamonds, San Pedro began to attract the attention of the baseball world. But baseball's roots there stretch back for almost a century, and its importance was well established long before the region became a pipeline for talent to the majors.

Introduced by Cubans and Dominican youth who had studied in the United States, baseball captured the hearts and minds of the Dominican people before the United States Marines arrived in 1916 for their eight-year occupation. Initially a game of the affluent classes, baseball soon became the people's game.

Baseball on the island never succumbed to a color line, and neither race, class, nor nationality deterred a club from recruiting a player. Early teams usually were either self-organized or backed by a commercial or political patron, with some developing a group ownership similar to that of European soccer clubs. In the 1940s, the government created a system of ostensibly amateur teams with regional leagues and national championship tournaments. At first organized on an ad hoc basis, semipro baseball gained a professional structure in 1951 with the creation of a Dominican summer league. Games were shifted to the winter to accommodate an agreement with the United States major leagues in 1955.[4]

Griffin overtakes a boy astride a horse-drawn cart loaded with cane cut into four-foot sections. Haitian women balance jerry cans of water on their head as they walk through the fields to their *batey*, a cluster of company-owned shacks. Their husbands and sons cut cane in fields that stretch as far as one can see on both sides of the road; they labor from sunup until sundown for about eighty cents a ton, cut and stacked. A decent day's work is three tons.

Traditionally, San Pedro's economy has revolved around its sugarcane industry. Initiated by Cubans fleeing the havoc of the Ten Years War (1868–1878), the sugar industry expanded greatly after the island's incorporation into the U.S. economic sphere early in this century. By the end of the Marines' occupation, U.S. capital dominated the industry, and the upgraded grinding mills sent their product northward.

An adequate supply of labor in this sparsely populated region was one of the industry's most pressing concerns, especially since Dominicans saw little incentive to partake of its hot, dangerous, and low-paying work. Ultimately, the industry turned to neighboring Haiti, whose miserable lot made even cane cutting seem a feasible alternative. But at the turn of the century, the cane cutters and *ingenio* workers came from elsewhere in the Caribbean. Alfredo Griffin's grandparents were among these migrants.[5]

Griffin slows to cross the tracks by the cemetery where Pittsburgh Pirate Alberto Lois lost a race with a train as he drove home from the ballpark one night. Lois's career ended on the spot, along with the lives of five of his passengers. In Consuelo, Griffin drives past the stadium where several youths practice under the watchful eyes of Boston Red Sox scout Rafael Batista. Griffin arrives at the home of his mother, Mary, where he unloads mitts and running shoes from the trunk of his car.

Mary Griffin lives in the house on Carty Street her son bought for her when he won Rookie of the Year honors in the American League in 1979. Although it was Rico Carty, the boy from Guachupita, who helped put Consuelo on the sporting firmament's map, it is his mother, Oliva, once the town's midwife, for whom the street is named. Carty Street stretches from Santa Ana Church to the *ingenio*, a century-old congeries of shops, giant grinding wheels, and centrifuges that make sugar out of the cane. Behind the mill lie Guachupita, La Habana, La Loma, Barrio Hato Mayor, and the other neighborhoods of company-owned housing.

Just as Carty Street ties Consuelo together, Rico Carty is the ballplayer who links Joseph's and Caines's generation with Griffin's. "My mother wanted me to be a doctor," Rico Carty recalled earlier as he sprawled across the rattan furniture in his San Pedro home, "but I didn't like that. My mother wouldn't let me go to the ball field, but I used to steal time to play. I tell my mother I going to school but I used to go to the river and swim and play ball instead. I would have ended up in the mill but for baseball."[6]

In the 1950s, after baseball's color line ended, Dominicans ventured north to the majors. Following the Cuban Revolution and the 1961 assassination of Rafael Trujillo, who had ruled the Dominican side of the island like a personal fiefdom since 1930, the country emerged as the chief source of Latin talent. Carty was part of that current. The grandson of St. Martin islanders, Carty's United States debut at the 1959 Pan American

Games in Chicago so impressed major league clubs that nine of them made him offers to play professionally. Carty accepted them all. "I just go ahead and sign 'cause all I want to do is play baseball. I get the baseball in my blood, and I keep on signing."

Rico Carty signed with all four Dominican winter clubs, too, and only the intervention of the president of the minor leagues saved him from permanent exile from the game. After Carty, whose .366 batting average led the majors in 1970, came his Guachupita *compañero* [companion] Pepe Frías, and then Rafael Batista, Griffin, Nelson Norman, Lois, Juan Samuel, Julio César Franco, and several score others who signed professional contracts. Other sugar mill town boys, like Rafael Ramírez, Rafael Santana, and Mariano Duncan, adopted a "Have Glove, Will Travel" approach and played for the *Ingenio* Consuelo "amateur" team, which sent five consecutive shortstops to the majors.

An idol to a generation of San Pedro youth, Carty retired in 1983, never missing a winter season. "I feel a real obligation to play here 'cause I owe my country a lot . . . because they pushed me so much here." Carty's debt is to men like Joseph, Caines, his uncle Luis Carty, Austin Jacobo, and a score of sporting elders who nurtured baseball during its early years in Consuelo.

These men were the sons of migrants of African descent who arrived in the Dominican Republic from St. Martin, Nevis, Tortola, Montserrat and the other, mostly British islands where the sugar industry was collapsing due to tariffs protecting the European sugar beet industry at the moment that the Dominican cane fields were expanding. At first, most came only to work during the harvest and returned home afterwards. But gradually, thousands of these men of African descent came to stay, bringing their families with them. They called themselves "the English" and settled in a part of San Pedro called Miramar and in the sugar mill towns that encircled the city—Quisqueya, Cristóbal, Colón, Angelina, Santa Fe, Porvenir, and Consuelo.[7]

"They were brought to cut cane on the estates," Roberto Caines explains in English with a West Indian lilt, "but they were scorned. It was a great trial to go to another country. We lived in barracks, four families to a house, with plenty bugs, plenty sickness and vermin. We had mostly English people here in Consuelo, but there were many, too, in San Pedro and the other estates—Santa Fe, Porvenir, Colón, and Quisqueya."[8]

Sipping wine, Caines continues: "They called us *Cocolos*, because many of the first English people here were from Tortola and the Dominicans had trouble saying that. They meant it as an insult and when a Dominican called an Englishman *Cocolo* it caused many a fight."

But this racial epithet subsequently became a term of pride as the English forged their own cultural definition of *Cocolo*, one that transcended their different islands of origin and places of residence and emphasized discipline and self-organization, at work and at play. Without these English-speaking, cricket-playing sojourners, Dominican baseball never would have become the best in the Caribbean.

"The only protection they have was to unificate with each other," Caines explains. "The first school we had here was the one we make in the yard under a tree to teach our children to read and write. And we make societies to care for people when they're sick and make the ceremony and carry them to the burial when they die."

These mutual aid societies were modeled after comparable British institutions. So, too, was their sense of sport.

"My father came from Antigua to cut cane," William Joseph offers. "They brought cricket with them from the islands and I learned the game from him. In this estate, we had two cricket clubs, the Ever Jolly and the Energetic, that began—whoooo!—long time ago. We got together with our small amount of money and sent for our gear from India. It took months! We made our own uniforms—all white, of course—and wore white sneakers and a sash with the club's colors. . . . After a while cricket was established in the Republic—wherever there were English to be found, wherever there were *ingenios*."

Cricket developed in a context of fraternal societies and race consciousness, with teams sometimes wearing the society's colors. One club, the Energetic, even organized its own benevolent aid society when its captain was seriously injured, and the players pooled their resources to help him.

"The children had sport crafted in them," Caines adds. "They were exposed to sport and taught that they must try not to fail or that the color will fail, too, and the race will be beaten. We never had no politics—the English were told to stay out of that—but we had the message of Marcus Garvey," the Jamaican-born leader of the Universal Negro Improvement Association (UNIA), the largest black nationalist organization of the century. "We always tried to maintain pride and heritage. We had a sense of discipline and organization with which we founded our clubs and societies, of good British discipline, of taking care of our people that have need."

Garveyism swept through the *ingenios* and San Pedro during the United States Marines' occupation. While the English generally refrained from choosing sides in a civil conflict that they saw as between Dominican factions, the Marine Corps kept close tabs on any expression of political sentiment. G. M. Kincade, the provost marshal for the district, wrote his commander that Marcus Garvey's UNIA, "if allowed to grow, inculcating Bolshevistic ideas to the ignorant, would soon become a menace to the peace of the community. . . . From appearances, it is a society for the uplift of the negro, but its ulterior motive is to engender racial hatred with an idea to ultimate domination of the white race." Garvey's appeal reflected the conditions that the English encountered at work and in the community as well as their sense of being a distinct, often abused group.

But open dissent had already lapsed before Rafael Trujillo took power in 1930, and English political activity after that historic divide all but ceased.[9]

"Trujillo!" sports activist Luis Carty exclaimed when asked whether the English protested their situation during Trujillo's thirty-one-year-long dictatorship. "He was too tough, man. Whooo! He was too tough. We would keep in the place. In the estates, everybody keep in their places and they didn't get mixed up in government affairs. No! No! No! Not the English people!"[10]

A network of cricket clubs took shape with each of the *ingenios* and the *Cocolo* community in San Pedro proper fielding at least one or two clubs. Consuelo, the largest mill, was represented by the Energetic, the Ever Jolly, and the Rattlers as well as two clubs reflecting the arrival of Hollywood in town, Metro-Goldwyn-Mayer and Twentieth Century Fox. Each was a self-financed, self-organized affair without sugar company backing. "We organized the teams," Coleridge Mayers, a seventy-three-year-old man of Antiguan descent recalled proudly on the porch of his Santa Fe *ingenio* home, across the street from where Pedro Guerrero grew up. "We even made our own pitch, exclusively. Cricket was the sport of the English people and the sugar estates then."[11]

A cornet player, followed by the queens of the clubs, led the players in a parade before the season's first match. Contests were on holidays and weekends, "But only during the *tiempo muerto*, the dead season," Joseph advises. "We didn't play at all during the *zafra*, the grinding season," when the shift was twelve hours a day, six days a week, for fifty cents a day. "You'd have nothing else to do in the *tiempo muerto* but play cricket," Mayers explained. "It kept people in touch, tied the English on the estates together."

"But cricket began to pass," Caines says with a shrug. "Those folks were getting old, their time was finishing and no one concerned themselves with cricket anymore. It was a great loss that cricket died out," Joseph concludes. "For many of us, it was our sport. But baseball becomes the English sport here and it almost teaches the same things as cricket did. The English gained acceptance by playing baseball and we found more benefit in it because in cricket we never were paid."

Cricket succeeded as the children of the migrants matured in a new society and became Dominicans with an English island heritage. Those born after 1920 grew up with baseball on the ascent. Some of the surviving English elders recalled the Marines playing baseball during the occupation, especially in Miramar, the *Cocolo* section of San Pedro where the troops where headquartered. But the pivotal event in tipping the balance from cricket to baseball might have been the national championships held on the island in 1936 and 1937.

The 1936 tournament featured Licey and Escogido from the capital, the Estrellas Orientales of San Pedro, and the Aguilas Cibaeñas of Santiago. When, to the horror of the capital, San Pedro's team won in 1936, Licey and Escogido were merged the following season to play as Ciudad Trujillo (as Santo Domingo had been renamed to further the glory of Rafael Trujillo). Each of the teams also stepped up its recruitment of foreign talent, a practice with some precedent. The best Cuban, Puerto Rican, and Venezuelan players, including Martín Dihígo, Perucho Cepeda, and Silvio García, were lured to the island. Recruiters, accompanied by Dominican consular officials, traveled as far north as Pittsburgh, and returned to the island with nine of the Negro National League's Pittsburgh Crawfords. Hall of Famers Josh Gibson, Satchel Paige, Cool Papa Bell, as well as a dozen other Negro Leaguers, jumped their circuit for the far more lucrative rewards of Dominican ball. The Crawfords were all but finished as a result, but island play that summer has yet to be forgotten.[12]

"My older brother used to carry me to those games on his shoulders, and they [the Negro Leaguers] came here to Consuelo to play on the estate's golf course—the only blacks to do that," Caines marvels. Coleridge Mayers recalls carousing with these foreign reinforcements at San Pedro dance halls during the week, cheering for them on the weekends, and finding a new allure to the sport of baseball. "Gibson could hit that ball from here to the sky!" Mayers exclaims a half century afterwards. "One Sunday, Bragaña [a Cuban pitcher] struck him out twice and he says to Paige, 'Goddamn, that ball is dropping hard, I can't hit him,' and Paige says, 'Stoop a little more.' Whoooooooo! It was the biggest home run I ever saw in all these Lord's days."

"Baseball overpowered cricket in Consuelo and the other estates," laments Joseph. The eclipse of cricket, meanwhile, channeled the English sporting energies and organization into baseball. The legacy of this cultural infusion can be seen on ball fields from San Pedro to San Diego.

As one generation of sportsmen put away its cricket bats and club sashes, their children picked up baseballs and gloves. While William Joseph, Leopoldo Carty, Albert Reed, Stanley Norman, Henry Conton, and their peers played for the Energetic, the Ever Jolly, Twentieth Century Fox, Metro-Goldwyn-Mayer, and Consuelo's other cricket clubs, Rico Carty, Alfredo Griffin, Nelson Norman, Chico Conton and their friends played baseball. In between, sporting cadre like Luis Carty, Austin Jacobo, and Roberto Caines carried the impulse that organized cricket into the Dominican pastime.

"All the great players around here are English or their descendants," Joseph attests. "It has to do with cricket. It's got to be that." Not all the ballplayers emerging from San Pedro's sandlots are of English descent, but few question that, historically, the chief concentrations of baseball talent in San Pedro have been on the estates with the most English and the best cricket. Son Howell, Garabato Sackie, Chico Conton, and Clemente Hart (all of whom played cricket, too) starred in Dominican ball in the 1940s and 1950s while the third generation of Griffin, George Bell, Pedro Guerrero, Juan Samuel, Mariano Duncan, Manny Lee, and José Offerman leads the current crop of San Pedro ballplayers in the major leagues. All four Dominicans at the 1987 U.S. major league All-Star game were from San Pedro, three of them grandsons of English migrants.

Most San Pedro natives, of English or Dominican descent, acknowledge the hegemony of the sons of the cricketers. They suggest that their family discipline, approach to sport, and affinity for organizing their lives amidst the deprivation of the *bateyes* and *ingenios* are the reasons why. "The adoption of cricket makes one more vigilant," argues eighty-three-year-old Sebastián "Basilio" Ferdinand, a former cricket arbiter, "and one could say that it is perhaps from the seed of cricket that baseball blossomed. The tradition coming down has made them better players."[13]

A half century ago, mill superintendent Edwin L. Kilbourne handed out the toys and sweets on Three Kings Day in Consuelo. Now, it is Griffin, clad in white from his polo shirt to his half-laced, high-top Reeboks, and with his close-cropped black hair and beard, reminiscent of an earlier sporting era. Griffin's grandparents migrated from Nevis to Consuelo and then to Angelina, the neighboring estate, where his father was born. Alfredo began life in the capital, Santo Domingo, but came to Guachupita after the 1965 Revolution. "I was a kid," Griffin remembers, "running up and down the streets. I wasn't scared of anything but my mother wanted to get me out of there." In Consuelo, Griffin played in the streets and fields in pickup games of Guachupita versus La Loma or Pueblo Nuevo [New Town] nines. "Then we'd go and cut a piece of cane and peel it with our teeth." He caught on to the tail end of the Santa Ana baseball club, perhaps the catalyst to Consuelo's evolution as a baseball breeding ground.

In 1947, Joseph Ainslie, a Canadian priest in the Scarboro Order, arrived in Consuelo. Forty years later, the man Consuelo remembers as Padre José sits in the rectory of his parish church north of Kingston, near where he grew up, and shakes his head in horror at the thought of the conditions he encountered there. "I had to get a technique to introduce myself to that melee. . . . Since I saw the obvious, that they loved baseball, I thought that this would help me infiltrate the people." Working with Luis Carty, Austin Jacobo, Caines, and other men, "mostly English, they seemed to understand organization better." Ainslie's ball club, named after the Santa Ana Church, was wildly successful. It gave the priest an entree that allowed him to mobilize for better housing, form cooperatives, and end usurious moneylending. Ainslie, who spent three years there before government and sugar mill pressures removed him from the country, is remembered with admiration. "He opened our eyes," Joseph recalls. Meanwhile, the team became a hothouse for nurturing outstanding players, of English and Dominican descent. It touched the playing or managing careers of many of the better players in the region.[14]

Later, seated in his den and clad in black shorts, thongs, and a gold pendant of a diamond-studded number four, Griffin connects himself to Consuelo's sporting continuum. "Austin Jacobo and Roberto Caines were working in the community, helping kids to play. Bibi (Caines) handled me for a while when I was a second baseman. . . . He was a big influence. Right now, he's one of the guys running my little league in Consuelo. . . . And Austin Jacobo would look at a kid and know when he was ready to play on a higher level. When I grew up, I realized that most of the kids from Consuelo that are professional ballplayers now are probably there because of him and the other men who worked and fought hard to have sport in Consuelo. The English people here had good ways to raise kids. They were very strict and the kids respect them. That was, for me, the main thing. If you have respect and discipline when you organize something, you gonna be successful. I guess it comes from playing cricket. . . . A lot of people ask me why so many players from Consuelo. For me, that's one of the answers."

Back at Tetelo Vargas Stadium, Pedro González stands behind first base, hands on hips, as three runners take staggered leads off the bag. It is ten in the morning, and the runners shimmer in the heat rising from the baked infield dirt. A hundred or so onlookers sit in the shade of the stadium's canopy. Most are male, many of school age, but the only students taking their lessons seriously this morning are those on the field, under the scrutiny of San Pedro professor Pedro González.[15] Soon González's Atlanta Braves rookie team will play against a squad of hopefuls from the Houston Astros. These contests are daily occurrences in San Pedro, where almost a dozen major league clubs maintain a constant presence. González, a former New York Yankee, is but one of San Pedro's many native sons who have joined its sporting professoriat in recent years as the city has become one large prep school for the baseball world.

González has the height and musculature that only the Dominican ballplayers of English descent seem to possess. An articulate, thoughtful man whose children attend medical school, González speaks to the forces that have made Macorís the most fecund source of baseball talent anywhere, anytime. "I think we have always been better," González says like a true Macorísano, "but lately, there's never been anything like it." Of the hundred plus Dominicans to have played in the majors by 1988, over a third came via San Pedro. And while the best Dominicans, like Juan Marichal and Tony Peña, initially came from elsewhere in the country, since the 1970s, San Pedro has provided the most bountiful harvests. "The people from the estates never had anything to do," González comments.

"You go there when the cropping season is over and you see the old men playing dominoes and younger people playing baseball. Once the season is over, what you gonna do, sit on your butt? No! You play ball, that's what you gonna do."

As is the case with González, perhaps half of San Pedro's baseball paladins have had English antecedents. And many of the non-English Macorísanos grew up on the estates alongside them, influenced by the *Cocolos'* approach to sport. The English have a very organized, very disciplined community," González avers. "They don't steal; they don't drink. They grow up with manners. If the father says nine o'clock in bed, it don't mean ten after nine. That carries over to baseball." And González concludes, "We are a big people. Look at Rico Carty, George Bell, Pedro Guerrero, myself. We all have English blood and we are each bigger than most Dominicans."

Heritage is of less and less consequence these days, González explains, because the highly competitive baseball culture in San Pedro has been stamped in the English mold. Discipline has become internalized as an item of faith; the distinction between English and Dominican has waned. "These boys are hungry," González declares with a gesture that encompasses the players and the growing number of spectators. "There's not a lot of work in San Pedro these days. And what job could pay what they can make in the majors?"

There is no comparable alternative to a baseball career, at least not a legal one, and the boys know it. Asked what he would do if he were not playing ball, one rookie responds "*Nada. No hay trabajo aquí.*" ["Nothing. There is no work here."]

But there is baseball—almost around the clock. Both the government and the sugar mills sponsor extensive amateur ball, while the camps run by major league teams train and evaluate prospects throughout the year. "This stadium is in use from morning to night almost every day of the year," González laughs. "Everywhere you look you find scouts. They don't miss a boy. And these boys are better prepared than we were."

Even the Japanese have gotten into the act. The Hiroshima Toyo Carp recently built a state-of-the-art training camp on the road to Consuelo, where they are intent on developing a few good Dominicans to play Japanese ball.

Since Rico Carty, San Pedro has sent César Cedeño, Joaquín Andújar, Alfredo Griffin, Pedro Guerrero, Juan Samuel, Tony Fernández, Julio César Franco, George Bell, and Rafael Ramírez to all-star careers. Hundreds of others played minor league ball, and thousands more are in training for a life in baseball. The town of 100,000 inhabitants remains perhaps the only one in the world that could form a credible major league franchise solely with local talent. While only the best and luckiest will make it, almost all will return to San Pedro each winter and after their playing days are over. These elder statesmen of the game give the youth of this town a tangible sense of the possibility of making it. And they provide a corps of talented advisors who frequently can be found at the ballpark or on the local sandlot.

Every boy who leaves the island and returns to San Pedro a major leaguer raises the town's fervor for the game another notch. Baseball is an ever-present preoccupation that shows no sign of abating soon. "Every boy grows up with a bat and a ball—it's the first present a male baby gets in his crib—and every one that wants the chance to play gets it," González affirms.

Ask any kid on any *calle* [street] where Andújar or Griffin live and they will escort you there personally. Go to a ball field and wait during the winter, and the chances are that a major or minor leaguer will soon appear and play alongside the boys who wish to join him in baseball's promised land.

The "miracle of Macorís," as San Pedro's pipeline to the majors has been dubbed, is a hybrid of the *Cocolos*' sporting offspring grafted to Dominican stock. The resulting progeny have flourished in the critical mass of competition that has taken hold in and around San Pedro. Now based on the sugar estates and in the major league camps, Macorís baseball has widened the game's traditional sources of talent and will shape its future on the field as much as any town in the world in the coming years.

If there is a secret to baseball in Macorís, it is perhaps that an informal network of boys and men built their own sporting life as part of the larger quest of the Dominican English to build a community in their new land. Putting aside cricket for baseball, their sons and grandsons Dominicanized their passion for sport as well as themselves and moved into the vanguard of baseball, both in the Caribbean and in the United States.

In part, the *Cocolos* developed a sense of themselves as a people from the oppositional nature of the dominant culture and the limited outlets for development that this culture permitted. Sport loomed in importance precisely because other avenues of advancement and expression were so often blocked. Cricket and then baseball linked the English together with a local pantheon of heroes. After the flush of the day's match had faded, the competition among the clubs from the different estates created a larger, more inclusive sense of solidarity. These events brought together crowds as large as a thousand to celebrate their sporting excellence and competence. And after baseball replaced cricket, sport served as a vehicle for "Dominicanizing" the English by allowing them to excel at the Dominican pastime and become heroes to the entire society.[16]

Back in Guachupita, William Joseph scratches the head of a ten-day-old goat kid as Roberto Caines carries the wooden chairs back to the kitchen. Arm-in-arm, they set off through the streets of the community which they helped build into a place to live and a place to play.

Notes

1. This article is based on research conducted for *The Tropic of Baseball: Baseball in the Dominican Republic* (Westport, CT: Meckler, 1991). The research was made possible by support from the Social Science Research Council and the National Endowment for the Humanities. Much of this material is based on extensive interviews conducted in the Dominican Republic and Tortola between 1985 and 1991.

2. The literature on sport's connection to culture and ethnicity is quite large. Among the best treatments are Peter Levine, *Ellis Island to Ebbets Field: Sport and the American Jewish Experience* (New York: Oxford University Press, 1992); C.L.R. James, *Beyond a Boundary* (New York: Pantheon, 1983); and Robert Whiting, *You Gotta Have Wa* (New York: Macmillan, 1989).

3. For material pertaining to San Pedro, see José del Castillo, *La inmigración de braceros azucareros en la República Dominicana, 1900–1930: Cuadernos del Cendia*, vol. 262, no. 7 (Santo Domingo: Universidad Autónoma de Santo Domingo); José del Castillo and Walter Cordero, *La economia dominicana durante el primer cuarto del siglo XX* (Santo Domingo: Fundación García Arévalo, 1979); and Julio César Mota Acosta, *Los Cocolos en Santo Domingo* (Santo Domingo: Editorial la Gaviota, 1977). Also based on three months of field work there.

4. For more on Dominican baseball history, see Cuqui Córdova, *Album del recuerdo*, 3 vols. (Santo Domingo: Talleres de Editora, 1981–1983); Tony Piña, *Los grandes finales* (Santo Domingo: Editora Colegial Quisqueyana, 1981); and Rob Ruck, *The Tropic of Baseball.*

5. Alfredo Griffin, interviews by author, June 1988, Pittsburgh; January 1989, San Pedro de Macorís, Dominican Republic.

6. Rico Carty, interviews by author, January 1988, January 1989, San Pedro de Macorís, Dominican Republic.

7. See del Castillo's and Mota Acosta's works cited above. See also Martin Murphy, "Historical and Contemporary Labor Utilization Practices in the Sugar Industries of the Dominican Republic" (Ph.D. dissertation, Columbia University, 1986).

8. Roberto Caines and William Joseph, interviews by author, June/July 1987, January 1988, June 1988, Consuelo, Dominican Republic.

9. Letter from G.M. Kincade, Provost Marshal, Eastern District to District Commander Eastern District, 21 September 1921, re: UNIA, in United States National Archives. The National Archives' holdings on the occupation dwarf the materials available in the Dominican Republic. For more on the occupation, see Bruce Calder, *The Impact of Intervention: The Dominican Republic during the U.S. Occupation of 1916–1924* (Austin: University of Texas Press, 1984).

10. Luis Carty, interview by author, January 1988, San Pedro de Macorís, Dominican Republic.

11. Coleridge Mayers, interview by author, January 1988, Ingenio Santa Fe, San Pedro de Macorís, Dominican Republic.

12. For the Dominican side of the 1937 tournament, see Ruck, *The Tropic of Baseball*. For the Pittsburgh perspective, see Rob Ruck, *Sandlot Seasons: Sport in Black Pittsburgh* (Champaign: University of Illinois Press, 1987).

13. Sebastián Ferdinand, interview by author, January 1988, San Pedro de Macorís, Dominican Republic.

14. Joseph Ainslie, interview by author, August 1987, Seeley's Bay, Ontario. A significant but little explored factor in baseball's evolution in the cane fields was the 1945–1946 sugar mill worker strike that led to the change from two twelve-hour shifts to three eight-hour shifts per day. That change allowed baseball to become more of a year-round game. See Ruck, *The Tropic of Baseball*, chapter 8.

15. Pedro González, interviews by author, June 1987, January 1988, June 1988, San Pedro de Macorís, Dominican Republic.

16. Janet Lever expertly analyzes this process for soccer in Brazil in her *Soccer Madness* (Chicago: University of Chicago Press, 1983).

6

Labor, the State, and Professional Baseball in Mexico in the 1980s

David G. LaFrance*

Baseball, Mexico's most widely played and followed sport after football (soccer), first entered the country in the late nineteenth century. It arrived from two directions: from the north, via U.S. miners and railroad hands who worked in Mexico; and from the east, from Cuba, which already had adopted the game and had close commercial ties with its neighbor across the Yucatán Channel. Today, baseball's popularity still reflects these origins, with its strongest presence in the north and northwest as well as along the Gulf coast. Like football, baseball also started out as an elite sport that eventually became part of mass culture. Players commonly came from small cities and towns scattered throughout the country's vast interior. Most of them played for the fun of the game. A few, however, made it into one of Mexico's organized professional leagues, and now and then one would even find his way to the big time, the U.S. major leagues. A recent example is Fernando Valenzuela, former All-Star pitcher for the Los Angeles Dodgers, who hailed from the village of Etchohuaquila, Sonora, in the far northwest.

On the whole, however, Mexican players, even those in the principal leagues, were not well treated. Neither owners nor the government saw them as true workers but rather as entertainers, who, because they were merely playing a game, did not warrant rights already gained by labor in general. Consequently, in 1980 baseball players initiated one of Mexico's only and most important strikes by professional athletes, thus forcing a reevaluation of this long-standing situation. Through a study of this strike

From *Journal of Sport History* 22, no. 2 (Summer 1995): 111–34. Reprinted by permission of the North American Society for Sport History.

*I would like especially to thank William B. Husband for critiquing a draft of this essay and my "lunch bunch" colleagues at Oregon State for their comments. Earlier versions of this essay were read at the Southern Historical Association, Charlotte, North Carolina, November 1986, and at the Conference on Popular Culture, East Lansing, Michigan, April 1989.

and its aftermath, David LaFrance demonstrates the close connection and important role that sport plays in the complex and multifaceted decision-making process regarding labor, the private sector, and government that ultimately has helped determine the economic and political development of the current Mexican state as it enters a privatized, global economy.

Introduction

Mexico boasts one of the most enviable records for political stability among developing nations over the past several decades. A central factor in that stability has been the role played in the nation's political system by the official party. Now called the Institutional Revolutionary Party (PRI), it grew out of the Revolution of 1910, was officially created in 1929, and has dominated the government since. As a result, party and government are so intertwined that for all practical purposes they are indistinguishable.

One key reason for the PRI government's effectiveness has been its special relationship to organized labor. Since the 1930s, most unions have enjoyed formal status within the party. In the 1960s they were gathered into a government-sponsored umbrella organization called the Congreso del Trabajo [Labor Congress—CT]. The Confederación de Trabajadores Mexicanos [Confederation of Mexican Workers—CTM], led by Fidel Velázquez, was the largest and most influential component of the CT.

Both sides benefited from this relationship, but it was not an equal one. Official unions received many perquisites, both economic and political, and enjoyed a relatively privileged position vis-à-vis labor as a whole. Government used labor to its advantage, co-opting union leaders and controlling such fundamental issues as the right to unionize, strike, and bargain collectively. Despite proworker rhetoric and sporadic populistic actions, over the long run the government sacrificed labor for the economic development of the country.

In the 1980s, Mexico suffered its worst economic collapse since the violent days of the Mexican Revolution early in this century. The reasons for the collapse were many and complex. In their analysis of them many economists and politicians began to question the viability of Mexico's corporatist, nationalistic, protectionist economic system. As a result, presidents Miguel de la Madrid (1982–1988) and Carlos Salinas de Gortari (1988–1994) attempted to resolve the crisis by modernizing Mexico's economy. They emphasized an individualisic, competitive, internationalist, free-market system that encouraged private-sector interests and downplayed government participation, including its connection to labor.

In this new environment, government called on labor to sacrifice for the good of the nation. Wages and benefits lagged behind inflation, and newly privatized companies shed their unionized workers. Labor leaders lost influence within governing circles. Unions' efforts to stymie this policy strained relations between government and workers' representatives. Meanwhile, government ties to the private sector became increasingly close and open. As a result, unions' traditional place within the PRI government came into question, thus threatening the political edifice that had governed Mexico since the 1920s.

In examining Mexican labor in the 1980s, studies have overlooked one of the most important movements of the decade, that of professional baseball players.[1] Their movement, which bridged the transition from the economic boom of the early 1980s to the depths of the crisis several years later, provided government with a golden opportunity to demonstrate its prolabor credentials, tame its opponents, and strengthen its political base. A whole new category of worker, the professional athlete, asked to enter the official fold. At the same time, baseball owners, wealthy, private-sector entrepreneurs who held absolutist control over the game and flaunted the law, could be tamed. Instead, the government rejected this chance.

A study of the Mexican baseball players' movement of the 1980s illustrates, then, the changing relationship between government and labor in the context of this free-market model of development. This impact was especially apparent in three areas: a deemphasis on labor recruitment, close and open government ties to private capital, and overt differences between government and the official labor sector. Traces of these characteristics, of course, had always existed to some extent in the government-labor relationship. Nevertheless, they became much more pronounced after 1982 as the effort of baseball players to unionize was among the first casualties of the neoliberal economic policies of the 1980s.

Background

Baseball in Mexico dates to before the turn of the twentieth century. The Liga Mexicana, the country's premier circuit, was created in 1925. By the 1940s, it had become well organized and a lucrative investment for its private-sector owners. The best-known power behind the league during that era was Jorge Pasquel, a multimillionaire who ran a customs brokerage firm that handled government business and who married the daughter of President Plutarco Elías Calles. Pasquel also controlled the *Novedades* newspaper empire and had close ties to President Miguel Alemán.[2]

When Pasquel died in 1955, another multimillionaire with close connections to the government, Alejo Peralta, took control of the Mexicana league. Also among Mexico's richest individuals, Peralta owned not only the Tigres baseball franchise in Mexico City but also teams in six other major cities, including two in Monterrey. In addition, he controlled over sixty companies including IUSA, Scovil, and Tehuacán and had close connections to the Japanese conglomerate, Mitsubishi. Reports linked him to powerful Mexican drug traffickers. He first gained public notoriety in the mid-1950s, when as head of the Instituto Politécnico Nacional, IPN, he called in the army to repress student protesters. Over the years, he served as a presidential advisor. In the José López Portillo administration (1976–1982), he had especially close ties to Arturo "El Negro" Durazo, Mexico City's notoriously corrupt police chief.[3]

Peralta, along with other private-sector owners, building on Pasquel's earlier efforts, reshaped the circuit, increasing its prestige and power. They gained its affiliation with U.S. AAA-level, minor league baseball. Peralta also created the Asociación de Ligas Profesionales de Béisbol de la República Mexicana [Association of Professional Baseball Leagues of the Mexican Republic], an owners' group that wielded political influence and adamantly opposed players' organizations and the formation of so-called pirate leagues. Baseball owners received the support of other sports executives who likewise feared athletes' groups.[4]

Owners viewed players more as expendable entertainers than workers. They felt little obligation to treat players according to the labor codes and had no intention to allow them to organize. Moreover, players' ability to challenge owners was impeded by the fact that most were of modest economic means, poorly educated, unskilled except for baseball, and inexperienced politically.

The idea of forming a professional baseball players' organization began in the 1940s. In the 1950s approximately one hundred players led by Jesús "Cochihuila" Valenzuela of the Tampico Alijadores attempted to form a mutualist society to provide health and pension benefits. Low salaries, particularly in comparison to foreigners, were also a concern. Pressure and threats from owners doomed the effort. Jorge Pasquel, along with executives from other sports, led the counterattack. A similar organization in 1961, called the Mutualidad de Peloteros Profesionales Mexicanos [Mutual Society of Mexican Professional Baseball Players], also failed when the owners refused to contribute to the society's fund and "froze out" the movement's leadership.[5]

Over the next two decades, profits from professional baseball as well as the conditions under which players performed, even according to some businessmen, warranted the formation of a players' association. The players' position seemed especially anachronistic when compared to their colleagues in other Caribbean basin countries such as the Dominican Republic, Puerto Rico, and Venezuela. In these nations, performers legally had formed unions that provided them with many of the same benefits that the Mexicans wanted for themselves.[6]

Mexican players demanded first and foremost to have their status as workers under Mexican law recognized, thereby gaining respect and implying their legal right to organize and receive benefits due all workers. The benefits included compensation for spring training, a paid vacation and one day off per week, the traditional end-of-the-year bonus [*aguinaldo*], and more money for food while on the road. Other improvements asked for were a retirement fund, the right to a minimum 25 percent of one's selling price when traded, veto power over trades, and improved hotel accommodations and transportation.[7]

In the face of owner opposition to players' associations, government only slowly extended basic labor rights to them. It was not until 1970, after the 1968 Olympic Games, hosted by Mexico, and a soccer players' protest focused attention on athletes' poor treatment, that the government amended the 1931 Ley Federal del Trabajo [Federal Labor Law] to include professional athletes.[8] Even then, change came slowly. Ten years later, only after word leaked that baseball players again were attempting to organize, owners finally agreed to comply with the section of the 1970 law calling for contributions to the national health system, Seguro Social, for athletes.[9]

Player frustration with owner disdain and recalcitrance and government indifference, led in 1980 to baseball players again attempting to organize, this time successfully. They created the Asociación Nacional de Beisbolistas [National Association of Baseball Players—ANABE]. Their subsequent strike against the Mexicana league and later creation of a rival circuit, the Nacional, dramatically changed Mexican baseball during the decade. Moreover, the ANABE's challenge brought to light a changing governmental labor policy.

The Strike

Two incidents in the spring and summer of 1980 provoked the formation of the ANABE and the subsequent strike. In April, Puebla, the previous year's Mexicana league champion and a perennial contender, became involved in a dispute with an umpire while playing in Veracruz. After the contest, one of the opposing team's officials induced local police to arrest the whole Puebla club, including its manager, Jorge Fitch. In the process, several Puebla performers were beaten. Although the squad was soon released thanks to the intervention of league higher-ups, the officials suspended Fitch and fined the players 3,000 pesos each. This move so angered the club's members that they refused to play the next series of games in Mérida. Only when league president Antonio Ramírez Muro threatened to disband the current team (by firing all the strikers and creating a whole new Puebla nine to be made up of men drafted from the other nineteen teams in the league) did the Poblano squad agree to return to the diamond.[10]

This brief but sharp confrontation with the owners galvanized the Puebla team into action. Led by one of its stars, Alfonso "Houston"

Jiménez, they sought to defend themselves against the arbitrary action of the league. Within a month some fifty players, including the whole Puebla squad, had taken the initial concrete steps to form the ANABE. They contracted a lawyer and chose a slate of officers headed by a president, Ramón "Abulón" Hernández, veteran shortstop for the Mexico City Diablos Rojos. When formally notified of the existence of the ANABE, league officials refused public comment; nevertheless, a blacklist containing ANABE players' names was already in the hands of team owners.[11]

Tension increased when owners threatened ANABE players with dismissal and traded deemed troublemakers to other teams in order to isolate them. Then, on the last day of June, the Mexico City Tigres owner, Alejo Peralta, fired catcher Vicente Peralta (no relation). Although officially dismissed because of his "inadequate performance," Peralta clearly fell victim because of his active role in the ANABE. Consequently, in solidarity with the fired Peralta, the next day, 1 July, ANABE president Hernández and the remainder of the Diablos Rojos team refused to play the Tigres in an all-important series between the two archrivals. That same evening Puebla followed suit in Poza Rica. The strike was on.[12]

The stoppage spread quickly. Eighteen-year-old Arturo Jiménez, who played for Yucatán, for example, upon receiving word of the strike, collected his paycheck and immediately flew to Mexico City to join the protesters. Within two weeks an estimated three hundred to four hundred players, a majority of them veterans, had joined the walkout, thereby incapacitating fourteen of the twenty teams in the leagues. The owners responded by firing all the strikers and forming a minileague composed of the six remaining clubs that would play out the remainder of the season. The league also induced key performers, including foreigners, to continue playing by offering them bonuses and plane flights to games. In early August, players on the six functioning squads formed a company organization, the Asociación Profesionales de Beisbolistas [Association of Professional Baseball Players—ASOBEPRO].[13]

The ANABE, lacking even such things as office equipment, no less a well-oiled organization, money, and political backing, took on the fight of its young life. While financial needs were met in part by playing exhibition games in various cities and through such gimmicks as selling autographed baseballs, ANABE's leadership soon realized that it was involved in much more than a simple dispute between labor and capital. It had entered the thickets of Mexican politics by directly challenging the longtime, expedient relationship among the government, the official union structure, and the private sector. This situation called for some very fast and adept maneuvering in order to survive.[14]

The first step had already been taken. Upon its formation the previous May, the ANABE petitioned to be recognized as a civil association (*asociación civil*) rather than a full-fledged labor union (*sindicato*) (civil association status was finally granted in April 1981). To get labor union recognition in Mexico was a long and generally complicated process with political costs. Registration as a civil association was easier to obtain, being somewhat analogous to a nonprofit organization. It also was viewed to be less adversarial than a labor union, thus making it, the ANABE calculated, more palatable to the owners and government.[15]

The second step was to reach out to the press. This was not an easy task in a political system in which much of the media practices self-censorship and curries the favor of the government and the private-sector establishment. As a result, most organs ignored or condemned the ANABE, but the association did enjoy the support of three sympathetic print sources in Mexico City—*Esto*, the nation's largest-circulation sports newspaper; *Uno Más Uno*, a left-leaning general news daily; and the influential weekly news magazine, *Proceso*. These sources and a handful of lesser ones kept the ANABE issue before the public and helped generate support for the striking players.[16]

The third step taken to gain political backing was a risky and audacious one. Because the ANABE was not a labor union it had only a very limited right to strike. Its action came under the category of a labor stoppage (*suspensión de labores*), giving it a mere nine days to solve the dispute or face the possibility of government sanctions. Therefore, the association went directly to President José López Portillo and asked for his personal intervention in the conflict. López Portillo proved reluctant to embrace the players and confront the owners. Nevertheless, the ANABE, supported by the official labor groups, the CT and the CTM, pointed out the president's hypocrisy. They cited his own rhetoric regarding workers' rights and the need to save jobs in the face of owner intransigence. Finally, López Portillo relented and personally received a group of ANABE representatives. After listening to their grievances, he promised his support.[17] López Portillos's acknowledgment of the players' cause gave the ANABE a modicum of official respectability and some desperately needed political maneuvering room.

The president called for the establishment of a governmental commission, headed by his brother Guillermo, to meet with the two disputing parties. At the talks, the owners insisted that in return for recognizing the players' demands the ANABE would have to be absorbed into the company association, the ASOBEPRO. The commission supported the league's position, but the ANABE refused to take such a step, fearing its demise. In a countermove, the ANABE asked the government for registration as a labor union. The ANABE's request initially received backing from the CT and one of its principal leaders, Fidel Veláquez. Nevertheless, López Portillo opted to back the owners by nixing the initiative and making it clear to both the ANABE and labor that union status would not be granted, at least not any time soon.[18]

Finally, in mid-August 1980, an agreement was reached. In it the owners recognized the players as workers and promised to treat them in accordance with the Ley Federal del Trabajo, something that they admitted they should have been already doing for years. As such, the owners agreed to provide a retirement fund; health care (Seguro Social); payment for trades; improved room, board, and transportation; a better schedule; and to take no reprisals against ANABE members. The accord did not, however, outline in detail the implementation of any of these provisions nor did it provide for collective bargaining—each player still had to negotiate individually his own contract. As a result of the agreement, then, the ANABE found itself in a troublesome position. Not being a union, it could not legally strike to force recalcitrant owners to comply with the federal labor law. Therefore, it was dependent on the goodwill of a less than fully supportive government to see that the statute was enforced.[19]

The ANABE quickly reaped the product of this weak agreement. Although the Mexicana league owners had consented to treat the players according to the law, nothing required that they deal directly with the ANABE, and they did not. Instead, they attacked the association and its members. Players' relatives, who in some cases worked in Alejo Peralta's factories, were threatened with dismissal. League executives used their political muscle to block government officials at the federal and state levels from meeting with ANABE representatives, and town fathers came under pressure to prevent the striking players from performing exhibition games in their communities. A negative press campaign orchestrated by the Mexicana and its media allies tried to make it appear that the ANABE refused to negotiate with the owners and was greedy for demanding more than the labor law provided. The owners warned that the financial demands made by the ANABE threatened the economic existence of several Mexicana league teams as well as entire minor league circuits. The threat was not an idle one. The Bajío and Noroeste leagues folded when the Mexicana and its allied winter circuit, the Liga del Pacífico, withdrew subsidies to their farm organizations. Later, four teams dropped out of the Mexicana, again depriving players of a large number of employment opportunities. When the question arose whether ANABE players would perform in the upcoming Pacífico season, one press source falsely claimed that 85 percent of the association's membership wanted to play, but its lawyers and about 25 recalcitrant activists were blocking an agreement.[20]

Liga del Pacifico

With the aid of government mediation, the ANABE and the Pacífico league came to an accord in early September. The ANABE felt pressure from its membership to provide jobs by playing in the winter league. This step was taken even though cardholders from the company union, ASOBEPRO, would also be performing and receiving the same benefits as the ANABE. The Pacífico, unlike the Mexicana, came to an agreement because some of its team owners could challenge the hegemony of Alejo Peralta due to their greater economic independence.[21]

Consequently, the Pacífico agreed to provide the benefits outlined in the federal labor law, including vacation days, better meal money, a housing fund (INFONAVIT), an end-of-year bonus, and health and retirement plans. These benefits came, however, at a price. The league claimed that its expenses rose some 40 percent because of the implementation of the law. Two of the circuit's teams, Tijuana and Los Mochis, folded. Rosters were cut from twenty-five to twenty layers, and deductions from players' paychecks increased from about 5 to 30 percent.[22]

Despite the Pacífico's promises, however, the agreement was not fully implemented. Not all teams provided health (Seguro Social) coverage, and the ANABE had to threaten the league with legal action before it turned money over to the government for the establishment of a retirement fund. A blacklist circulated among league officials, and ANABE members (fewer were actually hired than originally hoped) faced harassment, trades, and dismissal. In some cases, they were replaced with foreigners. Despite all the problems, the Pacífico completed its full schedule, capping the season with the traditional championship series in January 1981.[23]

Serie del Caribe

As the Pacifico league season neared completion, speculation mounted over the Serie del Caribe [Caribbean Series] scheduled for Caracas in early February 1981. Annually, the top team of the winter leagues of Mexico, Venezuela, Puerto Rico, and the Dominican Republic met to decide the Caribbean champion. With the creation of the ANABE, the players of the four countries were fully organized. Consequently, the ANABE joined the Confederación de Peloteros Profesionales del Caribe (CONPEPROCA), which demanded from the owners of the various teams participating in the series increased benefits. The owners balked, especially over the issue of radio and television revenue. Then, despite the intervention of Venezuelan president Luis Herrera Campíns, they canceled the series rather than meet the players' price. ANABE representatives traveled to Caracas to meet with the owners, but were refused an audience. One critic of the ANABE tried to smear the group by claiming that it received money from Fidel Castro's communist regime in Cuba to help finance the trip. By canceling the series, the owners lost an estimated 28 million pesos in revenues.[24]

Creation of the Liga Nacional

The cancellation of the Serie del Caribe did not bode well for the chances of a compromise between the ANABE and the Mexicana league over collective bargaining. During the fall and winter of 1980–1981, the Mexicana's principal officials, Alejo Peralta and Antonio Ramírez Muro, refused to deal with the ANABE. They said that their part of the previous August's bargain was simply to implement the federal labor law, and players, as individuals, could approach the league to negotiate a contract for the coming season. The Mexicana directors argued that the ANABE, because it lacked juridical personality (*personalidad jurídica*), legally could not represent players, and the league therefore had no obligation to bargain with it.[25]

The Mexicana also kept pressure on the ANABE in other ways. In addition to the loss of four teams, allegedly because of financial problems, Peralta arranged to move the Puebla franchise, whose players helped initiate the strike, to Campeche, thereby depriving one of the country's principal cities of a Mexicana team. To train new players and keep them out of the clutches of the association, Peralta established a baseball school, complete with full "scholarships." Funds for the players' retirement fund, due from the 1980 season, were not paid to the government. The league falsely claimed to have contracted several big-name Mexican and foreign players in an attempt to frighten ANABE performers into signing. Other key players, such as the ANABE's president, "Abulón" Hernández, were offered large sums to abandon the group and sign with a league team. The company union, ASOBEPRO, announced talks with the league and plans to allow its members to enter into contracts. Finally, Mexicana league managers sympathetic to the ANABE were fired.[26]

With the prospects of playing in the Mexicana looking dim, players searched for positions elsewhere. Some managed to land jobs in the Caribbean. Others looked to the United States. On a handful of occasions they signed letters of intent with major league organizations, but soon found that their careers were blocked north of the border, too. Upon joining the strike, all ANABE members had been fired from the Mexicana league teams and were, therefore, theoretically free agents. Nevertheless, Peralta and Bowie Kuhn, the U.S. baseball commissioner, adhered to a longtime agreement in which U.S. baseball clubs refused to hire any Mexican player without an explicit release from the Mexicana. ANABE appeals to the Mexican government to overrule the pact proved futile. Finally, only after the ANABE threatened to go to court to force Mexicana teams to hand over their financial records to the government, on suspicion of tax and revenue-sharing evasion, did the league relent. As a result, Eleno Cuen became the first ANABE player to sign with the major leagues, in this case the Pittsburgh Pirates. Still, few ANABE performers ever signed with the major leagues. Moreover, for those that did, Mexicana and major league teams reportedly avoided paying traded players the full amount due them by citing a low public figure while passing a large "under-the-table" sum between each other.[27]

The approximately three hundred members of the ANABE refused to succumb to the Mexicana league. The association even raised the stakes by taking a position that its members would be allowed to sign with the owners only when the August 1980 agreement was fully implemented, blacklists were ended, contracts outlined the working conditions for each player, and, upon signing, each performer be paid a 300,000-peso bonus. Part of this sum would go to the ANABE and the remainder to the player. In this manner, the ANABE argued, the performer would receive money that the league should have been paying him in the form of better salaries and benefits over the previous years. Moreover, the ANABE would gain financially and the league would be, in essence, recognizing the association. The league rejected these demands, thus ending any hope of reconciliation.[28]

As a result, in mid-February 1981, three weeks before spring training, the ANABE announced its plan to form its own circuit, the Nacional. Talk of exercising such an option in the face of owner intransigence had circulated for months. Squads of Anabistas had been playing exhibition games throughout the country since the summer of 1980 in an effort to raise money and to encourage local officials to consider the establishment of a team in their jurisdiction. Nevertheless, the ANABE wanted to ensure that an accord with the Mexicana was out of the question before taking such a consequential step. The association called upon its allies in the labor movement and appealed for support from other groups, including the private sector. It pointed out the economic benefits of having a team in one's community and promised to direct a portion of its income to local social causes.[29]

Efforts to create the new league met with relative success despite the Mexicana's opposition. Over the next three months the ANABE managed to form a two-division, eight-team circuit. The ANABE received aid from a variety of people and groups, and the motives for backing the venture were many. Nevertheless, most credit is probably due to labor's influence plus the desire of local and state officials to score political points. For example, the absence of a high-caliber professional team in Zacatecas prompted the governor and the state university to join hands to provide the facilities and ensure the financial backing (approximately 500,000 pesos for each franchise plus another estimated four million in start-up costs) necessary to create a franchise. In Puebla, anger over the Mexicana's abrupt transfer of its franchise to Campeche and the debts left in the wake of its departure prompted that state's chief executive to hand over the capital city's modern baseball park to the ANABE. Private interests, construction and metal unions, and the state university combined to back a team in Veracruz. The principal shareholder in Gómez Palacio was an individual with interests in two television stations in the state of Durango.[30]

Meanwhile, the Mexicana league acted to block the creation of the Nacional. The small number of pro-ANABE sportswriters, instrumental in drumming up public support for the upstart league, were blacklisted, harassed, and physically prevented from entering Mexicana league parks. Local officials, including ones in Mexico City, Monterrey, and Aguascalientes, were intimidated into refusing or reneging on agreements with the ANABE to allow Nacional teams to play in their jurisdiction. Although the Nacional included a Mexico City franchise, for example, the team could not get authorization to play in any park in the nation's capital, including the publicly owned Seguro Social park. It was forced to share ones in Puebla and Toluca. The Mexicana also used spies to gather information on its opponents.[31]

Despite the enormous difficulty of creating a whole new league, especially in the face of such formidable opposition, the ANABE finally succeeded. On 12 May, the first regular game of the Nacional league season took place in Puebla, where Veracruz won five to two before a full house. Three days later the remainder of the league's teams took the field.[32]

The Longer Term

The ANABE-manned Nacional league completed the 1981 season and four others before folding during the 1986 campaign. Despite its initial successes, the struggle to survive over the longer term proved to be exceedingly difficult. Three major factors contributed to the insurgent baseball players' eventual demise: a hostile economic and political climate, competition with and interference from the Mexicana league and its principal power broker, Alejo Peralta, and divisions within the ANABE-Nacional coalition.

The ANABE movement and its offshoot, the Nacional, came to life at a propitious time, at the peak of Mexico's petroleum-induced, deficit-financed economic boom of the late 1970s and early 1980s. This era of easy money helped the fledgling ANABE economically and facilitated support for it from a range of groups, including labor and, albeit reluctantly, the López Portillo government.

Two events, however, changed the relatively favorable economic and political equation in 1982. With the collapse of oil prices and rising international interest rates, Mexico could no longer service its debt and, for all intents and purposes, declared bankruptcy. The country entered its worst economic crisis in decades. Bankruptcy led to devaluation of the peso, currency and trade restrictions, rising inflation, and falling incomes. For the baseball teams, this situation proved to be a double blow. Devaluation and restrictions on currency movement (e.g., the limitations on the purchase of dollars) and trade raised the financial burden and logistical difficulty of paying for and of importing foreign-made equipment and non-Mexican players. At the same time inflation meant declining real income for both players and the general public, and government at all levels suddenly faced the need for economic retrenchment. Teams had little choice but to raise ticket prices to remain solvent, but this alternative further reduced attendance.[33]

Furthermore, a change in administrations occurred in the midst of this wrenching economic crisis. As a result, the new president, Miguel de la Madrid, had neither the economic means nor the inclination to look upon the plight of professional sports players with concern. Unlike his predecessor, he was no populist with plenty of cash on hand. He and his government saw less government and greater cooperation with the private sector as the keys to rescuing the economy. Labor activism had to be tamed. Moreover, viewed from this perspective, domestic "restlessness" became a national security concern as Mexico tried to project internationally an image of stability in order to encourage foreign investment and a renegotiation of the nation's huge debt. Consequently, De la Madrid assigned labor problems to the secretariat of the interior (*gobernación*), which was charged with internal security and headed by a hard-liner, Manuel Bartlett. The secretariat of labor (*trabajo*) normally would have handled such issues.[34]

Once the Nacional was created in 1981, the Mexicana and its officials, led by Alejo Peralta, continued to wield a wide array of measures designed to undermine the insurgent movement. Publicly ANABE's opponents conformed to the law, but privately they conspired to destroy the movement by both legal and illegal means. ANABE players remained blacklisted from the Mexicana and its allied circuits. United States baseball refused to recognize the Nacional and only reluctantly dealt with known ANABE members. Local government officials and private entrepreneurs, upon whom the Nacional increasingly depended for funding, also felt pressure to shun the league, while Peralta constantly juggled franchises in his own circuit to take advantage of the difficulties of his opponents.[35]

In an attempt to attract larger audiences at the expense of the Nacional, Mexicana owners hired additional foreigners and altered the game. They routinely ignored rules that limited total team salaries and foreigners' pay; the extra amounts were either paid under the table or hidden in bonuses and expenses. The teams' offensive capability, in an effort to make the game more exciting, was increased by pulling in the fences and tolerating the use of doctored bats and balls. As a result, hit, run, and home run totals dramatically increased.[36]

In the long run, the Mexicana's close links to and ability to influence the media proved especially damaging to the ANABE and its young circuit. Journalists either ignored the movement or increasingly projected a negative image of it, blaming it for "ruining" baseball and threatening the jobs of players. Carlos Calderón de la Barca, the editor of *La Afición*, one of Mexico City's major sports dailies with close links to the nation's industrial sector, also served as the head of public relations for the Mexicana's Diablos Rojos franchise in Mexico City and the Aguilas of Mexicali in the Pacífico league. Another important writer, Tomás Morales, with connections to both *La Afición* and the sports magazine, *Hit*, served as the Mexicana's official scorekeeper. Many other reporters, too, chose to accept the traditional *iguala* or stipend from those whom they covered rather than deal with the new league. Indeed, Mexico City journalists, who were notoriously underpaid, could pick up as many as three *igualas* each month (from the Diablos Rojos, the Tigres, and the Mexicana league) totaling several tens of thousands of pesos.[37]

The electronic media, too, succumbed to the Mexicana's influence. Before the strike, Mexican baseball did not appear regularly on television because of low audience ratings. Then in 1982 the Nacional gained access to the government network, IMEVISION, which broadcast weekend games. One year later, however, IMEVISION ended its relationship with the circuit when Peralta gave the network a transmitter on condition that it no longer carry Nacional games nor even report its scores on news broadcasts. In 1984, IMEVISION began showing Mexicana league contests on the weekends. Meanwhile, powerful radio station XEX, owned by the private media monopoly, Televisa, continued to broadcast Mexicana games on a daily basis. The Nacional, however, failed to find a regular radio outlet.[38]

Establishing a Mexico City Franchise

The deteriorating economic and political climates after 1981 combined with the wide-ranging attack on the ANABE and Nacional by its principal opponent, the Mexicana, resulted in constant insecurity and instability. Because of these factors, it was especially difficult to create stable franchises. Indeed, as of the start of the 1986 season, only two of the original eight teams, Durango and Zacatecas, were still laying in the league and several franchises had moved more than once.[39]

Perhaps best illustrative of the problems in establishing and maintaining a franchise was the effort made by the ANABE and Nacional to secure a viable presence in Mexico City. A team's existence in the capital not only enabled it to draw on a large pool of fans, but also provided ready access to the national media, the government, and labor unions, three potentially important allies.[40]

When the 1981 season opened, the Mexico City franchise of the Nacional, the Metropolitanos Rojos, had no home park in the city. Officials of the Federal District, over whom the president had ultimate authority, refused the Nacional team permission to use Mexico City's principal baseball facility, the publicly-owned Seguro Social stadium. There Alejo Peralta's two Mexicana teams, the Diablos Rojos and Tigres, played. The Metropolitanos then sought to gain permanent access to another city park, Magdalena Mixhuca. Although the team had been allowed to conduct preseason training sessions at the facility, its directors also denied the request. Finally, in late July, only after repeated entreaties from the CT, the Federal District relented and authorized the team to play in Magdalena Mixhuca.[41]

Meanwhile, the team's financial backers, two private-sector investment groups, failed to meet the two-million-peso monthly payroll and pulled out. The players frantically searched for additional gate receipts and new investors. As an inducement to fans, children were allowed into games without charge. Attempts were made to broadcast games over radio and sell stock to the general public. Talks began with labor unions. As a stopgap, the Banco Obrero offered a loan in return for the right to keep the team's books and promises from the other squads in the league to help pay off the debt. As a result, Anabistas on other teams contributed five percent of their salaries, not without some grumbling. Also, the Nacional contributed half of the proceeds from a league playoff game, held in October 1981.[42]

Financial problems continued to plague the Metropolitanos during the 1982 season. It sought backing from officials and business interests in Ciudad Sahagún, Hidalgo, as well as the many official labor unions in that industrial town, located north of Mexico City. The team held its spring training there and even talked of playing regular season games in the community. Nevertheless, the initiative failed, forcing the Nacional to turn again to the league's other teams which agreed to assume the Metropolitanos' expenses for food, housing, and travel.[43]

By the end of the 1982 season, Nacional officials decided that they could no longer maintain a team in Mexico City as long as it could not play in Seguro Social park. Because its present home, Magdalena Mixhuca, had no lights, all games took place in the afternoons. As a result, few of the club's mostly working-class fans could attend during the week. Therefore, when renewed efforts by the CT to help gain access to Seguro Social park again failed, the team moved. The stadium in the new host community, Chihuahua City, boasted lights, and the squad became the Centauros. The transfer was made in secrecy in order to foil the Mexicana league from placing pressure on Chihuahuan officials to sabotage the deal. Thus, the nation's capital hosted no Nacional league team during the 1983 season.[44]

Finally in 1984, under intense pressure from the labor movement and over the strenuous objections of the Mexicana, government officials agreed that a Nacional team could play in Seguro Social park. Nevertheless, in its zeal to gain access to the stadium, the ANABE and Nacional acceded to conditions that would soon haunt them. They agreed to vacate the park a minimum of three hours before a Mexicana game and maintain the facility's cleanliness. Moreover, the Mexicana retained preference for the scheduling of contests, meaning the Nacional franchise would again have to be satisfied with playing afternoon games during the week and at night during the weekend.[45] The new team, called the "Aztecas," was to be run as a cooperative with financing from the other teams in the league and the CT.[46]

The first game played at Seguro Social park, against Durango in March 1984, attracted several thousand fans. Nevertheless, the optimism generated by this turnout was immediately dashed. The Instituto Mexicano de Seguro Social [IMSS], the caretaker of the park, accused the Aztecas of several breaches of its contract including overstaying the allotted time for use of the facility and leaving the premises uncleaned. As a result, the Aztecas received a five-million- (later reduced to two-million-) peso fine, which it could not pay. The Nacional naively had fallen into a Mexicana-engineered trap.[47]

Several days later the Aztecas attempted to play a second game in the park. Despite the intervention of labor leader Fidel Velázquez, city officials ordered the field closed to the team until it paid the fine. In protest, some 1,500 angry fans tried to block traffic on Cuauhtémoc Avenue, a major thoroughfare that passes by the facility, but to no avail. In the face of subtle threats from secret police and with no possibility to appeal to President de la Madrid, who was conveniently absent from the country, the ANABE and Nacional leadership decided to avoid any further confrontation.[48]

Then, as a conciliatory gesture, the ANABE and Nacional offered eventually to pay the fine (one million pesos of which was paid within a week) and open negotiations on a new agreement. In response, the city and IMSS took a hard line, accusing the Aztecas of several additional infractions (including a lack of security at the park and the illegal sale of tickets) and demanding a ten-million-peso deposit plus additional fees for the scoreboard and sound system. One newspaper report claimed that Alejo Peralta used his close ties to police chief, Arturo "Negro" Durazo, to influence the IMSS. Again, the intervention of Mexico's labor movement on behalf of the Aztecas had little effect. Again, the CT, especially at critical junctures in the conflict, had proved unable to wield real power in the face of government indifference and owner hostility.[49]

Divisions

At this point the difficulties in establishing a viable franchise in Mexico City clearly exposed a slowly emerging breach between the ANABE and the Nacional league as well as divisions within the ANABE itself.

From its beginning, the Nacional had been a haphazardly run organization, dominated by baseball players, union activists, lawyers, and local and state officials, including university people, most of whom had little practical business experience. For example, the 1983 season roster of clubs and personnel as well as the official schedule appeared only six days before the opening game, because the league had no publicity officials. Moreover, these people often placed ideological and social considerations above practical economic needs. As much as making money, the ANABE attempted to improve the image of professional sports people and contribute to society by, for example, requiring that its members dress up while traveling, holding clinics for youths, and encouraging children to stay in school.[50]

This situation became clear with the ANABE's efforts to keep a team in Mexico City. By 1984, however, with economic conditions in the nation deteriorating rapidly, thus undermining the ability of unions, state and local governments, and universities to maintain their financial commitments to the game, many Nacional teams had fallen into the hands of private entrepreneurs who enjoyed much greater resources. These profit-minded owners, all located in the provinces, saw little reason to back a money-losing franchise in the national capital, especially when it faced brutal competition from fellow businessman Alejo Peralta. Moreover, it was highly influenced by unions, which the owners held in suspicion.

Therefore, when Mexico City officials denied Seguro Social park to the Aztecas and other teams in the Nacional were asked to come up with one million pesos each to keep the Aztecas solvent, several owners moved to nix the Mexico City franchise. This step provoked a direct conflict between the owners and the ANABE and its mainly labor-sector allies. In addition, charges flew that the Nacional owners' motivation for abandoning Mexico City was to make a deal with Peralta.[51]

Between March and July 1984, then, the Aztecas changed hands four times as the CT, backed by the ANABE, fought the owners of other Nacional franchises for control of the team. On the one hand, the CT and ANABE wanted the team in order to keep it in Mexico City as a show of commitment to the public and to demonstrate their resolve in the face of Mexicana league opposition. They failed, however, because they ultimately lacked the political backing necessary to gain access to Seguro Social park and the financial resources to administer the team. On the other hand, the owners sought the money-losing team in order to move it out of Mexico City to friendlier terrain or kill it. They had good reason to avoid further confrontation with and even to come to an accommodation with the powerful Peralta, seeing an opportunity to integrate their teams into his Mexicana league.[52]

When labor and ANABE mustered enough influence to prevent the team's transfer, the owners moved to strangulate it. They refused to invest any money in the franchise, including paying salaries and benefits and the remainder of the fine owed the IMSS. They blacklisted and attempted to trade ANABE activists. They threatened Dominican Republic players, who had arrived under an agreement with CONPEPROCA to play in the Nacional, with expulsion from the country if they played for the Aztecas. They placed pressure on other squads in the league not to play the Aztecas. And they refused to use the proceeds of an all-star game to pay off the Aztecas' debt, instead pocketing the gate receipts for themselves.[53]

By July, the Aztecas franchise was little more than a memory. Meanwhile, Jorge Ancer, owner of Nacional league teams in Monterrey and Reynosa, and former owner of the Aztecas, petitioned the Mexicana league to admit his two franchises for the 1985 campaign. The following month, reports surfaced that the Nacional was withdrawing its franchise in Puebla. This move opened the important city to a Mexicana league team, thus further pointing toward an accommodation of the Nacional with Peralta.[54]

The struggle to maintain a viable movement in the face of difficult economic and political obstacles eventually left the ANABE weak and internally divided. Even from early in the movement, the players had had difficulty maintaining a unified front in the face of generally united owner opposition, first from the Mexicana and then also from the Nacional. Serious differences within ANABE ranks began in 1983 when the leadership decided to play in the winter Pacífico league, despite it blacklisting of some players. Then, the problem of establishing a team in Mexico City exacerbated the differences within the union. ANABE head Ramón "Abulón" Hernández had moved with his team, the Metropolitanos, from Mexico City to Chihuahua in 1983. He came under criticism from union members because from there he was unable adequately to carry out his duties. The ANABE then created a full-time administrative position for him, but he delayed his departure for the nation's capital because the Chihuahua team paid him three times what the ANABE offered. Hernández also was accused of giving in too easily to Nacional owners' demands and even cutting deals behind the Anabistas' backs. Luis Meré, the ANABE's player representative and treasurer and the player-manager of the Aztecas, was one of Hernández' most vocal critics. However, Meré also came under attack from the rank and file for being absent from Mexico City and devoting too much time to his team, as the Aztecas wandered from city to city, always the visiting team with no home base. In July the ANABE ousted Meré for unauthorized use of one million pesos of the union's retirement fund to help prop up the Aztecas team.[55]

The End

Over the next two seasons, 1985 and 1986, the fortunes of the Nacional and the ANABE went from bad to worse. The league became so disorganized that it issued no official statistics (including scores and standings) until the middle of the 1985 campaign. Moreover, the person in charge did such a poor job that he was fired and as a result the numbers finally released were open to question. The league was so unprepared for the 1986 season that opening day had to be postponed for two weeks; as late as one week before the first game the official schedule had not been announced. Little information or publicity was forthcoming from either the ANABE or the league. All its games took place in the provinces, yet they failed to provide the results to important press outlets in Mexico City. Therefore, their isolation grew as newspapers such as *Uno Más Uno*, which had championed the movement's cause from its beginning, carried no results of Nacional league contests, except for an all-star competition held in Mexico City.[56]

At least some of the disorganization can be attributed to the poor economic conditions of many teams and ANABE's continuing problems. Several league franchises disappeared or moved as the country's economic situation deteriorated. Some teams did not know if they could play, only days before the season's beginning. Finding new homes also proved difficult, because of economic as well as political reasons, and moves did not necessarily enhance a squad's chances for prosperity and stability. The Puebla team, for example, transferred to the neighboring, but smaller, state capital of Tlaxcala for the 1985 season. Then in 1986 it journeyed to the isolated, tiny sugar mill town of Atencingo in southern Puebla, thereby finding a modicum of financial backing from the local union, but at the price of virtual obscurity.[57]

The ANABE, now estranged from the Nacional owners, remained divided internally and began to suffer erosion of its labor-based coalition. As a result it could no longer provide either the economic or the administrative stability needed to keep the league alive. Players continued to express discontent about the union, condemning the leadership for its lack of communication with the rank and file. In turn, ANABE officials, such as "Abulón" Hernández, criticized the payers for not taking a more active part in the organization, leaving the decisions up to him, and then finding fault with him. In the summer of 1985, the value of ANABE's links to the CT, its heretofore primary financial and political backer, virtually ended when a Cuban select team toured the country. The Cuban squad, world renowned for its quality, ignored the Nacional and only played Mexicana league teams. At the end of the junket, the CT attended a PRI-sponsored reception honoring the Cubans and officials of the Mexicana league.[58]

Until 1986, the Nacional provided most, but not all, ANABE members a job for several months of the year, however unsteady and poorly paid. Nevertheless, over time, the ANABE players and their families slowly but surely became tired of the fight, losing much of their original enthusiasm for the movement which demanded many sacrifices of them and furnished, given the difficult circumstances, only marginal returns. As the Nacional's fortunes fell, Anabistas began abandoning the league. Arturo Jiménez, for example, who had joined the ANABE in 1980 and then became one of the original players for Zacatecas in 1981, left for Mexico City. In the national capital he earned more money playing "amateur" ball than if he had stayed in the Nacional.[59]

Then, with the league's demise, all the remaining players had to seek employment elsewhere. Some left baseball altogether. Others entered the Mexicana where, if one were good enough, one could possibly sign a contract with a major league team. However, given the high signing price asked by the Mexicana, only a handful ever managed to play in the United States. A few others went to Europe, especially Italy. Most joined less prestigious regional circuits, particularly in the southeast of the country, where one could at least make a living. There the Mexicana league had only limited influence totally to control the sport.[60]

Ignored, isolated, indebted, and uncompetitive in the national sports market, the Nacional folded during the summer of 1986. Its disappearance was barely noticed in the midst of the celebration and publicity surrounding the soccer World Cup held in Mexico during the months of June and July.

Subsequent efforts to revive the Nacional or any other circuit using ANABE players were met with firm opposition by the Mexicana league and its monopolistic arm, the Asociación de Ligas Profesionales de Béisbol de la República Mexicana. In 1987, for example, the CT again attempted to use its political muscle to allow ANABE to play in Mexico City's Seguro Social park, this time featuring a group of Anabista stars in a series of exhibition games. The effort failed when the Mexicana demanded a high price for the stadium's use. Again, organized labor demonstrated its impotence vis-à-vis the private sector and an indifferent government.[61]

In 1989 the ANABE made one, last, desperate attempt to form a league, the Circuito Mexicano de Béisbol [Mexican Baseball Circuit—Cimebe]. It gained the backing of the former owners of teams in Tijuana and Guadalajara. Alejo Peralta had withdrawn their franchises because they contravened traditional Mexicana league practices: operating too independently of Peralta and being too generous to their players.[62]

Immediately the new circuit ran into problems. Francisco Eguiarte, the former Guadalajara owner who now ran the Cimebe, was an "unorganized dreamer" with little business acumen and not the best choice of a partner by the desperate ANABE. Moreover, in retaliation for his effort to revive the ANABE, the Mexicana arranged for its president, Ramón "Abulón" Hernández, to be fired from his position as player-manager of the Chinameca, Veracruz, team in the Liga Regional del Sureste [Southeast Regional League]. In addition, several cities came under pressure from the Mexicana. It promised Guadalajara, Puebla, and Veracruz teams for the next season if the cities forbade the establishment of a Cimebe franchise. In Guadalajara, Eguiarte already had a three-year contract to use the stadium at the University of Guadalajara for his former Mexicana franchise. When he attempted to house his Cimebe team in the facility, the University canceled the agreement claming that only a Mexicana team could perform in the park. Once the Cimbe started to play, the Mexicana tried to prevent umpires from working the games.[63]

Momentarily overcoming the difficulties, the Cimebe began action in September 1989 with six teams and a sixty-two-game schedule. Nevertheless, the league lasted only one season, even though it enjoyed the backing of the influential governmental body, the Comisión Nacional del Deporte [National Commission of Sports—Conade]. It succumbed, like its predecessor, to the relentless pressure of its principal antagonist, the Mexicana league and its owner-director, Alejo Peralta.[64]

Conclusion

Despite the ANABE's failure to unionize and its ultimate demise, it had an important impact on sports in Mexico. As the first group of players in any Mexican professional sport successfully to organize and strike, it gained modest yet concrete benefits not only for its own members, but for other players as well. In 1984, for example, the Mexicana provided a pension plan to its own players in an attempt to contain discontent. Then in 1989, the Mexicana announced the establishment of a life insurance program for players and petitioned the government to enforce the 10 percent per team limit on foreign players. Less concretely, it also established a precedent for future labor-community-press cooperation in the world of professional sports. Moreover, it served as an educative process that made players in Mexico more aware of the contradictions of their situation as athletes and as workers. This contradiction was amply underlined when, in direct response to ANABE, sports owners created a new antiunion group, the Consejo Mexicano de Espectáculos Profesionales [Mexican Council of Professional Spectacles—COMEDEP], made up of the heads of baseball, boxing, football, tennis, bullfighting, and acting.[65] Perhaps not surprisingly, no player associated with ANABE has been inducted into the Mexican baseball Hall of Fame and former leaders of the movement insist in 2001 that the league learned nothing from the experience.[66]

The ANABE experience also brought into sharp focus a changing labor policy of the Mexican government during the 1980s. The most salient aspects of this newly emerging policy, which reflected the implementation of a free-market economic model, beg a reevaluation of the continued viability of the traditional PRI-government-labor relationship: 1) government's unwillingness to recruit and protect labor, notably nonindustrial, nonpublic-sector workers, the ones least organized and therefore those with the greatest potential for organization, thus bringing into question government's future commitment to labor; 2) government's deference to capital, thus bringing into question the real extent of government's willingness and power to regulate the private sector; and 3) government's estrangement from its captive labor sector, reflected in public disputes and workers' declining political clout, thus bringing into question the well-being of the official governing coalition.

The professional baseball players' movement, and indirectly, professional athletes' organizational efforts in general, then, became the first major casualties of free-market reform. Government's treatment of athletes revealed, in turn, the emergence of a significantly different policy toward labor as a whole that undermined the traditional official relationship with workers, a relationship that had greatly contributed to the PRI-government's domination of Mexico. As this effort to modernize based on a neoliberal model continues, one must logically ask, does it jeopardize the entire governmental edifice of the twentieth-century, post-Revolutionary Mexican state?[67]

Notes

1. See, for example: Alberto Aziz Nassif *El estado mexicano y la CTM* (Mexico City: Ediciones de la Casa Chata, 1989); Dan La Botz, *The Crisis of Mexican Labor* (New York: Praeger, 1988); Dan La Botz, *Mask of Democracy: Labor Suppression in Mexico Today* (Boston: South End Press, 1992); Kevin J. Middlebrook. "The Sounds of Silence: Organised Labour's Response to Economic Crisis in Mexico," *Journal of Latin American Studies* 21:2(May 1989): 195–220; Kevin J. Middlebrook, ed., *Unions, Workers, and the State* (San Diego: Center for U.S.-Mexican Studies, 1991); Barry Carr, "The Mexican Economic Debacle and the Labor Movement: A New Era or More of the Same?" in *Modern Mexico: State, Economy and Social Conflict*, eds. Nora Hamilton and Timothy F. Harding (Beverly Hills: Sage Publications, 1986), 205–231.

2. William H. Beezley, "The Rise of Baseball in Mexico and the First Valenzuela," *Studies in Latin American Popular Culture* 4(1985): 3–13; Gilbert M. Joseph, "Forging the Regional Pastime: Baseball and Class in Yucatán," in *Sport and Society in Latin America: Diffusion, Dependency, and the Rise of Mass Culture*, ed. Joseph L. Arbena (Westport: Greenwood Press, 1988), 29–61; Michael M. Oleksak

and Mary Adams Oleksak, *Béisbol: Latin Americans and the Grand Old Game* (Grand Rapids: Masters Press, 1991), 49–52; Alan M. Klein, "Baseball Wars: The Mexican Baseball League and Nationalism in 1946," *Studies in Latin American Popular Culture 13*(1994): 33–56; *Current Biography,* 1946, 459–460; *New York Times* (9 Mar. 1955).

3. Interview with Victor Becerril, former sports reporter for *Esto* and *Uno Más Uno*, Mexico City, 24 Aug. 1987; *Proceso*, 29 Aug. 1983, 14–17, 23 Jan. 1984, 10, 13, 24 Aug. 1987, 12–13, 28 Sept. 1992, 16–19; *Excélsior*, 22 Aug. 1986; Luis Suárez, *Alejo Peralta: Un patrón sin patrones* (Mexico City: Editorial Grijalbo, 1992), 252. By 1992 Peralta reportedly owned 154 companies; see Suárez, 271.

4. Interview with Becerril, 24 Aug. 1987; *Proceso*, 7 July 1980, 46–47; *Siempre*, 16 July 1980, 14–15; *Uno Máis Uno*, 15, 25 July 1980.

5. Benito Terrazas, *Casa llena, bola roja: La lucha de los peloteros de la ANABE* (Mexico City: Editorial Leega, 1984), 31–33; *Esto*, 23 July 1980; *Hit*, 8 Aug. 1980; *Uno Más Uno*, 4–5 July 1980, 4 June 1983.

6. *Expansión*, 1 Apr. 1981, 40–47; *Uno Más Uno*, 11 July 1980.

7. Interview with Arturo Jiménez (former player and National Association of Baseball Players-ANABE member), Mexico City, 23 July 1993; Interview with Becerril, 24 Aug. 1987; *Hit*, 18 July 1980; *Proceso*, 7 July 1980, 46–47, 14 July 1980, 57; *Uno Más Uno*, 15 July, 6 Aug. 1980. Some regulars found themselves required to play in as many as 137 games in 138 days. Players in 1980 received 180 pesos per day, about eight U.S. dollars, but, given the overvalued peso, this amount was barely enough for a modest meal. Few teams provided air travel, except for certain foreign players, and bus rides of 12, 18 and even more hours were not uncommon—the trip from Chihuahua City to Mérida took 52 hours and upon arrival players often had to go directly to the park to play. This situation led to high levels of drug and especially alcohol use as players attempted to pass the long hours on the road. Salaries, too, played a role in the players' discontent, although not as much as the issue of workers' rights: A handful of star players made as much as 90,000 pesos (about 4,000 dollars) per month in 1980, but most regular, established ones received 30,000 to 35,000 (1,300 to 1,500 dollars), while rookies earned 7,000 to 9,000 pesos (300 to 400 dollars) monthly. Foreigners, however, received more money than even the best Mexican players and generally were paid in dollars. Former Boston Red Sox slugger George Scott, for example, earned 6,000 dollars a month in 1981 while playing with the Mexico City Tigres. These salaries were paid only for the regular playing season, which lasted from mid-March to mid-August. Some players, particularly those on teams near the U.S. border, trafficked in contraband goods in order to add to their salaries. Most performers, too, had to supplement their income in other ways during the off-season. The Mexican peso's value in 1980 was approximately 23 to 1 U.S. dollar. See: *Esto*, 7 July, 10 Aug. 1980; *Uno Más Uno*, 21 July, 26 Aug. 1980; *Chicago Tribune*, 16 June 1982; William Nack, "George Scott is Alive and Well and Playing in Mexico City," *Sports Illustrated*, 17 Aug. 1981, 42; Leo W. Banks, "South of the Border," *Sports Illustrated*, 30 Aug. 1982, 31; Steve Wulf, "Béisbol in His Blood," *Sports Illustrated*, 18 Aug. 1980, 26. Note that Mexican baseball players' demands did not include the more radical issue of free agency, which U.S. players first gained in 1975 and lay at the heart of the long and bitter 1981 strike; see James B. Dworkin, *Owners versus Players: Baseball and Collective Bargaining* (Boston: Auburn House, 1981); James B. Dworkin, "Results of the Professional Baseball Players' Strike of 1981," *Texas Business Review* 55:6(Nov.–Dec. 1981): 268–271.

8. Interview with Mariano Albor Salcedo (ANABE lawyer), Mexico City, 7 Aug. 1993. For a more detailed and legal consideration of the law and professional athletes, see: Mariano Albor Salcedo, *Deporte y derecho* (Mexico City: Editorial Trillas, 1989), esp. 272–290.

9. *Proceso*, 14 July 1980, 57.

10. Interview with Albor Salcedo, Mexico City, 9 Sept. 1986; *Hit*, 25 Apr., 2 May 1980; *Uno Más Uno*, 2 July 1980.

11. Interview with Albor Salcedo, 9 Sept. 1986: *Proceso*, 7 July 1980, 46–47; *Uno Más Uno*, 5 Sept. 1980.

12. Interview with Albor Salcedo, 9 Sept. 1986; *Esto*, 1, 2 July 1980; *Hit*, 18 July 1980; *Uno Más Uno*, 2 July 1980.

13. Interview with Jiménez; *Esto*, 6 Aug. 1980; *Hoy*, 14–20 July 1980, 16; *Proceso*, 7 July 1980, 46–47; *Uno Más Uno*, 3–11 July, 5 Aug. 1980; Wulf, 25–26; Suárez, 255. The six remaining teams were Ciudad Juárez, Laguna, Reynosa, Saltillo, Coatzacoalcos, and the Mexico City Tigres.

14. *Uno Más Uno*, 17 July 1980.

15. Interview with Albor Salcedo, 9 Sept. 1986; *Proceso*, 14 July 1980, 57.

16. Interview with Jiménez; Interview with Becerril, Mexico City, 8–9 Sept. 1986; Interview with Benito Terrazas (former *Uno Más Uno* sports reporter), Mexico City, 8 Sept. 1986; Interview with Albor Salcedo, 9 Sept. 1986. The contemporary popular press in the United States ignored the movement. As far as this author can ascertain, no U.S. news medium covered the 1980 Mexican baseball strike and its aftermath, although the U.S. had close connections to Mexican baseball for decades. Not even the *Sporting News*, the so-called “Bible” of U.S. sports, uttered a word about the action, despite the fact that it normally carried Mexicana league standings and that the stoppage received the public support of a number of U.S. major league players and paralleled their own movement which ended in a walkout a year later; see *Uno Más Uno*, 14 July, 19 Oct. 1980.

17. Interview with Albor Salcedo, 9 Sept. 1986; Interview with Becerril, 8–9 Sept. 1986; Interview with Terrazas; *Esto*, 8 July, 1 Aug. 1980; *Uno Más Uno*, 7, 15 July 1980.

18. Interview with Albor Salcedo, 9 Sept. 1986; Suárez, 254–256; Terrazas, 41–44, 71, 74; *Esto*, 12, 13 Aug. 1980; *Proceso*, 25 Aug. 1980, 23–24; *Uno Más Uno*, 16, 17 July, 12–14 Aug. 1980. The commission was composed of Guillermo López Portillo, director of the Instituto Nacional del Deporte [National Institute of Sport]; Pedro Ojeda Paullada, secretary of Trabajo y Previsión Social [Labor and Social Security]; and Alejandro Gertz Manero, head of the Procuraduría General de la Defensa del Trabajo [Attorney General for Labor].

19. Suárez, 256–261; Terrazas, 75; *Esto*, 8, 20 Aug. 1980; *Proceso*, 25 Aug. 1980, 23–24; *Uno Más Uno*, 20–21 Aug. 1980. In retrospect, one former ANABE member asserted that the organization’s lawyer, Albor Salcedo, made a mistake in not accepting the offer to merge the ANABE into the ASOBEPRO, as from that point forward the government did little to help and the Mexicana took an inflexible anti-ANABE stance that ultimately killed the movement; see interview with Jiménez.

20. Suárez, 258; *Hit*, 12 Sept. 1980; *Uno Más Uno*, 8, 15 July, 30 Aug., 1–2 Sept., 6 Oct., 19 Nov. 1980.

21. Interview with Becerril, 8-9 Sept. 1986; Interview with Terrazas; *Uno Más Uno*, 6 Sept. 1980.

22. *Hit*, 12, 19 Sept., 3 Oct. 1980; *Uno Más Uno*, 13 Sept., 1, 9 Oct., 24 Nov. 1980.

23. *Uno Más Uno*, 31 Oct., 1, 6 Nov., 3 Dec. 1980, 9 Jan., 2–3 Feb. 1981.

24. *Hit*, 16 Jan. 1981; *Uno Más Uno*, 11 Dec. 1980, 14, 16–17, 20, 22 Jan. 1981. The CONPEPROCA wanted 15 instead of 8 percent of the gate receipts, 30 dollars per day for food rather than 5, and 5 percent of the radio and television revenue from the series.

25. *Esto*, 16 Feb. 1981; *Uno Más Uno*, 16 Nov., 27 Dec. 1980, 12 Feb. 1981.

26. Suárez, 258–259, 269–270; *Hit*, 3, 20 Feb. 1981; *Uno Más Uno*, 20, 29–30 Jan., 4, 10, 14 Feb., 3 May 1981; *Wall Street Journal*, 28 Dec. 1987.

27. Terrazas, 106–108; *Esto*, 23 Feb., 11, 17, 31 Mar., 29 Apr., 1981; *Uno Más Uno*, 4, 16, 19, 26 Feb., 29 Apr. 1981. This agreement between Mexican and U.S. baseball, which disallowed Mexican ball players from negotiating contracts with U.S. teams without Mexicana league approval, began in the 1950s and grew out of a truce over the two countries' raiding of each other's players during the post-World War II years; see: Oleksak and Oleksak, 155–156; Klein, 33–56; Milton Jamail, "Put Baseball on the Free-Trade Agenda," *Washington Post* (26 Oct. 1991).

28. *Esto*, 17 Feb. 1981; *Uno Más Uno*, 4 Feb. 1981.

29. Interview with Jiménez; *Esto*, 21 Feb. 1981; *Uno Más Uno*, 6, 18, 20–21 Feb. 1981.

30. Interview with Jiménez; Terrazas, 80–83; *Esto*, 2, 5, 8 May 1981; *Uno Más Uno*, 6–7 Mar., 5, 7, 9, 20 May 1981. The Nacional was composed of teams in Durango, Gómez Palacio, Querétaro, and Zacatecas in the northern division and Mexico City, Puebla, Toluca, and Veracruz in the southern division.

31. Interview with Becerril, 8–9 Sept. 1986; Interview with Jiménez; Interview with Terrazas; *Esto*, 10, 23 Mar., 16 Apr., 14, May 1981; *Uno Más Uno*, 22, 26 Apr., 14, 30 May 1981. Meanwhile, the absence of the ANABE players, more than half of whom were former starters, hurt the Mexicana. Its owners attempted to fill their rosters through threats and bribes and the hiring of new players. While many Mexican rookies were contracted, agents also traveled to the United States to locate raw high school and college-level talent at a salary of 1,200 dollars per month. The owners tried to circumvent the law limiting the number of foreigners on a team's roster to 10 percent by passing off outsiders with Spanish surnames as Mexican citizens. See: *Esto*, 9, 20, 27 Mar. 1981; *Uno Más Uno*, 9 Apr., 25 Feb., 12, 17, 19, 26, 31 Mar. 1981.

32. *Uno Más Uno*, 13 May 1981.

33. *Uno Más Uno*, 22 Feb. 1982. The Mexican peso fell in value vis-à-vis the U.S. dollar from approximately 25 to 1 in 1981 to approximately 700 to 1 in 1986. Real wages fell by over 50 percent during the same period; see *New York Times*, 10 June, 23 Oct. 1986. Both leagues, of course, were affected by the deteriorating economic situation, but the lesser established Nacional doubtless felt the effects more. Ticket prices in the Mexicana, for example, rose from between 120 and 240 pesos in 1981 to between 700 and 1,000 pesos in 1986; see *Uno Más Uno*, 20 Mar. 1982, 17 Mar. 1986. The Mexicana first confronted the problem of importing and paying foreign players in "hard" currency. Nevertheless, the Nacional found itself in the same position when it began to look for foreign talent in 1984; see *Esto*, 1 Mar., 7 Apr. 1984.

34. Interview with Albor Salcedo, 9 Sept. 1986, 7 Aug. 1993.

35. Interview with Becerril, 24 Aug. 1987; Interview with Jiménez; *La Afición*, 4 Mar. 1983; *Excélsior*, 1 Dec. 1984; *Uno Más Uno*, 17 Mar. 1985, 13, 21 Mar. 1986, 12 Mar. 1989; *Proceso*, 11 Aug 1986, 62.

36. Interview with Becerril, 24 Aug 1987; *Esto*, 5 Apr., 8 May 1984; *Uno Más Uno*, 27 July 1983; *The Oregonian* (Portland), 13 Feb. 1987; *Proceso*, 11 Aug. 1986, 60–61; Banks, 33. One of the foreigners playing in the Mexican League in 1986, for example, was former Kansas City Royals star, Willie Mays Aikens; see

New York Times, 17 June 1986. Total team salaries were limited to 45,000 dollars per month and foreigners' pay to a monthly maximum of 3,500 dollars; nevertheless, outsiders received as much as 7,000 dollars per month. In 1986 an American, Jack Pierce, and two other players broke Hector Espino's 1964 home run record of 46 for a season; Pierce, who set the new record, hit 54 round-trippers.

37. Interview with Becerril, 24 Aug. 1987; Interview with Jiménez.

38. Interview with Becerril, 24 Aug. 1987; Interview with Jiménez; *Uno Más Uno*, 11, 17 Mar. 1984.

39. Terrazas, 80–83, 89–92; *Uno Más Uno*, 9 Mar. 1986.

40. Interview with Albor Salcedo, 7 Aug. 1993.

41. Interview with Jiménez; *Uno Más Uno*, 14 May, 2, 12, 15 June, 9, 15, 24, 30 July 1981, 9 Mar. 1982.

42. Interview with Jiménez; *Uno Más Uno*, 12, 19, 25 June, 11, 21 July, 8 Oct. 1981.

43. *Uno Más Uno*, 23 Feb., 9, 18 Mar. 1982.

44. Interview with Albor Salcedo, 7 Aug. 1993; *Uno Más Uno*, 4, 15 Mar., 30 Apr. 1983.

45. Interview with Albor Salcedo, 7 Aug. 1993; *Esto*, 2, 3 Mar. 1984; *Uno Más Uno*, 2, 3, Mar. 1984.

46. *Esto*, 10 Mar., 6 Apr. 1984; *Uno Más Uno*, 20, 30 Mar. 1984.

47. *Esto*, 13, 22, 29 Mar. 1984; *Uno Más Uno*, 22 Mar. 1984; Terrazas, 96–98. Estimates of the number of fans vary between 8,000 and 11,000.

48. Interview with Albor Salcedo, 7 Aug. 1993; *Esto*, 29 Mar. 1984; *Uno Más Uno*, 29 Mar. 1984; Terrazas, 96–98.

49. Interview with Albor Salcedo, 7 Aug. 1993; *Esto*, 30 Mar., 7, 11 Apr. 1984; *Uno Más Uno*, 30 Mar., 5, 7, 13, 18, 19 Apr. 1984. For more information on Durazo, see: José González González, *Lo negro del Negro Durazo* (Mexico City: Editorial Posada, 1983); David G. LaFrance, "The Myth and the Reality of 'El Negro' Durazo: Mexico City's Most-Wanted Police Chief," *Studies in Latin American Popular Culture* 9(1990): 237–248.

50. Interview with Jiménez; *Uno Más Uno*, 10, 15 Mar. 1983.

51. Interview with Jiménez; *Uno Más Uno*, 15 Apr. 1984; Terrazas, 98–100.

52. *Uno Más Uno*, 26 Apr., 14 June 1984.

53. *Esto*, 7 Apr., 2, 4 May, 3, 11 June 1984; *Uno Más Uno*, 27 Apr., 2, 3, 4, 19 May, 9, 13 June 1984; Terrazas, 98–100. Only after much pressure from the CT and the ANABE did the Nacional owners finally agree to hold another all-star game to benefit the association and the Aztecas team; *Uno Más Uno*, 15, 16, 28 June 1984. By July 1984 the Nacional league owed the ANABE nearly 9.5 million pesos for the players' retirement fund and other benefits: *Uno Más Uno*, 6 July 1984.

54. *Esto*, 22 June, 2 July, 20 Aug. 1984; *Uno Más Uno*, 18, 27 June, 29 Aug. 1984; Terrazas, 98–100.

55. Interview with Jiménez; Suárez, 266–267; Terrazas, 98–100; *Uno Más Uno*, 3, 19 May, 14, 18, 21 June, 6 July 1984, 3 July 1985.

56. *Esto*, 3, 7 Apr., 5, 10 May 1985; *Uno Más Uno*, 30 June 1985, 13, 21, 28 Mar., 10 Apr. 1986.

57. *Esto*, 5, 17 May 1985; *Uno Más Uno*, 14 July, 22 Aug. 1984, 3 July 1985, 4, 21 Mar. 1986. As of 30 June 1984, the Nacional had a debt that totaled 11.765 million pesos; *Uno Más Uno*, 23 July 1984.

58. *Uno Más Uno*, 3, 4, 16, 23 July 1985.

59. Interview with Jiménez.

60. Interview with Albor Salcedo, 9 Sept. 1986; Interview with Becerril, 8–9 Sept. 1986, 24 Aug. 1987; Interview with Terrazas; *Proceso*, 11 Aug. 1986, 62; *Uno Más Uno*, 12 Mar., 7 Apr. 1989. In 1985, of the 109 Latin American players in the U.S. major and minor leagues, only eight were from Mexico; *Uno Más Uno*, 29 Mar. 1985. By 1991, 38 Mexicans played north of the border, out of 585 foreigners, most of them Latin Americans; see Jamail. Also, see other articles by Milton Jamail on this topic in *USA Today Baseball Weekly*, 10–16 May 1991, 24 Feb.–2 Mar. 1993.

61. Interview with Becerril, 24 Aug. 1987.

62. *Excélsior*, 25 Jan. 1989; *La Jornada*, 13 Mar. 1989: *Uno Más Uno*, 4 Mar., 7, 8, Apr., 21 Aug., 30 Sept. 1989; *Proceso*, 6 Mar. 1989, 60–63.

63. Interview with Albor Salcedo, 7 Aug. 1993; *Diario del Istmo* (Coatzacoalcos), 2 Apr. 1989; *Uno Más Uno*, 3 Aug., 30 Sept., 6 Oct. 1989.

64. *Uno Más Uno*, 30 Aug. 18, 20, 21 Sept. 1989, 9 Mar. 1990.

65. Interview with Albor Salcedo, 7 Aug 1993; Interview with Becerril, 24 Aug. 1987; Suárez, 265–266; *El Nacional*, 26 Apr. 1984; *Proceso*, 10 Apr. 1989, 60–63; *Uno Más Uno*, 1 Oct. 1989.

66. *Proceso*, 1 July 2001, 90–93.

67. See, for example, the *New York Times*, 14 Dec. 1993, which comments on the fate of Mexican labor in the wake of the North American Free Trade Agreement (NAFTA).

7

Charreada: Performance and Interpretation of an Equestrian Folk Tradition in Mexico and the United States

Kathleen M. Sands

The horse has played a multifaceted role in Latin American history. On the negative side, one of the most widely accepted explanations for the rigid class structure of society originates directly in the relationship of horse and rider in pre-Columbian Spain. During the long years of warfare against the Moors in the so-called Reconquest of the Iberian Peninsula, to be able to ride a horse clearly separated a person of means from the masses. Subsequently, this outlook was reinforced in the Americas where the horse also elevated its European rider above the ranks of the large Indian population. A more positive interpretation of the horse's place, however, can be seen in its role in overall economic development and military feats related to nation building, such as the Mexican Revolution of 1910. The twentieth century witnessed a decline in the importance of these last two roles, but, ironically, the rider's social importance has gained strength as modernization has relentlessly penetrated the region. No longer, however, is the equestrian a symbol of division.

In a careful study of charreada, *or Mexican rodeo, Arizona State University professor Kathleen Sands, an avid equestrian herself, demonstrates how and why the horse and rider, in the context of stylized competitions, have taken on a significant and inclusive social-cultural meaning. She argues that* charreada, *by drawing on idealized traditions and practices, helps to reinforce a sense of common history and consequently cultural pride among Mexicans and Mexican Americans. In other words, in contemporary times the symbolism of horse and rider, as seen through a rose-colored prism of nationalism, helps people to cope with the great socioeconomic changes of recent decades.*

From *Studies in Latin American Popular Culture* 13 (1994): 77–100 (diagram and photos omitted). Reprinted by permission of *Studies in Latin American Popular Culture*.

Charreada, sometimes called Mexican rodeo, is the performance of a complex folk tradition that symbolically dramatizes the Spanish conquest of Mexico, the development of a colonial ranching culture, and the struggle for independence and national identity. It displays and upholds Mexican norms of bravery and patriotism, mastery of equestrian skills, family and community cooperation, and a distinct ethnic aesthetic. *Charreada* is a time for competition and celebration of horsemanship and courtly elegance within the Hispanic cultures of Mexico and the United States.

During a *charreada*, teams of riders called *charros* perform a series of scored events that test equestrian precision, style, smoothness, and flair. *Charreada* events combine the stately dignity of aristocratic ceremony and courtesy with the rough-and-ready excitement of rodeo. As folk performance, *charreada* provides a particularly good cultural text for the analysis of the adaptation of Old World tradition to a new landscape and offers an opportunity to trace some of the sources of contemporary cowboy culture in the United States.[1]

Furthermore, as social drama, it can be examined as a regenerative process which draws the community together to ritualize its collective history and reassert its ethnic identity. In anthropologist Victor Turner's terms, *charreada* is a "celebratory performance," which "rejoices in the values and virtues of the society that produces it, and in a history whose high points of success and conquest exemplify qualities of moral and aesthetic excellence."[2]

Charreada calls to mind a series of events and traditions that contribute significantly to Mexican self-definition, beginning with the conquest and colonization of North America. The Spanish expeditions to the New World owed their success largely to horses and skilled horsemen. So important was the horse to the conquest that Bernal Díaz, chronicler of the Cortés expeditions and battles, halted shortly into his narrative to list and describe ten stallions and six mares brought ashore at the first landing of cavalry on the mainland of Mexico in 1519. Throughout his memoir, Díaz emphasizes the importance of the horse, the care taken to keep them out of the hands of the indigenous population, and the grief felt when a horse was injured or died.[3]

Development of Mexican Riding Style

When Cortés landed in Mexico, "the *la brida* [bridle] school of riding which used very long stirrups and a stiffly erect posture was still in practice in Spain,"[4] a holdover from the medieval chivalric style. However, Cortés's cavalrymen used a modified *a la jineta* [horseman] riding technique. In this style, the result of the introduction of the agile Barb horse into Spain by Moorish conquerors, the rider used:

> a light saddle placed well up on the withers of the horse. The stirrups were so short that the rider seemed to be kneeling upon his mount. The rider rode with a high hand, that is to say, the short reins were held high because the horse was "bitted" on the neck; he was turned by the pressure of the reins on the neck rather than being guided by pulling at the corners of the mouth in the European fashion.[5]

To the New World, the conquistadors brought a modified Moorish saddle, lengthening the stirrups to accommodate rough country and long journeys. They also imported several Moorish riding techniques useful in battles with native populations:

> They never rode with the reins tied, because if they were dismounted in battle, the free reins, falling to the ground, were easier to catch, and there was less chance of their mounts running away. They also learned to tie a horse properly, so the knot neither ran hard nor slipped. They learned to mount in one motion, never standing in the stirrup with one leg posed stiffly in the air after the style of the [European] riding schools.[6]

Though the modified *a la jineta* style lingered after the initial stages of conquest, a new style emerged along with the development of the ranching economy that was to become the backbone of New Spain and independent Mexico. The new style, which would become the *charro* equestrian form, combines elements of both Old World schools to make it efficient for working cattle yet graceful and natural. It is a

> compromise between the long, straight-legged stirrup, which set the rider as dead weight upon a horse, and the extremely short *a la jineta*, a jockey-like length that placed the rider too far forward of the horse's center of balance. A stirrup that bends the leg slightly, giving the rider a slightly forward seat, helps him grip the horse's barrel in a natural manner. If the saddle seat is shaped properly, the horseman sits erect, yet without stiffness. He rides with resilience, is balanced in all gaits, and he is able to shift his weight with the changing movements of his horse.[7]

In the *charro* style, the rider is an extension of his horse. He rides with a high hand, neck-reining his mount, and controlling and guiding him with subtle and deft body cues.[8]

Charros claim to be the "finest, most elegant, and bravest horsemen in the world."[9] In Spain at the time of the conquest, "*caballero* [horseman] was the term for gentleman";[10] the term still applies to *charros* who are expected to exhibit propriety and panache in all their public acts. Their natural posture, balance, and rhythm evolves directly from their method of gentling and training horses. The process begins with roping a wild horse, then accustoming the animal to human touch by rubbing it all over before introducing it to ground work. As the animal becomes compliant, the trainer uses a halter and false reins tied to the saddle to introduce the animal to paces, turns, and stops, working the horse with an empty saddle. Before actually mounting, the trainer repeatedly places his weight in the saddle.[11] Each step is slow and patient; throughout the training, the trainer gives oral commands along with verbal encouragements and consistently rewards the animal.[12] *Charros* do not "break" horses but slowly bring them along, thus preserving their spirit while developing full command. Most contemporary *charros* prefer quarter horses because they are well-boned and muscular with the easy disposition and necessary speed, agility, and responsiveness for roping and other *charreada* events. Many *charros* ride stallions, harking back to the laws enacted during the reign of Isabella and Ferdinand in Spain which required gentlemen to ride stallions lest "they grow soft and womanly by riding gentle palfreys in their travels."[13]

Historical Dynamics of *Charreada*

Performance of *charreada* events has sources not only in cattle ranching activities but also in the equestrian games of Old World Spain. The elaborate celebrations of colonial Mexico often included *cañas* [canes] competitions derived from Moorish light cavalry exercises in which riders caught bamboo javelins in mid-air and threw them back at the opposition. Another game, *sortijas* [rings], goes back to medieval tournaments in which riders, using light lances, snared beribboned rings strung along a race course. These games had strict rules and violations could disqualify or penalize a rider. For example, in *sortijas*, the reins had to be held in the left hand and losing a hat or footing in a stirrup caused penalties.[14] These same rules apply to *charreada* events today.

The most important influences on *charreada* are, however, the day-to-day performance of stock management chores and the post-roundup competitions on colonial and post-colonial haciendas. The informal riding and roping competitions that drew vaqueros and hacendados from neighboring haciendas developed into more formal competitions in the late eighteenth century. By the early twentieth century, *charreada* events had become subject to complex regulations and reached a high degree of popularity under the wealthy old guard of Mexico. The 1910 Mexican Revolution contributed yet another aspect to *charro* tradition, as vaqueros and independent ranchers took up arms and joined the revolt against rich, and by this time, often absentee, landowners. Because of the crucial role *charros* played in the civil war for political reform,[15] today the *charro* is a symbol of Mexican patriotism and his costume includes a pistol.[16]

Despite the fact that the horse is often spoken of as the true hero of the revolution, and the *charro*, by extension, shares in that glory, the civil war actually threatened the survival of *charro* tradition. Battles decimated the horse population, breeders abandoned their haciendas, skilled saddlemakers and costumers died or fled, and interest flagged. Costumes were cheapened by adaptation to theater productions and use by nightclub musicians.[17] But with the return of peace and growing economic stability, interest in *charro* culture revived, though with significant changes. After the revolution, *charreada* became an urban sport as well as continuing to be part of local ranching tradition. The conversion of ranch work and pastimes into athletic competition brought a refinement of "accepted conventions and appropriate procedures"[18] by which the measure of dominance over animals and demonstration of elaborations on roping skills might be formally judged. By the 1920s, the *lienzo* [key-hole-shaped arena] replaced ranch-style corrals, and the competitions became very exacting with detailed procedures and official regulations covering everything from costume to event performance. In the movement from ranch to city, *charreada* events were no longer framed by cattle ranching activities like roundups and the space of the open range but identified by "demarcated times and places" and enclosed literally and figuratively within the border of the *lienzo*, "creating a set of expectations about the kind of behavior or conduct that should fill the encased space-time." This framing, according to Victor Turner, leaves the participants "free to fabricate a range of alternative possibilities of behaving, thinking, and feeling that is wider than that current or admissible in either the mundane world or the ritual frame." Removed from the requirements of managing livestock for sale, "disengaged from the 'business' of survival production and profit,"[19] *charreada* became a sport that could explore the limits of the skills of horse and rider in a sociable setting.

In 1921 the Asociación Nacional de Charros [National Association of Charros] formed, and in 1933, the Federación de Charros [Federation of Charros] began. The latter now includes over seven hundred local associations and twenty thousand members, among them eighty associations in the United States, primarily in the Southwest. Though public competition[20] has not received much attention outside the Mexican-American community, it is not new to the United States; *charreada* events took place north of the border for decades before the professionalization of United States rodeo, and *charros* regularly performed with such productions as Buffalo Bill's Wild West Show, gaining them reputation as the world's most skilled ropers.[21]

Despite a clearly traceable history of contributing factors, there is no single source for *charreada* and *charro* culture. Rather they evolved slowly over six centuries into a contemporary mixture of Old and New World equestrian traditions which only became distinctive in the Mexican landscape. Today the *charro* is a symbol of Mexican culture, but the term *charro*, like the term cowboy, did not originally carry legendary mystique. First applied to Mexican horsemen in 1829, the term originated much earlier in the Salamanca area of Spain where it described peasants and meant "crude and rustic." In Mexican culture it has undergone complete amelioration to denote the "stylish gentleman, skilled horseman, and patriot."[22] The term has a history much like that of the word cowboy, which was first used to refer to youngsters who herded milk cows, then to itinerant bronc riders. Not until the great trail drives of the late nineteenth century did the term cowboy acquire positive meaning, and not until the twentieth century has the cowboy become a national symbol.

American cowboy and Mexican *charro* traditions are both nineteenth-century adaptations of the Mexican vaquero. In central and northern Mexico and in the western United States, separate but related practices have developed to extraordinary levels of sophistication through public performance.[23] Examination of *charreada* performance makes the distinctions clear.

Charreada Performance and Interpretation

Horsemanship is the focus of every element of *charreada*. The horse elevates the *charro*, literally and symbolically, to a position of power and control that links him directly to the conquest of the Americas and the development of New World ranching. Semiotically, the *charro* is the culmination and enduring representation of five hundred years of Hispanic physical and cultural dominance of the landscape of Mexico and the southwestern United States. In the twentieth century, he is a popular symbol of Mexican nationality.

The events of the *charreada*, like those in rodeo, are based on the dominance and control of animals. However, while speed and endurance are the primary criteria in rodeo, style is the dominant criterion in *charreada*. No eight-second whistles signal the end of a bull or bronc ride and no prizes are given for the fastest time in roping events at a *charreada*. *Charros* compete strictly for the love of the tradition and the prestige accorded to those who give superior performances. To determine the level of each *charro*'s and each team's skill, judges add or subtract points for precision of maneuvers and elegance of costume and tack.[24] Nine competition events make up a *charreada*, plus an opening ceremonial parade of all contestants and officials, and frequently, a closing exhibition by an *escaramuza* [women's mounted drill team].

A *charreada* is a formal yet highly festive event.[25] Families of competitors and members of the local community gather in the grandstand to watch the competition, which is often followed by a fiesta with food and dancing. Before and during the *charreada*, mariachi musicians play traditional *charro* songs, the brass instruments enhancing the military overtones of the grand entry and enlivening the crowd during the competitive action. Vendors hawk food and drinks, families and friends visit, and children, often dressed in elaborate *charro* costumes, play in the grandstands. The integral audience, those familiar with the sequence of events and the criteria for good performance, alternate social interaction with attention on the arena when particularly dangerous events or an especially good performance occurs. Because they carry the sequence, scenography, and symbology of *charreada* at an unconscious level, they respond almost reflexively to cues from the arena.

The *charreada* begins with a *desfile* [parade] of participants, judges, association *reinas* [queens], and local officials. Designated riders carry the national flag—in the United States, both the Mexican and American flags. During the *desfile*, the arena is the landscape of Mexico on which *charros* and *charras* have played important roles in the struggle for independence and the revolution for political justice. The *desfile* is the most overtly military part of the *charreada*. The riders enter in parade ranks to martial music and fan out to the walls of the arena, saluting the audience before the national anthem(s) and holding the salute until it ends. The *mayoral* [arena steward] directs the riders and controls the flow of events; he must be well versed in the rules and is frequently, like the judges, a senior member of the community who has a distinguished record as a competitor.

Besides commemorating the military history of Mexico, the *desfile* offers an opportunity to display elegant costumes and horse trappings.[26] No rider may enter the arena without a sombrero and costume—no jeans allowed. Each *escaramuza* team has an array of colorful traditional dresses worn over crinolines and high boots. Each *charro* wears traditional conservatively colored pants decorated with embroidery and silver filigree buttons along the side seams. He wears ankle-length, flat-heeled boots with heavy silver spurs. The costume is completed by a fitted, waist-length jacket, butterfly tie, and stiff, wide-brimmed sombrero of either rabbit fur or tightly woven straw.[27] Each charro costume is unique—unlike the mariachi outfits modeled on them—but rich colors and fabrics, intricate silver and braid trim, and precision tailoring characterize all the costumes.

The horse's trappings are equally elegant. The saddle retains the Moorish cantle and the protective leathers of the Spanish saddle. It has a very sturdy pommel, which can withstand tremendous pulling strain and affords leverage useful in roping wild cattle and horses. Its flat seat allows ropers to move away from the rope as it is thrown.[28] The *charro* saddle is not an ancestor but a cousin to the American stock saddle, both having developed from Old World models modified for use in herding and roping cattle. Tied on the back of the saddle is a *serape* [bed roll], symbolic of working and living on the range. *Charros* usually use a light bit with elaborate cheek pieces, but as one observer remarked, "a strand of yarn would suffice to guide these horses."[29] Reins are traditionally woven from horse hair or made of braided leather.[30] The *charro* also carries a quirt and ropes on his saddle.

The *desfile* gives participants an opportunity to demonstrate the elegant manners respected by the community and to show off their horses, trappings, and costumes in a dignified tableau. The flavor is distinctly nineteenth century, but the contemporary character of *charreada* is clearly revealed in the pick-up trucks and stock trailers behind the *lienzo* and the coolers and video cameras and loudspeakers in the stands. Inside the arena is pageant, outside, real life. The demarcation is much clearer in an urban setting than on the ranch where sport and work blend and the physical space is used both for play and work.

Competition Events

With the exit of the parade riders, competition events begin. In the *cala* [reining], one *charro* from each of the two, or sometimes, three teams competes. The rider goes to the center of the arena, gives the *charro* salute, a touch of the back of the hand to the hat brim, open palm facing the audience. He then gallops to the far end of the panhandle of the *lienzo*, over one hundred yards. On a signal from the judges, he gallops down the alley and into the round arena, bringing his horse to a sliding stop, raising a cloud of dust. The rider then performs *cabriolas* [spins], making full and half turns in both directions. Judges score the horse and rider on smoothness and the number of rotations as well as on precision stops. Then the rider backs his mount out of the round arena and into the alley, a demonstration of complete control since horses dislike backing because they cannot see the terrain, and backing in a straight line is extremely difficult. The purpose of this event is to demonstrate the horse's complete and quiet compliance to minimal cuing and the rider's horsemanship. This event has no parallel in rodeo but is somewhat similar to horse show reining competition. The slide and spins are particular favorites with spectators who often count the number of rotations aloud and cheer enthusiastically.

The second event is *piales en el lienzo* [hind leg roping] in which three members of each team attempt to rope a running mare in order to bring it to a gradual stop. This event tests the capacity to rope in a confined area and control exceptionally long ropes. The competitors line their horses in the alley, rotating position with each new wild mare run. If a throw catches, the *charro* turns his rope around the dish-shaped saddle horn, and it sings and smokes when it pulls taut as the horse runs into the round arena and comes to a bounding halt. The point here, as in other roping events, is not to damage the animal—livestock is valuable and the concern for its welfare relates directly to ranching livestock management—but to stop the animal smoothly by playing out the rope evenly, much as a fly fisherman plays out his line. This event comes directly from ranching where roping in close quarters is required.

The third event is *colas* [tailing the bulls]. This activity harks back to the sixteenth century, before the introduction of ropes woven from *maguey* [century plant] cactus fiber, when steers on the range were struck with a club and pulled to the ground by the tail. Now the tailer salutes, taps the steer's back, grasps and wraps the tail under his right leg, and throws the bull to the ground, all while at a full gallop. To score well, the rider must avoid faults like touching the saddle or horse's mane; he must not use his quirt and must not raise his leg more than once to hook the tail. He must down the steer within forty to sixty yards, or approximately three to five seconds. Injuries, ranging from tail burns on the right hand to broken bones if the steer crosses in front of the horse and they collide, are a risk. Somewhat similar to rodeo bulldogging, *colas* require strength, speed, and daring.

Following *colas*, activities move into the *rueda* [round arena].[31] In the *jinete de novillos* [bull riding], the charro may use two hands, but he must remain on the animal until it stops bucking. Spurring the animal when it flags earns a higher score. Occasionally a bull will fall, and the rider, if he is very skilled, will stay on and continue the ride when the bull gains its feet, gaining high point standing and appreciative cheers. This event has much in common with rodeo bull riding, but the bull is smaller and the ride is usually a lot longer than eight seconds. This event is a demonstration of play, not ranching work; it is a test of the rider's strength, bravery, and agility.

Once the bull rider has dismounted, his team members begin the *terna en el ruedo* [team roping]. This event allows *charros* to show off their trick roping. As in rodeo team roping, the goal is to secure both the head and hind legs of the animal and stretch it out in the arena; however, in *charreada*, speed is not the point—ropers have eight minutes to complete their throws. They use the time to gain points by demonstrating intricate flourishes with their ropes; style is as important as accuracy and distance. This is the slowest event, appreciated most fully only by those who know the traditional rope flourishes and the difficulty of performing them horseback, but it can be spectacular as when, with a flick of the rope, the *charro* who has thrown the loop over the bull's horns, snaps it to form a halter over the animal's muzzle.

Encouraging cheers and appreciative applause mark a particularly good performance or compensate for a rider's bad luck in an event. Since scoring is very complicated, at small rural *charreadas* there is constant query as to team standings. At larger *charreadas*, an announcer keeps the audience up on team tallies; announcements and commentary in the United States are made in Spanish, reinforcing the Mexican identity of most of the audience and of the tradition.

The next event is the *jinete de yegua* [wild mare riding]. It is very similar to the bull-riding event, but relates directly to the taming of wild animals for use on a ranch. It also differs from rodeo bronc-riding events in which the cowboy attempts to remain on the horse for only eight seconds. The *charro* tries to ride the mare until it can be dismounted easily and quietly, much as a horseman on a ranch would do to domesticate a wild horse.

Once the rider has dismounted, the *manganas a pie y a caballo* [roping and throwing a wild mare from on foot and on horseback] begin. Here again, the ropers have an opportunity to demonstrate their expertise at flourishes. Each throw must be of a different style. *La máscara* [mask] requires the roper to twist his wrist so the palm faces upward when the loop is launched; it may only be used on the first attempt. In *la crinolina* [petticoat], a term originating in the era of hooped skirts, the loop whirls from left to right around the roper's body, then is raised upward and launched. Each rope flourish is named for its inventor, place of origin, or the pattern it traces, such as the basket or mirror.[32]

The other team members play a crucial role in the roper's success during *manganas*; they force the mare to a full gallop around the *rueda* wall so that the roper has the opportunity to perform flourishes and still throw the loop at exactly the right moment to catch the mare's forefeet and jerk her to a shoulder roll. There are many variations in both mounted and on-foot roping. The most dangerous and difficult requires the on-foot roper to place one end of the rope around his neck, cast the noose at the other end to catch the mare's forefeet, dig his heels into the dirt, and throw himself backward to jerk the mare into a roll. The most spectacular horseback-roping style requires the roper to stand on his horse while performing flourishes, often including jumping through the loop before throwing it; then he drops to the saddle to secure his rope around the horn and jerks the mare to the ground.[33]

Because the horse is the critical instrument for success in competition, it receives as much praise from knowledgeable spectators as the rider does. Riders may switch mounts for an event in which a particular horse has been trained and may ride horses owned by other members of the community though they generally prefer to ride horses they have gentled and trained themselves. Not only do especially expert *charros* become heroes, so do especially fine horses, and both or either may become the subject of folk stories or *corridos* [topical ballads].

The final event, *paso de la muerte* [pass of death], puts the contestant at great peril as he leaps from his bareback, galloping horse onto the back of a wild mare and rides to a stop. This event is particularly risky since the wild mare runs between the *charro* and the wall, so a miscalculation can leave the rider in jeopardy of being trampled either by the wild mare or by the mounted hazers urging her on. The *paso* evolved from the colonial period in Mexico when the *mesteñero* [mustanger] leaped onto a wild mare, rope in hand, and looped it over the animal's neck and nose in order to cut it away from the herd.[34] Today, *paso* is a symbolic test of courage, skill, and balance that, like bull riding, fits into the Mexican cult of machismo which honors daring and feats of masculine prowess.

Competition events recall the importance of ranching and horsemanship in the development of Mexico as a colony of Spain and an independent nation. They link the audience, many of whom have rural backgrounds and family ties, to the landscape of Mexico and remind them of the importance of horsemanship in the history of their homeland, giving them, as well as the performers, a means of expressing their ethnic heritage.

Women's Performance in *Charreada*

Performance by an *escaramuza* team often closes the frame on the *charreada*, reasserting the community's links to the military history of Mexico, since the term *escaramuza* means skirmish and evokes the role of women during the Mexican Revolution during which they gained fame for their equestrian skill as couriers and fighters. Riding *escaramuza* provides an opportunity for the young women of the community to demonstrate their equestrian abilities.[35] Members of the team, numbering from six to twelve, perform precision maneuvers at a full gallop, riding sidesaddle in traditional full-skirted costumes. Many of these young women also perform a modified *cala*, racing their horses to a sliding stop in the arena, and a few even perform spins. The drill patterns take discipline and courage, particularly *cruzadas* [crosses], which require the riders to alternate crossing each other's line of galloping horses; a second's miscalculation or a balk brings collision and certain injury to riders and animals.

To insure safe and expert performance *charras*, like *charros*, put in many practice hours. As with their male counterparts, cooperation, mutual trust, and equestrian grace and excellence are essential to success in the arena, but more broadly, these are values highly regarded within the culture, and by performing, *charros* and *charras* reinforce social norms and ideals of cooperation within the community.[36]

While *escaramuza* performance is very vigorous and requires strength and athletic ability, if done well, it looks smooth and reveals no strain or tension, pointing to the origins of the Hispanic women's equestrian tradition in the sedate aristocratic Spanish school of riding where young women were allowed to ride in processions on special feast days. The Mexican Revolution put women astride horses. Perhaps the most famous of these is Adelita, a legendary heroine often referred to as the originator of *escaramuza*; the dresses the *charras* ride in is called the Adelita costume. The revolutionary riding style, however, was not adapted since it clashes with traditional Mexican values concerning the roles of women. The graceful *escaramuza* costume and sidesaddle riding style preserve the appearance of a genteel tradition. Costumes, while colorful and ornate, remain modestly high-necked and long-sleeved. The wide sombrero protects delicate skin, and the ribbon under the hat holds the hair back from the face in classic Spanish style. The costumes and sidesaddle riding technique give the *escaramuzas* an air of aristocratic grace that masks their physical exertion and daring, much as the cult of domesticity and gentility in Mexican and Mexican-American cultures masks the power women hold.

Charreada Enacts Mexican Ethnicity

Charreada and the *charros* and *charras* who live the tradition serve as vital reminders of a shared historical past in the New World. Each *charreada* is a public manifestation of a much more complex matrix of culturally prescribed gender roles, family and community values, ranching practices and traditions, social protocols, ethnic identity maintenance systems, and components of national character. It preserves the baroque attention to style and ornate adornment typical of sixteenth- and seventeenth-century Spain, the influence of Moorish culture on Spanish equestrian style, the impact of a new landscape and economy, and the exuberant effect of independence and personal freedom on Mexican culture.

Just as rodeo gives Americans a unique sense of their historic past and national identity, *charreada* gives Mexicans and Mexican Americans a sense of cultural pride. These separate but related performances embody the values of the cultural communities that have created them and modified them over the years. In rodeo, individual action, speed, and strength dominate, reflecting the value Americans place on efficiency, practicality, self-sufficiency, and power. In *charreada*, style, team cooperation, and precision dominate, reflecting the emphasis Mexican culture places on elegance, colorful embellishment, community, and mastery. As Victor Turner notes:

> When a social group, whether it be a family, clan, village, nation, congregation, or church, celebrates a particular event or occasion, such as birth, harvest, national independence, it also "celebrates itself." In other words, it attempts to manifest, in symbolic form, what it conceives to be its essential life, at once the distillation and typification of its corporate experience.[37]

Charreada and rodeo, both developed in rural ranching communities, have now become sophisticated public performances of traditional skills molded by separate cultural preferences and values, but both symbolically demonstrate and celebrate the equestrian skills and human courage required for taming and controlling animals in the environment of the New World.

Notes

1. Both *charro* and cowboy are directly related to the working vaquero of the great haciendas of colonial Mexico. The history of the vaquero in Mexico, California, Texas, and other parts of the Southwest is much too complex to address in

this paper. The following sources provide context and background on the relationship of the vaquero equestrian tradition to *charro* and cowboy performance: Richard W. Slatta, *Cowboys of the Americas* (New Haven: Yale University Press, 1990); William D. Wittliff, *Vaquero: Genesis of the Texas Cowboy* (San Antonio: University of Texas Press, 1972); David Dary, *Cowboy Culture: A Saga of Five Centuries* (New York: Knopf, 1981).

2. "Introduction," *Celebration: Studies in Festivity and Ritual*, ed. Victor Turner (Washington, DC: Smithsonian Institution Press, 1982), 14.

3. *The Bernal Díaz Chronicles: The True Story of the Conquest of Mexico*, ed. and tr. Albert Idell (Garden City, NY: Doubleday, 1956), 38–39.

4. James Norman, *Charro: Mexican Horsemanship* (New York: G. Putnam's Sons, 1970), 2.

5. Ibid., 52.

6. Ibid., 53.

7. Ibid., 55.

8. For further discussion of trappings, see Daniel F. Rubín de la Borbolla's "Origins of Mexican Horsemanship and Saddlery," in *Man Made Mobile: Early Saddles of Western North America*, ed. Richard E. Ahlborn (Washington, DC: Smithsonian Institution Press, 1980), 21–38.

9. "*El charro: Lo más fino, lo más bravo, lo más elegante*," Museum Exhibit (Tucson: Arizona Historical Society, 1989).

10. Don Worcester, *The Spanish Mustangs from the Plains of Andalusia to the Prairies of Texas* (El Paso: University of Texas Press, 1986), 3.

11. Norman, 59.

12. Though each trainer's technique is somewhat different, there is a consistent pattern of gentling rather than breaking. As a result the mature *charro* horse is responsive to voice commands as well as very light body cues, is lively and attentive but easily controlled and directed. Preparing a new horse for competition usually takes about a year, and the *charro* horse is kept in constant training to correct performance errors and to reinforce patterns for performance events.

13. Worcester, 3.

14. Norman, 91–92.

15. A famous *charro* competitor in his youth, Emiliano Zapata is the most revered of all the *charro* revolutionary heroes; he is most often depicted in full *charro* costume.

16. *Charros* are the only civilians legally allowed to carry a sidearm in Mexico; this is because they are a reserve army that may be called to active duty in times of national emergency.

17. Norman, 87.

18. Clifford Geertz, *Interpretation of Cultures* (New York: Basic Books, 1972), 27. In this volume, Geertz argues that the "culture of a people is an ensemble of texts, themselves ensembles" that may be read without resorting to reductive formulas (452). He demonstrates his concept of "deep play" by analyzing Balinese cockfighting as performance text. Cockfighting is also a traditional sport in Mexican culture and often connected to *charro* culture, but the *charreada* offers a more complex performance for analysis, particularly in its historical symbolism.

19. Turner, 28.

20. *Charro* competition in the United States, as in Mexico, takes place at the local, state, regional, and national levels. The largest competition in the United States is the National Congress, which lasts four days each fall and draws the top teams from throughout the nation. The Mexican Congreso draws teams from both Mexico and the United States and lasts over a week.

21. For a full discussion of the history of *charro* competition in the United States, see Mary Lou LeCompte, "The Hispanic Influence on the History of Rodeo, 1823–1922," *Journal of Sport History* 12 (Spring 1985): 29–38, and Mary Lou LeCompte and William H. Beezley, "Any Sunday in April: The Rise of Sport in San Antonio and the Hispanic Borderlands," *Journal of Sport History* 13 (Summer 1986): 128–45.

22. "*El charro*," Museum Exhibit.

23. For a semiotic analysis of rodeo, see Beverly J. Stoeltje, "Riding, Roping, and Reunion: Cowboy Festival" in *Time Out of Time: Essays on the Festival*, ed. Alessandro Falassi (Albuquerque: University of New Mexico Press, 1987), 137–51; "The Rodeo Clown and the Semiotics of Metaphor," *Journal of Folklore Research* 22 (May–December 1985): 155–77.

24. Judges must attend seminars and pass rigorous tests before they may officiate at Federación-sponsored *charreadas*.

25. Descriptions of *charreada* events in this essay are drawn from several sources: personal observation of performances on both sides of the border; interviews with *charros* and *charras*, judges, and Federación officials in Mexico and the United States; and from the current Federación rule book. For a much more complete description and semiotic interpretation of *charreada* see Kathleen M. Sands, *Charrería Mexicana: An Equestrian Folk Tradition* (Tucson: University of Arizona Press, 1993).

26. Victor Turner offers a useful discussion of celebratory objects in his introduction to *Celebration: Studies in Festivity and Ritual*, 16–20. He notes that "celebratory objects are, first and foremost material objects, though they represent ideas, objects, events, relationships, 'truths' not immediately present to the observer, or even intangible or invisible thoughts and conceptions. Such celebratory symbols, moreover, usually stand for many things and thoughts at once." The tableau of the *desfile* presents celebratory objects to the audience, which, whether at a conscious or unconscious level, associates them with the historical and cultural context they represent. As Turner points out: "We are seldom dealing with separate symbols but with clusters made up of objects, actions, sounds, states, orders, contacts, each unit, act, or thing, at once itself and standing for more than itself, the ensemble making up more than the sum of its parts. In the celebratory process we cannot detach the participants from what they participate in, the subject from the object." The *desfile* brings all the visual, auditory, and other sensory symbols of *charreada* together, suggesting the historical context from which they derive.

27. Safety of both participants and livestock is an over-riding concern at all *charreadas*. The charro sombrero with its tall, stiff crown, which is as effective as a helmet in preventing head injuries, contributes to the safety of riders.

28. Rubin, 31–34.

29. Norman, 81.

30. Though they are not allowed in competition, many contemporary *charros* fashion reins from nylon rope for training, attesting to the enduring capacity for adaptation and innovation within the tradition.

31. This term is the source of the word rodeo.

32. Learning to perform rope flourishes is one of the mechanisms for introducing youngsters to the tradition. Many are proficient with the rope by age six or seven and perform at roping exhibitions both on foot and from horseback.

33. Rules changes in 1990 eliminated this variation from scored competitions, but it is still performed at exhibitions.

34. Norman, 102.

35. To compare the role of women in *charreada* with the role of women in rodeo, see Beverly J. Stoeltje's "Gender Representation in Performance: The Cowgirl and the Hostess," *Journal of Folklore Research* 25 (September–December 1988): 219–41.

36. Though social tensions do exist and antagonism occurs between *charro* associations, *charreada* unifies the participants and audience, at least for a couple of hours, in the act of celebrating a common culture. As Victor Turner observes: "Any major celebration, since it brings many members of a society into a single sociocultural space for a limited period of time, brings into proximity persons and groups with either endemic or transitory antagonisms. Celebration may be said partly to bring about a temporary reconciliation among conflicting members of a single community." For further discussion see Turner, 14.

37. Turner, 16.

8

Hosting the Summer Olympic Games: Mexico City, 1968

Joseph L. Arbena

Political leaders are seldom unaware of their own and their nations' standing in the international sphere, and most take reasonable measures to enhance that status. For many politicians, then, support for international sporting events becomes important. This process is encouraged by those who promote participation in the name of athletic excellence and global brotherhood, although in reality economic and political considerations carry more weight in pursuing such a policy. Winning a World Soccer Cup or accumulating a pile of medals in Olympic or World Games can "put a country on the map" or at least build upon an already formidable reputation. Likewise, successfully hosting an international event can greatly enhance a country's image.

As such, Mexico City took a significant risk in becoming the first Third World nation to welcome the Olympic Games. The country's leadership aimed to use the contest to help erase Mexico's generally unfortunate reputation as unstable and poor and to boost economic development via foreign investment and tourism. The bid nearly backfired, however, when student demonstrations, resulting in an unknown number of deaths, initially cast a pall over the event. Furthermore, not only did politics intrude upon the Games, but race, the debate between amateurism and professionalism, and the media also played negative roles. Nevertheless, in the end Mexico demonstrated that it successfully could organize and carry out such a complex undertaking. Although no other Latin American country has hosted the Olympics, many have boosted their images and economies, if only in the short run, by hosting the soccer World Cup/Mundial (Uruguay, Brazil, Chile, Mexico, and Argentina), the Pan American Games, and other international competitions such as the Bolivarian Games, the

Much of this chapter was published previously as "Mexico City, 1968: The Games of the XIXth Olympiad," in *Historical Dictionary of the Modern Olympic Movement*, ed. John E. Findling and Kimberly D. Pelle (Westport, CT: Greenwood Press, 1996), 139–47. Reprinted in this slightly revised and updated form by permission of Greenwood Press.

Central American and Caribbean Games, the Copa Libertadores, the Copa América, cricket test matches, Davis Cup tennis matches, and world championships in baseball, basketball, volleyball, and youth soccer.

The 1960s was a decade of controversy and conflict, of ferment and protest: The Vietnam War escalated; international condemnation of South African apartheid intensified; the rapid move toward independence altered the political map of Africa; civil war in the former Belgian Congo led to the death of United Nations Secretary General Dag Hammarskjöld; the Cuban missile crisis carried the world to the brink of nuclear war; student unrest shook France, Germany, Japan, and the United States; rebellious popular behavior provoked often brutal responses in such places as Brazil and Uruguay; and the black civil rights movement in the United States brought change along with serious white resistance. In 1968 alone assassins in the United States ended the careers of Martin Luther King and Robert Kennedy and violent confrontations marred the Democratic National Convention in Chicago, while in both France and the United States university students raised their outcries to new levels and in China the Cultural Revolution raged on. Also that year the Soviet Union invaded Czechoslovakia to suppress a nationalistic and ideologically deviant movement.

Host Mexico and the Summer Olympics scheduled for October 12–27 could not avoid those forces. Perceived as most dangerous was a predominantly student protest and demand for change that began as a meaningless fistfight between two secondary school students but that triggered an armed intervention by police and riot-control troops. University students, particularly at the National University (UNAM), began to organize for action, eventually directing demonstrations, some quite impressive, and calling a general strike that only partially, yet noticeably, materialized. In turn, the army occupied the UNAM campus and continued to harass student leaders. The climax came on October 2 when troops surrounded a group of students and sympathizers in the Plaza of the Three Cultures or Tlatelolco, for the name of the surrounding neighborhood, as the area was known in the fifteenth-century Aztec capital of Tenochtitlán. Without cause or warning the troops fired into the crowd, killing between 100 and 500 persons and wounding perhaps a thousand more. Following that "massacre" more protesters and suspected dissidents were arrested, tortured, and/or killed. Others were chased for several years.

Well before that confrontation, at its 60th General Session in Baden-Baden, Germany, on October 18, 1963, the International Olympic Committee (IOC) accepted Mexico's City's bid, initially submitted on December 7, 1962, to host the 1968 Summer Olympics, rejecting similar invitations from Detroit, Lyons, and Buenos Aires. In anticipation of this victory, in May 1963, then-President Adolfo López Mateos (1958–1964) had decreed the establishment of the Organizing Committee for the Games of the XIX Olympiad, though it was not formally constituted until after the IOC decision. Following the Baden-Baden meeting, the government created an Executive Commission directed by the longtime sports promoter General José A. Jesús Clark Flores; vice chairmanships were filled by Agustín Legorreta, for finance, and Pedro Ramírez Vázquez, for building, who were to be aided by eighteen specialized sections.

In June 1965 President Gustavo Díaz Ordaz (1964–1970) chose López Mateos to fill the still vacant chairmanship of the Organizing Committee, but due to declining health the former president stepped down after one year to be quickly replaced by the architect Ramírez Vázquez. In October 1966 the Committee created seven departments to carry out its functions: administration, sports technique, public relations, courtesies to visitors, control of installations, control of programs, and artistic and cultural activities. Now, with advanced computer assistance and the aid of numerous government agencies and private companies, serious work began. The Organizing Committee also initiated a sophisticated campaign of publicity and public relations.

As the new structure commenced its labors, it was viewed by many Mexicans as a means to advance their country's long attempt to raise its global prestige and thereby earn greater acceptance as a place safe for tourists and foreign investors. The student movement of July–October 1968 thus seemed to threaten those dreams, which explains, without excusing, the government's harsh reaction, especially at Tlatelolco. In addition to the 1968 Olympics, Mexican officials no doubt considered the impact of any social uprising on their obligation to host the 1970 soccer World Cup, another step in that long process of Mexican efforts to overcome five decades of foreign memory of its oft-cited Revolution (1910–1920) and its status as a Third World country. Overlapping this concern was the perception that any prolonged instability would bring into question the hegemony of the ruling Partido Revolucionario Institucional (PRI) [Institutional Revolutionary Party] and the authority of President Díaz Ordaz. Therefore, security for the Games was increased, whether necessary or not.

Meanwhile, within the IOC a potentially disruptive debate arose over the role of South Africa, which had been banned from Tokyo in 1964 because of racial policies offensive to the expanding body of black African states and to gradually more sensitive people in other world communities. Some eight months before the XIX Olympiad the IOC, based on a pledge from South African whites that they would modify their selection process to permit blacks to qualify, lifted the ban. In response, African nations announced plans to boycott the Games and soon had the support of countries in the Caribbean, the Islamic world, and Eastern Europe, bringing to around forty the number of countries expressing their willingness to be absent from Mexico City. Finally the Soviet Union threatened to stay home. Attempts to negotiate a compromise failed, so a divided and reluctant IOC voted to withdraw the invitation originally sent to Pretoria. The Mexicans also chose to deny entry to all Rhodesian athletes, despite their country's promise to send an integrated team, because of perceptions that the governing regime was composed of white racists and that black Africans would again be offended.

Less directly political were several issues facing the IOC before and during the Games. Performance-enhancing drugs were not yet a source of intense preoccupation, and irregular testing and observation brought only one expulsion: for alcohol abuse. Of greater importance to Olympic leaders was the suspicion (belief?) that not all female athletes were truly female, either because of genetic irregularities or medical treatments. Therefore, at least 640 females scheduled to compete were subjected to gender tests, but none of them was disqualified.

As at the 1968 Winter Games (Grenoble), the IOC struggled to abort the spread of commercialism, at least among athletes, and thus the decline of amateurism as defined by the IOC. But the IOC was virtually powerless to stop the trend and the Games, both Winter and Summer, generated a spate of stories about athletes who received gifts or kickbacks for their participation. A major source of income were the makers of sports equipment who paid athletes to wear their products and to conspicuously display their brand names. Pressure to do this increased as television became more intrusive. Mexico City represented the first serious attempt at live broadcasting for a major market, the success of which would generate a television explosion at future Games. At Mexico the scheduling of the Games and of some events was to a degree influenced by this desire to maximize the North American TV audience. The IOC wanted the revenue, the manufacturers wanted the exposure, and the athletes wanted pay for their cooperation. This alliance would eventually bring openly professional athletes to virtually all Olympic sports, as fans and sponsors sought the best athletes and the IOC could not disrupt the Games by banning so many obvious violators.

If Mexico's historic reputation and recent domestic unrest raised doubts about its ability to fulfill its Olympic responsibilities, even greater concern among some participant countries arose because of Mexico City's relatively high altitude of 7400 feet. Critics predicted that this site, by far the highest in Summer Olympic history, would physically harm the athletes and distort the competition. To equalize the competitors the British proposed that athletes be limited in the amount of time they could train above a certain altitude, an idea that received only mild support and was impossible to enforce. Mexican officials tried to reduce the nervousness by citing the number of local residents and foreign tourists who frequented the capital each year without obvious difficulty and by staging three pre-Olympic International Sports Competitions that experienced minimal problems; in the end, no nation withdrew from the Games because of the altitude issue. Of less concern then were the growing congestion and pollution caused by the city's nearly 10 million inhabitants—by 2000 more than doubled—in an environment with too little air movement; a few alarmists did call attention to the intestinal discomfort often cited as a problem among foreigners visiting Mexico.*

Ultimately, 113 countries sent 5531 athletes (4750 males, 781 females) to participate in 182 competitive events involving eighteen official and two demonstration sports. In the end, by whatever means, athletes from forty-four countries carried home 174 gold, 170 silver, and 183 bronze medals. Track and field, with 780 males and 239 females representing ninety-two countries, was the leading category of athletic performance. All sporting events were held in and around Mexico City, except the sailing competitions, which were assigned to Acapulco and its Yacht Club, 250 miles south on the Pacific coast. To house so many visiting athletes and conduct so many events the Mexicans needed to prepare adequate physical facilities. The decision was made to take advantage of space all over the sprawling city, to maximize intercultural contacts, and to risk organizing local services to meet the need: it was decentralized planning at its practical limits.

The Olympic Village for athletes was newly constructed south of the capital. The 5000-unit complex combined mass urban structures with varied open spaces, and provided facilities to entertain the residents, aid in their training, and encourage them to mix across national lines. Northeast was the new 22,000-seat Sports Palace, with its masonry base capped by a copper-covered dome. Another new facility was the Olympic Pool and Gymnasium, a compound structure with both an aquatic center for swimming and diving and a small arena for volleyball. Southeast, at the famous tourist site of Xochimilco, home of the floating gardens that date back to the fifteenth-century Aztecs, Mexico created a fine basin that served both rowing and canoeing. Other new structures included a prefabricated fencing arena, a velodrome next to the Sports Palace, and the partially roofed Aztec Stadium, the latter privately financed, used in 1968 for Olympic soccer, then fully exploited during the 1970 World Cup.

Among the several renovated structures the most used was the University City Stadium, renamed the Olympic Stadium, with its progressive design and its art work based on indigenous motifs. This was the site of the opening and closing ceremonies and most of the track and field competitions. The refurbished National Auditorium in Chapultepec, with its 12,800 seats, served successfully as the gymnastic venue. Weightlifting was held in the Insurgentes Theater, water polo in the UNAM pool, and target shooting on a military base.

*Through the 1960s Mexico City's population grew at an annual rate of 5.5%.

Expanding on the Games' athletic content, Mexican officials, with encouragement from the IOC, sponsored cultural and academic activities equal to the number of Olympic sports and often integrated with them. Thus the year-long "Cultural Olympiad," in which ninety-seven countries participated, offered such programs as: international festivals of the arts, folk arts, sculptors, and poets; exhibitions of Olympic philately and of the history and art of the Olympic Games; exhibitions on space research and nuclear energy; ballet; an international youth film festival; an international meeting of young architects; an Olympic camp for world youth; a presentation of the XIX Olympiad in motion pictures and television; and more. These events were held in museums and auditoriums, along busy thoroughfares, and in the city's green and spacious Chapultepec Park. One still visible example of this cultural cooperation were the nineteen abstract, monumental concrete sculptures crafted by an international team and erected along a seventeen-kilometer stretch of the southern Periférico (the circumferential highway around the capital) named the "Route of Friendship"; they straddled both sides of the Olympic Village. Avery Brundage, then president of the IOC, expressed hope that Mexico's expansive cultural program would mark a return to "the purity, beauty and simplicity" of the Olympic tradition.

Perhaps observers realized that this would be a special Olympic event when, at the opening ceremony, Norma Enriqueta Basilio, a twenty-year-old hurdler, became the first woman in Olympic history to bring the Olympic torch, which had entered the country through Veracruz, into the stadium and carry it up ninety-two steps to light the Olympic flame, a feminist prize even Brundage applauded.

Across the Games themselves, almost certainly the altitude did enhance performance, especially at the shorter racing distances and in field events, as well as among athletes who had trained extensively far enough above sea level; it often hampered those who had not. The sport that seemed to suffer most from the thin air was rowing, in which oxygen resuscitations were required on at least sixteen occasions. Still, uneven times and distances by athletes regardless of where they trained suggests a psychological dimension as well. For whatever combination of factors, these Games witnessed some remarkable feats, as 252 competitors surpassed previous Olympic records in those sports that can meaningfully be measured precisely in time, weight, or points. In total, competitors matched or surpassed twenty-four world and fifty-six Olympic records.

It was in track and field that so many records fell; only twelve of thirty-eight track and field competitions failed to tie an old or produce some new record. Besides the altitude, performances were surely improved by the new, all-weather synthetic track, called Tartan by the 3M Company, which developed and manufactured it. Its surface maintained uniform toughness and even resiliency, did not rut, and was impervious to weather. Competing mainly at the Olympic Stadium, men and women track and field participants combined to equal or exceed seventeen world and twenty-six Olympic records. In the five long-distance running events (1500 meters and up) athletes from Ethiopia, Kenya, and Tunisia swept the gold medals, demonstrating both the benefit of their longtime mountainous training and the increasing importance of their continent in the global sports arena. Highly acclaimed was Kipchoge "Kip" Keino (Kenya), whose 3:34.9 in the 1500 meters easily beat the Olympic record of Herb Elliot (Australia) and, in this race, his closest competitor, Jim Ryun (United States), by almost three seconds and twenty yards.

Surely the most spectacular of the records was set in the long jump. First the United States' Ralph Boston barely reached the world record in a qualifying leap on his way to a bronze medal. The next day he watched in amazement as the at-times erratic but recently very successful Bob Beamon, who had won twenty of his last twenty-one meet competitions, reached the incredible distance of 29-2 1/2, almost two feet over the existing record (27-4 3/4), setting a mark that lasted some twenty-five years. It was a humid, overcast day, ideal for the long jump, yet only Beamon put together the moves for so shattering an improvement.

Although aided some by the thinner air and lower gravitational force, Dick Fosbury and numerous pole vaulters, such as the United States' gold medal winner Bob Seagren, likewise benefited from new technologies and revised techniques. Gold medalist Fosbury forever changed high jumping with his head-first, stomach-up, flat-body leap, the "Fosbury flop," made less dangerous with the placement of a thick foam-filled landing pad instead of the traditional sand or sawdust pit; he won with a height of 7-4 1/2 feet. The vaulters at last learned to take advantage of the fiberglass poles introduced a few years earlier to rise to new standards. Nine men cleared the historic Olympic barrier of seventeen feet; Seagren won at 17-8 1/2. Less heralded but equally admirable was Al Oerter's fourth consecutive Olympic record and gold medal in the discus throw, a result of hard work and concentration.

In addition to the official Mexican desire to promote the host country and its willingness to spend for that purpose, the larger political atmosphere encroached on the Games in several ways, though local student activists who had generated such emotions over the previous two-and-one-half months were absent, due perhaps to a lack of organization, a fear of government brutality, or a sense of nationalistic interest in seeing the Games succeed; it will probably never be known for certain which determined the lack of further protest. What is certain is that spectators vigorously welcomed the Czechoslovak delegation and adopted as one of their special objects Vera Caslavska, its highly talented gymnast who became the symbol of suffering under Communist aggression and, perhaps more generally, of small country resistance to great power domination. While

Caslavska could never drive the Soviets from her homeland, she, her fans, and her countrymen could take pride in her outstanding performance: four gold and two silver medals and the individual title, topping three Soviet stars and two East Germans. Even some other Communist athletes cheered her on. After competing in three Olympics (1960, 1964, 1968), Caslavska was the recipient of seven gold and four silver medals.

Perhaps the most controversial and remembered political statement was that made by Tommie Smith and John Carlos of the United States. Teammates from San Jose State College, they had considered the suggestion of activist sociologist Harry Edwards to boycott the Games to protest mistreatment of blacks and denial of their human and civil rights and had helped him organize in 1967 the Olympic Project for Human Rights (OPHR). Eventually they chose to attend, though basketball great Lew Alcindor (later Kareem Abdul-Jabbar) did not, but still sought a way to express their deep convictions. They got their chance when, respectively, they won gold and bronze medals in the 200-meter sprint. On the victory stand, during the National Anthem, the two bowed their heads, closed their eyes, and raised their arms straight up, Smith's right and Carlos's left fist covered by black gloves, in the well-known Black Power salute; their shoeless feet showed only long black socks, a symbol of black poverty. For this act they were suspended from their national team and expelled from the Olympic Village. Silver medalist Peter Norman of Australia sympathetically wore during the awards ceremony a badge supporting the OPHR that he received in advance from Smith and Carlos.

As the two militants were preparing to depart Mexico, three of their black teammates, medal winners in the 400-meter final, expressed their sympathy by donning black berets when entering to receive their medals. After winning the 4x400 meter relay, those three and a fourth runner mounted the victory stand, left hands under their jackets, saluted, and assumed the military at-ease position during the playing of the Star-Spangled Banner. Bob Beamon later demonstrated his solidarity by wearing black socks while trying another jump following his record leap.

Whether the appeal of 1936 Olympic hero Jesse Owens for black moderation mattered or not, not all of the United States' blacks at the Games chose to protest. Wyomia Tyus impressively won the 100-meter sprint, becoming the first woman to win consecutive Olympic sprint titles, and later helped the 400-meter relay team to a gold medal, yet took no political action. Houston's George Foreman not only opposed the protest effort but personally marched around the ring waving a small U.S. flag after winning the gold medal in heavyweight boxing. Others may just have remained silent out of fear of retaliation or because of money offers from sports companies.

After the Games had ended and the foreign athletes and media had departed, Mexicans assessed the impact of that unique spectacle. Official reports indicate that expenditures were higher than those of Rome (1960) but well below those of Tokyo (1964). The total outlay in U.S. dollars was $175,840,000 (93.9% spent within Mexico): $53.6 million for sports installations; $16.56 million for city works, $16.08 million for athlete housing in the Miguel Hidalgo Olympic Village; $12.72 million for accommodations for the cultural delegations in the Narciso Mendoza Village; and $76.88 million for Organizing Committee direct expenditures. All but the last item represented investments in permanent constructions to benefit the city and country in the future and were spent in conjunction with various government agencies (e.g., Ministry of Public Works and Department of the Federal District).

To cover these costs the Organizing Committee derived income from a range of sources: The Mexican Government provided a subsidy equivalent to $56,816,000 U.S. dollars; Committee activities, including ticket sales, brought in an additional $20,064,000. Of the latter, $6.41 million derived from international television rights—ABC alone paid $4.5 million for the U.S. market and sent a staff of 450 to handle production and transmission—$3.89 million more from foreign services and royalty payments, while an additional $9.76 million came from local television rights, concessions, royalties, services, and contributions of in-kind goods and services by various private companies. To carry out its work the Organizing Committee for a brief period in October 1968 employed as many as 14,000 people, though the number was generally much less before September and dropped rapidly afterward. Independent of the Committee, expenditures of the participating nations were estimated at over two million dollars.

For this outlay Mexicans received not just the pleasure and profit of the Games themselves. In theory they indirectly benefited from the increased spending by visiting teams and tourists and an increase in tax collections. They also inherited a technologically superior television and communications system, a few pre-Hispanic archaeological ruins exposed during construction, housing units in the two abandoned Villages, numerous works of art created especially for the occasion and left for public enjoyment, an improved athletic infrastructure, vast experience in organizing and conducting an elaborate global festival, and a sense of national achievement and pride. Simultaneously, Mexicans cheered their largest Olympic squad ever, 300 athletes in eighteen specialties, who gave their country its best results ever: three each of gold, silver, and bronze medals. It was hoped thereby that they did in fact improve their country's international image and stimulate long-term tourism and economic activity.

Surely they paid a price, at Tlatelolco and in government spending. For many, apparently, it was a price worth paying. Unfortunately, Mexico has not since matched its athletic performance of 1968, winning infrequently at later Games; even with extensive help from Cuban coaches and advisers they won only four medals total at the last three competitions of the century. At Sydney in 2000 they improved to six: one gold (in women's weightlifting; the first gold since 1984), two silver, and three bronze. Tied to this athletic stagnation has been apparent incompetent administration of the national sports system and a deterioration of the facilities built or upgraded in the 1960s.

Despite the alarming warnings, threatening outside forces, and obstacles within Mexico City, in the words of Bob Phillips, writing in the British report on the Games: "The ultimate winners of the Games were the Mexicans themselves, and their organisation at every venue was virtually beyond criticism." These Games were, in short, "the biggest and the best" since the Olympics were revived in the modern era. It is hard to disagree.

Bibliography

Primary sources and selected printed materials related to the Mexico City Games are located in the research center of the International Olympic Committee in Lausanne, Switzerland, and in the Avery Brundage Papers in the archives of the University of Illinois at Champaign-Urbana. In Mexico the archives of the organizing committee are in the Archivo General de la Nación. Additional materials may be consulted at the Centre for Olympic Studies, University of Western Ontario in London, Ontario, Canada.

Among the published sources the place to begin is Beatrice Trueblood, ed., *Mexico 68* (1969), prepared by the Organizing Committee of the Games of the XIX Olympiad as its final report. Available in English, the four volumes cover, in order: The Country, The Organization, The Games, and The Cultural Olympiad. Before and during the Games the same entity published *Noticiero Olímpico* to communicate to the public its plans and scheduled events.

Additional insights into the construction projects completed for the Games are found in Barclay F. Gordon, *Olympic Architecture: Building for the Summer Games* (1983). A brief analysis, with numerous photographs, of one of the lasting cultural projects tied to the Games, is found in Karel Wendl, "The Route of Friendship: A Cultural/Artistic Event of the XIX Olympiad in Mexico City, 1968," *Olympika: The International Journal of Olympic Studies* VII (1998), 113–34. Brazilian experts look at the construction and other "technical" and "scientific" aspects of sports performance in Mexico in Arthur Orlando da Costa Ferreira et al., *Olimpiada-Mexico 68*.

For discussions of the contemporary political atmosphere in Mexico, especially the student protests of 1968 and the government excesses at Tlatelolco, consult Barry Carr, *Marxism and Communism in Twentieth-Century Mexico* (1992) and Elena Poniatowska, *Massacre in Mexico* (1975). More on the Mexican context of the 1960s is found in Ariel

Rodríguez Kuri, "El otro 68: política y estilo en la organización de los Juegos Olímpicos de la Ciudad de México," *Relaciones 76*, XIX (Autumn 1998), 109–29.

A consideration of how the 1968 Olympics fits into Mexico's long-term sports policy and its connection to larger domestic and foreign affairs is offered by Joseph L. Arbena, "Sport, Development, and Mexican Nationalism, 1920–1970," *Journal of Sport History* 18 (Winter 1991): 350–64. Armando Satow traces the expanding role of Mexico in the Summer Olympics in a series of twelve articles published in July 1980 in the Mexican newspaper *Uno Más Uno*. Mexico's long-term failure to build on its medal success of 1968 is highlighted in Francisco Ponce, "Después de los Juegos Olímpicos el gobierno no ha hecho nada," *Proceso*, 1147 (October 25, 1998), 75–76; Fabiola Zamorán, "Las ruinas olímpicas del 68," *Proceso*, 1244 (September 3, 2000), 90–91; and Mauricio Mejía, "México nunca aprovechó el entusiasmo de los Juegos de 1968," *Proceso*, 1244 (September 3, 2000), 92.

To put the Mexico City Games into the context of modern Olympic history, consult Allen Guttmann, *The Olympics: A History of the Modern Games* (Urbana, IL: University of Illinois Press, 1992) and Kristine Toohey and A. J. Veal, *The Olympic Games: A Social Science Perspective* (New York: CABI Publishing, 1999). Also check the Findling and Pelle volume cited on p. 133 in which an earlier version of this chapter first appeared. A critical view of recent Olympic administration is offered by Helen Jefferson Lenskyj, *Inside the Olympic Industry* (Albany: State University of New York Press, 2000).

Useful descriptions and analyses by foreign observers come from Bob Phillips, ed., *Official Report of the Olympic Games* (1968), a British document; Francisco Echeverría and José María Múgica, eds., *Juegos Olímpicos-Mexico 68* (1968), a Spanish summary; and Caetano Carlos Paioli, *Brasil Olímpico*, another Brazilian outlook. A more critical British perspective of the altitude and facilities at these "unfair" Games is found in Cristopher Brasher, *Mexico 68: A Diary of the XIXth Olympiad* (1969).

For an understanding of the meaning of the United States black protests in relation to the Games, consult Arthur R. Ashe, Jr., *A Hard Road to Glory: A History of the African-American Athlete Since 1946* (1988), the series of retrospective pieces contained in *Sports Illustrated* 75 (August 5, 1991), and David K. Wiggins, " 'The Year of Awakening': Black Athletes, Racial Unrest and the Civil Rights Movement of 1968," *The International Journal of the History of Sport* 9 (August 1992): 188–208.

9

Sport in Cuba: Castro's Last Stand

Paula J. Pettavino and Geralyn Pye

Uruguay's hosting of the first soccer World Cup in 1930, Guatemala's holding the Central American and Caribbean Games in 1950, and Mexico's hosting of the Olympic Games in 1968 and the soccer World Cup in 1970 and 1986 all gave those governments the opportunity to draw attention to both their nation and their state. Juan Perón's friendship with various Argentine sports heroes and his support of certain teams and games, and Mexican presidential candidate Carlos Salinas's photo ops with boxing great Julio César Chávez, illustrate ways in which political leaders have made sports work for them.

In recent decades, Latin America's most obvious and most successful example of the mixing of sport and politics has been that of Cuba. Since taking power in 1959, the Castro regime has been driven to restructure the island's sports culture by several motives: ideological principles, creation of the "new man," military preparedness, gender and racial equity, public health improvement, recreation and entertainment, domestic pride in the nation, and international prestige. As Paula Pettavino (American University) and Geralyn Pye (Flinders University) point out, the elimination of professionalism and the building of an elaborate amateur sports program have often fallen short, especially in the area of popular as opposed to elite sports, yet in international competition Cuba has become a major player and at home offers more opportunities to its population than at any time in its history.

Over the last decade, Cuba has maintained its international sporting stature. At the Atlanta Olympics of 1996, Cubans won nine gold (tied for seventh) and twenty-five total medals, placing them ninth overall; from Sydney in 2000 they carried home eleven gold and twenty-nine total medals, ranking them eighth in the world. Also, Cuban representatives in baseball, basketball, boxing, track and field, wrestling, weightlifting, and volleyball at other world and regional championships have won

From *Studies in Latin American Popular Culture* 13 (1994): 165–84. Reprinted by permission of *Studies in Latin American Popular Culture*.

numerous titles despite an economy that remains weak and unbalanced, though not as desperate as it appeared in the early 1990s.

At the same time, there have been some signs of displeasure with the sports system, or at least with life in general. In part for financial reasons and in part for love of their sport, an increasing number of Cuban athletes have defected, especially baseball players, some of whom have signed lucrative contracts and won titles and awards in U.S. major league baseball, but athletes in sports with lower monetary prospects have likewise abandoned their homeland. While many athletes express love of country and sympathy with the achievements of the Revolution as reasons for remaining on the island, the Castro government has made some adjustments to placate the more disgruntled athletes and fans. However, policies remain restrictive and erratic. In short, Cuba's sports success is bought at a price that more Cubans, athletes and others, are no longer willing to pay. Nevertheless, no major changes seem likely before Fidel Castro's departure.

Castro appears more successful than most politicians in earning praise at home and abroad for his sports policies. Yet, as in most other cases—from Argentina and Brazil to East Germany and the Soviet Union—it is doubtful if in the long run those achievements can offset inadequacies in other areas of life.

In the streets of Havana today, the *gua guas* [buses] pass in fewer numbers, but spewing ever bigger clouds of dark black smoke. Unlit streets in El Centro and Old Havana add to growing problems with assault and prostitution as Cubans seek ways to obtain material goods and the dollars to buy them. Shortages of food, clothing, gasoline, and electricity have reduced Cubans' quality of life. Even "activists" in government bodies and the Partido Comunista de Cuba [Cuban Communist Party, PCC] seek out (or at the very least accept with smiles) gifts from the growing number of tourists. Workers in tourism services accept tips previously frowned upon and even hand United States dollars to visitors willing to purchase in tourist shops goods that are scarce elsewhere on the island. The few cars (mostly Russian Ladas or forty-year-old American models) seem likely to crash into the multiplying numbers of bicycles without lights in the innumerable darkened, uneven, narrow streets in the crowded Cuban capital.

Such problems may make Cubans sports achievements seem insignificant or even irrelevant. Indeed, money spent on sports is likely to be cut. Yet, practicing sports is something in which Cubans may take pride, take part, and into which they may escape, at very little expense. The Cuban sports system built up since 1959 is indeed impressive and comprehensive in both mass participation and elite performance. This article focuses on the future of sport in Cuba in the current austere economic and political environment and in Cuba after Castro.

Cuba Today—Sports: Home Run / Economy: Strike Out

The Cuban Economy

There is a joke making the rounds in Cuba. "The three main accomplishments of the revolution are, as Castro says, education, medical treatment, and sports. The three main failures are breakfast, lunch, and supper."[1]

In order to understand fully the direction of Cuban sports policy, it is necessary to explore briefly the broader economic and political situation that is relevant to recent and future developments in Cuban sports.[2] The sweeping changes that occurred in the former Soviet Union and Eastern Europe disrupted the Cuban economy and created political pressures for major reforms in Cuba. The rapid pace of change in the old socialist bloc, in combination with previously existing economic problems, made it hard to establish a clear direction in Cuban policy. The Cuban response, in practice, if not rhetoric, was to attempt to reform the economic and political structures of Cuba within a socialist framework.[3]

Decreases in sugar and oil prices in the late 1980s contributed to a twenty-five percent cut in Cuba's hard currency earnings.[4] These developments, and reductions in Cuban tobacco and coffee production, added to the burden created for the island by other international events such as the devaluation of the dollar (the main foreign currency held in Cuba), increased protectionism in the West, and the tightening of the United States economic embargo.[5] In June 1989 Cuba's hard currency reserves had plummeted to a meager total of 87 million dollars (69 million dollars in cash), which was less than six weeks' worth of imports from the West.[6]

Since the mid-1980s, Cuba has been seeking new hard currency sources through tourism and new trading partners in Asia (especially China) and in Latin America (especially Brazil).[7] Between 1986 and 1992, Cuban tourism improved substantially, although services are still slow and prices have increased.[8] At the 1991 Congress, Politburo member Carlos Lage stated that tourism had earned over 400 million dollars for Cuba.[9] Joint ventures, sanctioned since 1982, have also received renewed attention, especially in recent years.[10]

At the end of 1990 austerity measures were expanded in Cuba under the rubric of "The Special Period in Peacetime," which temporarily ended the construction of schools, day care centers, polyclinics, and houses for two to five years.[11] The measures also included cuts in availability of gasoline, reductions in the number of publications, and an expansion of the rationed goods (including foodstuffs and clothing) list. The legal parallel markets that sold goods at higher prices than rationed goods were finally closed in November 1990 after previously being restricted to luxury items.[12] Moreover, use of fuels was cut as oxen and bicycles replaced tractors and cars.[13] In a ridiculous twist of old technology leading the new, the Cuban military has adapted horse-drawn carts and tricycles to transport supplies and heavy weapons, such as antiaircraft guns.[14]

By early 1992, taxi service was virtually halted (except for tourists), television broadcasting was restricted to five hours daily, and bus services were limited. Cinemas were open but only a few hours daily or one day per week, and air-conditioning and street lighting were reduced significantly. Even nighttime baseball games were halted![15]

These cuts are indicative of the severe economic (and possibly social) crisis facing Cuba as the new decade opens. With virtually no hard currency reserves and only seventy percent of expected imports in 1991,[16] there were growing external and internal pressures for far-reaching economic and political reforms.

Cuban Sports[17]

Yet even with the Cuban economy so badly tarnished, the sports system continues to shine brightly. After the 1987 Pan American Games in Indianapolis, a Cuban newspaper headline read, "CUBA: 7.5 Medals per Million Inhabitants. USA: 0.70."[18] For the last thirty years, the irony of Cuban sport has been that an island with a population smaller than several United States cities (almost eleven million people) has achieved such an astounding measure of athletic success. Despite a limited pool of talent and a notorious weakness in certain sports, Cuba has proven itself to be a sporting powerhouse.

Before the revolution, such wild success was limited to selected sports, such as baseball and boxing. Since 1959, Fidel Castro has presided over unprecedented growth and mastery of a long list of international sports. In baseball alone, Cuba amassed a record of 63–1 in regional and world championship tournaments from 1988 through 1992. It won gold medals in the last two Pan American Games, the 1988 and 1990 world championships, the 1987, 1989, and 1991 Intercontinental Cup Games, and in Barcelona, the first ever Olympic gold medal for baseball.

In other sports, Cuba had not been tested for a decade because it boycotted the 1984 and 1988 Olympics. Furthermore, because of the United States boycott of the 1980 Moscow Olympics, Cuba had not faced United States Olympic athletes since Montreal in 1976, when Alberto Juantorena won both the 400- and 800-meter races.

Then came the 1991 Pan American Games in Havana. The United States won the most medals (352 to Cuba's 265), but Cuba took home the most gold—140 to the United States' 130. This was the first time the United States had been beaten in the gold medal tally since the Pan American Games began in 1951. In the famous national pastime of both Cuba and the United States, sixty thousand Cubans watched their undefeated national team beat "los Yanquis," 3–2.[19]

Most recently, in Barcelona, Cuba claimed a respectable sixth place in the total medal tally with fourteen gold, six bronze, and eleven silver. Of the 172 countries participating, only the Unified Team, the United States, Germany, China, and Hungary won more medals. In gold medals alone, Cuba placed fifth, with three more than Hungary.[20] Clearly, in the area of sports at least, Cuba's revolutionary government has been doing something right.

Yet, despite this glowing success, the Cuban sports system is in jeopardy. One need look no further than those same Pan American Games held in Havana—at the juxtaposition of relative poverty for ordinary Cubans with ration books and relative plenty for the athletes. Despite Cuba's overwhelming economic problems, the Cuban government still spent an estimated 24 million dollars (in hard currency) and 100 million pesos (132 million dollars) to build athletic and residential facilities for the Pan Am Games. With the average Cuban waiting in line for basic goods (even sugar), there was understandable resentment throughout the island that seventeen thousand visitors were served all-you-can-eat buffets. While Castro was doing the "wave," ordinary Cubans were queuing up for their monthly ration of ten ounces of beans, six pounds of rice, four pounds of potatoes, and twelve ounces of chicken (including the bones), plus one piece of bread per person daily.[21]

Although the anticipated demonstrations against Castro did not materialize, one United States official pointed out that Fidel may still be generally popular, but "you can't eat charisma." One graduate of the University of Havana compared Cuba and the Games to the Roman Empire. "Remember the end of the Roman Empire—bread and circuses? That's the *Panamericanos*. Only soon even the *pan* [bread] will be gone." Yet, according to Gustavo Rolle, an official with INDER, the Cuban Institute for Sports, Education, and Recreation, there is no resentment because "the Olympics are important, especially in these difficult economic times." Besides, he said, Cubans clearly understand that "athletes need more food than the average person because of their high energy consumption."[22]

Yet observers at the Games spoke of the jarring contrasts: the shiny new facilities and the backdrop of decay; the official pomp and circumstance and the undercurrents of discontent; food lines, grim faces, and the omnipresent military. It is unlikely that athletes (such as boxer Teófilo Stevenson, who said that "We are all equals in Cuban society") have to wait in bread lines or ride on a bicycle through the polluted streets of Havana.[23]

Indeed, the athletes seem to want for nothing. They have all the food they can eat and, instead of the now typical bicycle, they have cars, drivers, and houses. According to José Fuentes, manager of the Cuban national baseball team, "Our government has a general assistance [policy] for all people who are outstanding. I think the people who do the greatest effort should be the prized ones."[24]

The last decade of major political and economic changes has been reflected in changing sport policies. An increased emphasis on defense expressed in the formation of military sports clubs in the 1980s reflected new security concerns, arising from the anti-Cuban foreign policy of the Ronald Reagan and George Bush administrations and the more recent withdrawal of much Soviet support for Cuba. Economic decline probably prompted cutbacks in sports expenditures (except for the 1991 Pan American Games) and a refocusing on popular sports participation in the mid-1980s. In the near future, Cuban leaders may try to use sport to break the political isolation that they now face, but the economic crisis could force the leadership to cut back on sports aid programs, teams sent to competitions, top athletic training, and programs for mass participation in sports.

The sports system has held a special place of honor in Cuban society since 1959. Such attention has paid off in both domestic and foreign policy; now it may pay off in the more literal sense. Sport may turn out to be a moneymaker as well as an image maker. Sport in Cuba is now self-supporting. According to Cuban officials, their 120-million-dollar-a-year sports and physical education program is self-financed. Income is generated from prize money won in international competitions, from the export of sports equipment, and from the contracting of Cuban coaches (who must give half of their fee to the Cuban sports program) to rival Olympic programs. For example, in Barcelona, nine of the boxing coaches for other countries were Cuban. In volleyball, Spain had never even fielded a team before 1992, yet under Gilberto Herrera Delgado, former coach of the Cuban national team, the Spaniards made the quarterfinals. A new policy permits Cuban athletes, coaches, and sports officials to charge some foreign television crews for interviews. And other countries have helped Cuba financially in sports; the Italian government in large part financed the Cuban baseball team's trip to Barcelona. Host countries typically pay for Cuban athletes to compete.[25]

For the last three decades, sport has been used by Fidel Castro to the utmost advantage. There is little evidence that he will break this record. Indeed, Fidel, unlike his colleagues in Venezuela, Peru, and Colombia, made a rare personal appearance in Barcelona. His extended trip, conveniently coinciding with the anniversary of his 1953 attack on the Moncada barracks, which sparked the Cuban revolution, was clearly a show of power. Unfortunately for Castro, however, the propaganda value of his effort was diluted when he rushed back to Cuba (to the astonishment of his Spanish hosts) amid talk of violence and troop movements at home. The rumors were apparently the work of the passionately anti-Castro Cuban exiles.[26]

Whither Cuba?

Castro's Last Days?

The future of Cuba depends in large part on four factors: (1) Castro himself; (2) United States policy toward Cuba and the active voice of Cuban exiles; (3) Cuban relations with the rest of the world; and (4) the resolve of today's Cubans struggling to survive. The Cuban response during the Special Period, of increasing voluntary labor in order to grow more food and of declarations that socialism would be maintained even if horsepower had to be used, could have several different results. First, there could be increased repression, which might prompt intervention by the United States and/or Cuban exiles. For example, at the end of 1991, three Cuban-Americans were caught trying to infiltrate the northeastern coast of the island, armed with forty-one explosive devices. After a trial in Cuba, one was executed, the others jailed. In May 1993, nine armed exiles, members of the militant, anti-Castro Alpha 66 group, were arrested in the Florida Keys. They were equipped with hand grenades, pipe bombs, AK-47 semiautomatic weapons, and a grenade launcher.[27]

Second, it could result in the further undermining of the legitimacy of socialism within Cuba, which is already evident in the emergence of human rights activists and in the burgeoning number of legal and illegal Cuban exiles.[28] At the end of 1991, five Cubans were arrested after allegedly killing three policemen in a foiled attempt to escape the island.[29] Several human rights activists were then arrested and one dissident claimed he had been beaten.[30] The Rapid Action Brigades, begun in concert with the Mariel boatlift in 1980, stepped up their harassment of dissidents.[31]

Within the last two years, dissident activity has clearly subsided. Like everyone else in this Special Period, human rights activists must spend the better part of the day and night standing in line, walking or hiking to work (if they have a job), and scrambling just to stay alive. Such a hand-to-mouth existence leaves little time for the luxury of dissent. According to Jorge Domínguez:

> Although many abroad expected that economic hardship would increase support for opposition groups, the short-term effects of this hardship have weakened and disorganized them, making it easier for the regime to endure. . . . Cuba's would-be Boris Yeltsins have thus far been cowed. Its would-be Violeta Chamorros and Václav Havels are in prison or in Miami.[32]

Third, despite its intention to do otherwise, United States policy could be leading toward a normalization of Cuban-United States relations. And Cuban rhetoric aside, internal liberalization of some form appears certain within Cuba. According to A. R. M. Ritter, "political pluralism and economic liberalization will come regardless of President Castro's current views on the matter."[33] The embargo, so strongly supported by conservative exile groups such as the Cuban American National Foundation

(CANF), is slowly—but equitably—starving everyone except tourists, the party elite, and, of course, the athletes. Cats are available for consumption for nine pesos per pound on the black market, compared to chicken or beef (when available) for thirty-five pesos per pound. Television programs show average Cubans how to make shampoo from eggs, how to fry grapefruit peel as a meat substitute, how to use tubers and common grasses in meals, and how to make candles. Cooking oil is almost nonexistent.[34]

Yet, like the invasion at Playa Girón thirty years earlier, the United States embargo has served to strengthen the resolve of the Cuban people as well as that of Fidel Castro. The one fact all Cubans—those in Miami and those in Havana—can agree on is that they are a very proud people. Current United States policy gives to ordinary Cubans a reason to support the call for austerity and to Castro his greatest psychological asset: the United States as the enemy.[35] Unsolicited, the CANF has prepared a "blueprint for a new government that it will present to whomever takes control in the void." Ex-patriots anxious to recapture their homeland frighten Cuban listeners of Miami radio "with the prospect of the return of exiles who will demand property restitution" and threaten members of the Cuban Armed Forces with promises of Nuremburg-like trials. Such rhetoric, along with Castro's execution of General Arnaldo Ochoa, ensures continued loyalty to the Castro regime on the part of those Cubans who might otherwise be willing to oppose him.[36]

The Cuban Democracy Act (also known as the Torricelli bill) was passed in 1992, signed by President George Bush, and endorsed by then President-elect Bill Clinton. Besides deepening the bite of the embargo, foreign subsidiaries of United States companies may now be prosecuted for trading with Cuba, a move that has been "denounced worldwide as an infringement on international trade law."[37] The most stinging indictment of this policy came with the 59–3 vote of the United Nations General Assembly for the resolution calling for an end to the embargo. Before the Cuban Democracy Act, it was Castro's Cuba that was isolated internationally. Current United States policy has swung the pendulum, with the two countries trading places in international public opinion; it may limit United States influence on a post-Castro Cuba.[38] Pulitzer Prize-winning journalist Andrés Oppenheimer calls the embargo "a Miami policy instead of a Cuba policy."[39] Despite the Clinton administration's support for the status quo, recent statements by United States officials again assured Cuba that there was no plan to invade and promised to punish any attempts to do so.[40]

Significantly, the Cuban exile community has started to show signs of severe schisms. A recent joint report issued by two human rights organizations accused the Spanish-language radio stations, the Cuban American National Foundation, and the Miami City Commission of "harassing political opponents with bombings, vandalism, beatings, and death threats."

It concluded that "Ironically, in their attitude toward dissenting viewpoints, many anti-Castro Miami Cubans have a good deal in common with the regime they loathe."[41]

Even those who for decades languished in Castro's prisons have finally begun to say *¡Basta!* [Enough!]. After twenty-two years of incarceration, Eloy Gutiérrez Menoyo recently founded a group called Cambio Cubano [Cuban Change], which works toward normalizing relations with Cuba. For his efforts, he has been denounced as a traitor by exiles who oppose a change in United States policy. Former Cuban pilot Orestes Lorenzo, after the daring rescue of his family on Cuban soil, quickly became the darling of the exiles. Yet after proposing a humanitarian people-to-people outreach with Cuba, he was vilified by the Cuban-American community. He moved his family to Orlando to "avoid the volatile cauldron of Cuban-American exile politics."[42]

Internal Cuban politics has shown signs of increased liberalization—within socialism—since the late 1980s. Reforms have focused on some liberalization within the economy as well as attempts to make Cuban officials more efficient and more responsive to public demands. For example, Cuba recently announced that it is cutting the size of its armed forces. At the same time, rhetoric tends to reaffirm a commitment to Marxism-Leninism. In practice, however, Cuban policy represents pragmatic responses to the economic difficulties encountered since the mid-1980s. The president of Cuba's State Committee on Economic Cooperation, Ernesto Meléndez, recently repeated Cuba's willingness to negotiate payment for United States properties nationalized in the 1960s.[43]

In an attempt to rejuvenate the political leadership, Castro dismissed several high-ranking officials. General Arnaldo Ochoa, hero of Angola, was executed in 1989 for "drug-trafficking and corruption." Carlos Aldana, former party secretary for ideology and international relations and among the most pragmatic and open-minded of the senior leadership, was dismissed in 1991 for corruption and negligence of duty. Aldana had greatly expanded his duties within the party and the government as recently as 1989.[44]

Politburo member Roberto Robaína González appears to be profiting from the recent shakeups. The thirty-seven-year-old leader of the Communist Youth organization was named Cuba's foreign minister, apparently to his own surprise. Analysts reason that the choice of Robaína is more important domestically than internationally. "With more than 50 percent of the Cuban population under 35 and nearly 40 percent between 14 and 30, the revolution definitely needs to be responsive to the younger generation."[45] Robaína recently spoke to journalists near the entrance to the United States Navy's Guantánamo naval base about normalizing relations with the United States. Perhaps with Robaína in mind, Castro has said he might be willing to step down in five years.[46]

Certainly, none of these steps is new, but "each side is choosing to emphasize the more positive aspects of its existing policies."[47] Cuban-United States relations may be on the verge of change.

The Collapse of the Socialist Bloc and Cuban Sports

The general economic situation and the radical changes in Eastern Europe and the Soviet Union make it likely that Cuban spending on sports will be reduced. Sport, as acknowledged by President Castro, is considered important but not first priority. Cuba is now forced to focus on meeting the most basic needs of its population. It is unlikely that Cuba will receive the (subsidized) technical and sports training facilities previously available to it from the socialist bloc, unless paid for in hard currency. This factor, together with the reduction of the sports equipment trade, has serious implications for Cuba's future capacity to maintain mass participation and top-level sports.[48] It will also make it difficult for Cuba to continue supporting sports development in other less developed countries, which may serve to increase the island's already substantial isolation.

Moreover, revelations of corruption in the former East German and Soviet sports systems, like exposures of party and state corruption in the old socialist bloc, will put increased pressure on the ideological underpinnings of political, economic, and sports structures in Cuba. The Soviet sports system, on which much of the Cuban system is modeled, came under considerable criticism during the processes of *perestroika* and *glasnost*. In 1991, contrary to official claims, only six to eight percent of Soviet citizens practiced sports.[49] Coaches and members of the Soviet Olympic Committee have been critical of policies that placed no emphasis on mass participation and concentrated on Olympic sports. The Committee allegedly used hard currency winnings from Soviet athletes (eighty percent of top athletes earnings[50] or about 100 million dollars) on foreign trips and bonuses for officials traveling overseas. Top athletes have sought to end this practice of hard currency winnings going into state coffers, with some tennis players merely ignoring these rules in recent years.[51]

Probably more threatening to Soviet sports strength (and most instructive for Cuba) was the decline of resources for sports and the exodus of athletes and coaches for the "riches" of professional sports in the West. Soccer players, a gymnastics coach, and water polo players are among former Soviet athletes who have left the Soviet Union.[52] The world record holder in the pole vault, Sergei Bubka, has also stated his intention to move to France, although he competed on the Unified Team at Barcelona.[53] In the meantime, he represents the Nike corporation and runs his own athletic school in Berlin.[54] Once-famous and well-funded sports clubs and schools are faced with shortages of money, equipment, and even food.[55]

Ethnic wars in the former republics of Moldova, Georgia, Armenia, and Azerbaijan blocked access to several important training sites. The gymnastics team, which shone in Barcelona, claimed to owe its success to the Italian Olympic federation, which hosted the Soviet team in the resort town of Porto San Giorgio. According to Vitali Scherbo, who won a record six gold medals, "Training facilities were excellent, the best we'd ever seen. It was an island of stability that helped us relax and concentrate on the Games."[56]

The Athletics and Soccer Federations have broken away from the centralized Soviet Sports Ministry *(Gosport)*, although seven percent of their earnings are still sent to *Gosport*. In athletics, competitors give ten percent of their earnings to the Athletics Federation. A gymnastics training center offers training camps for children from the United States for one hundred dollars per day.[57]

Although Cuban sport is not experiencing the same degree of turmoil, these developments in the USSR may well be repeated in Cuba should socialism begin to unravel there. It seems likely that some athletes would prefer to receive the money earned from their sporting efforts. René Arocha, a Cuban pitcher currently playing for the St. Louis Cardinals, claims that all Cuban ballplayers want to play in the United States. With a monthly salary of 230 pesos, players, unlike coaches and trainers, said Arocha, could not buy cars now nor could they purchase one at a discount upon retirement, as had been the case in the 1970s.[58] Allowing athletes to earn money from their sports could provide a source of valuable hard currency for the beleaguered Cuban regime. In 1991 there were frequent rumors that this practice would soon be permitted, but there so far have been no agreements. Moreover, in 1977, the United States outlawed the importation of Cuban baseball players and prevented baseball scouts from attending the 1991 Pan American Games held in Havana.[59]

Revelations of abuse in the former Soviet Union may prompt further reviews of Cuba's sports system and perhaps add to the current political isolation of the island.[60] Similarly, Cuba's substantial investment in high performance sports may stimulate criticisms within Cuba, especially with the intensifying economic pressures that threaten to destabilize the entire political system. Spending on elite sport is not likely to be applauded by Cubans facing increased rationing and a reduction in the availability of already limited consumer goods. Consequently, even if Cuba can survive the current economic turmoil, this situation may require not only massive cuts in the sports budget, including the diversion of athletes' earnings to other areas, but also longer working hours for less return, neither of which will serve to encourage an expansion of mass participation in sports among the island nation's population.[61] Thus far, however, there is limited evidence of a breakdown in traditional patterns within the Cuban sports system.

The Future of Cuban Sports

Yet regardless of the future of Cuban politics in either Miami or Havana, Cuban sport seems to have a life of its own. In an earlier time, sport was one area that allowed Cuba to break its circle of isolation. Now, in this era of flight from socialism in Nicaragua, Eastern Europe, and the Soviet Union itself, Cuba alone stands as a bulwark of Marxism-Leninism. Sport may once again be the precise tool for the job.

However, in this era of severe austerity in Cuba, the sports system may be one area from which Cuba could cut excess. In fact, the Cubans are being forced to do just that, even where it affects their national obsession. As the island moves further to conserve electricity, night baseball games have been canceled. Sports coverage in the newspapers has been reduced significantly because of shortages of newsprint. The main offices of INDER have had to move all of their computers into one room to save on air-conditioning costs. In addition, the shortage of gasoline recently caused the Cubans to cancel an annual bicycle race around the island. There was not enough fuel to transport the racers, staff, and their equipment during the event. The race will be replaced by an indoor competition.[62]

Yet these examples are illustrative of the Cuban ability to turn adversity into advantage, a talent finely honed for thirty years. Calling the 1991 Pan American Games a "Girón Deportivo" ["Girón Sporting Event"], Castro has almost elevated sacrifice to a virtue. Cuban foul balls, for example, are never kept by the fans who catch them, but rather returned to the field with a virtuous flourish. Baseball games have not been canceled, but are held during the daylight hours, and generally just on weekends.[63] The bicycle race was not discontinued, but rather converted into an event that used less of a precious resource. Sporting events play a tremendous role in sustaining Cuban morale; in this time of austerity, their complete cancellation would have far-reaching effects.

Cuba's leaders (and the population in general) have emphasized international sports victories as well as mass participation in sports. Almost all Cubans participate in some form of athletics at some point in their lives. In addition, the presence of outstanding athletes may inspire others to take up sports. These victories bring prestige to Cuba and demonstrate to both friends and enemies Cuba's achievements under a socialist system.

Yet Cuba has lost its ability to meet even basic human needs, much less provide sports equipment. Even Fidel, in an act of socialist anthropomorphic license, has taken to calling the now-ubiquitous bicycles valuable "daughters of the special period."[64] The Cuban sports system may be able to ease the situation. First, the system has continued to receive funding, although relatively modest, throughout the period of the revolution.

If needed, these resources, including athletes' and coaches' earnings now used to fund sports, could be redirected to more needy areas. Second, participation in sports and physical culture provides at little cost one area in which Cubans might temporarily forget their hardships and perhaps make themselves feel a little better.

Conclusion

The last decade has witnessed numerous changes in the sports policies on this Caribbean island. Currently, Cuba's leaders are hard pressed just to survive. Unless sports can be made a moneymaker through athletes' cash awards and the salaries of sports professionals overseas, it seems to be a likely and logical area in which to make cuts.

While sports may be a source of pleasure, serve as a temporary diversion from day-to-day life, and bring prestige to a country (all of which could cause Cuban leaders to seek its promotion), it is not likely to be at the top of the nation's list of priorities. Whether Cuba's leadership responds to the current crisis by a return to some form of capitalist economics, lesser reforms, or repression, economic survival will take precedence over other areas, including sport. This process is all the more likely if efforts are made to retain such social benefits as cheap education and free health services. The collapse of Castro's regime would mean a probable return to limited sports for many Cubans, depending upon who succeeds him. Likewise, an attempt to institute reforms such as self-financing of sports would probably result in a reduction of access to sports activities for less well-off Cubans. Hence, given the regime's survival and a desire to maintain mass sports, Cuba's leadership could be forced to cut its investment in elite sports even though this may reduce its ability to use sport as a vehicle for political prestige, for developing ties with potential new trading partners, and possibly for earning hard currency.

Alternatively, money earned through athletics, currently used to fund sports, may be used for more essential purposes, such as buying food.[65] The choice, if indeed there is a choice in the face of economic crisis and possible political upheavals, remains a double-edged sword for Cuba. Either elite sport suffers, bringing a loss of the prestige resulting from sports victories, or mass programs are reduced, adding to growing dissatisfaction.[66] The recent policy appears to be cuts in both areas, with the exception of spending on facilities for the 1991 Pan American Games.[67] Entry to the Games was free for Cubans and these facilities were to be opened to the public following the Games. However, such spending may provoke complaints among Cubans whose food rations have recently been reduced.[68] Neither sport nor the belief that it is a fundamental part of a well-rounded education can solve the more pressing economic and political problems that threaten to bring down socialism in Cuba.[69]

Athletes may well be asked to accept fewer privileges and to dedicate themselves even more to the revolutionary cause than is already expected. This could lead to pressures from athletes to be allowed to retain their winnings, as was recently the case in the Soviet Union. Economic and political pressures may weaken the impressive Cuban sports system, together with the varied domestic and foreign policy roles that it has traditionally played. Yet, at the same time, these same pressures could make the use of sport for political purposes more attractive to Cuba's embattled and isolated leadership.

Sports will almost certainly suffer as a result of current conditions in Cuba. If socialism disappears, it may be hard for any successor government completely to wind back the clock on physical culture in Cuba. Sport is an important part of many Cubans' lives and is clearly seen as a right of all people. As is evident in Eastern Europe and the Soviet Union, it is very easy to "throw the baby out with the bathwater." Much has been achieved in Cuban physical culture. While there are problems, the good features in Cuba's sports system would be unfortunate losses if the socialist system in Cuba collapses.

Notes

1. Douglas Farah, "Catering to Foreigners Instead of Cubans Puts Castro on Defensive," *Washington Post* (9 August 1992), A31.

2. Complete analysis of the economic and political setting has been done elsewhere. See, for example, R. P. Rabkin, *Cuban Politics: The Revolutionary Experiment* (New York: Praeger, 1991); S. Halebsky and J. M. Kirk, *Transformation and Struggle: Cuba Faces the 1990s* (New York: Praeger, 1990).

3. Discussion with Nieves Alemany (Secretary of the Cuban Women's Federation in Santiago de Cuba and a member of the Central Committee of the Cuban Communist Party until 1991) and Eva Seone Domínguez, Vice President of Instituto Cubano de Amistad de los Pueblos, at The Flinders University of South Australia with Geralyn Pye in October 1991. See also G. Gunn, "Cuba in Crisis," *Current History* 90:154 (March 1991), 104; R. Castro, "Llamamiento al IV Congreso del Partido," *Casa de las Américas* 30:180 (May–June 1990), 2–12; "Faintest Glimmers of Change," *Latin American Weekly Report* (24 October 1991), 3; Congreso del Partido Comunista de Cuba, 10–14 October 1991.

4. G. Gunn, "Will Castro Fall?" *Foreign Policy* 79 (Summer 1990): 134; M. Benjamin, "Things Fall Apart," *NACLA*, 24:2 (August 1990), 15. In 1979 the USSR paid 44 cents for a pound of Cuban sugar, which was 5 times the world price for sugar at that time. The Soviets charged Cuba $US12.80 a barrel for oil in 1979, that is, one third of the OPEC price in that year. R. Rabkin, "Implications of the Gorbachev Era for Cuban Socialism," in *Cuban Foreign Policy Confronts a New International Order*, H. M. Erisman and J. M. Kirk, eds. (Boulder: Lynne Rienner Publisher, 1991), 24. See also Jenkins, "Western Europe and Cuba's Development," in Erisman and Kirk.

5. Benjamin, 15; A. Zimbalist, "Introduction: Cuba's Socialist Economy toward the 1990s," in *Cuba's Socialist Economy toward the 1990s*, A. Zimbalist,

ed. (Boulder: Lynne Rienner Publisher, 1987), 4; A. Zimbalist, "Does the Economy Work?" *NACLA* 24:2 (August 1990): 18.

6. Further, because the Cuban debt is not held in United States dollars, the devaluation against other currencies hurts the value of the debt. N. Leon Cotayo, *Beleaguered Hope: The U.S. Economic Blockade of Cuba* (Havana: Editorial Cultura Popular, 1991), 60–61, 134.

7. Ibid., 137–38; Gunn, "Cuba in Crisis," 103. Cuban trade with Latin America in 1988 was worth $US1.33 billion; see Rabkin, *Cuban Politics*, 202. Relations between Cuba and China were fully normalized in August 1991. See "China, Cuba to Close Ranks after 30 Years," *The Advertiser* (5 August 1991), 6.

8. Workers in the tourist industry are fairly well paid (maximum = 325 pesos a month) and also have access to dollars through tips and possibly to goods in tourist shops. Workers are supposed to learn a second language by 1993 and are expected to be active revolutionaries who behave "correctly" with visitors. As jobs in tourism are now contracted for periods of a few years, workers behaving inappropriately may lose their employment. Discussions with Geralyn Pye and workers in the industry and noticeboard in the Hotel Lido, Havana, January 1992.

9. "Introducción a la discusión del Proyecto de Resolución sobre el desarollo económico, realizado por el compañero Carlos Lage Dávila," Congreso del PCC, 9.

10. Gunn, "Will Castro Fall?" 137–38.

11. Fidel Castro, Speech at the close of the 5th Congress of the FMC, 7 March 1990, in Fidel Castro, *Faithful to the Ideals of Socialism* (Havana: Editorial José Martí, 1990), 31.

12. C. D. Deere, "Cuba's Struggle for Self-Sufficiency," *Monthly Review* (July–August 1991), 60.

13. Gunn, "Cuba in Crisis," 104, 133.

14. *Cuba Internacional* (July 1992), cited in *Washington Times* (7 July 1992), A2.

15. NBC Nightly News (21 December 1991); C. Hughes, "Castro: Conditions to Worsen," *Times-Picayune* (19 December 1991), A26; "Cuba Cuts Electricity, Job Hours," *Times Picayune* (21 December 1991). Observations of Geralyn Pye, January 1992.

16. Discussion with Nieves Alemany and Eva Seone Domínguez with Geralyn Pye, Adelaide, Australia. See also S. Francis, "Awaiting a New Ally?" *Washington Times* (7 January 1992), F4.

17. For a complete treatment of sports in Cuba, see Paula J. Pettavino and Geralyn Pye, *Sport in Cuba: The Diamond in the Rough* (Pittsburgh: University of Pittsburgh Press, 1994).

18. Bill Brubaker, "Cuba's Renewed Mission: Olympic Glory," *Washington Post* (12 July 1992), D1, D6.

19. "Cuba Tops U.S. in Gold," *Times-Picayune* (19 September 1991), D1, D5; L. Hockstader, "60,000 Cubans Cheer Baseball Team's 3–2 Victory Over U.S.," *Washington Post* (12 September 1991), C1, C7.

20. "Medal Standings," *Washington Post* (10 September 1992), C8.

21. These Games were probably the major contributor to the 1991 sports budget of $150 million, a 50 percent increase on the 1988 budget, and a 12 percent increase on the 1990 budget of $117 million. Tom Knott, "Medals Won't Help This Tarnished Land," *Washington Times* (2 September 1991), D2; J. Powers, "On a Mission From Havana," *Boston Sunday Globe* (16 August 1987), 46; Spencer Reiss and Peter Katel, "The Only Dream Left Is To Get Out," *Newsweek* (12 August 1991), 38, 39; Douglas Farah, "Castro's Travels Connote a Tight Grip,"

Washington Post (27 July 1992), A10. The 1989 INDER budget was 116.2 million pesos. G. R. González González, L. Rubalcaba Ordaz, G. Díaz Cabrera, *El deporte cubano: Razones de sus éxitos* (Havana: Ediciones ENPES, 1991), 152 (hereafter referred to as *Razones)*; Warren Strobel, "Pan-Am Games Could Invite Cuban Unrest," *Washington Times* (2 September 1991), A5; George Vecsey, "Bay of Pigs Explains the Games," *New York Times* (12 August 1991).

22. Reiss and Katel, 38; Brubaker, "Cuba's Renewed Mission," D1; Strobel, A5.

23. Tom Knott, "Life Got You Down? Try Cuba's Wonders," *Washington Times* (20 September 1991), D1, D2.

24. Brubaker, "Cuba's Renewed Mission," D6.

25. Conversation between Basilio Gutiérrez and Geralyn Pye, 20 January 1992; William C. Rhoden, "You Need an Olympic Coach? Cuba May Have the Answer," *New York Times* (5 August 1992), Al, B10; Brubaker, "Cuba's Renewed Mission," D6.

26. Farah, "Castro's Travels," A10.

27. See *Plan de Alimentación* and *Plan Turquino*, Congreso del PCC, 10; Benjamin, 22; George Gedda, "U.S. Warns Exiles Not to Attack Cuba," *Times Picayune* (25 January 1992), A1; *Washington Post* (22 May 1993), A9; William Booth, "Cuban Exiles Still See War as Live Option," *Washington Post* (14 January 1992), A10.

28. Most of the human rights groups in Cuba are aligned in the Democratic Cuban Consortium (CDC) founded 4 September 1991. See *Latin American Weekly Report* (17 October 1991). On the issue of exiles, in 1990 nearly 20,000 Cubans emigrated to the United States. In 1991 some 15,000 had followed, leading the Bush administration to freeze visa applications in early August. "US Visa Policy Altered To Stem Flow of Cubans," *Times-Picayune* (4 August 1991); G. Gedda, "Castro Defies Fall of Communism," *Times-Picayune* (11 August 1991); Reiss and Katel, 38. In December 1991 a bizarre attempt to escape on a homemade swing tied to the wheel cover of a jet to Miami appeared to have been unsuccessful. "Addenda," *Washington Post* (28 December 1991), A9. Despite all this, there are still more Dominicans fleeing the Dominican Republic than Cubans fleeing Cuba. "More Dominicans Fleeing than Cubans," *Washington Times* (23 November 1992), A2.

29. Anna Husarska, "My Three Friends in Cuba," *Washington Post* (24 January 1992), A23.

30. Observations by a member of the Australian "Cruz del Sur" Work Brigade, conversations with Geralyn Pye, Havana, January 1992. See "Cuba Arrests 3 in Death of Agents," *Washington Times* (11 January 1992), A7; R. Castillo, "Exiles Are Skeptical About Bungled Cuba Mission," *Washington Post* (26 January 1992), A20; Pascal Fletcher, "Dissent Means Death, Cubans Warned," *Washington Times* (22 January 1992), A1; and C. Hughes, "Cuba Tightens the Screws on Dissidents," *Washington Times* (19 January 1992), A18.

31. Anne-Marie O'Connor, "Revolutionaries Joining Movement Against Castro," *Times-Picayune* (20 September 1992), A32; Lee Hockstader, "Own Revolution Fought by Castro's Daughter," *Times-Picayune* (15 April 1992), A15; Kevin Noblet, "Dissidents Pay Dearly To Oppose Castro's Regime," *Times-Picayune* (15 November 1992), A25; Fletcher, Al, A10; Douglas Farah, "Dissident Children of Cuba's Revolution," *Washington Post* (2 August 1992), A29, A31; Jorge Domínguez, "Secrets of Castro's Staying Power," *Foreign Affairs* (Spring 1993), 100.

32. Domínguez, 101.

33. A. R. M. Ritter, "Prospects for Economic and Political Change in Cuba in the 1990s," January 1991, unpublished paper written for the Latin American Studies Association Conference, 31.

34. A. M. O'Connor, "Cubans Start to Eat Cats as Food Rations Are Cut," *Times-Picayune* (14 October 1992); Douglas Farah, "Cubans Are Feeling Unempowered," *Washington Post* (21 December 1992), A15; Lee Hockstader, "Castro's Tenacious Talent for Survival," *Washington Post* (9 May 1992), A16.

35. Douglas Farah. "Castro Uses Stiffer U.S. Embargo To Justify Economic Straits," *Washington Post* (17 December 1992), A33, A44; Marcus Mabry, "Putting the Squeeze on Fidel," *Newsweek* (14 September 1992), 48; Steve Wulf, "Running On Empty," *Sports Illustrated* (29 July 1991), 60–70.

36. Domínguez, 103; Joan Treadway, "Hispanics Hope, Plan for New Cuba," *Times-Picayune* (date?), B1, B2; Joan Treadway, "Cubans Await Castro's Last Day," *Times-Picayune* (18 May 1992), B1, B2; Barbara Crossette, "Cuban Says Next Chief Shouldn't Be an Exile," *New York Times* (8 November 1992), 8; William Tucker, "Can Cuba Have a Velvet Revolution?" *Forbes* (21 January 1991), 54–56; Scott Sleek, "Mr. Mas Goes to Washington," *Common Cause Magazine* (January/February 1991), 37–40; George Gedda, "Tunnels: Cubans Dig Deep in Fear of Invasion," *Times-Picayune* (9 May 1992), A26.

37. Peter James Spielmann, "U.N. Panel Condemns U.S. Embargo on Cuba," *Times-Picayune* (24 November 1992), A10. Shawn Miller, "Castro's Cuba: Time to End the Embargo?" *Insight on the News* (23 May 1993), 8.

38. The vote also carried 71 abstentions, with only Israel and Romania aligning with the United States. Domínguez, 103, 104. Mabry, 48. Tom Carter, "Some Say U.S. Embargo Keeps Castro in Power," and Tom Carter, "Differing Dissident Harassed in Miami," *Washington Times* (9 August 1992), A9.

39. Miller, 7–14, 26–29.

40. "Cuba Says 'Adios' to Russian Troops, Cuts its Military," *Washington Times* (16 June 1983), A75.

41. "Rights Groups: Cuban Exiles Harass Foes," *Times-Picayune* (5 September 1992). See also Louis A. Pérez, Jr., "Cuba, Cubans, and the Climate of Intolerance," *LASA Forum* 23:4 (Winter 1993), 1, 3–6.

42. Tom Carter, "Lorenzo's Soil," *Washington Times* (18 May 1993), E1, E5.

43. "Cuba Trims Military, Seeks Talks." *Washington Post* (16 June 1993), A25; "Cuba Says 'Adios' to Russian Troops, Cuts Its Military," A7. See also Geralyn Pye, "Cuba: Prospects for the 1990s," *Current Affairs Bulletin* 69:8 (January 1993), 18–26.

44. Domínguez, 100; "Third Most Powerful Leader in Cuba Booted From Office," *Times-Picayune* (25 September 1992), A19.

45. Mimi Whitefield, "New Foreign Minister Climbs Ladder in Cuba," *Times-Picayune* (1 April 1993), A24; Hugh Davies, "Castro Protege Attempts To Save Collapsing Cuba," *Washington Times* (13 April 1993), A9.

46. "Cuba Seeks Talks on Normalizing U.S. Ties," *Times-Picayune* (13 May 1993), A6.

47. Gillian Gunn, quoted in "Cuba Says 'Adios.' "

48. Since 1988, imports of sports equipment from COMECON countries have fallen substantially. *Razones*, 152.

49. Ibid.

50. C. Brennan, "Mighty Red Star is Dimming," *Washington Post* (16 June 1991), A23.

51. V. Sysoyev, "Push for Olympic Gold Brings Drop in Sports Participation," *Survey* 133:5 (June 1990), 14, 16; "Champions Call for Sacking of Soviet State Sports Committee," *Survey* 12:9 (October 1989), 16.

52. Brennan, "Mighty Red Star," 6; "Official Says Soviet Sports Not Bankrupt," *Washington Times* (25 June 1991), D6, D7 notes. See also Christine Brennan, "Playing Catch-Up in a New Arena," *Washington Post* (18 June 1991), A14; Demak,

"Do Svidaniya Goodbye—Maybe—to the Great US-USSR Sports Rivalry," *Sports Illustrated* 75:11 (9 September 1991), 9; William Drozdiak, "A Team Unified by Individual Goals," *Washington Post* (4 August 1992), A1, A6. See also "Soviets Unite for Olympics," *Washington Post* (13 September 1991), F1.

53. Brennan, "Mighty Red Star," A23.

54. Drozdiak.

55. One club in Liebsk was forced to grow flowers and vegetables for sale in order to raise money to pay for a recreational park. Ibid.

56. Ibid.

57. C. Brennan, "Factory of Dreams Put in New Light," *Washington Post* (17 June 1991), A15. At a gymnastics competition in the U.S., Soviet coach Leonid Arkaev and gold medalist Dmitri Bilozerchev had a verbal fight over monetary winnings. C. Brennan, "For Soviet Athletes, to the Would-Be Victors Go the Sports," *Washington Post* (17 June 1991), A5.

58. See B. Brubaker, "Baseball Scouts Ready to Slide into Cuba," *Washington Post* (4 August 1991), D1, D10; Steve Wulf, "Sports People: René Arocha" *Sports Illustrated* (19 April 1993), 60; Tom Weir, "Arocha is Proof that Cuba Teems with Big-Time Talent," *USA Today* (7 June 1993), 7C.

59. Ibid.; "No Scouts, Please," *New York Times* (13 August 1991).

60. M. Janofsky, "Cubans Concerned about Definitions," *New York Times* (5 August 1987). Reviews of INDER have occurred several times. See particularly the highly self-critical 1987 Report. See J. Caminada, "Recuento de un análisis," *El Deporte* 20:203 (March 1988), 8.

61. Work hours have been cut to save electricity, but there is pressure to do more voluntary work. This work is often labor intensive because of the lack of petrol and spare parts for agricultural machinery.

62. NBC Nightly News (21 December 1991); C. Hughes, "Castro: Conditions to Worsen," *Times-Picayune* (19 December 1991), A26; "Cuba Cuts Electricity, Job Hours," *Times-Picayune* (21 December 1991). Interview with Orestes Vega, head of the INDER Section for Sports Automation, by Geralyn Pye, Havana, 24 January 1992. "Cuban Bicycle Race Runs Out of Gasoline," *Washington Times* (6 January 1992), A2.

63. Conversation between Gisela Labnada, ICAP, and Geralyn Pye, 24 January 1992.

64. Anna Husarska, "Soft Cell," *The New Republic* (27 January 1992), 15.

65. Conversation between Basilio Gutiérrez and Geralyn Pye, 20 January 1992. See also Bill Brubaker, "Cuba's Renewed Mission," D1, D6.

66. Dissatisfaction appears to be growing, especially among Cubans aged 15–30. This discontent is expressed through public drunkenness, money changing, prostitution or pimping, and requests to tourists for gifts. Observations by Geralyn Pye, Havana, 1988 and 1992. Crime was also a topic of some concern at the IV Congress of the PCC. The link between economic decline and rising crime seems evident in the fact that in 1990, 60 percent of crimes were property related. Gail Reed, *Island in the Storm: The Cuban Communist Party's Fourth Congress* (New York: Center for Cuban Studies, 1992), 96.

67. From 1987 to 1990, INDER budgets grew only slightly, from 112.3 million pesos to 117 million pesos. *Razones*, 152.

68. See George Vecsey, "Pins Are Toppling, Even If Castro Isn't," *New York Times* (11 August 1991), 8S; Benjamin, 15.

69. Conversation between Basilio Gutiérrez and Geralyn Pye, Havana, 20 January 1992; K. Hart, "Will Cuba Follow the Kremlin's Example?" *Swiss Review of World Affairs* 14:1 (April 1991), 10; Gunn, 104.

10

The Failure of Caribbean Integration: Lessons from Grassroots Basketball

Jay R. Mandle and Joan D. Mandle

The post-World War II world has witnessed the creation of many new, postcolonial nations. They may meet the nationalistic aspirations of their citizenry, but some of them are so lacking in the attributes of modern development or so small (ministates, if you will) that they find themselves marginalized both politically and economically. Consequently, leaders have searched for a solution to this problem through integration, joining other countries in order to form larger and more viable entities. One of the best examples of the effort to undertake this process has been in the Caribbean, especially among former British colonies. There, because of such common factors as language, culture, and history, it was thought that the chances for integration were bright. This prediction, however, has not been fulfilled.

Jay and Joan Mandle of Colgate University ask why this is the case and seek the answer through a study of basketball, one of the most popular and universally practiced sports in the region. If anything reflects attitudes and actions toward outsiders among a nation's populace, they assert, it should be international sports competition. Indeed, contrary to the conventional wisdom that such activities, despite the heat of the immediate competition, bring countries and their peoples together (one of the principal rationales for holding the Olympic Games), the Mandles find that the opposite is true for the Caribbean. There, they claim, contests among West Indian nations reflect a lack of interest and organization and even antiforeign attitudes. Moreover, inter-Caribbean basketball is further undermined by modern communications; many people pay more attention to the game as played in the United States, from where the sport is easily accessed via satellite television, than they do to that of their own region.

From *Studies in Latin American Popular Culture* 13 (1994): 153–64. Reprinted by permission of *Studies in Latin American Popular Culture*.

Writing in the aftermath of the 1962 collapse of the West Indian Federation, W. Arthur Lewis argued that "the case for West Indian federation is as strong as ever."[1] Despite the merits of this case, however, Caribbean regional integration has generally been an exercise in frustration. Subsequent attempts at regionalization have been disappointing. A Caribbean Free Trade Area (CARIFTA) was established among three countries in the region (Antigua, Barbados, and Guyana) in 1965, and nine years later the creation of an expanded Caribbean Common Market (CARICOM) deepened both economic and noneconomic regional cooperation. Even so, a group of experts commissioned by the region's heads of governments in 1980 concluded that "while some modest gains were made in the area of trade and functional cooperation, very little progress was made towards the achievement of major objectives."[2] Even more recently, Ramesh Ramsaran stated: "more than seven years after the expert group reported, there has been little improvement in the situation on both the economic and functional fronts."[3] Attempts at subregional integration such as the Organization of Eastern Caribbean States (OECS) also have experienced only limited gains in bringing together the islands of the Eastern Caribbean.

Yet as Anthony Payne has written of the Anglophone Caribbean, "the history of intraregional relations has come to acquire a schizophrenic character, exhibiting simultaneously the stamp of integration and fragmentation."[4] As if in confirmation of Payne's characterization, even as hopes for CARICOM and the OECS fade, new efforts at regional cooperation arise. In recent years the prestigious independent, though government-sponsored, West Indies Commission has held hearings throughout the region promoting integration and has issued a well-regarded report emphasizing the need for Caribbean nations to cooperate more closely.[5] Thus, despite the failure to overcome the parochialism of the nations in the region, the vision of a West Indian nation has not disappeared.

In this paper we explore the problems and opportunities of Caribbean integration as seen from the grass roots. We do so because it may not be possible to understand fully the contradictory dynamics at work in the region on this issue at the macro social level. For as Gordon K. Lewis wrote of the West Indian politicians who were involved in the failed Federation, they simply reflected the "basi[c] general prejudices of their electorates."[6] The problem therefore in accounting for the failure of the Federation and the limitations of other more recent efforts at integration lies in the nature of popular sentiment on the issue of regionalization rather than in the shortcomings of individual politicians.

The sources and content of political opinion at the grass roots are never easy to study or analyze. But an examination of the everyday lives of the Caribbean people, including aspects of their popular culture, may provide insight into attitudes concerning issues such as regional integration. In this way, we may be able to identify not only the level of regionalist support, but also the mechanisms that give rise to these sentiments in the West Indies. Our working assumption is that, to be successful, the kind of nation building which the theorists of regional integration have in mind must ultimately be attractive to the women and men of the Caribbean in their everyday lives.

In this study, we take as our vantage point the basketball leagues and communities of the nine nations of the Commonwealth Caribbean in which we have done participant-observation research since 1985.[7] Basketball is a form of popular culture which is growing rapidly in the Caribbean, especially in poor, grassroots communities. In volunteer-run leagues throughout the region, literally thousands of women and men play, watch, administer, and coach the game, and Caribbean basketballers have high aspirations for the continued growth and development of their sport.[8] Basketball therefore can serve as a useful laboratory in which to explore integration's attractiveness. To the extent that the participants in this grassroots activity find in integration a source of assistance and growth, the nation-building process can look to them for support. The opposite, too, is the case. If integration is either harmful or irrelevant to the aspirations of regional basketballers for the sport's development, then limited acceptance of regionalization can be expected from them. Our hope is that by exploring in this form of popular culture the microfoundations of either support or opposition to integration, we might cast light on the more general process of regional nation building.

Specifically, we analyze whether and how Caribbean fragmentation impedes the basketball community from achieving its desired ends. We then examine why a regionalist perspective is all but absent among this constituency. The costs and limited potential of federation are identified, and these then become the variables which account for the fact that most Caribbean basketballers are unenthusiastic about an integrationist perspective in the area of popular culture that interests them.

In principle, the regional integration of basketball might be attractive to its participants because it could better provide both the financial resources and motivation necessary to accelerate the sport's development. A centralized regional basketball structure might make fund-raising more efficient. To date, local Caribbean leagues and teams have been unable to raise the funds they need, and everywhere basketballers complain about problems resulting from severe financial shortages. Furthermore, throughout the region today leagues appear and collapse rapidly, thereby discouraging even strongly motivated donors from contributing to the sport. With the creation of an accountable central authority that would take fund-raising as part of its responsibility, both private and public donors might be more forthcoming than they are at present.

In addition, integration could facilitate a more rational allocation of those resources which are available to basketball. Because at present there are multiple decision-making units in basketball, it is impossible to ensure that resources are deployed in a way that maximizes their usefulness to the sport. A centralized structure could formulate a regional plan for basketball and provide training programs for players, coaches, officials, and administrators. Such activities could be arranged for locations that lack the resources to undertake them without assistance. Funding might also be provided to develop the sport in secondary schools, in that way contributing to the long-term development of basketball. Finally, the additional resources could be used to remunerate participants. By reducing the opportunity costs of basketball participation, such rewards might augment the number of talented athletes willing and able to participate in the sport.

Just as important as the providing of money, integration in basketball might also advance the quality of play through enhanced regional competition. The limited intra-Caribbean competition that exists at present quite clearly brings the best out of basketballers. The fevered pitch of excitement that occurs when, for example, arch-rivals St. Kitts and Antigua play each other, contrasts with the lower level of intensity that prevails in league play within either country. Thus by increasing the opportunity for regional play, integration might very well result in the development of skills which otherwise would lie dormant.

At present, however, the weaknesses of existing regional organizations such as CARICOM and the OECS have meant that the advantages associated with integration have only minimally been available to basketball. Occasional regional basketball tournaments stand as the sole exception to this pattern of neglect. But even with regard to these the experience has not been satisfactory. Although mandated as an annual tournament, in the thirteen years since its inception only nine CARICOM Basketball Championships have been held. The most recent competition, scheduled for the Bahamas in 1992, was one of those canceled at the last minute. Many of the tournaments' problems can be traced to the fact that, despite its name, the CARICOM Secretariat assumes no financial or organizational responsibility for this activity. Rather, CARICOM Championships are organized by a volunteer committee composed of elected representatives from participating national basketball federations. Unfortunately, communication among participants is inadequate, committee meetings infrequent, and funding insufficient. As a result, the tournaments have typically been poorly organized and their problems legion.

Often there is great uncertainty concerning both the dates and locations of the tournaments, and this confusion tends to reduce the number of participating nations. Thus, for example, in 1990, only five teams traveled to Trinidad and Tobago to play in the CARICOM Championship, largely because even the Trinidad organizers were uncertain up until the very last moment that they would be able to host the event. Other problems are equally serious. Since many of the smaller Caribbean countries find it difficult consistently to finance their national teams' travel outside the country, their participation is erratic. Athletes at the games constantly complain about the tournaments' inadequate food and accommodations, poorly trained officials, and inefficient transportation. Crowd control, too, is often a sore point, with disruptions sometimes occurring, as at one tournament where disgruntled fans threw bottles and chairs onto the court.

Basketball tournaments sponsored by the OECS are somewhat more frequent and do tend to be marginally better organized than the CARICOM events. This superiority is the consequence of the fact that the subregional OECS Secretariat includes a Sports Desk, a position not present in the CARICOM structure. The OECS Sports Officer works to raise funds from both private and public sources to sponsor tournaments and help support individual teams, chooses tournament dates and venues, hires referees, and coordinates with the local host committee in arranging team travel and other logistics. However, this officer is responsible for many more sports than basketball and must help to organize literally dozens of tournaments each year. As a result, he typically is able to do little more than provide for the general structure of each tournament, leaving the detailed work to local volunteers. Thus, finally, each tournament's success is dependent upon the organizational competencies of those local administrators who take on the multifaceted responsibility for arranging an event.

Not surprisingly, their performance has been uneven. Some OECS tournaments have run relatively smoothly. Others, however, have collapsed before the completion of the event. Disarray often is associated with unforeseen occurrences. A week of rainfall in Grenada in 1991 all but destroyed that year's competition. The one outdoor court available for the event flooded during much of the scheduled week of play, and the local organizers were unable to successfully arrange for an alternative site. The 1989 tournament, this time in St. Kitts, ended in chaos when the Antigua team stalked off the court during the final championship game, claiming that the referees, found to officiate the game only at the last minute, were incompetent. Most recently, at the October 1992 OECS Championship, the final game also was suspended early, this time because of uncontrolled fans. A regional newspaper described the situation as "a contentious play-off which later involved communication between the foreign ministries of the two territories [involved]."[9]

Despite its limitations, the existence of a Sports Desk in the OECS is not unimportant. It represents a commitment to the development of sports in the subregion which is lacking in the larger CARICOM. Nevertheless, that commitment has been insufficient in both financial and organizational resources, and as a result, the OECS has not significantly raised the performance level in the sport. Neither CARICOM nor the OECS, in short, has managed to establish that regional integration is capable of having a sustained and positive impact on the form of popular culture embodied in Caribbean basketball.

This failure is costly to Caribbean basketball. Because of the small population size of all of the West Indian nations, players rather quickly run out of new and exciting competitive opportunities. As a result, the development of their skills is prematurely stunted. This problem is illustrated in Tobago, an island of slightly more than 40,000 people. Basketballers in Tobago, who are proud of their thriving basketball league and which often boasts up to forty-five women's and men's teams, shared with us their concerns about the future of basketball on the island. In 1990, one informant, Pete, stated:

> We used to be able to go to Trinidad and play against their teams often. That helped us a lot because sometimes they were better than us and one of the coaches had training outside the country. But now the cost of the flight is so high we are only playing here in Tobago. The competition is not so good, there aren't too many new players, and the fans don't like so much to come and see the same thing all the time.

In Barbados as well, where there is a large and well-organized basketball association, we heard the same sentiment expressed by a longtime basketball organizer who told us, "We are stagnating. We're not going anywhere anymore because we need some better competition. The best players just can't get any better if they only play each other."

The question that arises in this context is whether, in light of the problems caused by the failure of regional integration, Caribbean basketballers themselves might become agents of change, erecting mechanisms linking the sport across the nations of the West Indies. The likelihood of such a development is not, however, determined solely by the many advantages to basketball that would seem to be associated with integration. Disadvantages and costs too are present. Indeed, it seems likely that it is these considerations that must account for the fact that Caribbean basketballers have shown little interest in building a regional basketball structure. Thus we turn to a discussion of the difficulties that tend to thwart efforts at creating an integrated form of the sport in the Caribbean.

Not surprisingly, the issues that seem to impede the regionalization of basketball are precisely the ones that are cited in the literature of the failure of integration generally.[10] These include the long-standing enmity that exists among the populations of at least some of the islands of the Caribbean, the likelihood of inequality in the distribution of the benefits derived from integration, and a dearth of the skilled organizational personnel required to construct such a structure. Each of these factors tends to raise the cost and reduce the probability of successful integration. In combination they seem strong enough to make it unlikely that an integrationist dynamic will emerge either in or from basketball.

Obviously, an effort at regional integration in basketball would be best promoted if organizers in all the countries believed that federation would strengthen the sport in their nation. But such a beneficent outcome for all is not the most likely result of basketball integration. In fact, it probably would be those countries with the weakest basketball that would benefit the most. The strongest would gain little and, when personnel and financial costs are considered, they might even be, on balance, disadvantaged by integration. If so, there is little incentive for them to support the regionalization of this form of popular culture.

This perverse outcome can be seen in the examination of two elements of integration: competition and financing. Countries where basketball is strong, as in Trinidad and Tobago or Barbados, would gain little advantage from competing against significantly weaker regional teams.[11] Conversely, that same competition against regional powers would undoubtedly help basketball in weaker countries such as Guyana, Dominica, and St. Kitts and Nevis, where players would benefit from being placed in a more competitive environment than they face at home. Compounding the problem is the fact that the strongest basketball countries are also the wealthiest in the region.[12] In a setting of basketball integration, these strong countries—particularly Trinidad and Tobago and Barbados—undoubtedly would be expected to provide a disproportionately large share of the resources that a transregional sport would require. In that case, integration will look to the basketballers of these two nations as an inequitable bargain. They would be asked substantially to finance an activity the benefits of which accrue to themselves only marginally. Under such conditions they can be expected to be reluctant to merge with other countries of the Caribbean where basketball stands at a lower level. Some of this may have motivated the rejection of the idea of regional cooperation by a veteran player in relatively affluent Barbados in 1989. "No, I really don't like the idea," he said in reply to our query. "I think Barbados should stay on its own. We'll do better that way than if we joined with other Caribbean countries."

This imbalance in benefits might not in and of itself doom integration. What does make federation appear remote is the fact that these inequalities in costs and benefits would be experienced in an environment characterized by mutual distrust among the populations of the participating units. It is difficult, of course, to measure the magnitude and impact of such attitudes. But of their existence there should be no doubt. Gordon K. Lewis, who remains the most sensitive interpreter of West Indian society, wrote of ". . . the mutual ignorance and sometimes mutual hostilities of the various island populations, even when they are all English-speaking."[13]

This hostility can show itself in seemingly unimportant incidents. At a tournament in Dominica, two Barbadian referees expressed their anger at the unwillingness of Trinidadian referees to help set up a scoring table each night in terms that far transcended the inconvenience caused by the oversight. One of the Barbadians, Sam, strongly concurred with the other's statement: "Those Trinidadians don't do anything; but that's what they're like—those people never do their fair share." We have heard these kinds of comments throughout the Caribbean as basketballers from one country make disparaging remarks about those from other islands. Worse still is that this antagonism sometimes spills onto the playing venue itself. During a regional tournament in 1992, for example, players from Antigua—even though they were losing—were mercilessly pelted by unripened mangoes thrown by Kittician boys perched on roofs overlooking the court. In this, the latter viscerally demonstrated that hostility toward the visitors and their nation that we had constantly heard expressed by both players and fans. Thus, the kind of mutually supportive environment that could facilitate regionalization in the context of inequality in the distribution of benefits simply is not present in the Caribbean.

A final factor militating against basketball's integration is the shortage of skilled organizational personnel present in Caribbean basketball associations. In some countries it is a crushing burden for basketballers to organize their own leagues and tournaments.[14] For them, the organization of a wider network of regional basketballers would be all but impossible. The experience of the CARICOM tournaments suggests that organizers available on a voluntary basis are not sufficient to sustain even so relatively simple a task as an annual tournament, let alone a much more complex level of integration. The same general pattern exists with regard to the Sports Desk of the OECS. While the individual who occupies this post is himself relatively competent, he is simply overwhelmed by the sheer number of his responsibilities and unable to supervise adequately his tournaments. Thus it is not clear that even with the best of intentions, a meaningful set of region-wide basketball activities could be adequately funded or would be within the organizational competence of basketball's administrators and managers.

Each of these problems tends to raise the cost or reduce the likelihood of success of regional integration in basketball. To the extent that they reinforce each other, the obstacles to cooperation become truly formidable.

The integration project is difficult enough on its own terms. But regionalization in Caribbean basketball involves the allocation of differential benefits and costs carried out in an environment that is structurally weak and poisoned by distrust. As such, it is hard to be optimistic concerning basketball's regionalist future.

These internal obstacles to basketball integration are reinforced by one further, external influence: the pull of the United States. While it would seem logistically and financially more advantageous to create ties among West Indian countries than to look outside the region for contact, in fact this has not been the route followed by Caribbean basketballers. From the inception of basketball in the region, the United States has exercised an important influence on the development of this popular cultural form. Opportunities to play the game against United States military personnel stationed in the Caribbean during World War II and films of and visits by the Harlem Globetrotters in the 1950s were important in the early development of the sport.[15] Furthermore, since the 1960s, almost every Caribbean country, at one time or another, has been the recipient of some United States foreign aid in the form of basketball instruction, although the level of such attention has been relatively limited. Nonetheless, Sports America, an agency of the United States Information Service, has sent basketball coaches and referees to work with the region's basketball leagues, and has even brought a few Caribbean coaches to the United States for instruction. We have ourselves encountered or heard about several Peace Corps workers who have also coached or helped out with local basketball teams during their Caribbean assignments.

But most important in establishing the influence of United States basketball in the Caribbean has been the enormous number of professional and collegiate games made available to Caribbean audiences by means of satellite television. From Barbados to the Bahamas, Caribbean basketball players and fans closely follow United States basketball. They have favorite teams and players; talk with great knowledge of standings, recruiting, and playoff prospects; and everywhere wear basketball shoes, T-shirts, and hats with logos and endorsements of National Basketball Association (NBA) teams and individual stars. Basketballers in the Caribbean frequently name their teams after those in the NBA. NBA and American collegiate rules are often used instead of or along with the international regulations that Caribbean leagues are mandated to employ, and players constantly compare themselves with and take on the nicknames of NBA superstars. The consuming interest in the NBA on the part of Caribbean basketballers was illustrated to us one evening in Tobago in 1989 when we inquired about the cancellation of an important Tobago league game. A player explained to us: "Of course we had to cancel the game. There's a NBA Championship on tonight. No one will come anyway [to the local game] 'cause they all be watching the game. Me too!"

If it were possible, most Caribbean basketballers would like even more contact with the sport in the United States than is the case at present. This is because they agree with the Antigua referee who flatly stated: "After all. United States basketball is the best in the world." Caribbean coaches are eager to receive the training and instruction available in the United States, and referees with whom we have spoken are anxious to attend instructional camps in that country. Players, of course, would like nothing more than to play their sport in its mecca. Caribbean basketball, in short, is eager to deepen its integration with United States basketball, even as it is cool to efforts at integration regionally.

The prognosis for a deepening of the relationship with basketball in the United States is, however, not good. For the simple fact of the matter is that basketball in the West Indies does not have enough to attract the sustained interest of representatives from the United States. If the region were shown to be a fertile ground for college basketball recruiters, interest would of course be high, but this is unlikely to occur, at least in the near future. Grassroots Caribbean basketballers are typically poor and poorly educated. Few graduate from secondary school, and even those who do so typically do not receive basketball instruction there. As a result, by the time players master their skills they tend to be in their mid-twenties, too old and too poorly educated to be actively recruited. In addition, the population size of the region is small. As a result the pool from which talented basketball players could be drawn is very limited. In thinking about recruiting, therefore, if only because of population size, Europe or South America likely would yield a larger corps of athletes than would the West Indies. Thus, basketball officialdom in the United States is unlikely to take much interest in the Caribbean. As a result, only a few individual West Indian basketballers can be expected to have success in breaking into basketball in the United States.

Not only is the desire for integration with the United States unlikely to be able to provide support for the development of basketball in the Caribbean, it also harms regional integration efforts. As noted above, basketballers look to the United States, not to each other, for support for the sport's development. This preference for forging ties with the United States erects yet another barrier to the development of a regionalization which could help basketball. To the extent that Caribbean basketballers focus their attention on the United States, regional basketball is viewed as a less worthy partner with which to affiliate.

We conclude pessimistically. The failure of Caribbean integration generally has severely handicapped regional basketball and thus the fulfillment of its participants' aspirations for the sport. Nonetheless, we do not believe that Caribbean basketballers in the future are likely to turn to regional integration as a means to stimulate further growth. Local organizational difficulties, imbalances in the distribution of costs and benefits, especially in the context of mutual distrust, and the weaknesses of the region's extant associations militate against such a development. The same obstacles, in short, that hamper regional integration generally seem to be at work in this sphere of popular culture. Furthermore, Caribbean basketballers' enormous interest in and, although limited, their ties with the sport in the United States further weaken their attitudes toward and the likelihood of their mounting a successful attempt at regionalization.

Thus in this area of popular culture, as in international relations generally, the nations of the Caribbean stand uncomfortably isolated. The difficulties associated with regional integration make that project unlikely, while at the same time the Caribbean's marginal status relative to the United States means that the latter will not pay much attention to it. We are forced therefore to conclude that basketball may tend to replicate the more general pattern present in Caribbean life. As in basketball, an insularity, not entirely its own doing, marginalizes the likelihood of federated activities in the region. The sport, though popular and vibrant at the grass roots, is unlikely to overcome the barriers to a regional integration that could help basketballers achieve their dreams for the further development of the sport. At present, therefore, there seems no obvious way for the people of the Caribbean to break out of the isolation that so frustrates their aspirations.

Notes

1. W. Arthur Lewis, "Epilogue," in John Mordecai, *The West Indies: The Federal Negotiations* (London: George Allen and Unwin, 1968), 461.
2. Ramesh Ramsaran, *The Commonwealth Caribbean in the World Economy* (London: Macmillan Caribbean, 1989), 171–72.
3. Ibid., 172.
4. Anthony Payne, *The Politics of the Caribbean Community, 1961–79: Regional Integration among New States* (New York: St. Martin's Press, 1980), 2.
5. Report of the West Indian Commission, *Time for Action*, 2d ed. (Kingston, Jamaica: The Press, University of the West Indies, 1993).
6. Gordon K. Lewis, *The Growth of the Modern West Indies* (New York: Monthly Review Press, 1968), 369.
7. Jay R. Mandle and Joan D. Mandle, "Basketball, Civil Society and the Post Colonial State in the Commonwealth Caribbean," *Journal of Sport and Social Issues* 14:2 (1990): 59–75.
8. Basketballers is the term that players, fans, and organizers use to refer to themselves.
9. *Jamaican Weekly Gleaner* (8 January 1993), 31.
10. Ramsaran; W. A. Lewis; Payne.
11. Mandle and Mandle.
12. Ibid.
13. Gordon K. Lewis, 18.
14. Jay R. Mandle and Joan D. Mandle, *Grass Roots Commitment: Basketball and Society in Trinidad and Tobago* (Parkersburg, IA: Caribbean Books, 1988); Jay R. Mandle and Joan D. Mandle, "Voluntarism and Commercialization in Basketball: The Case of Trinidad and Tobago," *Sociology of Sport Journal* 6 (1989): 113–24.
15. Anthony Clarke, *Basketball in Trinidad and Tobago: A Golden Era* (Trinidad: Anthony Clarke, 1991). Also, Mandle and Mandle, *Grass Roots*.

11

Sport in Nicaragua, 1889–1926

Richard V. McGehee

The decades of the 1880s to the 1920s were formative ones in terms of the adaptation and development of modern sports in Latin America. Although traditional pastimes remained part of the sport and recreational scene, particularly in rural areas and small towns, more urbanized parts of the region quickly adopted new versions imported from Europe and North America. In many cases these different worlds of sport came into conflict as society debated which ones should be practiced.

In this regard, Nicaragua was no exception, as shown by Richard McGehee (Concordia University, Austin), based on an exhaustive reading of mainly newspaper reports for the period. Its urbanites soon took part in a wide variety of up-to-date sports and related activities, largely downplaying older forms of recreation. Thus, Nicaragua demonstrates that even in a small and relatively poor nation with many political difficulties, modern sporting events of many types played an important role in socioeconomic development beginning in the second half of the nineteenth century.

In many ways, too, Nicaragua reflected development in the greater Caribbean Basin. North American business, diplomatic, and military personnel brought many sports with them, and English-language or at least English-language-based terms formed a large part of the sport vocabulary of the country. While certain sports started off with middle- or upper-class players and then spread down the socioeconomic scale, baseball became and remains the main one in Nicaragua, followed by soccer. Boxing and basketball also took on much significance.

Modern sports began developing in the late nineteenth century throughout Central America. The dates bounding this study are milestones in Nicaragua and the northern Latin American region: in 1889 baseball appeared in Nicaragua, and in 1926 the First Central American Games (the first International Olympic Committee-recognized regional "Olympics") were held in Mexico City. While the lack of sufficient information seriously limits the accuracy and completeness of a history of the development of Nicaraguan sport, the newspapers, magazines, and other archived materials that have survived bear witness to its importance.

Nicaragua experienced political turmoil during much of the period of study, intensifying in 1926. In that year there was widespread fighting, towns being first controlled by Liberals and then Conservatives. In May, Managua imposed a 9 P.M. curfew and young men probably stayed home as much as possible to avoid the "recruitment" that was going on; the city's parks and lakefront beaches were nearly deserted. The El Otro, Margot, and Variedades theaters were closed. Boxing in the Momotombo (baseball) field was suspended; its stands were falling down and horses and cows tried to graze on its little remaining grass. Soccer competition had been discontinued. Some news of the upcoming Central American Olympic Games in Mexico City was received in Managua, and it was even mentioned that Nicaragua's baseball players wanted to form a strong team to compete there. However, war conditions and the belief that Mexico was actively aiding the revolutionaries prevented Nicaragua's participation in that first IOC-recognized regional sport festival in the Western Hemisphere.

The geography of Nicaragua played an important role in the introduction and development of sports in the country. At the beginning of the century, the Caribbean coast area and much of the northern region were isolated from the more populated Pacific highlands and coastal plain. The major cities, roads, and rail lines were in the west. Although baseball, football, and basketball probably existed in the principal towns, most of the publicized competition took place among teams of Managua, Granada, Masaya, and, to a lesser extent, León, Chinandega, and Corinto. These six were the largest cities and were all connected by rail, with daily passenger service. Teams from Managua, Granada, and Masaya could easily travel by train for a Sunday game and then return home the same day.

Marines and Other American Influences

U.S. intervention in Nicaragua occurred occasionally in the nineteenth century but became chronic in the twentieth. The Marines were sent to Nicaragua to protect certain governments in power and thus stabilize desirable conditions for American business interests in the country. For that reason their presence was welcomed and defended by the government if not by the general populace. U.S. troops temporarily occupied ports on the Caribbean coast in 1909, and then from 1912 to 1933 there was a nearly continuous Marine presence on Nicaraguan soil. During this period, Americans ran the railways and collected the customs fees. From 1912 onward a force of at least one hundred U.S. Marines was stationed in Managua, in buildings and tents at the military field called the Campo de Marte. Apparently the first "international" baseball game took place in 1914, when Bóer eked out a victory over the Marines' team, Denver, which probably took its name from the U.S. warship *Denver*. Marines stationed in Managua fielded baseball teams and supplied officials for local baseball, boxing, and basketball competitions. Visiting crews from U.S. and British warships docked at the port of Corinto on the Pacific coast competed against the resident U.S. forces as well as with Nicaraguan teams. On December 30, 1920, athletes from the crew of the British cruiser *Cambrian* competed in fourteen events (most were probably track and field) against the American Marines. The Americans won thirty-six of the forty-two places, but the local reporter thought that the most interesting event was a boxing match in which a British sailor knocked out his Marine opponent in the first round. President Emiliano Chamorro attended this competition and Nicaragua's military band played. The team of Marines challenged Club Managua to a game for the July 4 celebrations in 1922, with a bet of 50 córdobas, but no report of the game was published.

American Marines served frequently as baseball umpires, but they were criticized for bad decisions and for calling balls and strikes from a position behind the pitcher. It is commonly thought that U.S. Marines brought baseball to Nicaragua and promoted its development there. Actually, the sport had arrived many years before the Marines; moreover, they apparently had little impact on promoting baseball. Their games had relatively low attendance and were reported in less newspaper space than that devoted to the principal Nicaraguan teams.

American officials, such as the director of railways and the collector of customs duties, as well as the Marines, were generally unwanted and disliked. However, when Marine ballplayers or baseball teams from warships docked at Corinto played against Nicaraguans, the atmosphere tended to be friendly and with mutual respect. Strained relations between the locals and Marines did not extend to sport events. Games were reported in a nonpartisan style, and Marines continued to be used as officials in baseball and basketball games despite a 1921 incident in which a group of Marines killed several Managua policemen and wounded a number of other people. Although probably not intended as such, the matches between Nicaraguans and Americans must have been good public relations for the United States, although the Nicaraguans enjoyed beating the Americans at their own game. There were also ex-patriot Americans such as A. W. Malcolmson, general manager of W. R. Grace & Company operations, and other foreigners who contributed to the development of Nicaraguan sport. It is likely that American sportsmen were the best ambassadors for the United States during the years of intervention.

Baseball

Unlike most Latin American nations, where soccer is king, baseball has been Nicaragua's national sport for over one hundred years. The national stadium in Managua is a baseball park. While the capital has other sport facilities such as soccer fields and tennis courts, as often as not these areas are occupied by pickup baseball games. In 1972 a terrible earthquake destroyed Managua. When the ruined buildings were dynamited and the rubble cleared away, the authorities decided not to restore the downtown area. The city was left with hundreds of acres of open fields separated by the decaying pavement of former streets and a few remaining shells of buildings. On every Saturday and Sunday these fields are the sites of neighborhood baseball games.

Why should baseball be more popular than soccer in Nicaragua? The nation's hot and humid climate is more suitable for baseball. A reporter covering a soccer game in 1917 suggested that the climate was too fierce to play halves of normal length and recommended that they be shortened to thirty-five minutes. Likewise, the baseball nation of Panama is near the equator and at low elevation. Mexico's Veracruz and Mérida, Cuba's Havana, and the Dominican Republic's Santo Domingo—traditionally strong baseball cities—are all near sea level and known for their heat and humidity.

In Nicaraguan Pablo Antonio Cuadra's analysis of his nation's preference for baseball over soccer, he mentions the factor of climate, but he prefers other, less prosaic explanations, such as the contrasting aspects of time in the two sports, the emphasis on individual play in baseball versus team play in soccer, and the fiction that baseball offers of a lonely hero who leaves his family and tours the world before returning home. Another factor in determining which sport became the more popular was the experience of Nicaraguan students abroad, who preferred schools in the United States, while Guatemalans and Costa Ricans studied in Europe.

Baseball was introduced in Bluefields, on the Caribbean coast, in 1889 and first played in Managua and Granada, two important cities of the more highly populated Pacific highlands area, in 1891. The sport's introduction in Bluefields is attributed to an American resident who wanted to lure the locals away from the cricket they had been playing. The first two teams in Bluefields had English names, Southern and White Rose. Bluefields at the time was so isolated from the western part of the country that the introduction of baseball in the west was probably a completely independent event.

Between 1888 and 1890 a Nicaraguan, David Arellano, attended St. John's College, a high school in Fordham, New York, and pitched for its baseball team. According to his great-nephew Jorge Eduardo Arellano, now director of Nicaragua's national library and archives, David Arellano even pitched a friendly game for Fordham against the New York Giants. Back home in 1891, Arellano and his brothers were active in founding a baseball team in Granada. In the same year a team was organized by the Recreation Society of Managua, a recently established club presided over by the former national president, Adán Cárdenas. The first game between these two clubs, on July 24, 1891, was pitched by David Arellano for Granada and Adolfo Cárdenas, son of the former president, for Managua.

These two teams continued home and home games until 1893. The players traveled on express trains between Managua and Grenada, where the visitors spent the night in the city's finest hotel and the losers paid for the next morning's breakfast before the visitors returned home. In 1893, during one of their customary post-game banquets, a joke turned into a battle royal among the players in the Granada hotel. The political chief of Granada forbade any further games there, and, for lack of opponents, play also temporarily stopped in Managua. According to Jorge Eduardo Arellano, the first baseball players in Granada and Managua were socially elite members of politically conservative families, but after the accession of liberal general José Santos Zelaya to the presidency in 1893, baseball's social base became more diverse.

In 1903 another alumnus of St. John's, Juan Deshón, while visiting his hometown during school vacation, introduced the American national sport to his fellow Chinandegans. Deshón returned to the United States to pitch for Cornell University and supposedly received offers to play for the New York Giants and Yankees. When he returned to Nicaragua, he organized the Titán Club in Chinandega. With Deshón as the only pitcher in the country throwing curve balls, his team remained invincible for some time.

Two baseball teams were organized in 1904 in Masaya, Japón, and Rusia. In contrast to the teams of Managua and Granada, which had good equipment imported from the United States, in Masaya, except for the catcher and first baseman, the fielders played without gloves. One of the most famous teams in Managua, Bóer, was founded in 1905 as a neighborhood club and supported by the U.S. consul, Carter Donaldson. About this same time, other new teams in Managua had the names Chicago, New York, and Manchester. The usual setting for the early games was the El Retiro field; it had no stands and no backstop, but good crowds turned out anyway. Baseball development was held up from 1907 to 1909 to devote more attention to the war with Honduras. The first organized league competition in Nicaragua was held in Managua in 1911–12 with the participation of the local teams Bóer, Manchester, Venus, Chicago, and Chile. Bóer was the winner, beginning a long tradition that would have its ups and downs but continues to the present. A former Bóer captain and pitcher founded in 1913 one of the most famous of the early teams, Managua, and it featured some of the greatest players of the time, including pitcher Chabelo Fernández and second baseman Carmen Quinto.

The year 1915 was one of baseball innovations. The first enclosed field opened, so admission to games could be charged. This was the Momotombo field in Managua, which remained the principal baseball facility in Nicaragua for many years. It belonged to and was managed by the Junta de Beneficencia, a quasi-governmental benevolent society. Income from ticket sales for sporting events was typically distributed to the competing teams after a certain percentage was taken by the junta, which used the money to help run the Managua hospital. Also in 1915 the first nationwide league play was held, featuring teams from Managua, Granada, Masaya, Chinandega, and León. Masaya combined three earlier teams into the San Fernando Club, which still exists. The Managua Club won the championship, but along the way San Fernando distinguished itself by winning twenty-four games in a row.

In 1916 many baseball clubs were active. Even the small towns of Bluefields, Boaco (Club Francia), and Camoapa (Club Masigüe) had teams. One Sunday in May three games involving five teams were played in Managua. The Bluefields team, whose members were always referred to as *negritos*, played in the capital this year, and on June 4 they beat Managua, the national champions, 15–4. One of Bluefields's most outstanding players was an outfielder—a small man with no right hand. A "select crowd of young ladies and gentlemen, who were treated to beer and ice cream by the Comandante, attended the game played between the Club Managua and 1915 in the Campo de Marte. Perfect order was maintained during play and the spectators were impressed with the decorum of the players." It was an open secret that Club Managua was subsidized by the Nicaraguan military during this period.

In 1917 the high society Athletic Club of Managua had both baseball and football teams. Possibly this club's most active member was the Grace Company's A. W. Malcolmson. A program held to raise funds for construction of new buildings and playing fields included singing, dancing, and a movie; it was opened with a rendition of the "Athletic Club March" by the nation's military band. President Chamorro, Archbishop Lezcano, and the Mexican minister attended the first game of the final series of the Liga Nacional for 1917, featuring Managua and América (of Granada) and won by Managua on June 17. Managua beat América again on June 24 and July 1 (a three-hour game) and then won the championship with their fourth consecutive victory on Sunday, July 15. At the end of the fourth and final game, Archbishop Lezcano, the honorary president of the Junta de Beneficencia, presented a silver cup to the vice president of the Liga, Juan Manuel Morales, who in turn presented it to the captain of the winning team, Pedro Ortega. Each of the nine players was given a medal, compliments of the Grace Company and Mr. Malcolmson.

The players were also awarded white sashes with black letters saying "Club Managua," and pitcher Chabelo Fernández received a crown of flowers sent down from the box seats by "distinguished señoritas." Fans set off fireworks and, to the sound of "inspired Spanish marches" played by the military band, a crowd of a thousand people marched behind the team to the cathedral to hear a *Te Deum* offered by several supporters in thanksgiving. The players were then treated to an elaborate lunch and spent the rest of the afternoon riding in carriages through the crowded streets of Managua. In September, members of the crew of the Argentinean frigate *Presidente Sarmiento*, guests of the government of Nicaragua, were entertained in Managua with a dinner, a dance, and a baseball game between Clubs Nicaragua and Sandoval, attended by President Chamorro and his cabinet.

Early in January 1918 a complete schedule of the Liga Nacional de Base-Ball for the year was published on the front page of a Managua daily. It listed fifty-six games to be played during the season, two on every Sunday from January 27 through August 4, one on each date in the Momotombo in Managua and the other in La Islita in Granada. Although they did not appear in the original schedule, other games were held in Masaya, so that there were three games on several Sundays. The eight teams were Managua, Nicaragua, Gigantes, Sandoval, San Fernando, Unión, Granada, and Países Bajos. Before the first league game in the Momotombo on January 27, Mr. Malcolmson provided his automobile to drive the players around the streets of Managua. The Italian owner of the Venecia restaurant offered a bottle of whiskey to the winning club, and other fans offered cash. As usual, the nation's military band played for the game in the Momotombo. The contest was interrupted toward the end of the first inning, when the band struck up the national anthem as Emiliano Chamorro entered the stadium and took his seat in the presidential box next to Archbishop Lezcano. For their game in Granada, some of Sandoval's best players missed the morning train, and the remainder of their team lost to Gigantes, 31–0. So many fans of Managua planned to travel to Masaya for their February 3 game with Gigantes that the railroad put on an extra car.

Neither Sandoval nor Países Bajos showed up for their March 31 games in Masaya and Granada, respectively. Países Bajos had lost their first three league games to Managua, 22–0, Nicaragua, 21–0, and Gigantes, 55–5. Sandoval and Unión also seemed to drop out of the league about this time, leaving the four strong teams to fight it out. The remaining league games were hotly contested, generally being won by a single run. At the end of a 1–0 game (with Gigantes) in Granada, San Fernando sent a telegram to the league secretary complaining of a bad call by the base umpire. They were allowed a second game (played in Managua), also won by Gigantes, 1–0. Sometimes in addition to the games played in each of the three cities on a single Sunday, the Momotombo featured both morning and afternoon contests. Newspapers sometimes reported the number of balls (usually two or three) used during a game.

The Bluefields team of *negritos* traveled west and, after losing its first game with Managua, won against Gigantes and Nicaragua. On June 9, after beating Nicaragua 3–2 in the morning, Managua eked out a ninth-inning victory over the U.S. Marines in the afternoon, with a score of 6–4. On June 30 the Marines were scheduled to play a team from the Escuela Estilo, consisting of a group of "apreciables y distinguidos artesanos" [esteemed and distinguished craftsmen]. As part of the July 4 celebration in 1918, an afternoon game was scheduled between the Managua baseball club and the Marines.

Gigantes (Granada) apparently won the 1918 league championship, although the precise organization with which the league began the year seemed to break down badly before the end of the schedule. Games were still being played in August, and the report of an acrimonious league meeting that month over an umpire's decision protested by Club Nicaragua implied that the latter club was competing with Gigantes for the championship. Very few games were mentioned after August. On Sunday, September 8, Gigantes, the 1918 champions, beat the 1917 champions, Managua, in a game with a side bet of 100 córdobas and the *dividendo* (a team's portion of the gate receipts). From September onward, an influenza epidemic seriously limited all public activities. Many people died, and the government closed schools and banned all types of public gatherings. The armistice in the European war was celebrated at U.S. Thanksgiving time with track and field events, boxing, and a baseball game involving the Marines in Managua as well as one between Gigantes and an all-star team from Managua.

Plans were being made early in January for the 1919 league, consisting of the teams Gigantes, Nicaragua, Nueve Fuertes (made up of former Managua players), and Los Atletas. Before the end of the month the Marines' team was admitted to the league, as well as Club Aguila from Managua and Club Centroamericano from Granada. In February, Nueve Fuertes and Los Atletas initiated league play, with President Chamorro pitching the first ball from the mound ("as is done in the United States"). However, only a few games were mentioned subsequently during the year. A variety of forces worked to reduce baseball and other sport activity. The influenza epidemic continued, 1920 presidential election politics occupied many Nicaraguans, and others participated in the ongoing revolution against President Frederico Tinoco in Costa Rica. In late May it was reported that in the next month a new attempt would be made to start a league, consisting of Nueve Fuertes, Aguila, and Gigantes. After late May there was little mention of baseball or any other sport in the newspapers. More games involving U.S. Marines were reported than in previous years, but from mid-June there are records of only four games involving the Marine team, which lost them all.

Baseball seemed dead at the beginning of 1920. The Momotombo field had been abandoned for a long time, and the junta considered selling it. The field was used occasionally for football in February and March, and finally baseball resumed in October, with games involving the new teams Xolotlán (a high-society club that also played football) and Denver (with Nicaraguan members), the American Marines, Aguila, and Bóer. The Marines' team continued in the news, winning two of the five games reported. In an October game against Aguila, one of the umpires was a Marine. After this contest, José Benito Ramírez, the junta's representative, awarded a prize of a Spalding baseball ("worth two dollars") to an Aguila pitcher for striking out fourteen batters and allowing only three hits.[1]

In December two more new clubs were organized ("by the best of our society"), Estaca and Naranja Agria. Also in December, another Managua club, called Espartanos, began organizing. They were to field both baseball and football teams and practice in the Campo de Marte. Perhaps to encourage renewal of interest in baseball, no admission seems to have been charged for any of the baseball games played in 1920. In several articles about upcoming contests, it was specifically mentioned that they would be free. On several Sundays, morning and afternoon games took place in the Momotombo, or there would be a baseball game before noon and a football match later in the day. All the baseball activity reported involved Managuan teams. It is almost certain that the game was played elsewhere during this period, but apparently something had happened to the intercity rivalries. Elections took place in 1920 (Diego Manuel Chamorro was elected president in early October), and the increased political activity may have interfered with sport. Also, continuation of the war in Honduras affected life in northern Nicaragua.

After over two years of rickety performance and in spite of war conditions during the latter months of the year, baseball experienced a temporary revival in 1921. When Xolotlán's new team debuted against San Juan, señoritas representing the best of society attended a baseball game for the first time. Club San Juan consisted entirely of players *del pueblo* [working class] and were supported by the common people of Managua. Several of the clubs had second teams. Aguila practiced every day against the Marines. In October, the disruptions produced by revolutionary activity in the country had abated sufficiently to give rise to a proposal that play in "two National Leagues" take place. Several games were held during the latter part of the year, but no league materialized.

Baseball activity during 1922 involved teams from Managua, Chinandega, León, Granada, and Masaya. The Xolotlán nine was said to be composed of "the best of the capital's society." The Marines were more active and more successful than in previous years. In January they beat Aguila, one of that season's better teams. At the beginning of the year nostalgic references were made to squads and games of two and three years earlier. Atleta of Granada included many former Gigantes and Japón players; its captain, Thomas Cranshaw, also headed the Granadan football club, Olímpico. Paco Soriano, Adolfo Solórzano (who also played football), and other top performers played for Xolotlán. Atleta lost to Xolotlán 5–2 in January and challenged them to a rematch with a bet of 100 córdobas, which they won 4–3. A new custom began of setting off fireworks to announce the arrival of Granadan and Masayan teams at the Momotombo in Managua.

Teams from the U.S. warships *Denver* and *Galveston* played Titán II in Chinandega. Denver and Titán II played an exciting 3–3 tie in February. The Chinandegans were not optimistic before the game because of the Americans' fame as baseballers, and they were pleased to have come out with an even score. The Americans allegedly had better skills, but the Nicaraguans were more clever and crafty because they managed to put out several base runners, who did not know the location of the ball. On March 5, Titán II took on the *Galveston*'s team. A Managua newspaper reported the action:

> The *Galveston* batters were seen to be much better than those of the *Denver*, and the largest crowd ever seen in Chinandega's field didn't think the locals had a chance to win. However, Titán was ahead 5–1 in the fifth inning. The Americans tied the game in the sixth, and both teams made two more runs in the seventh. In the eighth, center fielder Horacio Martínez made a tremendous catch of a ball that was heading for the *monte* [uncleared land] (sounds like there was no fence), but the Americans made two more runs. Titán then tied the game again at 9–9. Beginning the ninth, Galveston gets one superb hit after another, absolutely uncatchable, admirably placed. Titán is dragging. Although they run all over the field chasing powerful flies and make some tremendous plays, the charge of the yanquis is too much and they score six more runs. The huge crowd is sad; not a happy voice is heard. Titán seems defeated; but the nine Nicaraguan boys, as if in a war between races, exalted by their Nicaraguan pride, as though inflamed by powerful Indian blood, entered the bottom of the ninth with an enthusiasm spurred on by the screams of the crowd. At this point they were down 15–9.
>
> Titán falls on the ball with a terrible vengeance and makes two runs without any outs. It was beautiful. *Galveston* sees defeat coming but gallantly fights back and plays their last card by changing pitchers. Titán can't adjust to the new pitches and makes two outs. Hope dies in the thousands of spectators. But suddenly the batters regroup and attack furiously. The new pitcher watches his balls hit all over the field by the formidable Nicaraguan batters. A double by García ties it up 15–15. The spectators go crazy with emotion. With García on second, Cano hits a clean triple that gives the game to Titán.

Many officials, including the American vice consul, attended the game and afterward were treated to lunch. Also, in early March the thirteen-member squad from León played in the capital for the first time. Progress of their game with Aguila was reported in each inning by telephone from the Momotombo to the fans in León.

A legal dispute forced the suspension of games in the Momotombo during the spring of 1922. According to a Junta de Beneficencia representative, after the field was inaugurated in 1915, baseball ticket sales had risen, thus providing a good income for the hospital until 1918, when they began to fall off. Sales during 1919 remained poor. Therefore in 1920 the junta turned over the field's management for two years to a private individual, Benjamín Elizondo Rivas. In turn the junta was to receive 50 percent of the field's income. During this period, Elizondo delivered no money whatsoever to the junta and even contracted more games for the field after his two years had expired. A typical game grossed 250 córdobas in ticket sales. Therefore, after deducting 20 córdobas for expenses, half or 115 córdobas should have gone to the clubs and the other half to Elizondo. In April a judicial ruling took the field from Elizondo and turned it over to José Benito Ramírez, a member of Managua's Junta de Beneficencia. The stands were in poor condition and a section collapsed during the May rains.

In April baseball interest seemed to heat up, with wagers as high as 150 córdobas made on games and the larger bettors' names being published in the newspaper. Sometimes the two teams would "bet the dividend." The highest-ranked squads were Bóer and Aguila of Managua, Titán and Atleta of Granada, and San Fernando of Masaya. The famous old Club Managua reappeared, and a new Granadan team, Boston, was established in May. Boston's pitcher allegedly was the only Nicaraguan to throw the curve called *la cola del mico* [the monkey's tail]. The curve did the trick, and Boston beat Titán on May 7 in Managua. Then, reinforced by some of Titán's players, they took on Bóer. On May 21, El Atleta brought the best players of Granada to play Bóer. During seven innings nobody reached second base; in the eighth, Atleta loaded the bases with no outs but was retired with a triple play by Bóer shortstop Vicente Morales to stop the threat. They played on through fourteen innings with no score and then decided to suspend the game until the next Sunday (probably because Atleta had to catch the 2 P.M. train back to Granada). As the fans left the field, they encountered a great movement of people in the streets and the sound of gunshots—General Arsenio Cruz was attempting to overthrow the government. The next week, Atleta returned, betting the dividend, and with many individual wagers arranged, Bóer won, 4–2.

In June the Junta announced free games to be played every afternoon by Managua's better clubs. Bóer continued its string of victories with shutouts of Boston and its old rival Managua (twice, the second time with the stands full). Suspense was building for a confrontation between Bóer and Masaya's San Fernando. The latter had three strong pitchers: El Mono Negro [the Black Monkey] (Fernando Amador), El Mono Blanco [the White Monkey] (Julián Amador), and El Salvaje [the Savage] (Gilberto Miranda). El Mono Negro shut out Bóer in their July 11 game, which filled the Momotombo in Managua, striking out eighteen, including three in a row. With no score and two outs in the ninth inning, San Fernando's shortstop got on base and a ball hit over the fence by third baseman Gustavo Ochomogo brought in the winning run. Amid the din of fireworks set off by San Fernando's fans, the club's manager rewarded his team with a foreign-made bat. Over a thousand fans and the city's band welcomed their team at the train station in Masaya. The celebration included a speech in the central park and an evening concert. The last piece performed was "El Anunciado Capote" [The Predicted shutout], written by Masaya's well-known musician, Vega Matus.

Foreign bats, welcoming speeches, and concerts must not have been sufficient to keep the two Monos in Masaya, because at the end of July they had joined Club Managua. Gigantes of Granada was back in action, and in preparation for a July 30 game with Managua, they announced: "A giant strangles a monkey. There won't even be bones left to chew. We don't care about their batters, their game, their monkeys, etc. We are the ne plus ultra of humanity. We don't respect color or size. Anybody who sees us coming better get out of the way. The terror of Granada will arrive and beat the famous Club Managua, just as three and two make five."

Managua had eked out a 7–6 victory over San Fernando and El Mono Negro on July 23, but they may have anticipated needing a pitcher because there were rumors that Bóer was trying to get their star left-hander Argüello (and that Argüello had asked to be relieved from his position in the army's honor guard, probably indicating that Club Managua still had connections with the military in 1922). At the end of July, Bóer was touring western Nicaragua, and on July 23 they beat a combined team of the best players from León's Federal and Titán clubs, with a side bet of all the money they had taken in during their trip. Juan Deshón, the man who brought the curve ball to Nicaragua, pitched for León. In August a Marine team beat Bóer, 7–5, with Juan de Dios Rodríguez pitching for Bóer. Unlike most reporting of games involving Marines, the names of the American players were given in descriptions of their feats. The gate receipts were only 59 córdobas, in comparison with over 100, and sometimes over 300, for games involving two Nicaraguan teams.

When Xolotlán played a schoolboy team in September, "a few señoritas attended," giving the impression that women did not ordinarily attend baseball games. Also, in a Thursday game in September, Bóer avenged their earlier loss to the Marines, and a first for Nicaraguan baseball occurred when the Americans used a battery of two members of the president's honor guard, pitcher Díaz Solís and catcher Ramos. On the next day the Marines, using an American battery, lost to San Fernando. The Marine band attended both games and played the Nicaraguan national anthem before each one.

Bóer beat San Fernando 2–1 in September, "with the greatest attendance ever seen in the Momotombo field"—approximately 3,000 spectators (more than 500 from Masaya) and ticket sales totaling 409 córdobas.

This great mass of spectators caused a section of the stands to collapse, resulting in several injuries. The game started at 11 A.M. due to the late arrival of the train from Masaya, and it was interrupted at noon by a heavy rain. The contest ended around 3 P.M., too late for the Masayans to catch the afternoon train home. Each team received a dividend of 96 córdobas, more than the entire ticket sales for some games. Bóer's Argüello struck out fifteen, winning a one-córdoba prize and a bottle of whiskey for striking out three in a row. The single umpire was an American sergeant, who was given good marks for his calls (from behind the pitcher).

The game of the year was arranged for October 22—a rematch of Bóer and San Fernando. More than 2,000 tickets were sold, and a band and many fans were prepared to meet the Boeristas upon their arrival in Masaya. The contract specified that San Fernando would pay for the train fares and meals for the visiting team plus give it 45 córdobas from the ticket sales. On Saturday night, Bóer's representative called to notify San Fernando that due to the illness of one of their players, El Mono Negro would be their pitcher. San Fernando's representative replied that Bóer should not expose themselves to the disturbances that could result from their bringing El Mono, who was hated in Masaya (he was the traitor who had pitched a shutout against Bóer and then had deserted to the enemy). As no agreement could be reached between the two men, they decided to postpone the game for a week.

Thus, on Sunday, when no one in Masaya was thinking of a game that day, they were astonished to see the Bóer team arrive on the morning train. Surprise turned to anger when El Mono Negro appeared in uniform. Now the fans decided that the previous evening's telephone call had been a trick, because assuming that the game would not be held, the San Fernando players had spent the night partying in Masaya's fiesta of San Gerónimo. After the situation calmed down, the San Fernando fans walked with the Boeristas to the field to see the game, but then it was called off by some of the directors of Club San Fernando, who would not permit the presence of El Mono. Masaya's correspondent ended his article by expressing regret that the city's fans had not been more hospitable to their visitors. It was not the Boeristas' fault, he said, that such hostile feelings existed against El Mono, "who is as well liked as Mr. O'Connell" (the American director of the Nicaraguan railroad, who was blamed for a series of derailments resulting in injury and death). While El Mono's presence was being protested in Masaya, a good game was taking place in Managua, where the Gigantes shut out Club Managua 2–0. After the game, the Gigantes' president, Adolfo Benard, treated both teams to a lunch in the Estrella Hotel.

José Santos Ramírez, Nicaragua's premier sports promotor, made arrangements with two American tourists to bring their movie camera to an October game between Libertad (León) and Managua. All teams were requested to attend in uniform so that they and the game could be captured on film, "which would be shown all over the world." In this game an American sergeant served as umpire, and the writer complained that although the junta paid for his services, the umpire stood behind the pitcher instead of in the correct position behind the catcher and made several errors in calling balls and *strickes*.[2]

In November, Managua traveled to León for games against León and Libertad, whose pitchers, Deshón and Maqueado, respectively, were referred to by a Managua daily as "professionals." In December, Italian aviator Enrique Massi and his mechanic flew into Nicaragua (the first time anyone had entered the country by air). The manager of the Momotombo field moved a game between Bóer and Gigantes to the afternoon so that Massi could fly over Managua in the morning to shower the town with game programs, and then over the field to throw out some balls.

The social class of baseball players seemed to cover a wide range, and some entire teams apparently represented one extreme or another of society. The Club Managua squad consisted of military members and employees, who basically were paid to play. It was common for teams to have at least some working-class members. A benefit game was held in 1917 for a player who lost an eye on his job. A report in 1922 claimed that San Fernando players had little money, but being workers they at least had the means to earn a living at their trades. A reference to the victory of the Nicaraguan "national" team in the 1924–25 Costa Rican "Olympics" referred to the players as *obreros apreciables* [respected workers]. Members of the team Escuadra were referred to as *artesanos* [craftsmen]. Bóer players may have worked, but they evidently were able to practice regularly as there were almost daily complaints of balls falling on and damaging roof tiles adjacent to their training area. Moreover, a few teams consisted entirely of social elites.

Baseball activity in 1923 seemed normal during the first half of the year and then died for some reason. Basketball began to dominate the sporting news from March onward, and during the last half of the year basketball, boxing, and soccer dominated the press. The Marines' baseball team was more active and more successful than in previous years. They held their own with several Nicaraguan teams and also played squads from the U.S. warships *Tacoma* and *Cleveland*. In January, El Mono Negro was pitching well for Bóer, although two close games were lost to Gigantes. Club Managua then shut out Gigantes 7–0 with Argüello facing only twenty-eight batters, a Nicaraguan record. In Masaya, feelings about El Mono Negro's infidelity had mellowed sufficiently to permit Bóer to play there. During the week prior to a February game, handbills were distributed inviting people to the game and recommending courtesy and moderation among San Fernando's fans. Reinforced by a few star players from Club Managua, Bóer won 2–1, with El Mono striking out eleven batters. Two weeks later, Bóer won again in Masaya, 3–1. El Mono shut out San Fernando until the ninth inning, when 13-year-old Rodolfo Marín, Jr., drove in their lone run. Masaya's reporter noted that the visitors were treated very well, without the slightest hint of trouble at the game. Although Managuans viewed Masayans as semi-savages, the visiting players and fans could testify to the contrary.

Diminishing baseball activity may have been related to renewed litigation concerning the Momotombo field. In February 1923 a judge ruled against the junta and its manager and in favor of the former concessionaire. In March the opinion was expressed that most of the baseball clubs in the towns connected by rail did not like to play in the Momotombo because they received too little money there. For that reason, Gigantes and Bóer considered playing the next Sunday in Masaya, where, although the field was not as good, they were paid better, "which is what the players want." Then it was announced that the 1923 national league play would begin on May 1, with 50 percent of the ticket sales going to the teams and 50 percent to the junta. Clubs Bóer, Managua, Gigantes, and Libertad would most likely compete for the cup, which was presently held by Gigantes, although other clubs wishing to enter the league could also apply. In June, Managua won the championship with a victory over San Fernando. A Managua newspaper columnist seemed to echo the British public school ideal of sport when he stated in reference to the fans' interest in the championship game: "Of course, this spirit of competitiveness among the fans assures the continuation of a sport that serves to strengthen the physical endurance of our race. And for that reason, it does not matter which of our teams wins, as long as our young men are encouraged to participate in this type of exercise, which is of transcendental importance for the future of nations, as we are told by experts on the subject."

In late January 1924, fourteen Bóer players received passports to travel to El Salvador, apparently for a series of games with Salvadoran clubs. In addition to Fernando Amador (El Mono Negro), Salvador Argüello of Club Managua was carried as an additional pitcher. Newspapers that would have carried reports of this first Nicaraguan international baseball tour are not available. In the existing newspapers for 1924, only two games are reported, an 11–1 victory of the Marines over Bóer and a 7–1 Gigantes win against the Americans, both taking place in November.

A telegram from San José, Costa Rica, in January 1925 reported that the Nicaraguan team (which included pitcher Gilberto Miranda, El Salvaje) had won the baseball tournament in Costa Rica's "Olympics," beating the champions of the Canal Zone, 9–0. Salvador García Valery (who also accompanied the Bóer team that went to El Salvador in 1924) reported that the opposing club was magnificent—better than any seen in Managua. After the international baseball triumph in Costa Rica, interest in the sport seems to have faded temporarily in Nicaragua. With the exception of one baseball game in Granada between the local teams Colegio San Bosco and Marathon, the few newspapers available during the rest of 1925 report only on boxing and soccer. Continued political unrest in the country may have explained the dearth of baseball and other sport activity during the year. In late October, General Chamorro led still another attempt to overthrow the government.

In the midst of political turmoil and armed conflict in 1926, the teams Nacional, Margot, and Ferrocarril of Managua and Moderno and Coyotepe of Masaya played the only three games of the year reported in the newspapers available. The untiring promotional efforts of José Santos "Tex Rickard" Ramírez were not enough to revive the sport. Cleveland, Nueve Bates, teams of Marines from the warships *Tulsa* and *Galveston*, Imperio, Ferrocarrilito (composed of workmen from the railway shops), Boston, and Bóer were also mentioned as organizing, practicing, or planning games in 1926.

Football (Soccer)

Early in the twentieth century, Napoleón Parrales Bendaña, a native of Diriamba, introduced soccer into the town after having learned to play it in Costa Rica. In 1917 the Diriangén club of Diriamba became the first soccer team in Nicaragua. In the late 1910s and 1920s, adult and schoolboy teams existed in Diriamba, León, Granada, and Managua. While baseball players came from a range of social classes, soccer seems to have belonged exclusively to the elite. On a Sunday in June 1917, a game between Sporting Club of Granada and Atlético of Managua "was attended by a large and very select crowd," including the president of the republic, "the players belonging to the highest society of both cities." After the return match in Granada, a dance was held. In July, Club 15 de Setiembre of the Instituto Pedagógico in Managua beat Atenas, both *primeros equipos* [first-class teams]. In September 1917, Diriangén beat Atlético in Managua. The game was a fund-raiser for Club Atlético's building project. In a promotional article published prior to the game, Grace Company's Mr. Malcolmson, the club president, said that Diriamba had become the leading city in the country in terms of sport, with two first-class football teams, three baseball teams, the finest tennis court in the nation, a croquet lawn, and a young ladies' basketball team. Present at the game was President Chamorro as well as a great number of "beautiful and distinguished señoritas who added a note of spring-like aristocracy" to the spectators' boxes.

In March 1918 the Olimpic Club, national champions of Costa Rica, traveled to Nicaragua to play the teams of Managua, Granada, León, and Diriamba. The young men of the Costa Rican team represented "the most distinguished elements of San José's society, all educated in Europe, and some having played with French teams." After a May 1918 game between Olimpic of Granada and Atlético of Managua, the Granadan players were honored with a dance in the Club Social, attended by an "exclusive and numerous group of ladies and gentlemen."

In February 1919, Atlético invited players from El Salvador to visit Nicaragua, but no reports exist of what occurred thereafter. Finally, in February 1920, the first international football competition took place: a Costa Rican team played a Nicaraguan squad composed of the best players from Managua, Granada, and Diriamba, to a 1–1 tie in the Momotombo. "The best of Managua's society attended the game, and in the boxes there was exhibited the beauty of our best señoritas." Prior to the match, a newspaper article pointed out that a loss to the foreigners would cause Nicaragua to suffer, even though it was only a football game. Therefore, it advised the players to (1) practice an hour every day and afterward run around the field at least two times; (2) make sure their shoes were in good condition and not buy new ones without determining that they fit well; (3) abstain from all activities that might hurt their play, such as smoking, drinking alcohol, etc.; and (4) be sure to go to bed early and rise early as well.

New clubs playing football in 1920 included Xolotlán (Ricardo Nicol was a member, and the captain was Edmundo Bernheim, Jr.), Unión, Revolución, 1821 (students of the Hermanos Cristianos, or Christian Brothers), and Espartanos. In April, Thomas Cranshaw, a British resident of Granada and great advocate for sport in Nicaragua, tried to arrange for a Guatemalan football team to visit. Atleta (*sic*, probably Atlético) was also playing football. A New Year's Eve contest was scheduled in the Momotombo between the team of the British cruiser *Cambrian* and a Nicaraguan eleven.

There was no further news of soccer until July 1921, when Xolotlán played Ultramarinos as a benefit for the Gota de Leche [Drop of milk] program. In August, Xolotlán played Diriangén in Diriamba, and in October a combined team of Centenario (Chinandega) and Sporting Club (Corinto) played the Costa Rican national team, whose steamer had stopped over in Corinto. The Costa Ricans, en route home, had just dominated the Central American Games, which formed part of Guatemala City's centennial celebrations the previous month. They continued their string of shutouts by defeating the Nicaraguans, 11–0. Before the game, the Costa Ricans offered to pay five dollars for every goal made against them.

Football continued in 1922, but few games made the newspapers. In 1923, Club Metropolitan (León) was active. Club One Eleven, composed of "distinguished young men of Managua," was to play them in the Hipódromo field in León in January. A sportswriter called soccer the sport of fashion among young people. He dedicated considerable space to what he called the refined and cultured society of León who would attend the game—especially the incomparably beautiful señoritas, whose glances would defeat Managua's players even if the opposing footballers could not. The only soccer reported in the few available newspapers from 1924 was a game planned between Titán and Centroamérica in Granada. A Granada paper mentioned three contests in 1925.

Soccer activity picked up in 1926. In July, Ferrocarril and 1821 played on the field of the Escuela de Artes (the railway shops) in Managua. Other games involved Centroamérica and Oriental of Granada. Crowds of 3,000 and 4,000 attended two July games in Granada. Ferrocarril had a second team, called La Carraca, and Club 1821 had a second team, San Jacinto. Students in Managua organized a club called Stamford, and a new team appeared in Masaya called Atenas.

Under the direction of Granada's Thomas Cranshaw, a soccer league was organized for 1926. By mid-July he had proposed detailed rules for the championship, down to the celebration for the victors and the maximum cost of tickets for the banquet. When the list of players for Ferrocarril came in, Cranshaw pointed out that three of them did not work for the railway system and had not previously played on that team; moreover, he said, they were too good and would upset the balance in the league. Hence, Cranshaw ruled that only one man could be used, and less skilled substitutes would have to be found for the other two. Rufus Flint agreed to drop two of them, along with another excellent player, because they were members of Club Atlético, which was reorganizing its own soccer team. Because of war conditions and other conflicts, the championship became drawn out. By November, Club 1821 had dropped out of the league because its student players needed all their time to prepare for exams. Centroamérica won the first game of the finals against Ferrocarril on December 19, and the tournament was to be completed in late December or January of the following year.

Boxing

During the 1920s, previously dominant baseball and soccer had to share the sport scene with boxing, which also captured the interest of Nicaraguan athletes and spectators. As early as 1916, José Santos Ramírez began training Isabel Fernández, star pitcher of Club Managua, as a boxer. He predicted great success for Fernández, whose first match was scheduled in the Variedades theater against one of the best of the *negritos de Bluefields* boxers. Sunday afternoon boxing matches were held in the Variedades in 1918. The Nicaraguan pugilists were said to be improving; they tried to imitate American boxers but had not yet mastered the techniques. The resulting spectacular knockdowns were highly appreciated by the crowds, who found the locals' performances more entertaining than those of more skilled boxers.

Anastasio Somoza García was a great sports fan. After becoming president of Nicaragua, he had his own baseball team, Cinco Estrellas. As a young man he brought boxing gloves and rules from the United States and was said to have introduced the sport in Nicaragua, refereeing bouts in León, where he also judged football games. However, this would have been around 1919, and, as noted above, boxing existed in Managua before this date.

The popularity of boxing increased in the 1920s. Cables and articles on the July 1921 Dempsey-Carpentier match in Jersey City, New Jersey, were followed in October by showings of the fight film in two Managua and Masaya theaters as well as in the Campo de Marte. This contest was billed as the fight of the century "between the most colossal boxers human eyes have ever seen." Also in July, Santos Ramírez put on a Friday night program of boxing in the Variedades theater to follow the evening's movie. Managua's champion, Enrique Leal, was supposed to show up for a challenge from Francisco Ríos. There was to be one fight between the *marinos yanquis*, J. Fouty and S. Berger, and six more involving Nicaraguans. The American referee was referred to as the "professional," J. Moore. Jack Dempsey's film, *Muerto o Vivo* [Dead or alive], featuring staged boxing by the champion, was shown in two Managua theaters in September 1921.

Many of the participants and spectators in boxing probably were lower on the social scale than those in other sports. However, boxing champ Enrique Leal also kept goal for the society football club, Xolotlán. In Managua's Trébol theater on a Sunday in October 1922, Leal won by a TKO in the fourth round of a ten-round fight against the champion of León, Gustavo Chacón. Referring to the winning punch, which was to the throat, the reporter commented: "the practices of the Yankees are becoming more widespread all the time." In November, former baseball player Ceferino Centeno (Club Managua) began training for boxing and planned to challenge Leal in December. Three boxing matches were held prior to a soccer game in the Momotombo in November 1922, and the disapproving reporter grumbled: "We're making progress; we already had liquor, roosters, and bulls, and now, authorized fist fights."

The only sport photo in newspapers consulted through 1923 was a posed picture of boxers Enrique Leal and Simón del Carmen with promoter Santos Ramírez in February of that year. Leal and del Carmen fought on a Sunday afternoon that month in a ring erected in the Momotombo field. To follow their match, Bluefields pugilist Marcos Padilla had challenged "all the boxers in Nicaragua," offering to pay them 50 centavos for each round and 6 córdobas if they could beat him. Six fighters signed up to face him. The program also included two other fights, and the ticket sales totaled 340 córdobas.

Baseball player Ceferino Centeno of Club Managua began training as a boxer in November 1922, and in February of the next year he fought

Leal in the Trébol theater. At the end of seven rounds the referee, a U.S. Marine captain, declared the fight a draw. On the same card, Rosendo Rubí of León destroyed Juan de Dios Morales, winning by a TKO in the third round of their four-round match. Padilla, the Bluefields fighter, who was supposed to face five opponents, was defeated in the third round of his match with an "American soldier."

In June 1923, Moisés Gómez and Napoleón Tercero fought in the Salón Bertini of Granada, and in July a match was scheduled to be held in El Otro theater in Managua. The Junta de Beneficencia appealed to the city's political chief, citing a law that required all sporting events to be held in the Momotombo field. León's Rosendo Rubí beat the Managuan Centeno in August and then fought a ten-round draw with Leal in the Momotombo on Sunday afternoon, October 7. Before the Bóer-Colón baseball game in August 1923, there were to be five boxing matches. Boxing picked up in November, and a club with the name Polo Gron was established in Managua.

During 1922 and 1923, the principal Managua daily carried frequent news of foreign boxing, especially of Luis Angel Firpo and Jack Dempsey, and occasionally reported the activities of Nicaraguan boxers in other countries (for example, Guillermo Montenegro was successful in Guatemala). In February 1924 two Managua theaters showed films of the Firpo-Willard fight as well as another featuring Floyd Johnson and Jack McAuliffe. In April 1925 a film of the previous year's Firpo-Wills fight was shown.

Boxing remained popular in 1925, with the continued participation of Leal, Ruiz Simonson, Napoleón Tercero, and others, and the appearance of new boxers such as Ernesto Urbina, Chaparrón, and Kid Thomas. Rosendo Rubí (León) and Guillermo Montenegro (Masaya) were active in Salvadoran and Guatemalan rings in 1925. Baseball players continued to venture into the ring. Ernesto Urbina signed a contract late in 1925 to fight Gigantes pitcher Francisco Monterrey. Political unrest and military action may have been responsible for decreased boxing activity during 1926, although a few matches continued to be held in León, Granada, and Managua. Nicaraguan boxers increasingly participated in fights in El Salvador and Guatemala.

Santos Ramírez was the principal promoter of boxing in Nicaragua in the 1910s and 1920s. He also coached baseball and promoted activities as diverse as marathon dancing, bullfights, and contests between bulls and tigers. Known as the "Tex Rickard of Nicaragua," he was often referred to as "Tex" Ramírez. At one time he was also the director of a humor and sport weekly called *El Field*. He even tried promoting women's boxing, but it did not catch on. Nicaraguan women preferred tennis and basketball.

Basketball

Diriamba had a women's basketball team as early as 1917, but the sport demonstrated little activity before 1923, when teams were organized in several cities (including Managua, Granada, Masaya, Rivas, Jinotepe, San Carlos, and León). Most of the teams that received press attention were said to be composed of lovely señoritas of the finest ranks of society. The head of one of the more prominent clubs in Managua was the daughter of the nation's president. As of March 1923, basketball dominated sports news, specifically women's basketball. In the beginning all reports focus on the Managuan clubs Alpino and Deportivo. Alpino won the first encounter, 7–5, between these two clubs, a Sunday afternoon game held in the Momotombo, with the proceeds going to a church. The closeness of the score set a pattern of controversy over game outcomes and the performance of officials. A reporter praised the agility, skill, and valor of the "attractively uniformed, exquisite flowers, queens of gentility," but complained about the partiality toward Alpino of the line judge and timekeeper, who, he said, were members of that club. The same reporter had nothing but praise for the head official, the "cultured young man" René O. Wallace. When the two clubs played again, Alpino won, 18–12. The head official for that game and several future ones was a U.S. Marine officer, and the line judge and timekeeper were also not the same as those officiating in the first game.

A "beautiful fox-trot" was written for Deportivo, with the club's name as its title, and published in the magazine *El Pensador*. In articles on June 3 and 17, the sport of women's basketball was referred to as "aristocratic," and the spectators and players, "distinguished." President Chamorro and Managua's high society attended Deportivo's first victory over Alpino on June 19. The behavior of the "exclusive" crowd of fans, "although exuberant in their enthusiasm, befitted a cultured audience." The following week Deportivo, having finally won a game, was referred to as the "national champion." In August, Deportivo won again when Alpino disagreed with the official score and quit at the end of the first half. Many spectators complained of not being able to see the match after having paid for it.

Alpino went to Granada and lost to Blanco y Negro, 21–15, in mid-August 1923. The reporter complained that Blanco y Negro's baskets were too large and low and were enclosed by lateral boards, which guided the ball into the basket and made goals too easy. On Sunday, October 7, Alpino traveled to Masaya to participate in the inauguration of the Fénix Club, which played an intraclub game in the morning. Alpino did the same in the afternoon, and a grand ball was held in the evening. Although Alpino and Deportivo continued to dominate basketball news for the rest of 1923, with extensive reporting even of their intrasquad games, other teams also appeared in Managua. A basketball squad was to be organized in San Marcos, but the source did not indicate if it was to be male or female. Also, Jinotepe had its basketball club, Olímpico, which also was not by gender.

In October, President Diego Chamorro died after a brief illness. Former vice president Bartolomé Martínez took over as head of state, and within a week both Deportivo (whose president was Chamorro's daughter) and Alpino had named Martínez their honorary president. Another Managuan women's basketball team, Argentino, named General Emiliano Chamorro as an honorary member. These young women seemed to have a good grasp of political realities, as the general probably was the most powerful man in Nicaragua at the time. In late October, René Wallace, director of the basketball club Deportivo, received an invitation to select a national team to compete in Guatemala for the Central American Championships. In mid-November, apparently as a result of friction between Alpino and Deportivo, a group of young men suggested a tournament among those two clubs plus Capitalino and offered a basketball as the prize for the winner. Their objective was "to reestablish harmony among the players and prevent their giving up the sport of basketball."

In 1923, San Salvador was preparing to hold the second edition of a series of Central American Games, a multisport festival that had begun in Guatemala City in 1921. Nicaragua had been busy coping with revolutionary activity and did not participate in the 1921 competition. El Salvador's minister in Managua invited Nicaragua to the games, which were commonly referred to as the Central American Olympics. Nevertheless, he was surprised to find his invitation attacked in an article in a Managua newspaper, whose writer apparently thought that Olympic athletes still competed naked. The diplomat's reply, in the same paper, assured Nicaraguans that times had changed since the ancient Greek games, and nobody's modesty would be offended. He pointed out that the Salvadoran president's daughter was on one of their basketball teams, and the Nicaraguans could count on the high cultural level of all competitors.[3]

Although they did not receive attention in the newspaper, men also played basketball in the 1920s. Managua's Sporting Club had the first men's team. At the time, basketball was considered a women's sport, and some people questioned the masculinity of males who played the game. A men's basketball game (along with a boxing match between Enrique Leal and Juan Matus) inaugurated the Sporting Club in June 1923. The national military band entertained during the day's activities, and the women's basketball clubs of Alpino, Deportivo, and Margot, as well as many "distinguished señoritas," attended. Men's teams also were referred to in March 1923, when it was suggested that the half-time rest period of the women's games be extended from fifteen to twenty minutes so that the male basketball clubs could play during that time.

The only reports of basketball available for 1924 concern social events and intrasquad practice games of Alpino and Argentino. In 1925 there is one brief note about the celebration of Alpino's third anniversary; in the following year, however, basketball regained some of the prominence it had had in 1923. In May, Alpino had been reorganized, yet in spite of extensive praise and encouragement in the press, its members never seemed to be very active. New teams included Railroad Star, Nacional, and Valentino (Managua) and Flor de Lis and Sultana Five Stars (Granada). There were also teams in León (Metropolitano and Blanco y Negro) and possibly in Diriamba (Olímpico). Newspapers frequently featured their activities, although the only games (five-member teams) reported were intrasquad practices. Warfare within Managua was cited as holding up further developments among the women's basketball teams. Railroad Star was organized in late June and practiced in an area adjacent to the field of the soccer club, Ferrocarril (also sometimes called El Tren). Adolfo Cárdenas, manager of the railway system, and his assistant manager, Carmen Díaz, were great basketball enthusiasts and supporters of the team. For the inauguration of the club, their coach, Rufus Flint, presented them with a new ball, which was christened with a bottle of champagne; Carmen Díaz had a "boudoir" (furnished with towels, soap, powder, umbrellas in case of rain, etc., and kept in perfect order with maid service) constructed adjacent to the court, so the women would have a place to freshen up; a team anthem, with music composed by Carlos Tünnermann and words by Adolfo Calero Orozco, was played by the nation's military band; and fine, smooth sand was spread on the court so the women would not hurt themselves if they fell. By the end of September, Railroad Star had five coaches, each working one week in rotation. At this time the team still had not played a game with any other club.

In December 1926 officials began planning for a women's basketball league for 1927, which would constitute the first formal women's sport tournament in the history of Nicaragua. Thomas Cranshaw, coach of the Flor de Lis team, wrote the league rules, which were sent to eight teams and three Managua and two Granada newspapers.

Tennis

Toward the end of August 1917 a doubles tennis tournament was held at the Campo de Marte. Two Marine officers organized the event, and most members of the fifteen teams participating also were Marine officers or noncoms. Colonel Ham, the customs office director, and Mr. Lindberg, his first assistant, won the contest, while second place went to two Marine officers and third to an American sergeant and corporal. At least one team—Rosendo Chamorro, who had to withdraw due to injury, and Luis

Jiménez—apparently was Nicaraguan. Chamorro was reported to be among the best players in the tournament.

In October 1917 a group of tennis enthusiasts from Managua, León, and Corinto met in Managua where they founded the Asociación Nacional de Lawn Tennis de Nicaragua. The group elected F. A. Lind president, and J. L. Griffith represented Corinto; the others had Spanish surnames. One of the founders, A. E. Bradley, donated a silver cup for their national championship, based on home and home matches to be played among the three cities of the founders.

The tennis club of León visited Managua in 1918 for a weekend of matches against Club Atlético. President Chamorro attended (also the minister of war, the American minister's wife, and Marine commander Harrison and his wife), the government band played, and between matches there was dancing on the court. Three of the six visiting players had Spanish surnames, as did one of the Atléticos. Atlético won all five matches and retained possession of the Bradley Cup. José Benito Ramírez presented a dozen tennis balls to the winning team

In 1919 a series of tennis doubles matches was held on the court of the Banco Nacional with a silver cup donated by the American minister, Mr. Curtis. The winners had Spanish surnames, but no Nicaraguans participated in a Central American lawn tennis championship held in November in San Salvador. In December the same invitation was extended for the championship of the following year. In 1925 the Granada Tennis Club built a court for its members, and by 1926 the number had expanded to three. The Railroad Tennis Club was established in Managua in 1926, and its members included both Nicaraguans and foreigners.

Cycling and Other Sports

The only mention of cycling in newspapers was an outing from Managua to Masaya by Club Veloz in January 1918 and of the founding of Club Central Ciclista in December 1919, with the purpose of staging *carreras de cintas* [ribbon races] to earn funds for the charity, Socorro Infantil [Children's Aid Society]. Chess, commonly considered a sport in Latin America, was reported in 1908 (including a match by mail between Granada and Masaya) and in 1921, when contests between the Social Clubs of Managua and Granada were conducted by telephone. Horse racing in Granada and Managua was reported as early as 1907. Swimming and boating in Lakes Managua and Granada were occasionally mentioned, but usually as recreational activity rather than competition, although in 1926 the "swimming champion of Managua," Juan Bonilla, was challenged by Granada's Enrique Marín for a race. Also, plans were made to found a swimming club in Managua. A billiards match took place in 1921, while another, in Granada in 1925, was canceled. Dancing was considered recreation, and dances were frequently held to celebrate team victories and the inauguration of new sport clubs. Marathon dancing competitions also were reported; this endurance event was referred to as a "yanqui sport." In 1926 the Social Club of Managua, safeguarding the morals and decorum of its members and visitors, banned the shimmy and the Charleston.

School Sport

School sport and other physical activity were probably very minor. The 1918 yearbook of a private boys' school in Granada included photos of gymnastics. The school also had an enclosed area in Lake Nicaragua for swimming (a wire-mesh fence protected swimmers from the lake's freshwater sharks). Other activities at this school included hockey and stilt walking and stilt fighting. In November 1920, to celebrate the birthday of its director, the school held a track and field meet, called "Olympic games," which had a program of nineteen events. In 1921 the undersecretary of public instruction advocated that "Olympic games" and other sports be established in the principal schools, but no money was available to support them and nothing more about them showed up in the press.

Most school physical education likely involved exercises rather than sport or games. In December 1920 the Instituto Pedagógico in Managua held a school fiesta in honor of President Chamorro, who was shortly to leave office; the program included Swedish exercises. The Colegio de Señoritas de Managua listed physical exercises as one of the numbers in its program at the end of the 1922 school year, and its final program in 1923 included calisthenics. Some private secondary schools did offer competitive baseball and soccer. In 1925 the Colegio Centro América of Granada held an "Olympic Games" competition for its students. Events included rowing and swimming in Lake Nicaragua, equestrian events, races and jumps, gymnastics, pole vaulting, springboard jumping, stilt fighting, a "fatties' race," and revolver shooting (at 25 meters). The "most select of Granada's society" attended, and the president of the republic awarded prizes such as cameras and silver watches to the winners.

Traditional Sport and Festivals

In addition to playing and watching sports, recreation in early twentieth-century Nicaragua included private parties, public concerts, movies and live entertainment (singers, dancers, opera, plays) in theaters, an occasional circus, and a variety of activities that took place in the annual *fiestas patronales* [patron saint celebrations] of each town and sometimes even within neighborhoods. While the activities of "modern" sport were more characteristic of the larger cities and middle and upper classes, the popular sporting pastimes of the common people occurred principally during their patron saint festivals and included *carreras de cintas*, horse races, cockfights, and bullfights.

The local festivals were probably the high points of the year. They lasted one to a few days each and, in addition to religious ceremonies, featured drinking, gambling, and a great variety of recreational activities. Although local in nature, all Nicaraguans were invited; even poor people were able to attend several each year. Government officials nationwide, for example, granted 150 permits for such festivals in 1923 alone between July 25 and August 10. Typically a wooden bullring (*barrera*) would be erected, as would temporary stands (*chinamos*) for selling food and drinks and running games of chance. Toreros included locals as well as Spanish professionals, who made a living traveling from town to town.[4]

For Corinto's May fiesta in 1918, there were to be concerts, dances, regattas, shooting contests, and cockfights. Organizers expected bets of more than 200 córdobas on the cockfights and invited owners of fighting roosters from the entire country to compete for the championship and the money. The fiesta of Santa Ana in Chinandega in 1918 had *carreras de cintas* for bicycle and horseback riders, sack races, climbing the greased pole (*palo lucio*), concerts, free movies (some to be attended by the "principal señoritas" of the city), and a "magnificent dance, attended by the most select society." The 1919 fiesta of San Jerónimo in Masaya was to feature bullfighting by Spanish toreros, cockfights with bets of 200 córdobas, a sack race with a prize of 20 córdobas, climbing a greased pole, and catching greased pigs (*chanchos lucios*).[5] In the evenings an eight-act drama was presented in which all twenty-nine actors died each night as the final curtain fell.

In January 1919, the village fiesta of Acoyapa, on the north side of Lake Nicaragua, advertised the usual horse races, cockfights, greased pole climb, movies, and fireworks. Additional attractions, however, included a bullfighter who would place *banderillas* [barbed darts] and pole vault over the bull, *carreras de gatos* [cat races], rockets tied to dogs, the *triángulo* [triangle], magicians, soothsayers, singers, a circus, a huge game of chess with the pieces represented by señoritas from the cream of society, an exhibition of a tailless monkey with the face of a rooster, a flight of a Guatemalan airplane, and *juegos de sport* (baseball?). As a "great surprise," the village would be illuminated by electric light produced by a generator on loan from a local farm.

The August fiesta of Santo Domingo in Managua in 1920 had horse races with bets of 100 and 200 córdobas.[6] *Carreras de cintas* were also usually featured in Managua's celebrations. The 1921 fiesta of Santa Ana in Niquinohomo included the traditional activities as well as baseball games with teams from Granada and Masaya playing against the locals. For the July 1922 fiestas in Somoto, there were to be *carreras de cintas*, bulls from Olancho, Honduras, fought by Mexican toreros, movies, *paraguas japonés* [Japanese umbrellas], masquerade balls, and theatrical productions. Two rows of wooden houses were built for the use of visitors from all Nicaragua. The fiesta of Paso de Panaloya in May 1925 included bulls from Chontales, *ola giratoria* [revolving wave], *paraguas japonés*, *los caballitos* [the horses], *palo lucio*, *triángulo*, *chinchines*, *carreras de cintas*, carousels, horse races, cart races, cockfights (a rooster belonging to Juan José Morales was named El Firpo), movies, fireworks, the Circo Nacional Mejicano with its excellent performers, and aviator General Humberto Pasos Díaz with his airplane ("he'll do lots of aerial tricks, including *la hoja seca* [the dry leaf] and many others of which we are ignorant").

Carreras de cintas were also held on other occasions, particularly as fund-raisers for churches or charities. While some of these events were high-society affairs, they frequently involved working-class people. In the traditional *carreras de cintas*, young men rode horses at high speed, holding a small rod, which they tried to insert in suspended rings. Young women prepared sashes (the term *cinta* could refer both to the sashes and to the ribbons that held the rings), which they awarded the winners. Each ring matched one of the *cintas*. Usually the man who speared the greatest number of rings won the privilege of naming the day's queen, who would be honored at that evening's dance.

Newspaper announcements and reports of *carreras de cintas* always noted the social class of the participants. Working people were referred to as *artesanos* [artisans], *obreros* [laborers], *obreritas*, and *mengalitas* [servant girls or working girls]; society participants were called *caballeros* [gentlemen] and *señoritas* [young ladies]. The winner of a June 1919 *carrera de cintas* in León, held at a farm rather than in town, was Anastasio Somoza, Jr. He may not have been exactly high society himself at that time, but *señorita* Margarita Debayle, whom he selected as queen, certainly was. A June 1919 *carrera de cintas* in Masatepe also involved the upper classes.

Earlier in 1919 a *carrera de cintas* was organized in Managua by obreros in honor of "distinguished *obreritas*." President Chamorro and his wife attended this event, held to raise funds for building the church of San José, and he awarded the winner a medal. Another young man speared the white *cinta*, which gave him the right to name the queen, an attractive *mengalita*. A newspaper in León also reported this event and called the queen a "regia morena" [splendid dark-skinned woman]. For the January 1923 fiesta of San Sebastián in Diriamba, the mayor judged a *carrera de cintas*, and the queen was described as a "niña muy apreciada en el elemento obrero" [girl highly thought of in working-class circles]. Many of the beautiful señoritas involved in the *carrera de cintas* would be attending the next Saturday's dance, organized by *obreros* of Diriamba. A *carrera de cintas* in Managua in March 1923, a benefit for the church of San José, was to be attended by Archbishop Lezcano.

Occasionally bullfighting and cockfighting were attacked for being inhumane. Bullfighting, for example, was not allowed in Managua's August festival in 1917. The organizers pointed out, however, that the law only banned bulls and that they, instead, had lined up four *vacas bravas* [courageous cows]. In 1918 the congress approved a decree that levied a fine of one córdoba on spectators at cockfights. In January 1923 the new mayor of Diriamba banned cockfighting in that town, joining Managua, which had already done the same. Later that month the controversy over cockfighting again reached the national congress, where a bill to ban it was debated in lively fashion. Opponents argued that cockfighting was cruel to the roosters and dehumanizing for the spectators, who frequently ended up battling among themselves. Supporters pointed out that it was a tradition loved by the people, who had little else in their lives for entertainment, and that it involved no harm to anyone (other than the roosters, "who were born and lived precisely for the purpose of fighting"). The argument was advanced that cockfights were a part of the national culture, having been brought by the Spanish conquerors, and that small communities needed them to bring in money during the annual fairs. It was also pointed out that most of the trouble among spectators was caused by excessive consumption of alcohol, and that it would be illogical to ban cockfighting when the law permitted prizefights between men. Moreover, a supporter of the bill said that alcohol could not be banned because taxes on its sales were the nation's chief source of revenue. The vote turned out 20–14 to ban cockfighting. Ironically, the same newspaper that reported this congressional debate also announced a program of boxing matches to take place the next Sunday in the Momotombo.

Conclusion

Sport developments in Nicaragua in the late nineteenth and early twentieth centuries were similar to what was going on in Mexico and the rest of Central America. Nicaragua, however, was unusual in that baseball remained the most popular men's sport, a situation that continues to the present. Boxing was also popular early and retains its status in the nation today. In their initial phases, soccer and women's basketball were played by social elites. Modern sports gradually came to coexist with traditional recreational activities and replaced them for many people, especially in the cities.

Notes

1. The junta awarded prizes as early as 1917. Prizes in 1922 included: home run = 1 córdoba, three consecutive strikeouts = 1 córdoba, triple play = 1 córdoba, triple = 50 centavos, double play = 30 centavos, double = 20 centavos. The córdoba was at par with the U.S. dollar, Cuban peso, Guatemalan quetzal, and Panamanian balboa in 1925.

2. English terms and English-based terms were used in all sports in early twentieth-century Nicaragua. Examples include the following: *Baseball*: base ball, base-ball, basse ball, field, bases, flies, pitcher, catcher, strick (strike), team, score, out, umpire, fielder, short stop, hit, play, inning, faul ball, home rum, sior (short stop), run. *Boxing*: boxeo, ring, clinch, fould (foul), knock-down, rabbit-punch, match, round, referee, time-keeper, knock-out, nockeado, boxer. *Football (soccer)*: foot ball, foot-ball, balompié, gual (goal), goald (goal), goal, refereé, off-said (off-side), shoot (shot), center-forwars, footballistas, halfback, forwards. *Basketball*: basket ball, basket-ball, goal, doble (field goal), baskets, foul, referee. This phenomenon of foreign-language use in sport has been described as cultural imperialism. However, the practice seemed to be by choice rather than due to any type of coercion. Throughout the twentieth century, Hispanic athletes and reporters have themselves preferred to use imported sport language even when equivalent Spanish terms exist.

A purely political article in a Managua daily, which predicted the imminent fall of some politicians named Tijerinos, used baseball images and language in its explanation of what had happened to them: "In the political game the Tijerinos, having struck everybody out (*dejado a todos en el guante*) to ensure their victory, sent up a high ball (*fly*) that should have given them a home run (*home rum*), but a fielder (*filder*) snagged the fly (*fly*) in the instant that the runner arrived at home (*home*)—the runner who was called out (*out*) representing in this case the Tijerinos." The expressions in parentheses are those used in the original text. *Dejado en el guante* literally translates as "left in the glove." In the early years of Nicaraguan baseball it meant striking out a batter. Another note, referring to students who had failed their exams in the School of Medicine and Pharmacy, said they had been *noqueados* [knocked out]. For a discussion of foreign-language use in sport, see Joseph L. Arbena, "Sports Language, Cultural Imperialism, and the Anti-Imperialist Critique in Latin America," *Studies in Latin American Popular Culture* 14 (1995): 129–41.

3. Later in June, news was received that El Salvador's Olympics had been postponed to 1924. However, they were not held in that year either. In 1923, Nicaragua was the only Central American nation that had never participated in an Olympics-type festival. In 1918, President Chamorro had proposed that January 6 each year be "sport day" in Nicaragua, with an "Olympic" program to be organized by "clubs de basse ball, foft ball, law tennis [*sic*]" and workers' societies, but there is no evidence that this took place. Nicaragua had not attended the 1921 games in Guatemala due to revolutionary turmoil at home. In fact, Nicaragua's own centennial activities, which had been planned to include sporting events such as target shooting, regattas, a marathon, and tennis matches, were postponed until hostilities had died down late in the year. The three days of festivities that took place in December 1921 included no sporting events. Neither did Nicaragua accept Brazil's invitation to send a delegation for athletic games commemorating the Brazilian centennial of independence in 1922, with free housing in Rio de Janeiro during the entire month of September to be provided by the host country. Costa Rica invited Nicaragua to its year-end 1924 "Central American Olympics."

Events were to include soccer, baseball, basketball, and a full track and field program, with living costs in San José to be paid by Costa Rica for up to forty-five athletes from each invited country (the five Central American republics, Panama, and the Canal Zone). A subcommittee was set up in Managua to facilitate planning for Nicaraguan participation in the games. The government offered the small sum of 1,000 pesos (córdobas) for travel costs, and in the end only a baseball team (Bóer) attended.

4. Nicaraguan bullfighting was entirely different from the spectacle known in Spain and in some parts of Latin America. Within the temporary corral erected for the local fiesta, the bull was tied to a thick post (*bramadero*). A barefoot rider (with spurs tied to his bare feet) mounted the bull, and the "bullfighters," holding red blankets, took positions around him. When the bull was released into the ring, he immediately began bucking and wheeling, trying both to unseat the rider and charge the toreros, who simultaneously attempted to encourage his charges and avoid being caught. The spectators were delighted when the rider was thrown off and attacked, along with the toreros, by the enraged bull. A bull that did not throw the rider was considered worthless and was whistled at (that is, booed) by the crowd. In 1918 an American Marine tried to ride one of the bulls in Managua's Plaza de Santo Domingo during the city's August festival. After he was quickly thrown and kicked in the chest, his companions placed blankets around him and carried him from the arena. The Nicaraguan crowd believed him dead. Then, when he appeared among them, much the worse for wear but laughing about his experience, they cheered and hugged him and brought him water.

5. The *palo lucio* was a thick tree trunk (around one-half meter in diameter and 6 to 8 meters tall, with bark removed so it was completely smooth) coated with wax, grease, and/or soap to make it as slick as possible. Nailed to the top was a board on which was placed or tied a variety of prizes, such as shirts, pants, handkerchiefs, soap bars, and envelopes containing money. Youngsters spent hours trying to climb the pole and claim a prize, but none was successful until finally the pole lost some of its slipperiness. The crowds were entertained by the boys' spectacular slides down it. For the *chancho lucio* event, a pig was shaved and greased or waxed and released, to be chased around the plaza by a crowd of boys. The one who caught and held onto the pig got to keep it.

6. Horse races had been a Managua tradition since the days of the Spaniards. Activities of Managua's June celebration dedicated to San Juan, abandoned after colonial times, included: a blindfolded and disoriented man wildly swinging a machete, trying to behead a rooster buried up to its neck in the ground; the *corrida de patos*, in which horsemen, racing under a pole from which a duck was suspended by its feet, attempted to pull off the duck's head; and tilting at a ring, another full-speed charge by horsemen who tried to spear a gold ring with a small rod held in the rider's hand, with the winner keeping the ring.

Bibliography

This article is based principally on primary sources, mainly original copies of newspapers housed in Managua, Nicaragua, in the Hemeroteca Nacional and Biblioteca Nacional and the libraries of the Banco Central and the Universidad Centroamericana. Additional minor newspaper holdings are found at the University of Texas at Austin and Tulane University, New Orleans. In Nicaragua, newspaper collections are very incomplete, and as a result of the hot, humid climate much of the older print material has deteriorated. However, they are by far the best source of information about early sport in Nicaragua. The principal newspapers consulted were *El Diario Nicaragüense* (Granada), 1886, 1888; *El Diario de Granada*, 1907, 1908; *Diario Moderno* (Managua), 1911, 1912, 1924; *El Imparcial* (Managua), 1917; *El Heraldo* (Managua), 1916–1919; *El Comercio* (Managua), 1918–1926; *El Cronista* (León), 1919; *El Pacífico* (Managua), 1922; *El País* (Granada), 1922; *El Correo* (Granada), 1925; and *La Prensa* (Managua), 1927. References are seen to the Managua newspaper *El Duende* (its director complained of the dangers of allowing baseball to be played in the streets in 1893) and to a sporting magazine, *El Field*, which was published in the early twentieth century. No known copies of these publications still exist. Magazines that occasionally featured news of sport and even sports-related photographs included *Nicaragua Informativa* (Managua, 1917, 1918) and *El Gráfico* (Managua, 1926).

There are few secondary materials available, and they tend to carry little or no documentation. Carlos J. García's *Reseña de cien años de béisbol en Nicaragua* (Managua, 1991) briefly outlines some of the developments in baseball between 1889 and 1989. Luis Mojica Sánchez relates the origins and early history of soccer in *Una historia de gol y pasión: Los setenta y ocho años del club Diriangén* (Diriamba, Nicaragua, 1995). Information about basketball in the 1930s and 1940s is given in Carlos F. Vallejo, *Guía y reglas del basket ball en la América Latina: Dedicada a Nicaragua, C.A. con la historia de la X Serie Mundial de Base Ball* (Monterrey, Mexico, 1948). Jorge Eduardo Arellano describes the role played by his great-uncle in establishing baseball in Granada in *El doctor David Arellano, 1872–1928* (Managua, 1993). Chale Pereyra Ocampo wrote two volumes of his own and others' memories of sport figures and incidents, published as *Anécdotario / Kaleidoskopio* (Managua, n.d.). Pablo Antonio Cuadra's *El nicaragüense* (Managua, 1993) describes his countrymen's infatuation with baseball. Traditional sport and recreational activities are described in Heliodoro Cuadra, *Historia de la Leal Villa de Santiago de Managua*, vol. 1 (Managua, 1939); María Berrios Mayorga, *Juegos nicaragüenses* (León, 1960); and Enrique Peña Hernández, *Folklore de Nicaragua* (Managua, 1968).

The U.S. Marines' presence and activities in Nicaragua are treated in Richard Millett, *Guardians of the Dynasty: A History of the U.S. Created Guardia Nacional de Nicaragua and the Somoza Family* (Maryknoll, NY: Orbis Books, 1977); Ivan Musicant, *The Banana Wars: A History of United States Military Interventions in Latin America from the Spanish-Amercan War to the Invasion of Panama* (New York: Macmillan, 1990); Allan Millett, *Semper Fidelis: The History of the United States Marine Corps* (New York: Free Press, 1991); and Lowell Thomas, *Old Gimlet Eye: The Adventures of Smedley D. Butler* (New York: Farrar & Rinehart, 1933).

12

The History of Peruvian Women's Volleyball

Abelardo Sánchez-León

Despite a five-hundred-year history since the arrival of Europeans to Latin America, a number of countries in the region are still searching for what it means to be a nation. Countries appear on nicely colored maps with precisely drawn boundaries, but that does not mean that they function as coherent, integrated wholes in which their residents are fully woven into the political as well as socioeconomic fabric. One of the best examples of this incomplete process is Peru. In this breathtakingly beautiful and varied country, there exist deep cleavages based on race, ethnicity, religion, culture and language, gender, geography, and even one's relation to the world beyond its borders. How to overcome these seemingly insurmountable obstacles is of great concern and debate, which profoundly divides this so-called nation. In the 1980s and 1990s, for example, a virtual civil war erupted over these issues between the government, led by President Alberto Fujimori, and a guerrilla movement, the Sendero Luminoso [Shining Path], headed by Abimael Guzmán Reynoso.

Within this cauldron of complex and competing interests over how to form the nation, Peruvian journalist and authorAbelardo Sánchez-León examines how sport, and particularly women's volleyball, reflects this process. Peruvians, it is clear, are desperate for athletic victories on the international scene, as success helps to mitigate feelings of inadequacy or inferiority. As such, perhaps more than anything, Sánchez-León demonstrates how fleeting and, indeed, fragile such success can be in a poorly integrated country with an inadequate infrastructure. Gains in Peru were made via volleyball, for example, not only in terms of sport but also in the areas of women's place in society, racial and class tolerance, international recognition, and feelings of nationalism. Nevertheless, for its accomplishments, Peru paid a high price: expending valuable resources, depending upon the outside world for much of its good fortune, and in the end losing nearly everything (save for a lingering nostalgia for the good

From *Studies in Latin American Popular Culture* 13 (1994): 143–52. Reprinted by permission of *Studies in Latin American Popular Culture*.

times of the past), including the players themselves. Worst of all, no concrete legacy of an infrastructure, volleyball or otherwise, was created upon which to build a future. In a sense, Peruvian women's volleyball is a metaphor for the country's attempt at nation building; small, specific gains are possible, but the molding of them into something that is cumulative and more than the sum of the parts is yet to be achieved.

One of the most notable differences between North and South America, with the possible exceptions of Brazil and Argentina, is the social attitude toward victory and defeat. This is even more so in the case of the Andean region and, above all, in Peru.

The history of Peru is a lamentable story of consecutive defeats, a history that began a good four and a half centuries ago, in 1532, when Pizarro and 150 soldiers initiated the conquest of an empire, albeit divided by internal rivalries and a civil war, of ten million people. To this day, Peruvians—in their complex makeup—still do not know whether to side with the conquerors or the conquered. As mestizos, in any case, they feel the pain of the defeated.

Defeat has come to establish itself as a kind of collective identity, which, nevertheless, has been tinged with an aristocratic air: a certain generosity, a certain indolence, and a certain distance from a competitive attitude. Defeat, especially in sports, is justified by the rejection of a disciplined effort to attain goals which, in the end, are not justifiable. Traditionally, in Peru, there have been two sports in which the people have believed they could triumph: soccer and volleyball. In other disciplines they have serious doubts, since they know that these other areas require technological support, which the nation lacks, or innate skills that are not part of the people's physical makeup. An extremely rare exception is in target shooting, a sport in which Peru has won three of its four Olympic medals. The other was won in none other than volleyball, a silver medal in the Seoul Olympics. Peru won the medal after being defeated in the fifth set, 16–14, by the Soviet Union. For the Soviets it was one more medal. For Peru it was the only medal the country won.

In soccer, a sport that has not given a great deal of satisfaction to Peruvian society, Peru has ceased being competitive. It is true that the soccer team was present at the World Cup in 1970, 1978, and 1982, but at the present time the sport finds itself among the least favored in the Latin American region as a whole. The only remaining hope is volleyball, and women's volleyball at that, because of its strong female contingent in Peru. Peruvian women are proud of these twelve athletes and constantly poke fun at those men who, in their own right, are associated with soccer. While the women win, the men lose. And this affiliation by gender has expanded to the whole society; since the 1980s there has been a categorical increase in the presence of women in various social sectors. There is a strong presence at the intermediate and high-level posts of the Shining Path and the Túpac Amaru Revolutionary Movement (MRTA); a monopoly over women's volleyball in South America; prominent positions in public administration, such as the National Treasury and the General Comptroller; a massive presence in universities; control over urban development organizations. Thus, more and more, Peruvian women are beginning to be associated with discipline, perseverance, and the ability to work, while the nation's men have resigned themselves to the thought that quality, geniality, and good fortune do not require continued effort or work, thus producing fruits of dubious quality, especially in sports, as has been demonstrated in soccer.

A Bit of History

Women's volleyball in Peru entered the competitive level in the mid-1960s when the sports federation decided to hire a Japanese expert, Akira Kato. In contrast with all other sports, volleyball maintained this same coach, replacing him only after he became gravely ill. At that point the federation contracted another trainer, this time a South Korean national, Man Bo Park, who was referred to affectionately by the athletes as Mambo, like the rhythm that the legendary Dámaso Pérez Prado popularized. Since 1964 the Peruvian women's volleyball team has had only two coaches.

This continuity is extremely rare in a country that is not familiar with political or economic stability, one accustomed to coups and among those with the most inflated economic indices in the world, something close to two thousand percent monthly in 1989. The soccer team is an example of the exact opposite of this scenario. The young soccer star José del Solar has remarked publicly that on the six occasions he played for the national team he did so with different coaches. Women's volleyball adopted, interestingly, a long-term approach, a plan of action for reaching world-class level. In a country like Peru this feat is difficult to comprehend, because it is a country that has accustomed its people to a perennial state of economic crisis, officially declared in 1975, as well as a state of political crisis since 1980.

How was it possible, Peruvians asked themselves, that these twelve women, from the same country, living there, eating like them, could be among the five best teams in the world, which include enormous and populated countries like China, the Soviet Union, Brazil, and the United States, not to mention Japan and Canada, which, though not as talented, are equally large and affluent? And it was true. These women were South American champions for years, almost always Pan American runners-up, among the four best Olympians—and runners-up in Seoul, thus filling Peruvians with emotion, astonishment, and curiosity. The emotion came because Peruvians knew the difficulties of training. Astonishment occurred because

Peruvians realized it could be done if there were a miracle, desire, and a dose of sacrifice. And curiosity arose because Peruvians wanted to understand the mystery of the historical gap between the athletes and themselves, the rest of the Peruvians.

Within the most respected academic circles, three working hypotheses to explain the phenomenon were presented: a) that the athletes were Peru's best; b) that they were not Peruvian; c) that they were good, in spite of Peru.

This essay defends the third possibility. But before developing this point, it will return to the origins of this exciting sport.

The origins of women's volleyball are closely tied to an old school located in the center of Lima, the Divino Maestro, whose director, Enrique Castañeda, was the primary force behind this pedagogical-volleyballistic institution. The trainer is a robust man named Enrique Aguayo. The Divino Maestro was not only an educational center but was also home to volleyball players from the provinces, above all from Ica, an area south of Lima, with a large black population. The principal Peruvian volleyball players are black, but this is by no means exclusive; the Peruvian team became skilled at maintaining a broad racial representation of the country on the court: its Chinese, Japanese, and European origins were combined with mestizos in a rich and varied gamut intended to demonstrate to the country the possibility for harmonious coexistence in a society characterized more by stagnation, social stratification, and racial tension. While Cuba put six black athletes on the court, Peru exhibited its intricate rainbow. A great number of Peru's stars have emerged from that ancient school on Camaná Avenue.

For the early years various interpretations can be used to explain the link between volleyball and women in Peru, because one cannot ignore the fact that in other countries volleyball is also a men's sport. For Enrique Castañeda the explanation is rooted in the fact that "a woman is more flexible than a man. A man needs to earn his living, and the young man, by eighteen, must already think about his future and cannot dedicate as much time to sports as he would like. A woman has more time, does not feel the same urgency to support herself. Parents pressure their sons but they are less demanding of their daughters."[1]

Certainly this interpretation is not necessarily the correct one, although it comes from someone associated with the sport. The Peruvian woman, above all the one who comes from the working classes, has responsibilities within the home. From adolescence she assumes the kitchen and baking duties, cares for younger siblings, and bears domestic responsibilities that the son does not, but it is also true that there has been a transition in women's expectations that has slowly allowed them to leave behind home life and enter into the public sphere. One possibility for mobility was education, the other sports.

With regard to sports there were only three alternatives: athletics, basketball, and volleyball. All three were amateur sports and none guaranteed a living, but in contrast with the other two, volleyball was adopted by the working classes as their own. It was fairly easy, low cost, and a park or field could offer a convenient practice site. Basketball was heavily associated with private clubs and high society. In any case, basketball and volleyball were competitive, because in a country where tall women are scarce, there was little possibility of having tall women in basketball and volleyball. Volleyball became the bridge, as it were, which would lead the Peruvian woman out of domestic labor. It was a form of modernity, a form of female success, independence.

Sports, anatomically speaking, do not tend to be very democratic. They demand precise physical adaptation and volleyball, in this sense, requires attributes best suited to blacks and whites. In Peru both elements have coexisted in greater harmony with each other than with mestizos or Andeans, perhaps because both are coastal or "*citadinos*" groups. The Andean harbors, it is said, a resentment of invaders and thus has developed an unsociable and distrustful personality. The Andean, male or female, is best at the marathon, an ancient discipline, which in Peru goes hand in hand with those solitary, introspective people in whose lives time is measured with patience.

Nevertheless, for many years, the entire decade of the 1970s, female volleyball players remained amateurs and trained under terrible conditions. There was no coliseum in Lima; there was no suitable practice location, and the athletes were referred to as the "golden girls" for their devotion and generosity. Although this situation was not very modern, it was romantic, patriotic, and feminine; their work continued without any economic recompense.

From a different perspective, it has been said that the working-class backgrounds of the first volleyball players instilled in them a capacity for work and discipline never before seen in a country as disorganized and lax as Peru. Soccer players, who in fact were professional, did not have the stamina of the volleyball players, and this provided a certain amount of pride, nationwide, in women who, for the first time, were able to make up for a kind of approved male supremacy in Peruvian society. These women, without earning any money, put their souls into training and into their official teams. This perspective thus concludes that without access to other options, volleyball was a woman's best track for social mobility, just as soccer or boxing had been for men.

Akira Kato and his successor Man Bo Park have maintained strict discipline. Both have projected an image of themselves as serious men, strong, strict, and rigorous, even to the point of physical pain. They also exhibit a fatherly image, one who is understanding, quiet, who would never shout or even raise his voice in anger. These two men with elongated eyes, trim and svelte, of very few words, who speak in a language not their own, contrast with the image of the common Peruvian man: drunken, boisterous, and disorderly, with the obvious exceptions of the writer Mario Vargas Llosa and the secret leader of the Shining Path, Abimael Guzmán Reynoso. And, obviously, with the exception of President Alberto Fujimori Fujimori, who is as Eastern in his manners as Akira Kato and Man Bo Park.[2]

The 12 September 1992 capture of Guzmán alters, in part, his image. On 13 September he appeared on television—in a very well-edited montage—half-naked, undressing and dressing himself. An earlier video showed him drunk, dancing, and surrounded by women. Alberto Fujimori—who, like Mario Vargas Llosa, neither drinks nor smokes—positioned himself, as of 5 April 1992, head-to-head with Guzmán in a political boxing ring. Once Fujimori had captured Guzmán his goal was to humiliate Guzmán. Fujimori sought to remove Guzmán from his legendary pedestal and to Peruvianize him, to make him submissive and pathetic. But Guzmán, at the time of his capture, proclaimed, like Atahualpa: "today was my turn to lose." Could he be referring to the rebirth of the myth of the Inkari or the Inka-King?

Throughout the course of the women's volleyball team's history it is possible to detect certain changes in its composition. There is an evident rise in the number of women who came not from the working- or middle-class sectors—as in the cases of Pilancho Jiménez, Irma Cordero, or Norma Velarde—but rather from the upper classes. The most famous cases, chronologically speaking, are those of Cecilia del Risco, Natalia Málaga, Alejandra de la Guerra, Gaby Pérez del Solar, and Paola Paz Soldán. Not only were white women being integrated into a team of mestizos and blacks, there were also blondes from the upper classes. Volleyball had achieved the miracle of San Martín de Porres in a country marred by racial misunderstanding. Peru was in the 1980s.

From a sociological perspective, and therefore with some suspicion, we may ask ourselves what expectations these women had when they joined a sport run with an iron hand by a South Korean trainer considered among the best in all America? It could not have been as a mere pastime, even though they love to play. During that decade volleyball was a high-level sport, disciplined, demanding, rigorous, a rare example in a chaotic country not accustomed to adapting to athletic efforts. Evidently, by all rights and with reason, volleyball had become a way of life. Although it was an amateur sport, there were opportunities for economic and social benefits: prizes, employment, travel, recognition, and tradition. Whoever joined the team entered a perfect microcosm with established rules wherein the quality and dedication of a person superseded skin color or economic status. All of Peru coexisted on that team, with the grave exception, perhaps, of the Andean woman, whose presence, like that of the Andean man, has been limited for the aforementioned reasons.

This essay now addresses the third possible analysis: the volleyball players were Peruvians in spite of Peru! This means the team became a national cultural ensemble that did not live in Peru. The team was invited to Asian, European, or North American tournaments. The national women's volleyball team could not play in Peru if it intended to remain among the best in the world. It was a traveling country. Peru followed the squad by cable. And the populace welcomed the women—thrilled—when they spent their vacations in the country. In that way volleyball was transformed into a modern activity for Peru's women, who displayed their beauty in selected attire.

This modernity was possible only upon leaving the country, something akin to what Martín Adán, the celebrated, solitary, drunken, and extraordinary poet from Lima jokingly said: "to grow one must travel to Europe." To be a female volleyball player, a soccer player, a doctor, an engineer, or a painter one must migrate to Europe, for the only ones who willingly remain in the country are the narco traffickers or the subversives, who are incapable of developing a public culture that relates to their activities. These women were, originally, volleyball players in spite of Peru and then—ciao, baby—outside Peru.

This situation changed radically when Italian professional volleyball tempted the team members. In astonishment, Peruvians wondered how their idols could sign foreign contracts. Cecilia del Risco was one of the first to leave, but she went to Spain. Later the majority emigrated to Italy, returning only to represent Peru in South American or Pan American tournaments. At one point Man Bo Park suggested that he could go to Milan, in place of their returning to Peru, and they could train in Milan as opposed to Lima. All the players, almost without exception, were given the nickname "the Italians." They lived in pleasant villages, they had juicy contracts, they modelled, they amazed Peruvians, and they sent photos. Peruvians felt betrayed, but deep down, like the good promoters that they are, Peruvians understood the women's reasons. Man Bo Park stayed behind, alone in the El Olívar coliseum.

This stage, with its successes and fluctuations, culminated at the Seoul Olympics (1988). The players all returned, trained with fervor and decided to win the gold medal. They were on the verge of accomplishing just that. The score moved capriciously: the first set, Peru's; the second set, Peru's; the third set, the Soviets'; the fourth set, the Soviets'; the fifth set, the Soviets' . . . 16–14. And then they returned to Italy. Cecilia Tait, the major star, the golden brunette, the golden southpaw, disdainful and jovial, later opted for Brazil, delving into modeling and video clips. Previously, when they had been world champion runners-up in Lima, each player was given an apartment and a car. Volleyball was now a way of life, a way to make a living, to be a woman in Peru.

Three Women

Luisa Fuentes

Akira Kato sculpted Luisa Fuentes's life with oriental patience. Fuentes will be eternally associated with the origins of competitive volleyball in Peru. Born in Ica, dark-skinned and robust, incredibly strong, she played only five minutes for a team from Ica against a Japanese squad touring the country. Those five minutes were enough for her to be contacted by Akira Kato. The Japanese coach would teach her all his secrets by way of a training that, at times, seemed like punishment.

Luisa Fuentes—"Lucha" to Peruvians—exemplified absolute dedication and total obedience: a love life and motherhood were left behind. Some analysts believe that the social backgrounds of the early players left them no other option; the dilemma was to remain in rural areas or become volleyball players.

Those were the days when volleyball was played in exchange for very basic financing: fading uniforms that the players themselves had to wash, travel, and meal money. In 1982, Luisa Fuentes mistakenly believed that the players training for the world championships of that year would never play volleyball for fourteen years as she had done. But she was wrong because the majority has continued doing so, perhaps because they have found a way to make a living in volleyball. The professionalization of volleyball abroad, above all in Italy, permitted their continuation in the sport.

Cecilia Tait

Cecilia Tait's private life is a sea of mysteries, and I will not be the one to expose them—even if I knew them—in this vignette. The daughter of a Panamanian, she lived in the company of a middle-class family from Lima, which afforded her the opportunity to develop various aspects of her own potential, including a beautiful figure, and a proud and, at times, unpleasant personality. Everything about her, even these characteristics, fascinated men, be they Peruvian, Mexican, or European. Her romantic life would appear in newspapers, which she, in comparison with Luisa Fuentes, could not ignore. An Italian was one of her better-known lovers, as was a German with whom she now lives abroad.

Cecilia Tait is an attractive brunette who debuted at the Junior World Championships in Mexico. She was the golden southpaw of Peru's team for more than fifteen years. She suffered a serious cartilage injury and had surgery under modern conditions in the United States. She has reaped fame, admiration, and fortune. She has modeled, although she herself dismissed that possibility when she was young, and she manages her own businesses.

In her opinion the presence of Akiro Kato and Man Bo Park has been essential for the team: "if you want," she says "your son to be educated, responsible and disciplined, then you need to work and to work you need to teach your children and that is what has occurred with us. From the time you begin to play you have been taught discipline, which you now must demonstrate as an adult."[3]

Gabriela Pérez del Solar

Gaby, a tall girl of more or less 1.9 meters, was Man Bo Park's athletic daughter. Her unique quality—to be tall in a land of short men and women—was transformed into an endless number of virtues: a spiker and a blocker at the net, in addition to her dedication to the other volleyball players. Like Lucha and Cecilia, Gaby did not know how to play volleyball. Cecilia Tait confesses that at the beginning the trainer classified her as a "clown," and Gabriela Pérez del Solar was considered a "giraffe." In contrast with soccer, where men believe that technique equals ability, female volleyball players have learned to play volleyball; they have learned techniques; ability is grounded exclusively in possessing specific physical characteristics. Volleyball is practically the only sport in Peru that is considered a slow, patient, planned learning process,

Gaby is a white woman with the face of an eternal adolescent, who comes from a comfortable middle-class family. She has gained, like Lucha Fuentes and Cecilia Tait, the admiration of her fans; they love her, idolize her, and would imitate her if they could be as tall. There is a famous photograph of Gaby with former president Alan García, in which, perhaps because of her curly hair, she is taller than he by a few centimeters. Currently she plays in Italy. She has delved into the modeling business, not as a model, but as a clothing manufacturer.

Ill-Fated Days, the Criticisms of a Few Specialists, the Future Smiles at Peru Once More

After the Seoul Olympics there was a complete exodus; the twelve team members, including the alternates, left for Italy to play, make money, and live as independent women. This created a vacuum, which many specialists classified as Man Bo Park's fundamental error, having produced athletes but neglected to develop the sport.

Countries like Cuba, for example, can boast about having developed sports in their societies through athletic schools for players and trainers, schools whose success is measured by their ability to export coaches. Cuban athletics or boxing is Cuban, as is its volleyball or its baseball. The development of athletic infrastructures—playing grounds, clinics, trainers, schools—guarantees the continuation of athletic disciplines. When the twelve volleyball players left Peru, there was a sense of abandonment apropos to orphanhood. Peru had to begin anew, with young women, in the lower divisions, meaning a need for time for them to mature.

The misery came to an end with Brazil's defeat of Peru at the 1991 South American qualifying tournament for the Barcelona Olympics. Brazil, a giant in almost all South American athletics, was not that in women's volleyball. After so many years of Peruvian hegemony, Brazil succeeded in defeating Peru and preventing it from qualifying. Later Peru sought a place at the World Championships but could not qualify; it was eliminated by the United States. After having participated in the Olympics at Mexico, Munich, Montreal, Moscow, Los Angeles, and Seoul—a long tradition—Peruvians were, or so they thought, the grand absentees in Barcelona. A void had been created. Sometime earlier Man Bo Park was questioned about his high salary. Man Bo Park, with his still flawed Castillian, has become a naturalized Peruvian and is now the owner of a pharmacy; he loves Peru with its uncertain future and has rejected several offers from abroad.

Why do the women leave and why does he stay? Because to be a champion in Peru is an incomparable ecstasy. In this country the coach is also a father, the father that Franz Kafka never had, a combination of rigidity and bonhomie, subject to the rules and to affectionate patience. The Peruvian father—I know that is another story—is either a screaming authoritarian or irresponsible. The majority of coaches in Peru are foreigners: Barotti, Didi, Tim, and now Popovich in soccer, and Man Bo Park in volleyball. (Fujimori Fujimori is another matter. And Guzmán Reynoso, he had a father and a stepmother, etc., etc.).

Recently a new South Korean trainer, Dung Jung Park, took charge of the current junior team. He uses mime, hand signals, English, Italian, and a rudimentary spattering of Spanish to communicate with the girls. Judging by recent results they seem to understand him. And thus the enigma remains alive: Asian trainers, Peruvian women, volleyball as a sport, and Peru as a country may be the exotic or explosive formula that Alberto Fujimori, from one trench, and Abimael Guzmán Reynoso, from another, are trying to reproduce. Women's volleyball may be a kind of answer to this country's uncertain future. For now, the amalgam of races and social classes coexist in that microcosm, like a part of Peru, linked to the outside world as though it were an enterprise.[4]

Notes

1. José María Salcedo and Abelardo Sánchez-León, "Volibol peruano: Matar por amor al arte," *Quehacer* (Lima) (18 August 1982): 67–83.

2. Luisa Fuentes, the best-known star from volleyball's early years, says: "I do not have an ideal man, but he would be a good man, who loves me, good-natured. With that I would be satisfied. But the majority of Peruvian men are not like that. They need to work a bit more. The Peruvian man is lazy, womanizing. He should set some goals for himself and try to become better each day." Ibid.

3. Ibid.

4. Additional background on Peruvian women's volleyball is found in *Sobre la net: Itinerario de victorias* (Lima: Edición Copi, 1983).

13

In Search of the Latin American Female Athlete

Joseph L. Arbena

Over the long run, success in sport may be like the proverbial tree falling in the forest; if no one is there to witness the event, who can prove that it occurred? This parallel is true for sports in general in Latin America, where thus far only limited attention has been paid to its role in society, a situation that pertains particularly to the case of female athletes. Women are out there: they perform in at least modest numbers, and they win, but few people report on them; seldom do they receive international coverage or provoke scholarly analysis. Nevertheless, this does not mean that sport is not playing an important role in the broader realm of gender relations in the region, or that women athletes are always ignored or denigrated, as Abelardo Sánchez-León demonstrated in the previous selection.

Joseph Arbena, an authority on the literature of sport in Latin America, summarizes the current state of studies about women athletes and probes some of the reasons why so little has been written about them. Despite the usual excuses and obstacles—alleged physiological differences from men that make women inferior, household and workplace duties, male chauvinism, second-rate facilities, and more—Arbena finds that the field is not totally barren either of performers or coverage of them. In conclusion, he urges that more work be done regarding the study of women in sport as, he predicts, such an endeavor could reveal some surprises in what heretofore has been considered largely an all-male world.

It is no doubt revealing that in her otherwise comprehensive and highly useful sourcebook on Latin women of the Americas, Lynn Stoner failed to include a chapter on women in sports.[1] When I asked her about this void, she explained that there appeared to be few publications on Latin American female athletes and that no one to her knowledge was working in the field; thus, to commission such a contribution would have been

An earlier version of this article was presented at the annual meeting of the North American Society for Sport History, Auburn, Alabama, May 24–27, 1996.

meaningless. In their subsequent bibliographical survey, Edna Acosta-Belén and Christine E. Rose praised the growth in the number of works on women's studies, yet included no references to sports or athletes.[2] Likewise, Allen Guttmann, in his sweeping survey of women's sports, cites few Latin American athletes beyond those emerging from the special case of socialist Cuba after 1959.[3]

My own 1989 bibliography of Latin American sport included, much to my disappointment, only twenty-one entries with specific reference to female athletes, their training, and competition,[4] a fact commented on critically and justifiably by one reviewer of that volume, who found it "difficult to accept the small handful of items relating to women" in sports throughout the region.[5] Even fictional literature, before and after 1989, has yielded nothing about female athletes, although there are references to women in the lives of male athletes. My entirely new 1999 edition produced thirty-five index entries, hardly a major leap forward.[6] In short, I conclude that this dearth of bibliographical citations is a combined result of a shortage of first-class female athletes and a related lack of interest in the subject. The two reinforce each other.

Among the limited materials I had located by the time my first bibliography went to press and among those cited by Guttmann is a rare biography of a female athlete, Cuba's María Caridad Colón (b. 1959). In a simplistic, almost juvenile account, Frank Guiral summarizes the pro-Castro views of Cuban sport as seen in the life of a pretty girl of modest origins who goes from a small eastern city to win gold medals in the javelin at the Central American and Caribbean Games, the Pan American Games, and the 1980 Moscow Olympics, among others. In addition to expressing the revolutionary sports program, its training methods, and its linkage to the now-defunct Eastern European sports systems, Cari Colón allegedly represents Cuba's best as daughter, sister, student, wife, and mother as well as hard-working athlete.[7]

Later, as half of a two-part survey of the Cuban sports scene, S. L. Price introduced readers of *Sports Illustrated* to few female athletes beyond Ana Fidelia Quirot, age thirty-two in mid-1995, earlier the world's top runner at 400 and 800 meters, ex-wife of a world champion wrestler, and later lover of high jumper Javier Sotomayor. Once beautiful and vain, she was badly scarred and lost an unborn child in a 1993 accidental kitchen fire. But she had bounced back through hard work and was aiming at the 1996 Olympics, for which efforts she earned private hospital visits by the bearded leader and later his unlimited public praise. She is, says Price, "the prize product of Castro's socialist plan" and Fidel's "favorite athlete." In exchange, Quirot remained dedicated to her sport, loyal to her country, and faithful to her friends and former lovers. And she won the silver medal in the 800 in Atlanta.[8]

The question still remains whether these and other shining examples demonstrate that socialist Cuba has erased all vestiges of sexism in its impressive athletic system. Defenders of the revolution tend to answer in the affirmative; critics say the contrary.[9] In their impressive survey of Cuban sport, most notably in the post-1959 era, Paula J. Pettavino and Geralyn Pye take the cautious middle ground, probably with good cause. Although growing on both the elite and mass level, "women's participation in sports has always been much less than men's." In part, this results from the continued "popularity of sports that rarely include women," in part from the concentration on preparing to compete internationally in more glorious sports, and in part to a sense that "men only" sports provided implicitly a feeling of cultural continuity in a society often marked by rapid and disruptive change. On top is the hard truth that "despite the liberation that came with the revolution, Cuban women, like those in other societies, found limited time for sports, after working, caring for husbands and children, doing housework, and waiting in lines for rationed goods." While race, class, gender, or age is no longer a formal obstacle to sports participation at any level in Cuba, it is obvious that some problems persist due to uneven resource allocation and lingering social attitudes. And given Cuba's floundering economy, things are not likely to improve in the near future.[10]

Another limited yet encouraging study found even before my first bibliography appeared was a thin survey of great Chilean athletes. It was encouraging because, among its sketches of various men, it included a chapter devoted to Ismenia Pouchard, a "tall, beautiful, and intelligent" basketball player of "European ancestry" who, at the time of that study (1972), had been playing for twenty-two years, most of them with Santiago's top-level Colo Colo Club, and had been a member of the national team for eighteen. While emphasizing the subject's athletic skills and the international successes, if only on a limited scale, of her Chilean squads, the author could not resist describing "the other Ismenia," the one who worked for the Banco del Estado, read a lot, wished that she had a child to fulfill herself as a human being, and lamented that basketball had not left her enough time to enjoy the "beautiful side of life" that is the "tranquility of the home." But, at least, "basketball has taught her to be strong in the face of [such] adversity." Similar insights did not appear in the sketches of male sportsmen.[11]

In a brief epilogue, author Patricio Manns also praises Anita Lizana, probably Chile's best female tennis player ever, although she spent most of her competitive years (1935–1939) in England and eventually married an Englishman. During that brief span she won 107 out of 117 sets and fifty-three of fifty-nine matches; she captured the U.S. Open at Forest Hills in 1937. She had the advantage of having a prominent tennis coach for a father and of training in Argentina. But she must have been a special talent, since at least a few other players have enjoyed similar privileges without gaining as much success.[12]

I was also slightly rewarded in my bibliographical search by an inexpensive Peruvian publication devoted to women in sports. Unfortunately, while there are quick references to such little-known Peruvian female athletes as Ruth Jamie (marathon) and Fina Salazar (table tennis), most of the volume focuses on such non-Peruvians of international renown as Billie Jean King, Sonja Henie, and the Brazilian María Esther Bueno. But it concludes that the importance of women in sports is increasing and offers suggestions for how they can get and stay in shape.[13]

Beyond those, my pre-1989 inventory offered examples, even when they did not cite specific athletes, of the debate over the proper place of physical activity in women's lives. Representative of the traditional view was a book by a Spaniard that went through at least four editions in Chile; it contends that sports are important only as they contribute to work and that women are not meant to be participants, at least not in those of the physical variety.[14] Two Uruguayans, in contrast, asserted that women's functionality is not inferior to that of men, considering that women were for so long denied access to competitive sport, thanks to unscientific arguments.[15] Most positive was a Venezuelan tract arguing that women need to be involved equally in sports; they thus far have been denied such equality because they do not appear to the market economy to have sufficient commercial value. But they should exercise more to improve their health and use sports as a means to inculcate positive values in their children, even if society does not encourage them.[16] How influential any of these were is hard to say, although the fact that the negative item went through multiple editions suggests that it had some importance in its day. The last two, similar as they are to other observable changes, for example, in physical education and recreation programs, may mean that they reflect somewhat different times for women athletes.[17] I end this introduction to mostly older materials by noting that my initial bibliography also cites a few runs of sports magazines that contain materials on women's sports and recreation—untapped sources for someone hoping to construct a history of women's athletics in Latin America, however limited that history might be.[18]

~

Beginning in the late 1980s perhaps no single Latin American female athlete received as much press coverage as Gabriela Sabatini,[19] who drew on a long tradition of women's tennis in Argentina.[20] Attractive, personable, talented, and financially very successful both on and off the court, the Argentine never quite achieved as much athletically as observers had predicted. Still, writers in many countries found her "alluring," noted her appeal for commercial endorsements,[21] and hoped that she would serve as an example for other Latin American women who needed to break out of traditional restraints and work to enjoy the opportunities for athletic development available in the United States and Europe.[22] Yet they remained perplexed and disappointed by her frequent and extended slumps.[23] One Colombian suggested that her periodic lapses on the court resulted from her tendency to think of those "other things" that gradually intruded into her life.[24] And, despite an obvious contrast between capitalist and socialist drives, perhaps instead motivated by cultural bonds, even a Cuban writer could lament Sabatini's inability to defeat Steffi Graf and others with sufficient frequency to become number one in the world.[25]

Another stimulating contribution to the search for the Latin American female athlete is found in Kathleen Sands's work on Mexican *charrería*, an equestrian folk tradition with roots in Ibero-Mexican history and ranching and with links to North American rodeo. *Charrería*, as explained in the selection by Sands in this collection, is a male-dominated activity or sport, women's role being more aesthetic than competitive, although competition does exist. In their event, the *escaramuza*, "women ride only sidesaddle and in decorous costumes," although the drill patterns they perform require as much athletic skill and disregard for danger as in the men's events. Women also serve as *reinas*, or queens, of *charerría* associations, a post requiring both grace and equestrian abilities; with age they are supporters of present and "mothers" of future male and female performers. Their roles are festive, colorful, and important, but their status is secondary.[26]

There are also reports of women's entry into less traditional athletic roles. Laura Serrano García, in 1995 a 27-year-old law student and one of only twenty professional women boxers in Mexico, won the WIBF women's world boxing title at 130 pounds, despite the fact that only three Mexican states permitted female boxing and the federal boxing commission refused to acknowledge either the sport or the title. Later, Mexico City boxing authorities created a special commission to study the question of female boxing and finally recognized the sport but only at the amateur level.[27] Serrano, frustrated because "in my own country they shut the doors on me," packed up and moved to the United States where she found more tolerance of her sport and greater athletic and, thus, financial opportunities.[28] This despite reports that as early as 1930 Mazatlán native Margarita Montes, under the alias of "La Maya," had a brief career as Mexico's first female boxer, and that numerous male boxers, including national hero Julio César Chávez, have at times employed women as sparring partners.[29]

In Argentina, according to a report in the youth supplement of the widely read Buenos Aires daily, *Clarín*, young and attractive females are gradually moving into sports once practiced exclusively by men: specifically, auto racing, soccer, boxing, weightlifting, even polo. The number of participants is low, and funding and training resources are limited; jokes and insults are common.[30] For many Argentines, in the sporting world "the woman is still a complement to the man, not his equal." The soccer ritual, for all its changes regarding women, remains a process of social reproduction of male dominance. And those women who are penetrating the soccer or other sporting spheres must be careful not to lose their own gender identity.[31] Similarly, in Brazil, where girls were long discouraged, even banned, from playing soccer and women were rarely seen in soccer stadiums, females have become more expressive fans and some have begun to play, to the extent that Brazil now has a competitive national women's team. However, these advances have been slow and are resisted by men who consider the sport inappropriate for women, by women who fear the behavior of men in stadiums, and by a sexist language that reinforces masculine exclusivity on the field and in the stands.[32]

Not the object of much verbal abuse for much of the last two decades has been the Peruvian women's volleyball team whose success has been, as Peruvian journalist and poet Abelardo Sánchez-León contends in an article reprinted in this volume, contrary to the country's "lamentable story of consecutive defeats" and is possible only because the players learned to be good "in spite of Peru and then . . . outside Peru." In the process the players, most of them of modest origins, have become models for other Peruvian women who "are beginning to be associated with discipline, perseverance and the ability to work."[33]

Two nonscholarly Argentine periodicals with a strong female presence further suggest a slight opening: *Cuerpo & Mente en Deportes*, in 1995 in its tenth year of publication, and *Cuerpo & Mente en Aeróbica*, was launched in that same year and uses glossy paper and color photos. The former contains articles about prominent athletes, competitive sports, and even sport theory and history, but both its text and its advertisements reflect a strong interest in gymnastics, bodybuilding, health, and beauty. The latter is devoted entirely to the application of aerobic techniques to the maintenance of strong bodies and minds. The latter, exceeding the former, likewise had in its first issue about equal numbers of male and female writers and the same distribution of its photographs. Some of these illustrations bordered on soft pornography, so it is difficult for me to speculate about the intended market. Still, the two magazines together imply that someone believes that women as well as men are interested in reading about strenuous physical activities, participating in such activities, and buying products to aid in such participation.

In January 1990 the Mexican feminist magazine *Fem* published a collection of short pieces, most by Guadalupe López G., about the place of sports and recreation among the nation's women. This was a logical follow-up to two earlier *Fem* essays: one lamented that Mexican women not only lack free or leisure time to rest their bodies and develop human capabilities but they also are not even aware that they deserve such time or conscious of how to use to its fullest advantage what little they do get;[34] that article accompanied a second piece calling for specific research on aspects of these questions, realizing that not enough factual data yet existed to support more than speculative answers.[35]

In her half-dozen short essays, López G. concludes that some progress has been made toward increasing women's participation in sports, but that practice still does not match legal standards and administrative rhetoric. Thus, Mexican women are not deriving equitable benefits from sports programs and sports medicine, reflecting the unequal role this society has imposed on them: women are discouraged from participating in those sports considered for men only, women are not supposed to be aggressive and competitive, women are confined to the home, thereby enjoying less time to participate and enjoy. Sexism, prejudice, and a feminist focus on other issues have kept them underrepresented in athletic competition and, even more so, in sports leadership positions. And those few Mexican women who have achieved modest athletic success are not publicized and are not considered heroes. In short, while these new commentaries provided little hard data, they did at least raise some provocative questions and hypotheses and exposed some little documented ideas obviously circulating among Mexican women.[36]

After that special issue, *Fem* writers continued calling for nonsexist, non-role-defining toys and games that would permit children to develop the imagination, creativity, and skills necessary to become complete human beings and, citing cases from Mexico and elsewhere, have warned of the danger, especially to women athletes, of taking drugs and of undergoing such illegal or unethical medical treatments as radiation doses to stunt growth and planned pregnancies to increase short-term strength and speed.[37] In fact, since late 1994 *Fem* has made its column on women's sports a regular monthly feature, touching on such issues, in addition to those cited elsewhere, as pioneer Mexican women participants in the marathon (Alicia Villa) and speedboating (Lilián Arens),[38] the need to include more women in the upper levels of sports administration,[39] and the belief that women are in no greater danger than men of psychological stress or physical injury in the practice of sports.[40] Throughout, the ultimate message of *Fem* has been that women are first of all women; that they are athletes because they wish to excel, not because they wish to be men; and that they defend their right to pursue whatever sports they desire, even if they are accused thereby of losing their femininity.[41]

As an aside, I should note that for this paper I am not including the Anglophone Caribbean in my definition of Latin America. However, it would be an error not to mention the work of Jay and Joan Mandle, now of Colgate University, who have done so much to reveal to us the place of basketball in the often fractured societies of that region; an example of their work is found in this book. Over the years, one interesting sub-theme of their analysis has been the important, if secondary, role of women as both participants and spectators in Caribbean grassroots basketball.[42]

Slightly more afield has been the work of Eduardo Archetti who has sought, among other things, to identify the sexual content and symbolism in the totality of (especially) Argentine soccer.[43] More recently, Archetti and Jeffrey Tobin have linked soccer to such traditional masculine activities in Argentina as the tango and the *asado*, or outdoor barbecue. Women are, at best, a marginal part of that world and, at worst, objects of domination or even violence.[44] While this does not focus on female athletes per se, it does draw our attention to the potential gender meanings of all sporting behavior, proposes ways in which cultures constantly reaffirm or redefine their gender perceptions and roles, and raises speculation about what might occur in Latin American society should women ever gain a preeminent place on the athletic field.[45] In sum, with notable exceptions, works both before and after 1989 that study Latin American female athletes are brief, isolated, come as part of works more generally devoted to men, and are often sexist, or at least condescending, in tone.

~

These works are why Liliana Morelli's 1990 volume, despite its limitations, is so important. *Mujeres deportistas*, one of a series of books on Argentine women in various fields, looks at the personalities, personal lives, and athletic careers of eighteen women, two of whom are Swedish and only one, Gabriela Sabatini, truly active in the 1990s, who have made significant contributions to Argentine sport in the twentieth century.[46] Their areas run the gamut from aviation[47] to swimming, fencing, track and field, rowing, golf, both auto and horse racing, roller skating, and tennis. Using mainly interviews and press accounts, Morelli notes the sacrifices that most of her subjects endured, often choosing sport over schooling and/or family as they struggled to find both time and facilities for their training and competition. She also finds reflected in these women's lives a qualitative difference between the older "amateur" system and the more intense, even dehumanizing professional regime. Most of Morelli's sportswomen trained and triumphed for the love of sport; most failed to gain and hold the reward or recognition they deserved. Similar problems hampered the career of roller skater Nora Alicia Vega (b. 1961, Mar del Plata) who still managed to win five world titles, eight Pan American Games medals, ten South American Championships, and some fifty national tournaments.[48] Yet, despite its rich factual content and lively spirit, Morelli's narrative will disappoint most scholars: it has no footnotes, no bibliography, and no discussion of methodology or theoretical design.

Still, we can hope that Morelli's work represents a change in attitudes that will generate more studies of Latin American female athletes both inside and outside the region. Encouraging is the essay by Brazilian sociologist and University of Florida faculty member Glaucio Ary Dillon Soares, who, in a survey of women athletes in the modern Olympics, concluded that they have markedly closed the gap between their performances and those of men, often surpassing men's marks from all but the most recent Games. Also, women in countries such as the United States frequently approach or even exceed the best men in countries such as Paraguay. Consequently, he asks if men's traditionally better performances result from genetic differences or from such factors as number of performers, years of involvement, levels of support, and societal values.[49] Similar views, with pronounced support for greater gender equity in sports, are expressed by Claudio Tamburrini, an Argentine moral philosopher resident in Sweden, who cites the recent success of women's tennis as a model for the future when "female athletes will compete equally with men."[50]

Unfortunately, such views as those of Morelli, Soares, and Tamburrini may not yet prevail among Latin American journalists, scholars, and sports administrators. For example, writing less than a decade ago in what I consider a moderately liberal historical journal, Argentine author Pablo Ramírez offered an "homage" to the female athlete who "logically" performs in "man's shadow" because nature conferred on her a special role in the creation process: "women should always symbolize the delicateness, the tenderness of life." Ramírez himself had a "marvelous mother" to whom he owes "the pleasure of existence," because of whom he has enjoyed many of life's "highest and most beautiful things," and in whose memory he prepared his essay.

Not surprisingly, Ramírez does not like women's soccer or boxing, or female sports photographers; such are not proper feminine roles. For him, and perhaps correctly, "the greatest feat achieved by an [Argentine] woman" athlete was jockey Marina Lezcano's 1978 quadruple crown in Argentine horse racing.[51] This was to him clearly superior to the successes of Gabriela Sabatini who, for all the international recognition she brought to her country and the money she earned, played against only other women, while Lezcano defeated men. And Ramírez's few other specific female examples were cited more for their grace, dedication, or "spiritual strength" than for their pure athletic ability.[52]

In a similar vein, one Colombian educator argued that, given its value in the development of the individual and in the national culture, soccer must be properly integrated into all physical education programs. Unfortunately, only men play soccer. Attempts have been made to change this, but around the world these have been a "complete failure": women's play "has lacked power, skill, and understanding; in all female experiments [with soccer] there is insufficient impulsion and effort to generate corporal force."[53]

In 1995 a Nicaraguan author, possibly a medical doctor, highlighted the accomplishments of the country's various female athletes, including those who have represented Nicaragua in the Olympics, and called for more support for future sportswomen. Nevertheless, he went to great lengths to point out what he considers the physiological and psychological differences between men and women, differences which make it difficult for women to perform at the same level. Women have less muscular, cardiocircular, and respiratory capacity than men; they are more intellectual than combative; and their periods of tension and menstruation seriously reduce their athletic abilities. Above all, it should not be forgotten that the reason women were created was maternity, their "protagonist role . . . in the reproduction of the species." The myths and stereotypes persist.[54]

~

Despite Ramírez and people like him, the world is changing, as the editors of *Fem* have suggested. Limited evidence of this is found in the results of the 2000 Summer Olympic Games, where women athletes from Latin America and the Caribbean won fourteen individual and eight team medals. However, seven of those went to Cuba, five to Jamaica, four to Brazil, and two each to Argentina and Costa Rica; neither a geographical nor demographic balance was achieved. Perhaps the most surprising achievement was by Soraya Jiménez Mendivil (Mexico) and María Isabel Urrutia (Colombia), who each won gold medals in women's weight lifting (an Olympic sport for the first time in Sydney) and became national heroes back home.[55]

Obviously, however, the women's sports scene in Latin America is changing only slowly, and I fear we will have to wait some time before large numbers of the region's females come to the top of international elite sports and before more serious studies of female Latin American athletes come out of the region itself. And, it hurts me to report that I know of no North American scholar who is entering the field. Thus, in the near future, coverage in Spanish and Portuguese will continue to be limited, though with gradually more attention in the press. For coverage in English we apparently must depend on irregular journalistic accounts and on passing references in writings with a different focus.

Further, few Latin American female athletes have gained international recognition, although a surprising number have gained respect and praise from their own countrymen. Clearly, many more have labored anonymously in both the amateur and professional spheres, winning at times but earning little. We need to know more about these individuals: their social backgrounds, their objectives, their training methods, their self-perception, their place in the larger athletic community, their destiny after leaving sport. No doubt, due to a lack of both will and resources the entire sports structure in Latin America is less developed than those in North America and Europe, and women have surely suffered from this more than men. Nevertheless, I suspect that serious research would reveal some surprises about female athletes in the supposedly "male" world of Latin America. The record suggests, however, that such research awaits both expanded personnel and revised attitudes.

Notes

1. K. Lynn Stoner, ed., *Latinas of the Americas: A Source Book* (New York: Garland, 1989). For the purposes of this paper, I accept the categorization of female/woman based on self and peer identification. For a critique of recent literature on gender and sex differentiation and the complex problems involved in defining such terms, see John Hood-Williams, "Sexing the Athletes," *Sociology of Sport Journal* 12, no. 3 (1995): 290–305. For one example of the difficulties involved in working out these problems in the real world of the Olympics, see Denise Grady, "Sex Test of Champions," *Discover* 13 (June 1992): 78–82. A Mexican feminist comment on the difficulties that female athletes have faced in trying to prove they are truly women is offered in Elina Hernández [Carballido], "El examen de la feminidad: Un problema deportivo aun sin solución," *Fem* 18, no. 139 (September 1994): 40–41.

2. Edna Acosta-Belén and Christine E. Rose, eds., *Researching Women in Latin America and the Caribbean* (Boulder, CO: Westview Press, 1993).

3. Allen Guttmann, *Women's Sports: A History* (New York: Columbia University Press, 1991).

4. Joseph L. Arbena, *An Annotated Bibliography of Latin American Sport: Pre-Conquest to the Present* (Westport CT: Greenwood Press, 1989).

5. David M. K. Sheinin, "Assessing Recent Reference Works on Latin America," *Latin American Research Review* 27, no. 2 (1992): 264.

6. Joseph L. Arbena, *Latin American Sport: An Annotated Bibliography, 1988–1998* (Westport, CT: Greenwood Press, 1999).

7. Frank Guiral, *María Caridad Colón: La jabalina de oro* (Havana: Editorial Científico-Técnica, 1985).

8. S. L. Price, "The best little sports machine in the world," *Sports Illustrated* 82, no. 19 (May 15, 1995): 60–78; "Back in the Running," *Sports Illustrated* 82, no. 20 (May 22, 1995): 48–55. In his latest, highly personal commentary on sports under Castro, Price says virtually nothing about female athletes, although he did visit with Quirot several times; see, *Pitching around Fidel: A Journey into the Heart of Cuban Sports* (New York: Ecco Press, 2000). Another sympathetic profile of Quirot is offered in Elizabeth Royte, "Return of a Scarred Fidelista," *New York Times Magazine* (June 23, 1996): 42–43.

9. Eric A. Wagner, "Sport in Revolutionary Societies: Cuba and Nicaragua," in *Sport and Society in Latin America: Diffusion, Dependency, and the Rise of Mass Culture*, ed. Joseph L. Arbena (Westport, CT: Greenwood Press, 1988), 123–27; Joseph L. Arbena, "Sport and Revolution: The Continuing Cuban Experience," *Studies in Latin American Popular Culture* 9 (1990): 319–28.

10. Paula J. Pettavino and Geralyn Pye, *Sport in Cuba: The Diamond in the Rough* (Pittsburgh: University of Pittsburgh Press, 1994)—for a summary discussion of the debate over problems in promoting mass participation in Cuban sports, see pages 121–26; idem, "Sport in Cuba: Castro's Last Stand," *Studies in Latin American Popular Culture* 13 (1994): 165–84. For an earlier and somewhat

more optimistic picture of the women's sports system in Revolutionary Cuba, see Karen Shaw, "Cuban Sportswomen," *Cubatimes* 3, no. 3–4 (1983): 31–32.

11. Patricio Manns, *Grandes deportistas*, No. 31 in *Nosotros los chilenos* (Santiago: Editora Nacional Quimantú, 1972), 55–62.

12. Ibid., 93. For brief sketches of thirty-two Chilean athletes, including some females, see Carlos Guerrero, *Grandes del deporte*, No. 15 in *Nosotros los chilenos* (Santiago: Editora Nacional Gabriela Mistral, 1975).

13. Lidio Gallo Antoniotti, *La mujer y el deporte* (Lima: Ediciones y Promociones Futuras, 1978[?]).

14. Gregorio Marañón, *Tres ensayos sobre la vida sexual*, 4th ed. (Santiago: Editorial "Cultura," 1934 [1926]).

15. Gaetano Carlevaro Pérsico and José Laurino, *Blanco, mestizo, negro en el deporte* ([Montevideo]: Pozzetto, 1984).

16. América López de Gouverneur, *La mujer y el deporte* ([Caracas: n.p., 1975]).

17. For comments on one typical law that requires a country to provide physical education for all its children, see Donna Cleland, "Educación Física in Costa Rica," *Journal of Physical Education and Recreation* 51, no. 7 (September 1980): 63–66.

18. *Vida Sportiva* (Rio de Janeiro, 1917–1920); *Aire Libre* (Lima, 1923); *Encestando* (Bahía Blanca, Argentina, 1965–); *Full Speed* (Lima, 1980s).

19. For a brief time there was interest in Costa Rican swimmer Silvia Poll, but that did not last, no doubt a reflection of the nature of her sport; Matt Kenny, "Costa Rica's Golden Girl Makes a Splash," *Américas* 40, no. 4 (1988): 53–54. Younger sister Claudia Poll never attracted the same attention, despite winning a gold medal in Atlanta and two bronze medals in Sydney; she even had trouble getting recognition and praise in her own country.

20. Mauricio Cohen Salama et al., *Cien años del Buenos Aires Lawn Tennis Club, 1892–1992* (Buenos Aires: Buenos Aires Lawn Tennis Club, 1992). The club's first tournament for women was held in 1903, following the men's by only a decade.

21. Elizabeth Comte, "The Allure of Gabriela Sabatini," *Parade Magazine* (September 3, 1989); Fabián Waintal, "Gaby," *Sport* 81, no. 6 (June 1990): 96–99; James Brady, "In Step With Gabriela Sabatini," *Parade* (November 22, 1992): 18.

22. Elmo Valencia, "La mujer en los deportes," *La Guía de Bogotá* 13, no. 80 (October–November 1986): 29–31, 34.

23. Sally Jenkins, "Gabriela Sabatini," *Sports Illustrated* 80, no. 22 (June 6, 1994): 60.

24. "¿Qué pasa con vos, Gabriela?" *Semana* 621 (March 29, 1994): 92–94. In an earlier piece, Carlos Briceño attributed some of Sabatini's inconsistency to poor conditioning; "Gigi, Mary Joe & Gabriela," *Hispanic* (July 1988): 28–33.

25. Jorge Alvarez, "La pesadilla Graf," *Prisma Latinoamericano* 15, no. 203 (August 1989): 54.

26. For a more complete discussion, see Kathleen Mullen Sands, *Charrería Mexicana: An Equestrian Folk Tradition* (Tucson: University of Arizona Press, 1993). Related, though much less focused on Latin America, is Mary Lou LeCompte, *Cowgirls of the Rodeo: Pioneer Professional Athletes* (Urbana: University of Illinois Press, 1993).

27. Francisco Ponce, "Con su campeonato mundial, Laura Serrano espera abrir las puertas al boxeo femenil en México," *Proceso* 966 (May 8, 1995): 74–75; Elina Hernández Carballido, "El boxeo: un deporte, un arte . . . es pasión: Laura Serrano García, la mejor deportista mexicana de 1995," *Fem* 19, no. 153 (December 1995): 46–47.

28. Michelle Sánchez, "Laura Serrano emigró a Las Vegas, decepcionada," *Magazine Deportivo* no. 197 (February 2001): 50–52. For an introduction to the emerging world of women's boxing in the United States, see Richard Hoffer, "Gritty Woman," *Sports Illustrated* 84, no. 15 (April 15, 1996): 56–62.

29. Marco A. Maldonado and Rubén A. Zamora, *Cosecha de campeones: Historia del box mexicano*, vol. 2, *1961–1999* (México, D.F.: Editorial Clío, 2000), 78–79.

30. Natasha Niebieskiwiat, "Mujercitas," *Sí: Suplemento Joven de Clarín*, July 14, 1995. On females in polo, see Paula Varsavski, "Amor al juego," *American Airlines Nexus* (October–December 2000): 61–68.

31. María Graciela Rodríguez, "Territorio unisex," *Perfil*, May 9, 1998.

32. Janet Lever, *Soccer Madness* (Chicago: University of Chicago Press 1983); Larry Rohter, "Brazil Averts Its Eyes," *New York Times*, July 4, 1999.

33. Abelardo Sánchez-León, "The History of Peruvian Women's Volleyball," *Studies in Latin American Popular Culture* 13 (1994): 143–52. An example of uncompromised praise for the Peruvian squad is found in *Sobre la net: Itinerario de victoria* (Lima: Edición Copé, 1983).

34. Matilde Terán, "Tiempo libre . . . ¿cuál?" *Fem* 13, no. 80 (August 1989): 18–20.

35. Elsie McPhail, "El tiempo libre," *Fem* 13, no. 80 (August 1989): 10–17.

36. The six short articles by Guadalupe López G. are found in *Fem* 14, no. 85 (January 1990): 10–24.

37. Mayleth Echegollen Guzmán, "¿A qué jugamos?" *Fem* 16, no. 118 (December 1992): 17–18; Elina Hernández Carbillido, "El doping en el deporte," *Fem* 19, no. 142 (December 1994): 47–48, and "Laboratorios femeninos," *Fem* 19, no. 143 (January 1995): 46–47. As a feminist with athletic interests, Hernández Carbillido also expresses her longtime and continued admiration for Romanian Olympic gymnastics champion Nadia Comaneci and North American "Super Woman" Babe Didrickson; see "Nadie como Nadia Comaneci," *Fem* 19, no. 141 (November 1994): 48, and "Mildred Didrickson: 'La Super Hembra,' " *Fem* 19, no. 144 (February 1995): 44–45.

38. Elina Hernández Carballido, "Una lucha por 42.195 kilómetros," *Fem* 19, no. 149 (August 1995): 47–48, and "Una mujer en el agua enfrenta a la velocidad," *Fem* 20, no. 154 (January 1996): 46–47.

39. Elina Hernández Carballido, "La mujer en la administración del deporte," *Fem* 19, no. 152 (November 1995): 47–48.

40. Elina Hernández Carballido, "La psicología en ayuda del deporte (I)," *Fem* 19, no. 148 (July 1995): 47–48, and "Lesiones en deportistas," *Fem* 19, no. 145 (March 1995): 47–48.

41. Elina Hernández Carbillido, "Deportes no femeninos: Machismo o falta de costumbre," *Fem* 19, no. 147 (June 1995): 48, and "La psicología en ayuda del deporte."

42. For recent summaries of their ideas and citations of their earlier publications, see Jay R. Mandle and Joan D. Mandle, *Caribbean Hoops: The Development of West Indian Basketball*, Vol. 8 in *Caribbean Studies* (Langhorne, PA: Gordon & Breach, 1994), and "The Failure of Caribbean Integration: Lessons from Grass Roots Basketball," *Studies in Latin American Popular Culture* 13 (1994): 153–64.

43. For examples of Archetti's reasoning, see "Fútbol, violencia y afirmación masculina," *Debates en la Sociedad y la Cultura* 2, no. 3 (April–May 1885): 38–44, and "El fútbol y el otro machismo," *Palabra Suelta* 1 (1987): 12–16. For an analysis of an Argentine literary comment on related phenomena, see Geralyn

Pye, "Political Football: Sports, Power and Machismo in Luisa Valenzuela's *The Lizard's Tail,*" *Studies in Latin American Popular Culture* 13 (1994): 115–27.

44. See Eduardo P. Archetti, *Masculinities: Football, Polo and the Tango in Argentina* (Oxford, UK: Berg, 1999), and Jeffrey P. Tobin, "Manly Acts, Buenos Aires, 24 March 1996," Ph.D. diss., Rice University, 1998.

45. Seven decades ago Philip Guedalla speculated on the ways that playing golf at the country clubs might be changing social values and family patterns among Argentina's upper-class ladies; *Argentine Tango* (New York: Harper & Brothers, 1933), 164–65.

46. Liliana Morelli, *Mujeres deportistas* (Buenos Aires: Editorial Planeta, 1990).

47. For an introduction to another early Argentine female aviator, see Julio A. Luqui Lagleyze, "Amalia Celia Figueredo de Pietra, primera aviadora argentina y sudamericana," *Todo Es Historia* 25, no. 291 (September 1991): 72–80.

48. Lorena Costanza et al., *Nora, la vida sobre patines* (Buenos Aires: Ediciones Corregidor, 1997). Interesting is the story of the impact of the change from traditional to line skates.

49. Glaucio Ary Dillon Soares, "A mulher nas Olimpíadas," *Ciência Hoje* 8, no. 43 (June 1988): 34–43

50. Claudio M. Tamburrini, *¿La mano de Dios? Una visión distinta del deporte* (Buenos Aires: Ediciones Continente, 2001), 121–70, 182–83; quote from 182.

51. Lezcano is one of Liliana Morelli's subjects; see *Mujeres deportistas*, 163–72.

52. Pablo A. Ramírez, "Las deportistas," *Todos Es Historia* 25, no. 335 (June 1995): 38–41.

53. Tucídides Perea Rosero, *Fútbol: Educación y cultura* (Bogotá: Editorial Deportiva Colombiana, 1990), 194. For brief comments on the beginnings of women's soccer in Mexico around 1970, see Elina Hernández Carballido, "Inicios del futbol femenil," *Fem* 19, no. 146 (April/May 1995): 46–47.

54. Edmundo Quintanilla M., *Antecedentes históricos, mitos y realidades sobre la práctica deportiva en la mujer* (Managua: Instituto Nicaragüense de Estudios Socio Políticos, [1995]); quote from p. 39. My thanks to Richard McGehee for bringing this title to my attention.

55. Fabiola Zamorán, "Soraya Jiménez, primera pesista mexicana en Juegos Olímpicos," *Proceso* 1212 (January 23, 2000): 76–77. For one of many postgame Mexican comments on Jiménez, see the "Sydney: Suplemento olímpico" published by *El Universal*, October 2, 2000.

Suggested Readings

A selection of recent publications in English on aspects of sport in Latin America follows. For additional sources, check the notes and bibliographies cited in the chapters of this book.

Alabarces, Pablo, Ramiro Coelho, and Juan Sanguinetti. "Treacheries and Traditions in Argentinean Football Styles: The Story of Estudiantes de la Plata," in *Fear and Loathing in World Football*, ed. Gary Armstrong and Richard Giulianotti, 237–49. Oxford, UK: Berg, 2001. The rise and decline of the controversial Estudiantes team in the late 1960s paralleled the policies and fortunes of the Onganía dictatorship.

Alabarces, Pablo, and María Graciela Rodríguez. "Football and Fatherland: The Crisis of National Representation in Argentinian Soccer," in *Football Culture: Local Contests, Global Visions*, ed. Gerry P. T. Finn and Richard Giulianotti, 118–133. London: Frank Cass, 2000. Soccer may no longer be enough to overcome Argentina's lack of sources of national identification and unity.

Arbena, Joseph L. "The Diffusion of Modern European Sport in Latin America: A Case Study of Cultural Imperialism?" *South Eastern Latin Americanist* 33, no. 4 (March 1990): 1–8. Considers why European sports have been so widely adopted in Latin America.

_______. "Generals and *Goles*: Assessing the Connection between the Military and Soccer in Argentina," *International Journal of the History of Sport* 7, no. 1 (May 1990): 120–30. How the Argentine military leadership sought to use soccer for its economic and political benefit.

_______. "History of Latin American Sports: The End before the Beginning?" *Sporting Traditions* 16, no. 1 (November 1999): 23–31. Cites some useful new approaches to the study of sports in Latin America.

_______. "Meaning and Joy in Latin American Sports," *International Review for the Sociology of Sport* 35, no. 1 (March 2000), 83–91. Are sports understood better as a form of pleasure or as part of a sociological model?

_______. "Sport, Development, and Mexican Nationalism, 1920–1970," *Journal of Sport History* 18, no. 3 (Winter 1991): 350–64. Using sport to rebuild after a decade of revolution.

_______. "Sport and the Promotion of Nationalism in Latin America: A Preliminary Interpretation," *Studies in Latin American Popular Culture* 11 (1992): 143–55. Governments have tried to use sports to promote national unity and political stability, but often without success.

_______. "Sport and Sport Themes in Latin American Literature: A Sampler," *Arete: The Journal of Sport Literature* 5, no. 1 (Fall 1987): 143–59. Soccer, boxing, baseball, and other sports have found places in some Latin American literary writings, including those of several prominent authors. See Henager, P. Eric; and Perri, Brad, cited below.

______, comp. *An Annotated Bibliography of Latin American Sport: Pre-Conquest to the Present.* Westport, CT: Greenwood Press, 1989. Cites 1,379 titles, mainly in English, Spanish, and Portuguese.

_______, comp. *Latin American Sport: An Annotated Bibliography, 1988–1998.* Westport, CT: Greenwood Press, 1999. Cites 1,098 titles, mainly in English, Spanish, and Portuguese.

_______, ed. *Sport and Society in Latin America: Diffusion, Dependency, and the Rise of Mass Culture.* Westport, CT: Greenwood Press, 1988. Eight original essays treating modern sports in Latin America.

Archetti, Eduardo P. "Argentinian Football: A Ritual of Violence?" *International Journal of the History of Sport* 9, no. 2 (August 1992): 209–35. Links soccer/football to masculine ritual and expressions of public and government violence in the 1970s and later.

_______. "In Search of National Identity: Argentinian Football and Europe," *The International Journal of the History of Sport* 12, no. 2 (August 1995): 201–19. Can soccer provide Argentines with a source of national identity?

_______. *Masculinities: Football, Polo, and the Tango in Argentina.* Oxford, UK: Berg, 1999. Sport and dance are tied to Argentine gender roles and national identity.

_______. "The Moralities of Argentinian Football," in *The Ethnography of Moralities*, ed. Signe Howell, 98–123. London: Routledge, 1997.

_______. "The Spectacle of a Heroic Life: The Case of Diego Maradona," in *Sports Stars: The Cultural Politics of Sporting Celebrity*, ed. David L. Andrews and Steven J. Jackson, 151–63. London, UK: Routledge, 2001. In both triumph and joy, tragedy and grief, Maradona remains the quintessential Argentine "*pibe*," or spontaneous youth, and thus the ideal(ized) national symbol/hero.

_______, and Amílcar G. Romero. "Death and Violence in Argentinian Football," in *Football, Violence and Social Identity*, ed. Richard Giulianotti, Norman Bonney, and Mike Hepworth, 37–72. London: Routledge, 1994. Examines four cases of deadly violence at Argentine soccer stadiums (1958, 1967, 1976, 1983).

Beckles, Hilary [McD.]. "Brian Lara: (Con)testing the Caribbean Imagination," in *Sports Stars: The Cultural Politics of Sporting Celebrity*, ed. David L. Andrews and Steven J. Jackson, 243–56. London, UK: Routledge, 2001. The best cricket batsman in the world, as captain of the West Indies team, multimillionaire Lara has been the source of controversy, a consequence of his symbolizing a new paradigm in the region's national identity in a global age.

______, ed. *An Area of Conquest: Popular Democracy and West Indies Cricket Supremacy.* Kingston, Jamaica: Ian Randle, 1994. Highlights the crucial role of cricket in the Anglophone Caribbean as both sport and an expression of popular culture and identity.

______, and Brian Stoddart, eds. *Liberation Cricket: West Indies Cricket Culture*. Manchester, UK: Manchester University Press, 1995. More of the above.

Beezley, William H. *Judas at the Jockey Club and Other Episodes of Porfirian Mexico*. Lincoln: University of Nebraska Press, 1987. Sport was one important expression of an attitude about progress in late nineteenth-century Mexico.

Bestard, Miguel Angel. *International Football in South America, 1901–1991*, trans. Helen Bonser. [n.p.]: Soccer Book Publishing Ltd., 1992. Tables and short comments provide details of international competitions by the national teams of ten South American countries.

Bjarkman, Peter C. *Baseball with a Latin Beat: A History of the Latin American Game*. Jefferson, NC: McFarland & Co., 1994. A useful combination of details, human interest, and interpretation.

Bretón, Marcos, and José Luis Villegas. *Away Games: The Life and Times of a Latin Baseball Player*. New York: Simon & Schuster, 1999. Traces the career of Dominican shortstop Miguel Tejada in the context of Latinos in major league baseball.

Briley, Ron. "Houston's Latin Star César Cedeño and Death in the Dominican Republic: The Troubled Legacy of Race Relations in the Lone Star State," in *The Cooperstown Symposium on Baseball and American Culture, 2000*, ed. William M. Simons, 219–36. Jefferson, NC: McFarland & Company, 2001. In their treatment of César Cedeño and other Latino players, Houston Astro officials have shown a lack of full enthusiasm or respect.

Brock, Darryl. *Havana Heat*. New York: Plume/Penguin, 2001 [2000]. A baseball novel set partially in Cuba in the early twentieth century.

Brunt, Stephen. *Second to None: The Roberto Alomar Story*. Toronto: Penguin Books, 1993. A member of a well-known baseball family, Puerto Rican All-Star second baseman Alomar helped lead Toronto to the World Series championship in 1992. He later played with Baltimore and Cleveland.

Burns, Jimmy. *Hand of God: The Life of Diego Maradona*. London: Bloomsbury, 1996. Praises Maradona's skills but criticizes his character.

Cantor, Andrés, with Daniel Arcucci. *Gooooal! A Celebration of Soccer*. New York: Simon & Schuster, 1996. A commentary on soccer by a popular Latino sportscaster.

Chávez, Luciana. "A World Away," *The Sporting News* (February 19, 2001): 46–49. A look at Montreal Expo Vladimir Guerrero in his Dominican Republic home and community.

Duncan, P. J. *Sosa! Baseball's Home Run Hero*. New York: Simon & Schuster, 1998. Also published as *¡Sosa! El héroe del jonrón,* combined in a bilingual edition. A positive picture of Dominican and Chicago Cubs slugger Sammy Sosa.

Evanson, Philip. "Understanding the People: *Futebol*, Film, Theater and Politics in Present-Day Brazil," *South Atlantic Quarterly* 81, no. 4 (Autumn 1982): 399–412. Critics often overlook the importance and possible political value of soccer's popularity in Brazil.

Fainaru, Steve, and Ray Sánchez. *The Duke of Havana: Baseball, Cuba, and the Search for the American Dream.* New York: Villard/Random House, 2001. The story of Orlando "El Duque," Hernández who fled Cuba and became a star pitcher for the New York Yankees.

Galeano, Eduardo. *Soccer in Sun and Shadow*, trans. Mark Fried. London: Verso, 1998 (1995). A leading Uruguayan intellectual and fanatical soccer fan offers an insightful, at times humorous, critique of soccer past and present.

Giulianotti, Richard. "Built by the Two Varelas: The Rise and Fall of Football Culture and National Identity in Uruguay," in *Football Culture: Local Contests, Global Visions*, ed. Gerry P. T. Finn and Richard Giulianotti, 134–54. London: Frank Cass, 2000. Uruguay's days of international soccer glory are past.

Goldemberg, Isaac. *Play by Play*, trans. Hardie St. Martin. New York: Persea Books, 1985 (1984). Uses a soccer match to comment on life in Lima for people of mixed ethnic and cultural identity struggling to get ahead, as is Peru the nation.

González, G. Leticia. "The Stacking of Latinos in Major League Baseball: A Forgotten Minority?" *Journal of Sport and Social Issues* 22 (May 1996): 134–60. Latinos are overrepresented in core on-field positions, but there are virtually no Latino managers.

González Echevarría, Roberto. *The Pride of Havana: A History of Cuban Baseball.* New York: Oxford University Press, 1999. Comprehensive and detailed; a monumental work.

Goodall, Lian. *Maradona: The Man with the Magic Feet.* Toronto: Warwick, 1999. A juvenile biography of the Argentine soccer star whose drug use shortened his brilliant professional career.

Granger, Bill. *The New York Yanquis*. New York: Arcade, 1995. The greedy owner of the New York Yankees recruits an entire team of Cubans from Castro's island in hopes of cutting costs and possibly winning more games. A humorous fictional comment on cultural differences and the state of professional baseball in the 1990s.

Guttmann, Allen. *Games and Empires: Modern Sports and Cultural Imperialism.* New York: Columbia University Press, 1994. Includes numerous references to the diffusion of modern sports to Latin America as part of a global process.

Henager, P. Eric. "Physical Competition and Identity in '*Día Domingo*' and '*Final Del Juego*,' " *Aethlon: The Journal of Sport Literature* 17, no. 2 (Spring 2000): 77–91. Looks at the role of sport in short stories by two prominent Latin American writers.

Hoffer, Richard. "Spurred to Greatness," *Sports Illustrated* 94, no. 20 (May 14, 2001): 54–58. Félix "Tito" Trinidad, perhaps the best boxer on the current scene and one of the best of all time, is a popular hero in his native Puerto Rico.

International Baseball Rundown (1992–2001). ISSN: 1097–1688. Recently ceased publication, but over the years it contained numerous reports on baseball in Latin America.

Jamail, Milton. *Full Count: Inside Cuban Baseball.* Carbondale: Southern Illinois University Press, 2000. Reinforces the traditional image of baseball's importance to Cubans. The author has contributed often to *USA Today, Baseball Weekly*, and *The Sporting News.*

Joseph, Gilbert M. "Documenting a Regional Pastime: Baseball in Yucatán," in *Windows on Latin America: Understanding Society through Photographs*, ed. Robert M. Levine, 76–89. Coral Gables, FL: North-South Center, University of Miami, 1987.

Kinsella, W. P. "Searching for January," in *The Dixon Cornbelt League and Other Baseball Stories*, 111–20. New York: HarperCollins, 1993. Whatever happened to the body and spirit of Roberto Clemente on December 31, 1972?

Klein, Alan M. *Baseball on the Border: A Tale of Two Laredos*. Princeton, NJ: Princeton University Press, 1997. An ethnographic study showing how baseball contributes to nationalism on different levels across the U.S.-Mexican border.

______. "Borderline Treason: Nationalisms and Baseball on the Texas-Mexican Border," *Journal of Sport and Social Issues* 23 (August 1996): 296–313. If you cannot read Klein's *Baseball on the Border*, at least read this article.

______. "Culture, Politics, and Baseball in the Dominican Republic," *Latin American Perspectives* 22, no. 3 (Summer 1995): 111–30. Highly popular, baseball plays various roles in Dominican society.

______. "Latinizing Fenway Park: A Cultural Critique of the Boston Red Sox, Their Fans, and the Media," *Sociology of Sport Journal* 17, no. 4 (2000): 403–22. The success and popularity of a Latino star such as Pedro Martínez does not mean that Anglo fans are more tolerant of all Latinos.

______. *Sugarball: The American Game, the Dominican Dream*. New Haven: Yale University Press, 1991. Dominicans love the game but also seek success for financial reasons.

Knisley, Michael. "Everybody Has the Dream," *The Sporting News* (February 19, 2001): 50–54. The dream of money and the joy of the game drive Dominican youth to play baseball and scouts to follow them everywhere.

Kramer-Mandeau, Wolf. "Tradition, Transformation and Taboo: European Games and Festivals in Latin America, 1500–1900," *International Journal of the History of Sport* 9, no. 1 (April 1992): 63–82. Diffusion and fusion mark the spread to and adaptation of European games and sports in pre-modern Latin America.

Krich, John. *El Béisbol: Travels through the Pan-American Pastime*. New York: Atlantic Monthly Press, 1989. A good example of how not to write about a sport in a culture that one does not understand or appreciate.

LaFrance, David G. "A Mexican Popular Image of the United States through the Baseball Hero, Fernando Valenzuela," *Studies in Latin American Popular Culture* 4 (1985): 14–23. Fernandomania from the Mexican point of view.

Le Batard, Dan. "Real Simple," *ESPN: The Magazine* 4, no. 5 (March 5, 2001): 64–69. Hitting sensation Manny Ramírez grew up in poverty in the Dominican Republic, left Cleveland for $160 million to play in Boston, and remains a "simple," even humble person.

Lever, Janet. *Soccer Madness: Brazil's Passion for the World's Most Popular Sport.* Rev. ed.; Prospect Heights, IL: Waveland Press, 1995 (1983). A look at soccer as a unifying force in Brazil.

Longoria, Mario. *Athletes Remembered: Mexican/Latino Professional Football Players, 1929–1970.* Tempe, AZ: Bilingual Press, 1997. More Mexicans and Latinos have played professional American football than is often realized.

Magazine, Roger. " 'The Colours Make Me Sick': América FC and Upward Mobility in Mexico," in *Fear and Loathing in World Football*, ed. Gary Armstrong and Richard Giulianotti, 187–98. Oxford, UK: Berg, 2001. Support for América FC is associated with fans who seek vertical mobility as opposed to those who desire horizontal solidarity with groups of similar class or values.

Mandle, Jay R., and Joan D. Mandle. *Caribbean Hoops: The Development of West Indian Basketball.* Langhorne, PA: Gordon & Breach, 1994. Basketball is becoming a game of the people in the Anglophone Caribbean.

______. *Grass Roots Commitment: Basketball and Society in Trinidad and Tobago.* Parkersburg, IA: Caribbean Books, 1988. Basketball is a basis for community organization and class and ethnic conflict in this island nation where cricket historically dominates.

Mangan, J. A., and Lamartine P. DaCosta, eds. *Sport in Latin American Society: Past and Present.* London, UK: Frank Cass, 2001. Nine essays tracing aspects of the diffusion and adaptation of modern sports. Touches on soccer, baseball, the Olympics, national identity, racism, class consciousness, politics, foreign influences, and more.

Manley, Michael. *A History of West Indies Cricket.* Rev. ed.; London: André Deutsch, 1995 (1988). An important political figure surveys his region's major participant and spectator sport.

Mason, Tony. *Passion of the People? Football in South America.* London: Verso, 1995. South Americans have learned to love the game that they adopted from the British and modified to be their own.

McGehee, Richard V. "Latin America and the Caribbean in the Modern Olympic Movement," *Journal of the International Council for Health, Physical Education, Recreation, Sport and Dance* 32, no. 4 (1996): 12–15. With minor exceptions, Latin America's place in the Olympics has not been significant.

______. "The Origins of Olympism in Mexico: The Central American Games of 1926," *International Journal of the History of Sport* 10, no. 3 (December 1993): 313–32. With support from the International Olympic Committee, Mexico tried to offset its recent violent history and assert some regional leadership.

______. "Revolution, Democracy, and Sport: The Guatemalan 'Olympics' of 1950," *Olympika: The International Journal of Olympic Studies* 3 (1994): 49–81. Guatemalan leaders sought to promote national stature and support for their "revolutionary" government as part of hosting the Central American and Caribbean Games.

______. "Sports and Recreational Activities in Guatemala and Mexico, Late 1800s to 1926," *Studies in Latin American Popular Culture* 13 (1994): 7–32. A fitful beginning in both countries, although Mexico had more resources except during the revolutionary decade of the 1910s.

Miller, Tom. *Trading with the Enemy: A Yankee Travels through Castro's Cuba*. New York: Atheneum, 1992. A contemporary picture of Cuba pays special attention to the central place of baseball.

Moss, Stirling, and Doug Nye. *Fangio: A Pirelli Album*. London: Pavilion Books, 1991. The legacy of Juan Manuel Fangio, the great Argentine race car driver.

Murray, Bill. *The World's Game: A History of Soccer.* Urbana: University of Illinois Press, 1996. Includes much on Latin America; highly readable.

Musick, Phil. *Reflections on Roberto.* Pittsburgh: Pittsburgh Associates, 1994. Memories of Roberto Clemente by a Pittsburgh sportswriter.

Oleksak, Michael M., and Mary Adams Oleksak. *Béisbol: Latin Americans and the Grand Old Game.* Grand Rapids, MI: Masters Press, 1991. A history of baseball in the circum-Caribbean area and of Latin players in the North American big leagues.

Pérez, Louis A., Jr. "Between Baseball and Bullfighting: The Quest for Nationality in Cuba, 1868–1898," *Journal of American History* 81, no. 2 (September 1994): 493–517. Baseball became part of Cuba's struggle for cultural and political independence from Spain.

______. *On Becoming Cuban: Identity, Nationality, and Culture.* Chapel Hill: University of North Carolina Press, 1999. Contains long section on the place of baseball in the development of Cuban national identity and culture.

Perri, Brad. "Disappearing Regions: Charles Atlas, the United States, and Nicaraguan Identity," *Aethlon: The Journal of Sport Literature* 16, no. 2 (Spring 1999): 35–46. Sergio Ramírez's short story "Charles Atlas Also Dies" is more about the "colonial" relationship between Nicaragua and the United States than about the well-known bodybuilder.

Pettavino, Paula J., and Geralyn Pye. *Sport in Cuba: The Diamond in the Rough.* Pittsburgh: University of Pittsburgh Press, 1994. A comprehensive picture of the Cuban sports structure under Fidel Castro.

Price, S. L. *Pitching around Fidel: A Journey into the Heart of Cuban Sports.* New York: Ecco Press, 2000. Based on personal observations of Cuban athletes, administrators, and fans: baseball and more.

Regalado, Samuel O. *Viva Baseball! Latin Major Leaguers and Their Special Hunger.* Urbana: University of Illinois Press, 1998. Latins in pursuit of baseball careers for money and love of the game have faced and overcome major obstacles.

Rendall, Ivan. *Ayrton Senna: A Tribute.* London: Pavilion Books, 1994. An introduction to a popular Brazilian race car driver, tragically killed on the track in 1994.

Ruck, Rob. *The Tropic of Baseball: Baseball in the Dominican Republic.* Westport, CT: Meckler, 1991. Baseball's popularity in the Dominican Republic derives from various historical factors.

Rucker, Mark, and Peter C. Bjarkman. *Smoke: The Romance and Lore of Cuban Baseball.* Kingston, NY: Total/Sports Illustrated, 1999. Useful text and magnificent photos based in part on recent fieldwork.

Sands, Kathleen M. *Charrería Mexicana: An Equestrian Folk Tradition.* Tucson: University of Arizona Press, 1993. Imported from Spain and adapted to New World conditions, this Mexican sport and performance event carries national significance. See the author's article in this collection.

Scarborough, Vernon L., and David R. Wilcox, eds. *The Mesoamerican Ballgame.* Tucson: University of Arizona Press, 1991. Technical and theoretical analyses of an important and pervasive sporting activity with political and economic implications dating from long before the Spanish conquest.

Shah, Diane K. "Same Old Bull," *ESPN: The Magazine* 4, no. 6 (March 19, 2001): 64–68. Twenty years after he touched off Fernandomania, "El Toro" Valenzuela still gets batters out and puts fans in the stands for Hermosillo in the Mexican league because he "love[s] this game."

Shirts, Matthew. "Playing Soccer in Brazil: Sócrates, Corinthians, and Democracy," *Wilson Quarterly* 13, no. 2 (Spring 1989): 119–23. Politics in a popular Brazilian soccer club is linked to politics, and more, in the larger society.

Sosa, Sammy, with Marcos Bretón. *Sosa: An Autobiography.* New York: Warner Books, 2000. The life and career of the Dominican hitting star, based on extensive interviews with the subject. Juvenile market.

Sugden, John. *Boxing and Society: An International Analysis.* Manchester, UK: Manchester University Press, 1996. Contains a provocative ethnographic essay on boxing in Havana, Cuba.

Tobin, Jeffrey P. "Manly Acts, Buenos Aires, 24 March 1996." Unpublished Ph.D. thesis, Rice University, 1998. An ethnographic look at soccer, tango, and *asado* (barbecue) and the construct of masculinity in Buenos Aires, Argentina.

Torres, César R. "Mass Sport through Education or Elite Olympic Sport? José Benjamín Zubiaur's Dilemma and Argentina's Olympic Sports Legacy," *Olympika: The International Journal of Olympic Studies* 7 (1998): 61–88. The career and educational philosophy of an Argentine educator who served in name on the International Olympic Committee.

Van Hyning, Thomas E. *Puerto Rico's Winter League: A History of Major League Baseball's Launching Pad.* Jefferson, NC: McFarland & Co., 1995. The Winter League launched the big-league careers of countless players from both the island and the mainland.

Van Mele, Veerle, and Roland Renson. *Traditional Games in South America,* trans. Rita Wellens. Schorndorf, Germany: Hofmann, 1992. ICSSPE *Sport Science Studies,* Vol. 4. The threat to and persistence of traditional games in different areas.

Wagenheim, Kal. *Clemente!* Maplewood, NJ: Waterfront Press, 1984. A biography of one of Puerto Rico's greatest sports heroes.

Wendel, Tim. *Castro's Curveball.* New York: Ballantine Books, 1999. A fictional look at the Cuban Revolution and Fidel Castro's alleged baseball skills.

Wilson, Suzanne. "Por amor al juego (for the love of the game)," *Sports Illustrated Women* 3, no. 7 (November 2001): 90–93. Despite decreasing resources, women's sports in Cuba continue to produce international winners, raise popular enthusiasm, and encourage younger females to share the excitement of competitive athletics.

Winegardner, Mark. *The Veracruz Blues.* New York: Viking, 1996. A novelized account of the 1946 attempt to upgrade the Mexican League to major league baseball status.

About the Editors

Joseph L. Arbena holds degrees in Latin American studies from The George Washington University and the University of Virginia. He began as a specialist in Colombian and Panamanian history but shifted his focus to sports while directing the Clemson University Conference on Sport and Society. He later served as editor of the *Journal of Sport History*. Along with numerous articles on Colombian politics and diplomacy and Latin American sports, Professor Arbena has compiled two annotated bibliographies of Latin American sports (1989 and 1999). His current research looks at the links between sport and politics in Latin America. Since 1965 he has been on the faculty of Clemson University, where he teaches Latin American history and geography and modern sports history.

David G. LaFrance earned his Ph.D. at Indiana University, is presently research professor in the Benemérita Universidad Autónoma de Puebla, Mexico, having previously taught in universities in Ecuador, Poland, and the United States. He has published articles and books on Mexican political history and popular culture, including *The Mexican Revolution in Puebla, 1908–1913* (1989) and, with Guy P. C. Thomson, *Politics and Popular Liberalism in Nineteenth-Century Mexico: Juan Francisco Lucas and the Puebla Sierra* (1999). He has recently finished a second book on Puebla during the Revolution of 1910 and is currently working on a comparative history of the textile industries in Puebla and Lodz, Poland.